India and Pakistan

After three centuries of British domination, the two new democracies of India and Pakistan, with a combined population of almost half a billion people, are struggling to gain economic and political stature in one of the most complex and troubled areas of the world.

Here is their story—the story of India and Pakistan, past and present—of their people, their leaders, their culture, their economy, their government, their politics and particularly . . . of the religious heritage that made partition a necessity.

T. Walter Wallbank analyzes the historic trends in the fabric of Hinduism and Islam. He compares the basic beliefs and attitudes of each religion towards the caste system, the status of untouchability, non-violence, child marriage, deity worship.

He evaluates the forward steps that India and Pakistan have taken since independence . . . and he discusses the economic and foreign policy problems which face India and Pakistan—the solution of which will affect the future of the world.

T. WALTER WALLBANK *is a professor of history at the University of Southern California. In 1951-1952, he was a Fulbright Lecturer at Fouad University in Cairo. In the fall and spring of 1956-1957, he made a research trip to India and Pakistan, under the auspices of the Rockefeller Foundation, to obtain material for this book.*

A SHORT HISTORY OF

India and Pakistan

AN ABRIDGED EDITION
OF *INDIA IN THE NEW ERA*,
COMPLETELY REVISED AND UP-TO-DATE

———◆———

T. WALTER WALLBANK

A MENTOR BOOK
Published by THE NEW AMERICAN LIBRARY

COPYRIGHT © 1958, 1965 BY SCOTT, FORESMAN AND COMPANY

Previous Copyright, 1951, by Scott, Foresman and Company
under the title *India in the New Era*

Published as a MENTOR BOOK
by arrangement with Scott, Foresman and Company,
who have authorized this softcover edition.

FOURTH PRINTING (REVISED), FEBRUARY, 1965

Maps by Arnold Ryan
Illustrations by Franz Altschuler

The author wishes to acknowledge the courtesy of
The Bodley Head, London, who have granted permission
to reprint passages from Jawaharlal Nehru's
Autobiography, the English title of *Toward Freedom*.

MENTOR TRADEMARK REG. U.S. PAT. OFF. AND FOREIGN COUNTRIES
REGISTERED TRADEMARK—MARCA REGISTRADA
HECHO EN CHICAGO, U.S.A.

MENTOR BOOKS are published *in the United States* by
The New American Library of World Literature, Inc.,
501 Madison Avenue, New York, New York 10022,
in Canada by The New American Library of Canada Limited,
156 Front Street West, Toronto 1, Ontario,
in the United Kingdom by The New English Library Limited,
Barnard's Inn, Holborn, London, E.C. 1, England

PRINTED IN THE UNITED STATES OF AMERICA

Preface

In the years immediately following the end of World War II, Asia with its half of the population of the globe was convulsed with social and political revolution. Colony after colony became free of imperialistic control—as in the cases of Burma, Pakistan, Ceylon, Indochina, Indonesia, and India—or, as in the case of China, overthrew its government and embarked on a sweeping and bloody revolution. It is likely that this Asian Revolution or Awakening will continue its dynamic course for several decades, and people of the Western world must take note of its objectives, aspirations, and accomplishments.

The purpose of this volume is to present the important facts and movements—past and present—in the story of Pakistan and India. We will be concerned with their ancient heritage, with their tutelage under British rule, and finally with independence and full nationhood.

India and Pakistan are vitally important to the United States with its program of containing Communism and advancing the economic well-being of the world's underdeveloped peoples. India and Pakistan together, after China, have the largest population mass in the world, about 450 million people. Potentially they possess economic resources which may ultimately transform these nations into great industrial powers. Most important, India and Pakistan are pledged to the democratic way of life—to the rule of parliaments responsible to the people.

If India, the foremost nation of southwest Asia, succeeds in making herself a great industrial power providing expanding economic horizons for her people, it will be a sign to all Asia that the good economic things of life need not be purchased at the cost of individual liberty.

The present offers but a few shadowy outlines about the future of India and Pakistan. But no matter whether success or failure comes to their present course of action, either way there is every reason to believe that these nations will influence in substantial measure the course of the Asian Awakening and with it a goodly portion of world events.

Contents

Contents

I. The Facts of Indian Life

As a sequel to World War II, nationalism reached its highest peak of intensity in the Indian subcontinent. The demands for independence came to a head just at a time when Great Britain was emerging from a world conflict weak and impoverished and in no condition, even had she so wished, to maintain her imperial control over 400 million unwilling subjects. In 1947 she gave up all authority in India.

The question naturally arises, What was undivided India like in the year of her independence after nearly two centuries of British rule? What were the problems faced by her two new states of Pakistan and the Union of India when British governors, district officers, and their regiments sailed from Bombay and Karachi in the fall of 1947? The Indian subcontinent is racially, religiously, and linguistically one of the most complex areas in the world. Even to the English, to whom it should be best known, India has in many respects remained a mysterious and incomprehensible land, while to most Americans it has been a distant and strange country compounded of such elements as the Black Hole of Calcutta, the Taj Mahal, the Burning Ghats, and the enigmatic figure of Mohandas Gandhi.

To people of the Western world, and especially to those in the United States, it is becoming more and more evident that myths and ignorance about Asia, and especially India, must be superseded by adequate unbiased knowledge and sympathetic interest. One must, therefore, on the eve of independence, go figuratively into the 700,000 villages in the Indian subcontinent and its great cities to discover how farmers, businessmen, and industrial laborers lived.

9

If a map of the Indian subcontinent were superimposed on one of Europe, it would stretch north to south from Norway across the Mediterranean and almost to the African coast; and east to west it would cover an area from within England to well inside Russia. This subcontinent has an area of 1,600,000 square miles, as large as western Europe without Russia, nearly twenty times the size of Great Britain, and about half the size of the United States. The large land mass stretches over twenty-nine parallels of latitude, with its northern area in the same zone as California or Virginia and its southern in the same as Nigeria or Venezuela.

The Indian subcontinent is a huge peninsula jutting down from its massive mountain base into the Indian Ocean and shaped like a great triangle. No country has ever been more influenced by its geographical features. India's hot climate has undoubtedly conditioned the social organization of its people and their attitude toward life. Its dependence upon the monsoons—the seasonal winds that bring life-giving rains—has always given nature a cruel whip hand over man. Above all, the Himalayan mountain chain has walled India off from neighboring lands and made it a distinct geographical entity. While not offering complete protection from invasion—for many invaders have come through the passes—the Himalayas have isolated India and go far to explain both her distinctive culture and the remarkable continuity of her civilization.

The Land and the People

India can be divided into four main regions. The hill country and mountain zone in the extreme north contains such great peaks as Everest (29,141 feet) and Kanchenjunga. This wild and beautiful section, while sparsely populated, has valuable forests and great water-power resources. At the foot of the hill country lie the great northern plains, stretching two thousand miles and watered by three river systems—the Indus, the Ganges, and the Brahmaputra. These plains can be thought of as stretching, crescent fashion, west to east, from the Arabian Sea to the Bay of Bengal. The plains of the Indus are largely barren. Rivers are used for irrigation in what is known as "Dry India," and the Indus River serves the same function as does the Nile in Egypt. The eastern half of the plains country is the fertile Ganges valley. Enjoying plentiful rainfall and endowed with rich alluvial soil, it is one of the most productive areas in the world, with a population estimated at almost 175 million. All this plains region has been known throughout history as Hindustan and has been the traditional center of Indian culture. Directly to the south of Hindustan is the great table-land of the Deccan. Shaped like the larger triangle of the Indian subcontinent, its base is formed by the rugged Vindhya Mountains, which separate it from the plains country. Not far from the coast the walls or scarps, called Ghats, of the Deccan fall abruptly down to sea level. The soil of the tableland is not rich, but it possesses great mineral resources.

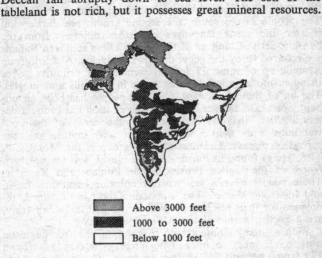

Above 3000 feet
1000 to 3000 feet
Below 1000 feet

Between the Ghats and the sea is yet another region, the long and narrow coastal plains, and in the far south, where the eastern plain broadens out somewhat, is an area called Tamil Land.

The population of India [1] in 1941 was 389 million, constituting one of the three great population masses of the world. Perhaps the most striking feature of its people is their diversity in culture, race, and religion. India has well been called one of the greatest ethnographical museums in the world. The reason lies in the many streams of invaders who have come through the mountain passes. An English anthropologist well expressed this fact when he declared, "The subcontinent of India has been likened to a deep net into which various races and peoples of Asia have drifted and been caught." [2] Three of the main racial groups of the world, the so-called yellow, black, and white, are repre-

[1] Hereafter, "India" will mean the entire subcontinent. After partition, in 1947, the term will be used to refer to a political entity, a part of the subcontinent.

[2] J. H. Hutton, *Caste in India* (Cambridge: Cambridge University Press, 1946), p. 1.

sented in India, and these in turn have been further divided into seven distinct racial types.

Perhaps the most simple classification would be as follows: First, there are Indians, many of whom are tall, fair-skinned, and long-nosed, whose language is derived from Sanskrit. Known as Aryans or Indo-Aryans, these people live mainly in the north, and most of the high castes belong to this group. The people in the south, the second group, are darker and shorter and speak languages altogether different from the Sanskrit-derived tongues of the north. These southern Indians are referred to by the generic term Dravidians. A third group is made up of some 25 million members of primitive tribes living in more or less isolated areas in the hills and jungles. The lot of these backward, childlike people has been an unhappy one. The impact of modern civilization has brought demoralization, the loss of their land, the decay of their old traditions with their ancient dances and myths, and the spread of disease. The fourth racial group is the Mongoloid. This type is found in Burma, Assam, Nepal, and the northern fringe of the United Provinces, the Punjab, and Kashmir. These people have a yellowish complexion, beardless faces, and high cheekbones. The mountain Gurkhas of Nepal, renowned for their military prowess in the British Indian army, are a good example of this Mongoloid type.

With so many ethnic groups it is natural that the linguistic situation is most complex. One language survey has found 179 languages and 544 dialects in India. This analysis, however, tends to overemphasize language complications, as many of the dialects are spoken by only a few tribes, and at least two dozen of the languages are relatively insignificant. There are only fifteen major languages, the most important of which is Hindustani. This language in its spoken form is understood by 150 million people. Unfortunately, its written form is divided ino High-Hindi, using the Sanskrit script, and Urdu, based on Persian script. Hindustani and related Indo-European languages are spoken by 70 per cent of the Indians, and these languages "are so closely akin that a quick-witted man who speaks one of them can with very little practice understand most if not all the others." [3] In the south of India, people speak Dravidian tongues, their users numbering some seventy million people.

During the past century English has occupied a unique place in India. It has been the lingua franca in what otherwise would have approached very close to a Tower of Babel, enabling educated men from all parts of India to understand

[3] H. N. Brailsford, *Subject India* (New York: John Day Co., 1943), p. 119.

each other. In 1931 out of 28 million who could read and write, 3.5 million could speak English.

While there has been a tendency on the part of English writers to exaggerate the linguistic complexity and for Indians to gloss it over, there is no doubt that the language problem is a serious one in India. There is no getting around the fact that in 1941 the All-India Radio was broadcasting in sixteen languages. We will return to this language problem in a later chapter, when we will see that it caused much controversy in the Indian Union after independence.

Most of India is either subtropical or intertropical. Generally speaking, it is an extremely hot land. The plains of the north are much warmer than the same latitudes in North America, the temperature often reaching 125 degrees Fahrenheit. Briefly summing up, it can be said that in the north the short winters are moderate but during the rest of the year temperatures are very high, and elsewhere—although the temperatures are not so extreme as in the plains—it is always hot.

India is dependent upon the monsoons for its rain, especially the moisture-laden winds from the southwest that start in May. The months from June to September are always anxious ones in India, for if the monsoon fails famine results. An Indian geographer discussing the monsoon observes:

> In a variable climate, such as we find in India, one year may be warm and wet, and full of crops, and another hot and dry, and famine stricken, one region may be inhabited by a healthy and prosperous peasantry, such as we find in the Punjab, and another by a half-starved mass of humanity, such as we notice in Central India.[4]

All in all, India is one of the most complex and diverse countries in the world. In its geography there are all kinds of contrasts: aridity and the heaviest rainfall in the world; lands of eternal snow and the humid, baking plains of the south; the highest of mountains and the flat plains at their feet. Racially and linguistically the human material is infinitely complicated. There are wide differences in the culture levels of the people. Professor E. J. Rapson has pointed out:

> We now find, at one extreme of the social scale, communities whose members are contributing to the advancement of the literature, science, and art of the twentieth century, and, at the other extreme, tribes still governed by their primitive constitutions, still using the implements and weapons, and still retaining the religious ideas and customs of their remote ancestors in the Stone Age.[5]

[4] A. M. Lorenzo, "Atlas of India," *Oxford Pamphlets on Indian Affairs*, No. 16 (Bombay: Oxford University Press, 1943), p. 8.
[5] *Cambridge History of India*, I (Cambridge: Cambridge University Press, 1922), p. 38.

As subsequent chapters will show, there are additional complications in human organization in India. There is caste, for example, and in religion there is more diversity than in all of Europe. India, with its immense size and population and its many contrasts in geography, race, and culture, is a fascinating land and one that has a strong lure for its thinking sons and daughters, who are deeply moved by its rich variety. Jawaharlal Nehru had all this in mind when he wrote:

> When I think of India, I think of many things: broad fields dotted with innumerable small villages; of towns and cities I have visited; of the magic of the rainy season which pours life into the dry, parched-up land and converts it suddenly into a glistening expanse of beauty and greenery, of great rivers and flowing water; of the Khyber Pass in all its bleak surroundings; of the southern tip of India; of people, individually and in the mass; and above all, of the Himalayas, snow-capped, or some mountain valley in Kashmir in the spring, covered with new flowers, and with a brook bubbling and gurgling through it.[6]

The Political and Economic Map of India

A political map of pre-independent and unpartitioned India presented a bewildering mosaic of British provinces and Indian princely states all jumbled together in a confusing patchwork. Slightly more than half of the total land area of India had by conquest and annexation come under the direct rule of the British government. Known as British India, and usually colored red on the map, its territory often surrounded or mingled with that of the princely states, which were ruled by Indian maharajas and nawabs under the benevolent protection of Great Britain.

At the outbreak of World War II, British India was administered by the Government of India Act of 1935 and consisted of eleven provinces, among them Bombay, Madras, Bengal, and the Punjab. Some of these provinces were as large as a single European nation of fair size and supported a comparable population. Madras, for example, was as large as Italy, with a population of 47 million. Within these provinces, which had their own legislatures and provincial officials, there was a considerable degree of autonomy. However, their executives, the British governors, were endowed with special powers enabling them to intervene in the event of a deadlock in the legislature or in the case of a threatened breakdown of law and order.

[6] Jawaharlal Nehru, *The Discovery of India* (New York: John Day Co., 1946), p. 51.

Apart from the provinces, where the people were British subjects and the land was British territory, were the princely states, 562 in number, comprising an area of 715,000 square miles inhabited by 90 million people. More than half of the area of the states belonged to the twenty-four largest; some of them, like Hyderabad, Mysore, Travancore, and Kashmir, were veritable countries. Hyderabad, for example, had an area of 82,000 square miles, with a Nizam—the ruler—who had 16 million subjects. On the other hand, many of the states were quite diminutive, incongruous vestigial remnants from a remote past. More than three hundred of them had altogether a land area of barely 6,000 square miles with a population of less than a million. In some instances the state might consist of only a few acres with a population of less than fifty.

Generally speaking, the people of the princely states were less influenced than those of British India by the impact of Western civilization brought in by the European rulers. In the states much of the color, the picturesqueness, and sometimes the barbarity of medieval India lingered on. Here the courts of the maharajas, supported by prodigious funds supplied by poor peasantry, sponsored costly festivals, tiger shoots, elephant processions, and entertainment for visitors on a lavish scale. Outside the courts of the rulers the rich traditions and culture of the past survived among the people in their handicrafts, their colorful costumes, and their ancient ceremonials.

Much has been said and written in denunciation of the princes, whose domains have been defined as "anachronistic pools of absolutism in the modern world." [7] The best of the maharajas were benevolent despots presiding over progressive and well-governed states such as Baroda, Mysore, and Travancore; the worst of them were cruel tyrants or irresponsible spendthrifts. Many of the maharajas lived like English country gentry. They traveled widely and were quite at home on the boulevards of Paris or in Park Lane in London. Great sportsmen, they spent huge sums on their stables and frequently were mighty hunters, stalking the lion, tiger, hippopotamus, and buffalo. Above all, a native prince was proud of the gun salutes accorded to him by the British. Only those princes with an eleven-gun salute merited the title of "Highness." There were only five rulers enjoying what was the ultimate in status—a twenty-one-gun salute; and of the entire number of princes almost three-quarters, regarded as small fry, were granted no right to gun salutes whatsoever.

[7] John Gunther, *Inside Asia* (New York: Harper and Brothers, 1939), p. 444.

The princely states, as will be seen in succeeding chapters, originated in their modern form when their rulers in the latter part of the eighteenth century and early in the next accepted the suzerainty and protection of the British crown. While in a sense independent, the princely states had to recognize what came to be known as the principle of paramountcy, by which Great Britain controlled the foreign affairs of each of the states and also reserved the right to interfere in a state's domestic affairs in the event of maladministration and gross injustice on the part of its ruler. Such interference was rare, however, and most states ran their own affairs. The position of the princely states in relation to Great Britain has been expressed by an Indian publicist thus:

> Though they vary in size, population, revenue, and the extent of the rights they enjoy, there is one fact which is common to them, that is, their territory is not British and their people are not subjects of the Crown. British Indian Courts have no jurisdiction inside even the smallest States and the laws passed by the Indian legislature do not, except in certain cases in relation to British subjects, extend to the states. Legally, they are foreign territory.[8]

Of all the princely states, Hyderabad was regarded as the most important. Only Kashmir exceeded it in area, by a few thousand square miles, and in population and wealth it was without question the premier state. Its ruler, the Nizam, occupied an office that had first been established by the Mogul emperor in 1713. This potentate was often referred to as the richest man in the world; his treasure in gold bars alone, excluding fabulous wealth in jewels, was estimated to be worth 250 million dollars. Until 1911 Hyderabad was a pure autocracy, but in 1919 an executive and a legislative council were set up. The powers of these bodies were limited, however, so that in practice the authority of the Nizam remained absolute. While there was little government by the people, the rule of the Nizam was benevolent. About 40 per cent of the public revenues were earmarked for public departments, such as health and education, that served the people. Much attention was given to irrigation projects, and industry was encouraged. As for the capital, the city of Hyderabad, it ranked as the fourth largest in India and was the home of the famous Osmania University, an institution sponsoring writing and research in the Mohammedan language of Urdu. The last striking feature to comment upon in Hyderabad is the fact that the Nizam and his 2 million Mohammedan coreligionists

[8] K. M. Panikkar, "The Indian States," *Oxford Pamphlets on Indian Affairs*, No. 4, 1942, p. 3.

constituted the administrative hierarchy over some 13 million Hindus. This fact was to have signal importance in affecting the destiny of Hyderabad in the post-independence era.

Another princely state deserves attention. Kashmir covers an area of 85,000 square miles tucked away in the northwest corner of the Indian subcontinent. This state is sometimes called the "House of Many Storeys," composed as it is of lovely valleys, inviting lakes, and snow-capped mountains. It is famous for its scenery and for the artistry of its handicrafts. In Kashmir the religious problem was the opposite of that in Hyderabad, for here the great majority of the people were Muslims and their ruler was a Hindu maharaja. There was much dissatisfaction, with occasional revolts on a minor scale by the Muslims against the maharaja and the ruling Hindu class. A serious uprising in 1932 resulted in the British government's creating a commission of inquiry which exposed the corruption of the police, the lamentable neglect of education, and the resort of officials to forced labor. Like Hyderabad, Kashmir was to play an exceedingly important role in the Indian drama immediately following independence.

It should be understood that in the 1930's there was no organic political integration between British India and the princely states. Under the Government of India Act of 1935, however, there was provision for the establishment of a federal structure in which the states and the British provinces were to be dovetailed into a common central government. This objective of federalism was not realized before World War II, but with the achievement of Indian independence in 1947 the question of the political future of the states was to become a major issue.

While India in the decade preceding its independence enjoyed a considerable measure of self-government, the ultimate authority lay with the viceroy, who was the highest executive official and the representative of the British government. Assisting the viceroy were less than three thousand British officers, for the great bulk of the administrative staff in the 1930's was Indian. In all of the country there were only 117,000 persons of British stock—men, women, and children —and this figure included 70,000 troops. The Indian civil service, the inner steel frame of the entire administration, was staffed less than half by British officials, who in such services as the medical, the police, and the railways, formed a small minority. Though the percentage of British officials in the Indian government had steadily declined after World War I, as India had become more self-governing, the fact is that even in the heyday of British rule in the nineteenth century the English controlled India with amazingly few men. Indeed, in the long history of imperialism there has been nothing approaching British control of India. For the fact was that a nation of some 40 million living on a small island off the coast of western Europe was able to project its power six thousand miles to govern more than 300 million subjects.

Great Britain, that nation of traders and shopkeepers, had good reason to maintain its position in India. Apart from the value of this country as a market for British goods, huge sums had been invested there. In the 1930's the British stake was around 3.5 billion dollars, of which some 2 billion was invested in public utilities and British-owned companies doing business in India, the remaining 1.5 billion dollars constituting the public debt owed by the Indian government to Britain. Loans had been raised on the London market, and the great bulk of the funds had been used for productive purposes, such as building railroads and irrigation projects. The interest on this debt ran to 50 million dollars yearly. But while the British investment in India was considerable, its importance has often been exaggerated. Excluding the sterling debt owed to Britain, that country's investments in India were matched approximately by sums in Canada, Australia, South Africa, and Argentina.

Partly as a result of these investments, India, though still predominantly agricultural, had by 1930 undergone a kind of industrial revolution that made her an important element in world trade. In fact, judged by her external commerce, India was surpassed as a world trader only by the United States, Great Britain, Germany, France, and Canada. As an Asian economic power India was not in the same industrial category as Japan but was well ahead of China. India's railway mileage was five times that of China, and in mileage of paved roads the superiority was again almost five to one.

Up to 1914 Indian industry was limited mainly to cotton textiles, coal, and iron, and in that year the number of workers in factories employing more than twenty hands was only 951,000. In the 1920's, however, industry forged ahead in steel, glass, soap, jute, sugar, leather, and cement. By the 1930's, large-scale industry employed 2 million workers and India was rated as one of the eight industrial powers of the world. Compared with her huge population and with her resources, however, the degree of industrialization was quite meager and insufficient. The only great industries employing more than 100,000 by 1940 were the cotton mills engaged in spinning and weaving, the mills ginning and pressing cotton, the factories processing jute, and the railway shops.

The growth of industry was accompanied by a trend toward urbanization. During the decade 1921-1931, city population increased more than 6 million, to a total of nearly 40 million town dwellers. In the 1930's the rate of increase became more rapid, cities of 100,000 increasing in number from thirty-five to fifty-eight with a total population of 16.5 million. Calcutta almost burst at the seams as its population passed beyond the 2 million mark, and Bombay's figure increased to 1.5 million. Other cities, such as Cawnpore, Ahmadabad, and Jamshedpur, also made important population gains.

Rural life is, however, still dominant. As we have already seen, the population of India in 1941 was 389 million—one and a half times that of the Western Hemisphere and, next to the Chinese, the greatest population mass in the world. The great majority of these millions were peasants living in more than 700,000 villages. Out of every 100 people in India, 90 lived in the villages, and of these, 72 were directly supported by agriculture.

Life in Village and Town

To know undivided India one must understand her villages, for here lived the bulk of her many millions, and here existed in their strongest form the basic institutions of the Hindu way of life. The average village consisted of a few hundred acres supporting perhaps fifty to one hundred families. In the typical village one saw no paved roads, no running water, and no modern system of sewage disposal. Glancing about, one found that, while certain signs of modernity might be noted, village life had changed little in fundamentals during the past five hundred years. Cattle lived practically as part of the family. Sugar cane was crushed in a hand mill, wooden plows were used, bullocks at harvest time accomplished the threshing by treading out the grain, and in harvesting people squatted on the ground using sickles.

The huts—one could not dignify most of them by the word "house"—were ramshackle structures of mud and thatch with no chimneys or windows. Inside there were dirt floors, rarely tables and chairs, often no beds, and only a few chests and brass pots and pans. Filth and smells were everywhere. Sewage ran along the narrow alleyways. During the rainy season there were noxious pools full of mosquitoes. Garbage and filth littered the village. A recent American observer of Indian village life has given us a graphic and repulsive picture of its dirt, disease, and dung. He writes, "The smells rose too, smells of spice and of urine, of garlic and curry powder and dysentery stools, all the assorted smells of the Indian village, all the smells of life, decay, and death." [9]

[9] John Frederick Muehl, *Interview With India* (New York: John Day Co., 1950), p. 30.

The village, however, was changing. Events in the outside world, especially the influences of modern business and city life, were causing it to alter its ancient ways. But the tempo of change was slow. The villagers were the most immobile of all the people; many lived and died without traveling as much as fifty miles from the place of their birth. The village was the great fortress of conservatism. Without benefit of education, only vaguely understanding the slogans of his political leaders, and suspicious of new methods of agriculture, the Indian ryot, or peasant, dimly appreciated the fact that his standard of living was tragically low, but at the same time he was often the despair of those who tried to improve his lot.

India had her thousands of villages but, at the same time, she had great cities such as Calcutta, a metropolis second only to London in the British Empire. In these cities one saw great government buildings, banks, hospitals, factories, and slums—especially the last. For the impact of Western civilization, particularly that of its economics, during the past half-century upon urban life in India had been singularly uneven, leading to all kinds of contrasts, some good and some evil. In the great cities, elements of the old and new existed side by side or mingled to form unhappy combinations heretofore unknown in either India or western Europe. Within the city were smartly dressed businessmen attired in Western clothes; there were also Indians wearing the traditional *dhoti,* or dressed in a form of loose pajama-like trousers and jacket. Here and there were scantily clad coolies and practically naked fakirs. At night hundreds of people slept on the pavements. Automobiles mingled with bullock carts. Hawkers shouting their wares passed by ultra-smart Western-style shops, and from time to time a sacred cow meandered down the street.

Like any city in the United States, the Indian city had the usual economic classes, from bankers, manufacturers, professional men, and shopkeepers to factory workers. The last-named class was by far the most numerous and its status the most unsatisfactory. The urban worker usually arrived in the city with little knowledge of its conditions, especially its snares and pitfalls. Failure of his crops, loss of his land, or even threat of actual starvation had driven him to the city for employment. Work could be secured only through a middle-man, the jobber (known variously as the *maistri, sirdar,* or *mukadam*). Payment of a kind of bribe put the new worker into the debt of the jobber, a condition in which he often remained permanently. The jobber was actually employed by the factory management and in a sense was an essential inter-mediary between the employer and his men; in fact, he was usually a petty tyrant who got rich on bribes and frequently graduated into the ranks of the moneylenders.

Wages, housing, food—these elements constitute a basic economic trinity which may or may not mean happiness and the good life for the urban worker. As far as housing was concerned, the situation in the 1930's was tragic. In most Indian cities housing for the workers was squalid, unhealthful, inadequate as to space, and unbelievably expensive. Bombay had its *chawls,* blocks of flats, in which there was little ventilation for the middle rooms, lavatory facilities were insufficient, and most household filth and refuse was dumped outside. One-third of the population lived in rooms occupied by more than five persons. A large number, estimated to be 80,000, existed in rooms which were occupied by from ten to nineteen persons. And some people did not even have hovels and had somehow to live on the streets; and so one reads of the "night population" and of the "pavement sleepers." A graphic picture of these housing conditions is given by an Indian investigator:

> In one room on the second floor of a *chawl,* measuring fifteen by twelve feet, I found six families living. . . . On enquiry, I ascertained that the actual number of adults and children living in this room was thirty. . . . Three out of six women were shortly expecting to be delivered. . . . When I questioned the nurse who accompanied me as to how she would arrange for privacy in this room, I was shown a small space 4 feet by 3 feet which was usually screened off for the purpose. The atmosphere of that room at night, filled with smoke from the six ovens and other impurities, would certainly handicap any woman with an infant both before and after delivery.[10]

Similar conditions were found in the industrial slums of other large cities such as Cawnpore, Calcutta, and Ahmadabad. In Madras the slums were called *cheries,* and consisted of dilapidated hovels constructed of mud and kerosene cans. In one area it was estimated that there were only 460 faucets for 183,000 people, and everywhere there were open sewage, garbage, filth, and flies. In spite of the squalor the rents were high, and the Indian landlords often secured a return of 35 per cent on their investment.

Trade unions for workers came relatively late to India, the first being organized in 1918. In 1935 only 270,000 workers were members of permanent unions. Many serious obstacles hindered the growth of unions in India. Much of the in-

[10] Quoted in B. Shiva Rao, *The Industrial Worker in India* (London: George Allen and Unwin, 1939), pp. 108-9.

dustrial labor was migratory, responsible leadership was lacking, and workers were too poor to pay dues and too ignorant to understand what a union proposed to do. A further obstacle was the opposition of jobbers, of employers, and, on occasion, of the government.

In 1934 a fairly adequate Factory Act was passed which reduced working hours, provided for better working conditions, and limited all adult labor (fifteen years and over) to a ten-hour day and a fifty-four-hour week. This act, unfortunately, did not apply to "unregulated factories," i.e., establishments employing less than twenty workers or not utilizing mechanical power. In these small workshops, where millions of workers were employed, operations were carried on twenty-four hours a day. The rooms were dark and poorly ventilated, the floors were often of mud, and it was not uncommon for children of five to work twelve hours a day under the strictest discipline.

As might be expected, the wages of the Indian urban worker were miserably low. Children got from ten to seventy-five cents a month, an average wage for a factory worker was a dollar and a quarter a week, and a casual farm laborer got five to eight annas (about ten to fifteen cents) a day.

In most cities there was a disparity in numbers between males and females, the former sometimes exceeding the latter two to one. Often a villager would leave his wife behind, or a young bachelor would come to the city with the idea of saving a small sum and then returning to the village. In any case, this sex disparity encouraged immorality; and, in addition, squalor of surroundings and lack of adequate recreation encouraged workers to drink to excess and to take drugs, such as opium. On the whole the state of the urban worker was a desperate one, and his condition was perhaps more degraded than that of most of his fellows whom he had left in the village.

The Arithmetic of Impoverishment

In 1930 the average per capita income in India was reckoned at twenty dollars, a figure exceeded seventeen times in England and twenty-two times in the United States. There have been numerous studies dealing with the income of the peasants. One such estimated that an average ryot had an annual income of about one hundred dollars (to estimate the money worth of his small crop). Above what he and his family needed for food he was able to sell thirty-nine dollars' worth of produce. With this cash sum in his pocket he was able to pay his land tax of six dollars, leaving a little more than thirty dollars for the clothing, amusements, and medicines needed by his family. But the ryot was in debt to the sum of eighty dollars to the moneylender, or bania, who demanded the exorbitant sum of twenty dollars each year for interest. Thus the peasant was not even able to pay the annual interest, but each additional year settled more and more securely into the clutches of the bania.[11]

With low income necessarily comes inadequate diet, and in this respect the Indian masses suffered both qualitatively and quantitatively, from not enough and from the wrong kinds of food. In certain sections of India the average daily intake of calories for an adult male was estimated at only 1700, while the number required to maintain health would be 2500. In 1939 the director of the Indian medical service calculated that 39 per cent of the people were well fed, 41 per cent poorly nourished, and 20 per cent near a starvation diet. It was estimated that 20 per cent of the population were always hungry.

The food that was consumed was not well balanced. The diet showed a deficiency of fats, vitamins, and proteins. Little milk was consumed, and not enough green vegetables, eggs, fish, and fruit. Meat was an unknown item to the great majority of Hindus, because of both economic and religious factors. Actual experiments have been carried out to test the dietary habits of various sections of India. One such experiment used rats of the same size, weight, and age, and gave to some the best diets found in the country, to others the poorest. It was found that the weight differential after 80 days ran from 155 to 235 grams. There can be no question that India was a poorly nourished nation, with the inevitable evil results upon physical stamina, health, and life expectancy.

Every year nearly 6 million deaths resulted from preventable disease. Chief among these was malaria, which infected 100 million persons a year; only 10 per cent of these were able to secure adequate treatment, and 1 million of them died annually. Other diseases, such as tuberculosis, hookworm, leprosy, cholera, smallpox, and typhoid, took a heavy toll. The factors which brought about heavy decimation from otherwise preventable disease were (1) contaminated water, (2) lack of sanitary facilities, (3) bad housing, (4) mosquitoes and flies, and (5) malnutrition.

As long as malaria, fevers, and tuberculosis took life prematurely by the million, India had one of the lowest rates of life expectancy in the world. The general death rate in 1941 was estimated to be 21.8 per thousand and for infants under one year, 162. For New Zealand the corresponding figures

11 C. F. Strickland, "The Indian Village and Indian Unrest," *Foreign Affairs*, X (October 1931), pp. 70-80.

were 9.1 and 31, for Australia 9.4 and 38, and for the United States 12 and 55. The life expectancy at birth in New Zealand and Australia was, respectively, 65 and 63 years; in India, by contrast, it was 26. In India 65 per cent of the people died before the age of 30, and no mother had a better than even chance of raising her child to adulthood. It was also pointed out that, of every 100,000 babies born alive, only a little more than 50 per cent lived over five years.

India desperately needed adequate public health facilities. But there was only one doctor available to every 6000 people, one nurse to every 43,000, and one dentist to every 300,000. The country also needed adequate education, for much of the disease resulted from ignorance and superstition. In 1941 only 12.5 per cent of the population of British India were literate in their own language; only 2 per cent were literate in English; and for all of India only 14 per cent were estimated to be literate. While the number of literates increased from 23 million to 47 million during the decade 1931-1941, the number of illiterates increased from 315 million to 341 million. Merely to hold her own in the race between literacy and illiteracy India must educate 3.5 million of her youth each year to read and write. Most serious was the lack of schooling for girls. In the 1920's only 35,000 girls were in classes above the elementary school, and in the latter the usual ratio is one girl to four boys. In 1941 barely 5 per cent of all women were literate.

A basic problem in Indian education was the large percentage of students who left school in the upper grades of the elementary schools. Half-educated, these boys returned to their villages with their lack of books, newspapers, and any form of adult education, and they naturally lost what little learning they possessed. Commenting on this matter, a school inspector observed:

> The great majority of our ex-students, in less than ten years after leaving school, can neither read, nor write, nor cipher. From having nothing to read, having no occasion to write, and no accounts to keep, they gradually forget whatever they learn, and are as ignorant as if they had never been at school.[12]

All this was part of the arithmetic of impoverishment: low income, poor diet, ravages of disease, inadequate public health facilities, illiteracy, and low life expectancy. The overall picture was a melancholy one. After studying these prob-

[12] Quoted in *Cambridge History of the British Empire* (Cambridge: Cambridge University Press, 1932), V, p. 342.

lems, not by benefit of statistics on the printed page but by the observation of daily life in India, an American writer, appalled by what he had seen, expressed his reaction thus:

> It was the fact of the atrocious poverty of village India; even starvation and famine could not measure its depths, for it was like something malignant with a life of its own. This memory I could no longer differentiate; it was a mass of hoarse cries and protruding bones, the smell of disease in a thousand villages, the smoke of a hundred burning ghats. . . . India was neither simple nor happy but complex and miserable, involved and squalid, the breath of its people coming labored and uneven through the weight and mass of superstition and ignorance.[13]

Religion: The Great Divider

India, like ancient Egypt, was a land saturated with religion; its people were obsessed with the destiny and status of man in the hereafter. Nearly every aspect of life, every thought and action, was conditioned by faith and dogma, whether in business, in politics, or in social behavior. The dominant religious community in India was the Hindu, whose members in 1941 constituted 65 per cent of the entire population, whereas the Mohammedan community represented 25 per cent. Hinduism is impossible to define in a terse and neat statement, for it comprehends a way of life, rather than a narrow, church-going creed, and affects a man's social status, his marriage, the very food he eats, the friends among whom he can mingle, and the occupation he follows. In the following chapter something will be said of the origin and development of Hinduism and its theological and philosophical beliefs. At this point, however, a discussion of the caste system is appropriate, for it is the structure within which Hinduism has its being and at the same time the machinery which gives practical effect to the objectives of this faith.

In the caste system all individuals are classified according to the occupation they traditionally follow, the circle within which they must marry, and the group with whom they can mingle socially. Birth lays down the caste to which a Hindu belongs, and there is no possibility for him to switch to another. In ancient times, as will be explained in the next chapter, there were four basic castes—the Brahman, the most revered; the Kshatriyas, the nobles and warriors; the Vaisyas, the traders; and the Sudras, the serfs. Today, however, this fourfold classification has been blurred and complicated by the development of more than three thousand separate caste groups. The easiest way of understanding the status of these

13 Muehl, *op. cit.*, p. 298.

many castes is to know that there are three main caste categories. The first group includes the Brahmans; the Rajput clans,
representatives of the ancient Kshatriyas; and the traders who
claim descent from the Vaisyas, all of whom constitute the
Twice-Born. The second group embraces the traditional Sudra
castes that are now all lumped together as being not Twice-
Born. At the bottom are the Untouchables, also known as the
Depressed Classes or Scheduled Castes. There is, consequently, a definite hierarchy from the debased and "unclean"
ranks of the Untouchables up through the higher castes of
those not Twice-Born, on into those who are, culminating in
the Brahman castes. So ingrained is this concept of differential status that there are even various grades among the
Untouchables, "each superior grade considering the inferior
. . . as polluting as the highest class of the caste Hindus
regard the worst grade of Untouchables. Further, among the
same grade of Untouchables there are sections, each considering itself different and distinct from any other, prohibiting inter-dining and inter-marriage." [14]

Each caste is an exclusive group. It is endogamous, for a
man must select his bride from within his own group. Furthermore, each caste has its *dharma*, its rules regulating the kind
of food that may be eaten, the manner of its eating, and with
what other castes there may be social intercourse. Rules of
eating are especially complex, dictating the people from whom
one can take water, the correct ritual at the table, the specific
people who can cook one's food, and the companions one
may have at the table.

Closely related to caste is the traditional Hindu institution
known as the joint family, which consists of a father, his sons,
and his grandsons, together with all their womenfolk until
they are married and enter other joint families. The family is
joint in food, worship, and estate, and the income of the an-
cestral property and the current earnings of all members
are placed in a common fund.

Traditionally each caste followed a specific occupation,
but new castes are constantly growing up and a caste may
also take up a new occupation. Unless there is a rapid decline
in the occupational characteristics of the caste system, it is
possible that the growth of industrialism in India may result
in a further bewildering multiplication of castes to conform
to the complex variety of modern industrial occupations.
One American correspondent observes: "So far no subcaste of
typists or airplane mechanics or locomotive engineers has
been reported. But it could happen." [15]

---

[14] Quoted in Rao, *op. cit.*, pp. 81-82.
[15] Robert Neville, "Caste Is the Curse of India," *Life*, XXII (May
19, 1947), p. 106.

At the bottom of the caste system are the Untouchables, some 50 million people, described as "the largest subordinate racial group in the world." [16] They are the menials of India, doing the dirty and degrading tasks, being the scavengers, the tanners, washers of dirty clothes, and handlers of dead carcasses. Untouchability has been defined as "Jimcrowism on a fantastic scale." [17] Untouchables must live apart, segregated from the rest of their fellow villagers. Their touch, contiguity, and sometimes even their shadows are considered to be polluting to the higher-caste Hindus. In the past they were denied access to Hindu temples, they could not draw water directly from the village wells, and their children could not attend school along with the other Hindu students. They have even been forbidden to walk on the public roads. In many villages the higher-caste Hindus have done many things to stress the inferiority of the Untouchables. These unfortunates are not supposed to dress well, may not ride on a horse, cannot build a two-story house nor use brass vessels in their kitchen. It is natural that the Untouchables as a class usually have a bare subsistence living and are paid pitifully low wages. If, as sometimes happens, a member of the Depressed Classes is able to obtain a good education and make a mark for himself as a businessman or lawyer, despite all the culture and the wealth that may be accumulated this "self-made man" remains an Untouchable, the social inferior of the higher castes who is barred from their society. This is somewhat less true today than in the past, especially since the legal abolition of Untouchability.

As we will see in the next chapter, certain deep and ingrained beliefs cause the vast majority of Hindus to accept their caste status without question. In most castes there is also the governing body, the Panchayat, which meets like a court of law—or, one might perhaps say, like the executive committee of an American trade union—to punish any rash members who have broken the traditional rules of their caste. Punishable offenses might be breaches of caste etiquette, killing a sacred animal, and breaches of the marriage law.

Like all human institutions, wherever found, caste did not just happen. Originally it served a positive function, and even today it has certain commendable features. The Hindu emphasizes the fact that as a result of numerous racial invasions of his country, which will be discussed in later chapters, India became inhabited by many people with various levels of culture, and it was the caste system that enabled all the various groups to live together. In Western countries, backward peoples in like circumstances were either extermi-

[16] Louise Ouwerkerk, *The Untouchables of India* (London: Oxford University Press, 1945), p. 3.
[17] Gunther, *op cit.*, p. 397.

nated or enslaved. In its operation today Hindus point out that a caste is a kind of brotherhood, democratic within itself, within which all the members are equal regardless of their wealth.

> Caste moderates personal ambition and checks the bitterness of competition. It gives a man, whatever his station in life, a society in which he can be at home even when he is among strangers. For the poor man, it serves as a club, as a trade union, and a mutual benevolent society, all rolled into one. It ensures continuity and a certain inherited skill in the arts and crafts. And in the moral sphere it means that every man lives content with that place which Destiny has allotted to him, and uncomplainingly does his best.[18]

There may be mitigating features in the caste system, but on balance it is a way of life utterly inconsistent with the basic forces that are now influencing our contemporary world. Nehru, India's renowned statesman, has written that "in the social organization of today it has no place left," and that it "has to change completely, for it is wholly opposed to modern conditions and the democratic ideal." [19] One of the crusades of Mahatma Gandhi was against Untouchability.

Is caste declining? In the 1941 census there were nearly 7 million Hindus who refused to indicate any caste membership, and in the past half-century it is indisputable that the impact of British rule and Western influences in general have weakened to some extent the hold of caste. Marriages outside caste have been legalized, and the law protects the property of a caste renegade who is threatened with punishment by his caste Panchayat. Above all, modern conditions of life, especially in the city, where trains, buses, and factories throw people of all castes together, tend to break down the old system. Many Hindus are increasingly ignoring the old food taboos and restrictions, and from time to time there are intercaste marriages. Despite these changes, however, caste is still the most powerful institution, and its essential principle, that of caste endogamy, has been little weakened. The most recent trends in the fabric of Hinduism—i.e., the strength of the caste system, the status of Untouchability, and the future of the joint family—will be discussed in Chapter 9.

While religion has divided Hinduism within itself, there is at the same time a wide fissure between Hinduism as a whole and Islam. In 1941 there were 95 million Muslims, equivalent to 24 per cent of the population. The great majority were of the same stock as their Hindu neighbors, and in the province of

---

[18] Quoted in Lord Meston, *Nationhood for India* (London: Oxford University Press, 1931), p. 51.
[19] Nehru, *The Discovery of India*, p. 532.

the Punjab, where there was the largest percentage of foreign origin among the Muslims, such origin was computed at only 15 per cent. A later chapter will show that the bulk of present-day Muslims are descendants of Hindus who accepted Islam voluntarily, often to escape low caste status, or who chose it as the preferable alternative to death at the hands of the invading Muslim hosts or discriminatory taxes by Muslim rulers.

If Islam were primarily and exclusively a matter of theology, the unfortunate rivalry and even hatred that developed between it and Hinduism in the present century might not have come about. Like Hinduism, however, Islam is more than a religion; it is a way of life, a veritable culture all its own. Unlike the former, it believes in the fundamental equality of all men and repudiates any notion of caste. Islam is iconoclastic, an idol-smashing faith, in contrast to the voluptuous polytheism of Hinduism with its variegated array of deities. The Muslims reject child marriage and eat meat, especially that of the cow.

Because of the exclusiveness of the caste system, there could be little or no contact between these two religious communities, and intermarriage is out of the question. It has been pointed out that even in the case of the long traditional enemies, France and Germany, a young Frenchman going to the latter country to study might easily secure residence with a German family and eventually marry the daughter of the house. No Muslim could live on such terms in the large majority of Hindu homes. A Muslim leader has commented:

> Any of us Indian Muslims travelling for instance in Afghanistan, Persia, and Central Asia, among Chinese Muslims, Arabs, and Turks, would at once be made at home and would not find anything to which we are not accustomed. On the contrary in India we find ourselves in all social matters total aliens when we cross the street and enter that part of the town where our Hindu fellow townsmen live.[20]

In contrast to the contemplative and elaborate edifice of Hinduism with its many gods, Islam is simple, unadorned, and dynamic. The Muslim creed tersely affirms, "There is no God but Allah and Mohammed is his Prophet." In addition there is simply the belief in Allah's teachings as revealed in the Koran and in a final resurrection and judgment.

During the seventy-five years before independence, differences and rivalries between the Muslim and Hindu communities grew ever keener. The former lagged behind the latter in taking up the new Western education, thus giving

[20] Quoted in Sir John Cumming, ed., *Political India, 1832-1932* (London: Oxford University Press, 1932), p. 104.

the Hindus a monopoly in governmental service and in the professions. The Muslims were also disinclined to go into business, one important reason being the Koran's prohibition against lending money for interest. Naturally, Hindus came to dominate business, to be the moneylenders and landowners. More and more the Muslims came to resent being the "House of Have-Not" in India, and much of the mutual antipathy undoubtedly had some economic source.

Muslims ate the flesh of the cow; Hindus regarded this animal as sacred and not to be killed under any circumstance. The matter of the cow played an important part in stirring up trouble between the two religious groups. Once a year good Muslims celebrated the anniversary of Abraham's sacrifice on Mount Moriah. Several Muslims would come together and buy a cow for the rite. In the process Hindu neighbors were often baited and mocked, and when the animal was decked out in garlands and led noisily to slaughter through the streets, a first-class riot ensued. On the other side, Hindus took an impish delight in conducting their noisy religious processions, including the loud playing of musical instruments, just outside the local mosque where the faithful were at prayer. The Muslims rushed out to protest, stones were soon substituted for words, and another communal riot began.

In addition to the two dominant socioreligious communities, the Hindus and the Muslims, there were four minority groups that deserve brief identification. The Parsis, a small community of about 100,000, were centered largely in Bombay. Originally they were followers of Zoroaster and their home was in Persia, which they left in the eighth century to escape coming under the rule of Islam. While almost a microscopic element amid India's millions, the Parsis have exerted an extraordinary influence on the cultural and economic life of their adopted country. They have proved themselves to be an unusually intelligent and enterprising group and were among the first communities to take to Western science and culture. One of the greatest political figures in the early days of Indian nationalism, 1890-1910, was the Parsi Dadabhai Naoroji, who was a prominent member of the Indian National Congress. In the field of business the reputation of the Parsis was known throughout the Far East. The great Tata Iron and Steel Company, for example, was founded by a Parsi, the late J. N. Tata.

The members of the Sikh community, defined as "neither a race, nor a nationality, nor a caste, but primarily the followers of a religion," [21] numbered almost 6 million, concentrated primarily in the Punjab. This sect traced its history back to the founder, *Guru* (Great Teacher) Nanak, who

[21] *Ibid.*, p. 124.

lived in the fifteenth century and who opposed caste, idolatry, and the supremacy of the Brahmans. Known as Sikhs, and led by a line of famous *gurus,* his followers fought back against the persecution of Muslim Mogul emperors who were ruling the country at that time. Gradually the Sikhs developed into a strong, militant brotherhood, famous throughout India for their military prowess. Early in the nineteenth century they gave evidence of becoming a strong imperial power in northern India, but they were conquered by the British. Their military tradition, however, was perpetuated by their service in the British Indian army, where the Sikhs gained fame for their heroism and soldierly qualities. They not only served in the Indian army but became a familiar sight as policemen in such British colonies as Singapore and Hongkong.

One result of British conquest and rule of India was the creation of a small community of mixed blood known first as Eurasian and after 1911 officially as Anglo-Indian. Never numbering more than 150,000, this group has illustrated, sometimes tragically, the effects of a biological blending of two proud peoples, both of whom often rejected the product of the union. The Anglo-Indians usually thought of Britain as their spiritual home and tried to associate themselves with the English community in India. The English, however, wanted little to do with them, while the Indians tended to despise this hapless group as renegades supporting the rule of the alien imperialist. So difficult was the economic status of the Anglo-Indians that the British sought to guarantee employment for them, mainly in the postal service and on the railways. As the day for Indian independence approached in the mid-1940's, the leaders of the Anglo-Indian community began to urge its members to forget their British inclinations and to go with the new India as loyal sons and daughters.

Christian missionary enterprise has been very active in India, not only spreading the Gospel but making significant contributions in education, establishing pioneer printing presses, and developing the Indian vernaculars into literary languages. By 1941 Christianity, while very small in following compared to Hinduism and Islam, had reached the position of the third religious community in India, with a little more than 6 million members. Most of the converts came from the lower castes, especially the Untouchables. Compared with the population as a whole, the Indian Christians were remarkably advanced, especially in education. Their rate of literacy was far above the average.

Factors in Indian Poverty

Why was undivided India so poor? There have been in the past two basic approaches to this problem. The nationalistic school has argued that all of India's problems, especially economic impoverishment, have sprung from the evils of British rule. It is argued that British imperialism has discouraged industries, prevented the creation of necessary tariffs to encourage Indian industry, established a parasitic landlord—zamindar—class, taxed the Indian masses too much, and neglected social services, such as education. The other school found the causes of Indian poverty in fields other than the political or strictly economic, maintaining that it sprang from socioreligious traditions and customs within the pattern of Indian culture. To this school it was naïve to believe that a fundamental improvement in standards of living could be secured merely by adopting a new constitution without a thorough reconstruction of Indian society. As later chapters take up in detail some of the charges made against British rule, it is appropriate at this juncture to comment upon socioreligious factors in Indian life that bear upon the problem of poverty.

Of utmost importance in its bearing upon the economic well-being of the masses was the prevailing attitude toward life inculcated by Hinduism in general and the caste system in particular. Later chapters will refer to the passivistic attitude, the principle of the unimportance of this life, and the spirit of resignation, all of which spring from Hinduism and its doctrine of transmigration. Nehru bitterly complained of the undue influence of religiosity and the obsession with the supernatural that prevented Hindus from utilizing their energies in scientifically studying the socio-economic problems around them and kept them from seeking to control the forces of nature to serve the legitimate needs of man.[22] Many Indians besides Nehru also criticized the Hindu outlook as not conducive to progress; one of them declared:

> The general outlook upon life in India is too gloomy to permit sound individual or social development. Far too common is the belief that life is merely a transitory state in the passage of the soul to another world. That notion chills enthusiasm, kills joy and promotes fatalism. In some cases the joint family system tends to produce drones; some Indians actually take pride in the number of persons they maintain in idleness. While Indians feel that life is a burden, people in the West are full of hope and are intensely active.[23]

Some authorities maintained that it was not so much overpopulation, landlordism, or chronic indebtedness that explained the poverty of the peasant but rather his psychology

[22] Nehru, *The Discovery of India*, p. 520.
[23] Sir M. Visvesvaraya, quoted in G. Findlay Shirras, *Poverty and Kindred Economic Problems in India* (Calcutta: Government of India, Central Publication Branch, 1932), p. 10.

and how he looked at life. The Indian ryot was bound down by custom, caged within the confines of his caste, and usually a slave to tradition. Like so many backward people, up to quite recently at least, he tended to be satisfied with a bare minimum of subsistence, and he has in the past shown little interest in improving his lot. It has even been asserted that the Indian ryot seemed to exhibit a kind of masochistic satisfaction in grumbling about the many evils that preyed upon him.[24] Of all the cultural groups affected by the Asian revolution, the Hindu masses were most insulated by religion and custom against the suffering caused by their debased economic status. It follows that they would be the most difficult to arouse to the necessity of basic reforms.

There can be little argument that before independence the village was the citadel of conservatism in India and that from the caste system with all its ramifications there stemmed many forces, usually malignant from the Western point of view, that operated to bring about the tragically low standard of life in India. It is mainly by reference to Hindu beliefs that one can best understand the tremendous pressure of population in India; appreciate the economic waste associated with the sacred cow and the principle of the sanctity of all life; and study the poverty of the average Indian village, which springs from debt created by uneconomic religious festivals and the wasteful fragmentation of agricultural holdings. Above all, there has been the depressed status of Indian women, who have been discouraged and even barred from making their potential contribution to the progress and wealth of their motherland. In discussing India's social problems it has well been said, "Of all the many changes likely to improve the welfare of Indian society, none is more important than these two—female education and marriage reform." [25] These problems of population pressure, the status of women, reform of the caste system, and the uneconomic use of the country's animal population will be discussed in greater detail when we take up the stage when, in 1947, independent India had both the challenge and the opportunity to embark on the great task of reconstructing the pattern of life of her masses.

24 Muehl, *op. cit.,* p. 126.
25 Sir Edward Blunt, ed., *Social Service in India* (London: His Majesty's Stationery Office, reprinted 1946), p. 74.

Brahma

2. Historical Ingredients of Modern India and Pakistan

MODERN INDIA as we knew it before independence and division into two nations was a product of the preceding century and a half. The process of its creation began in earnest shortly after 1800 and advanced rapidly after reaching the mid-point of the nineteenth century. It is with this latter phase of modern nation-making in India that this volume is mainly concerned. To understand the India of Mohammed Ali Jinnah and Mohandas K. Gandhi, however, one must know something of what it started with late in the eighteenth century, on the eve of the British conquest. For it was out of the historical ingredients existing at that time, found by the officials of the English East India Company, together with what British rule added, that modern India came to be shaped.

Archeology has given us the clue to the oldest chapter in Indian history yet found. As late as 1921 an important discovery was made of the remains of an ancient civilization in the Indus Valley. The specific sites were at Mohenjo-Daro (Mound of the Dead) in the province of Sind, and at Harappa in the North Punjab. Excavations under the direction of Sir John Marshall proved that India could well claim to be one of the "mothers of civilization." At a time when comparable achievements were being registered in the Nile Valley, in Mesopotamia, and along the Hwang-Ho in China, life in the Indus Valley had shifted from a nomadic existence to urban dwelling, and writing, the use of metals, and the organization of government on a complex scale were achieved.

The life span of this fluvial culture of the Indus has been estimated to run from 4000 to 2500 B.C.

Although the writing at Mohenjo-Daro has not been deciphered, much has been learned of life in India some five thousand years ago. We know that the people lived in large cities probably not duplicated at that time anywhere else in the world. Mohenjo-Daro had well-planned streets, houses several stories high made of kiln-fired bricks, and large, pillared halls that were probably municipal halls or palaces. There was a fine drainage system, and the most imposing edifice was a great municipal bath.

The state of the arts was well advanced in this ancient Indus Valley culture; there were skilled industries and an active commerce. Smiths worked skillfully with bronze and made beautiful beakers of copper, silver, and lead. Potters used the wheel in their craft and also were familiar with glazes. Cotton was grown and woven two thousand years before this textile was used in the West. The archeologist's spade has unearthed numerous beautiful carved soapstone seals and amulets or charms. The representation of animals on these seals is excellent. In addition we have beautiful small figurines and samples of delicate jewelry.

What caused the downfall of the thriving cities in the Indus Valley? No one knows, but the end apparently came swiftly and completely about 2500 B.C. but, though some disaster seems to have overwhelmed Mohenjo-Daro, its culture in some unexplained fashion lived on. One of its deities apparently was a prototype of the Hindu Shiva, and various other elements in the Indus culture were passed down to the present pattern of Indian life. "We must therefore hold," writes an Indian historian, "that there is an organic relationship between the ancient culture of the Indus valley and the Hinduism of today." [1] This fact gives to Indian civilization an almost incredibly long continuity, a fact that naturally gratifies and stirs the modern Indian nationalist. Nehru in one of his books speaks of the thrill he felt standing on one of the mounds at Mohenjo-Daro and realizing that its ruins represented a civilization that was well developed five thousand years ago.

The next act in the drama of ancient India was the appearance of vigorous nomads who pushed through the mountain passes from central Asia in successive waves from 2000 to 1000 B.C. Belonging to the Indo-European family, and thus related to the Greeks, Persians, and Romans, these Indo-

[1] R. C. Majumdar, H. C. Raychaudhuri, and K. Datta, *An Advanced History of India* (London: Macmillan and Co., Ltd., 1946), p. 21.

Aryans, as they are called, were fair-skinned, fine-featured, and tall. As they pressed down into the northern plains, the Aryans came into conflict with the Dravidians, who apparently were the most numerous indigenous group at this time. The invaders described these Dravidians as short, dark, and ugly and contemptuously referred to them as *Dasyu* or slaves. The Aryans set about the task of conquest with a will and "with the ferocity of the American pioneers in their struggles against the Redskins." [2]

The dark-skinned Dravidians were driven south down the Indian peninsula, where their descendants are mainly concentrated today. But in spite of this retreat there was considerable fusion of both blood and culture between the conquering Aryans and their foes. In order to try to preserve to some degree Aryan racial purity, a barrier which gradually developed into the complex caste system as we know it today was set up, apparently on a color basis, between the two races. It is believed that the Dravidians had a higher level of culture than their conquerors and that the Aryans borrowed numerous aspects of their pattern of civilization.

Our knowledge of the long period of conquest and Aryan settlement, 2000 to 1000 B.C., comes from the sacred Vedas, a mass of material handed down for centuries by word of mouth. The common usage is to classify this ancient literature into four Vedas (*Veda* means "wisdom"), the oldest being the *Rig-Veda*. This consists of 1028 hymns, addressed mainly to the gods, dealing with nature worship and prayers for long life, good cattle, and victory in war. In the *Rig-Veda* we find a brooding, probing spirit concerned with the mysteries of life, and we note the element of mysticism that was to become so characteristic of Indian culture. Rabindranath Tagore, the famous Indian poet, has described the Vedas as "the poetic testament of a people's collective reaction to the wonder and awe of existence." [3]

The next important period in the development of Aryan civilization in India is called the Epic Age (1000-500 B.C.), mainly because our knowledge of events is gleaned from two famous epics. The *Mahabharata*, the longest poem in the world, made up of 100,000 couplets, glorifies war as does the *Iliad* of the Greeks. The most famous part of this epic is the *Bhagavad-Gita* ("The Lord's Song") of some seven hundred verses, the most beloved gem of Hindu literature and a piece of profound philosophy in poetic form. The *Gita*, as it is called, has been greatly admired in the Western world

[2] H. G. Rawlinson, *India: A Short Cultural History* (New York: D. Appleton-Century, 1938), p. 21.

[3] Quoted in Jawaharlal Nehru, *The Discovery of India* (New York: John Day Co., 1946), p. 69.

and has been translated forty times into English, the most famous translation being *The Song Celestial* by Sir Edwin Arnold. The second epic is the *Ramayana,* which has been likened to the Homeric epic, the *Odyssey.* This poem deals mainly with peace and domestic devotion, with the wanderings of the hero and the dutiful steadfastness of his wife.

It has been said that perhaps no other pieces of literature have influenced so many people for so long a time as have these Indian epics. In a sense they are what the Bible, *Pilgrim's Progress,* Milton, and Shakespeare have been to the English-speaking people. Everywhere in India their characters are sculptured in the temples, carved in the woodwork of houses, or painted on the walls. Common people all over the land know and love the old plots and characters of these epics.

> Nightly to listening millions are the stories of the *Ramayana* and *Mahabharata* told all over India. They are sung at all large assemblies of the people, at marriage feasts and temple services, at village festivals and the receptions of chiefs and princes. Then, when all the gods have been duly worshipped . . . a reverend Brahman steps upon the scene . . . and sitting down, slow and lowly begins his antique chant, and late into the starry night holds his hearers, young and old, spellbound.[4]

These epics give us a vivid picture of life in India from 1000 to 500 B.C. By this time the Aryans had ceased to be nomads and the village had become the basic cell of society, as it has remained to this day.

Expansion by the Aryans was also taking place eastward along the Ganges, and numerous small kingdoms were established. Trade expanded and cities were built. By this time a fusion of cultures between invader and vanquished had been accomplished. This is referred to as the Aryo-Dravidian Synthesis, and was something like the fusion that took place between Roman and Germanic elements in Europe following the fifth century A.D. or the mixing in England between Saxon and Norman following William the Conqueror's victory in 1066. During the Epic Period caste began to harden. The four traditional castes crystallized: the Brahmans, or priests; the Kshatriyas, or soldier class; the Vaisyas, farmers and merchants; and the Sudras, or serfs. Beneath this caste hierarchy was the submerged group, the Untouchables. And, as we have seen, this caste system became closely tied in with religion.

Hinduism, or the Hindu way of life, is one of the most important historical ingredients of modern India. We say "Hindu way of life" because it is more than a religion as the term

4 Herbert H. Gowen, *A History of Indian Literature* (New York: D. Appleton-Century, 1931), p. 251.

is usually understood. Hinduism has been termed a working hypothesis of human conduct; it took at least a thousand years to develop, but its seminal period was the Epic Age just discussed. It was during this period that the *Upanishads,* prose religious writings, were formulated. Philosophical in nature, these writings deal with the basic problems of existence and are replete with awe, wonder, and inquiry. This spirit is expressed in their words: "Lead me from the unreal to the real. Lead me from darkness to light. Lead me from death to immortality." [5] All of the main scaffolding of Hinduism is found in the *Upanishads.*

We may list these main elements in the structure of Hindu religious thought: (1) Life is evil. All things material are *Maya,* that is, illusion. In Christianity eternal life may be secured with the promise of individual existence; in Hinduism separate individuality is lost. The goal is not being but non-being, not separateness but absorption in the absolute. (2) The main object of true religion is *Moksha,* or deliverance, by which the soul becomes absorbed in the world soul or *Atma.* (3) This release is part of a cosmic and complicated process. The individual soul must go through a long series of wanderings and of earthly reincarnations from body to body. The status of a man at any particular time is no fortuitous lot but depends on his soul's actions in previous existences. "At the moment of death, then, there is an accumulation of the consequences of past action, which determines the condition of the individual in the next birth, whether as a man or as a higher or lower animal." [6] Caste is the essential machinery for what is, in effect, the educative process of the soul as it goes through the infinitely long succession of rebirths from the lowest category in caste to that of the Brahman, who presumably is near the end of the cycle.

Hinduism has no canon, no precise doctrine, and it has room for the most primitive idol worshiper and at the same time for the believer in the most profound philosophy of monotheism. There are literally thousands of deities and godlings worshiped in India. One worships what or whom one pleases. Perhaps the essential characteristics of a Hindu are that he usually accepts the leadership of the Brahman caste and is usually content with his own position in the caste structure.

Pervading Hinduism is a passive attitude, a feeling of resignation, and a belief that death is only an essential incident in

[5] Quoted in Nehru, *The Discovery of India,* p. 81.
[6] W. H. Moreland and Atul C. Chatterjee, *A Short History of India* (New York: Longmans, Green and Company, 1945), pp. 20-21.

the foreordained cycle of rebirths. Quoting from the *Bhagavad-Gita:*

. . . . the wise in heart
Mourn not for those that live, nor those that die.
Nor I, nor thou, nor any one of these,
Ever was not, nor ever will not be,
For ever and for ever afterwards.
All, that doth live, lives always! to man's frame
As there come infancy and youth and age,
So come there raisings-up and layings-down
Of other and of other life-abodes,
Which the wise know, and fear not.

. . . .
Nay, but as when one layeth
  His worn-out robes away,
And, taking new ones, sayeth,
  "These will I wear to-day"
So putteth by the spirit
  Lightly its garb of flesh,
And passeth to inherit
  A residence afresh.[7]

Quite early in its development Hinduism appeared to some of its votaries as too priest-ridden, too much concerned with ceremonies and sacrifices. In the sixth and fifth centuries B.C., therefore, a reform movement arose to challenge the dominance of the Brahmans. Led by the famous teacher Gautama Sakyamuni, later the Buddha, this movement denied the necessity of rituals and priests, fought against the dogmas of the Brahmans, and opposed caste. The gist of Buddha's teaching was that sorrow existed in the world; that it sprang mainly from individual self-seeking and love of material things; and that sorrow would continue as long as the individual was chained to the Wheel of Birth and Rebirth. Only successive life experiences could teach man's soul the illusion of self-seeking and show him that, finally, rest and peace would be achieved by reabsorption of the soul into universal life or the state of nirvana.

It is too often not understood that the distinction between Buddhism and Hinduism was fundamentally, in India at least, only sectarian. Some of the basic ideas of Hinduism were accepted by this reform movement, such as *Maya* and rebirth, and Buddha was regarded as a Hindu saint. Buddhism was a vital force in Indian religious life for almost a thousand years, but it was ultimately absorbed there by Hinduism, while it continued to live on in such areas as Ceylon, Tibet, and China. Although repudiated as a distinct sect in the land of its

[7] *The Bhagavad-Gita*, translated by Edward Arnold ("The Harvard Classics," XLV; New York: P. F. Collier and Son, 1910), pp. 806-807.

birth, it did exercise profound influence upon Hindu thought, especially in the realm of pacifism or *Ahimsa* (non-violence). In the final chapter we will see how Buddhism is again exercising profound influence upon Indian thought.

The first recorded contact of India with the West came in the sixth century B.C., when the Persian emperor sent out an explorer who sailed down the Indus to its mouth, and thence up the Red Sea to the present site of Suez. Shortly afterwards the Persians captured the Punjab, which became a satrapy (province) of their empire. The fourth century B.C. was destined to record momentous events. The Greek city-states collapsed, Macedonia rose to power, Rome began its amazing march to world empire, and Alexander the Great toppled over the mighty empire of the Persians. After this last feat, Alexander moved eastward and conquered first Afghanistan and then the Punjab. His aim was to conquer the rich Magadha Kingdom in the Ganges valley. The conqueror, however, confronted with discontent and possible mutiny among his homesick troops, had to return to the West, and in 323 B.C. his grandiose plans of further conquest ended with his death. Alexander's Indian conquests were taken over by one of his generals, Seleucus.

It was at this time that a young man named Chandragupta Maurya appeared on the scene. Ousting the Greeks, he next conquered Magadha and established a great empire in north India. We have a vivid picture of his capital at Pataliputra from the pen of Megasthenes, ambassador from the court of Seleucus. The most illustrious member of the Maurya dynasty was Asoka, grandson of his house's founder, who became emperor in 273 B.C.

We know more about Asoka than about any other early Indian ruler. At the outset of his reign he was eager for military glory, but during one of his campaigns he experienced a revulsion against war and bloodshed, and was converted to Buddhism. Abhorring the idea of taking any form of life, he went so far as to discontinue the royal hunts and forbade the kitchens of the palace to kill animals for the table. A devout Buddhist, Asoka sent numerous missions to various lands to propagate his faith. Missionaries were sent to Ceylon, to south India, Burma, Egypt, and Kashmir, and had great influence in disseminating Indian civilization.

Asoka stands out par excellence as one of the best examples in world history of the benevolent ruler who had no thought but the welfare of his subjects. Acting as the servant of the people, he liberalized the laws, set up hospitals for the sick, and dug wells and planted shade trees along the roads. He was an eager builder, the first to use stone in India. His great palace, now no more, was in its day the wonder of the Chinese pilgrims. Asoka built many memorials, called stupas, to Buddhist saints. They were solid-domed structures of brick and stone built on a round base with beautifully carved balustrades and gateways. In addition to these the principal remains of the reign of Asoka are his magnificent pillars, huge sandstone monoliths, forty to fifty feet high, weighing some fifty tons. The pillars were surmounted by capitals ornamented usually by symbolic figures. The most striking of these capitals is the one at Sarnath, with its four magnificent lions, which is now used by the government of the Union of India as a symbol of the state. The late Dr. V. A. Smith has said, "It would be difficult to find in any country an example of ancient animal sculpture superior or even equal to this beautiful work of art, which successfully combines realistic modelling with ideal dignity and is finished in every detail with perfect accuracy." [8]

Under Asoka the Maurya Empire reached its height, including Hindustan in the north and much of the Deccan. In 232 B.C., however, the great ruler died, and the empire began to decline immediately with his passing. By 185 B.C. the Maurya Empire had collapsed. It fell before renewed invasions of central Asian tribes, especially the Scythians, who in turn were overrun by Asian nomads called Kushans. After the extinction of the Maurya authority, with the exception of two relatively short periods, there was no political unity in north India for 1400 years.

The Kushans referred to above were invaders who took over the civilization of the people they conquered in north India. Under Kanishka (120-162 A.D.) they set up a large border state including northwest India and a large area of central Asia comprising Afghanistan. The Kushan capital was located near Peshawar. This state was the meeting place for many races and cultures; contacts with China were encouraged, and this was the beginning of a continuous interchange between the two countries, while Kushan relations with Rome were also very cordial. Kanishka became a Buddhist and a patron of the arts and of learning. Especially famous is the distinctive school of art, called the Gandharan, that flourished at this time. This art was Greek in technique but Indian in spirit, and its most important gift was the evolution of an image of the Buddha. Gandharan art spread through Turkestan to China and even to Japan.

After the death of Kanishka, events in northern India

[8] Quoted in Majumdar, Raychaudhuri, and Datta, *op. cit.*, p. 226.

shaped themselves into a pattern that was to recur over and over in the political annals of the country. The Kushan Empire broke up and another dark period ensued. Little is known of the political history of northern India until the advent of the Gupta Empire in the fourth century.

While the invasions through the mountain passes spent their main force in the plains of Hindustan and interfered little with central and south India, political unity was just as evanescent in the Deccan and in Tamil Land as it was in the north. From time to time flourishing kingdoms arose giving promise of unifying south India, but this object was never achieved. The history of the Deccan and Tamil Land is the story of the rise and fall of kingdoms and of constant warfare.

Among the most important kingdoms of the south in Tamil Land were those of the Pandyas, Cholas, and Pallavas. In general, Tamil civilization was very advanced, based as it was on a flourishing sea trade. Tamil rulers, especially the Cholas, had great fleets which sailed to Ceylon, Burma, Java, and even the Far East. In 45 A.D. the use of the monsoon in navigation had been discovered and, taking advantage of these prevailing winds, ships could now cross the Arabian Sea instead of hugging the coast. The trade of Tamil Land with Rome was particularly active, as Europe greatly prized the spices, perfumes, precious stones, and textiles of south India. Several Roman colonies were set up in Tamil Land, and it has been estimated that the annual drain from Rome to India approximated 4 million dollars.

While, politically, kingdoms rose and fell and there was a fatal fragmentation, culturally the Tamil cities were on a par with the most advanced urban civilizations in the world. Flourishing cities were built, huge irrigation projects constructed, and remarkable progress made in architecture, as is attested by the temples at Tanjore and Madura. We are fortunate to have a picture of south India from the pen of Marco Polo, who visited the area on his return from China in 1293 A.D.

To return to north India, political disunity and confusion gave way in the fourth century A.D. to the orderly rule of one great paramount power. The dynasty known as the imperial Guptas began its rapid rise in 320 A.D., and by the time of its greatest ruler, Chandragupta II (not to be confused with Chandragupta Maurya), who was on the throne from 380 to 413 A.D., nearly all of north India was united in one empire. The Guptas gave India a glorious period of civilization, one which is to this land what the Periclean Age is in the annals of Greece.

A graphic picture of the glories of the Guptas has been handed down in the journal of a Chinese pilgrim, Fa Hian. He writes of an empire peaceful, prosperous, and well-governed. Art at this time enjoyed its classical period as definite types, conventions, and ideals of beauty crystallized. Gupta art, in keeping with fundamental esthetic Indian canons, was subjective and always sprang from a religious urge. This was the greatest period in Indian sculpture, and the artists of this time developed the standard type of divinity, both Buddhist and Hindu. Perhaps the Buddha images found at Sarnath, near Benares, constitute the finest sculpture yet found in India. Few examples of Gupta painting survive, the most famous being the Buddhist frescoes on the walls and ceilings of the Ajanta caves. The subjects of these paintings are the life of Buddha and scenes from court and domestic life in India. This most famous body of surviving painting gives evidence of having been done over a period of five hundred years, and its scenes are valuable in giving us a picture of Indian social life fifteen hundred years ago. As for Gupta architecture, there is nothing to compare with the sculpture of Sarnath or the Ajanta frescoes, for little has survived. We know that spacious buildings were erected and imposing palaces built, but all these were destroyed by the ravages of the Muslim and Hun invaders.

The Gupta period witnessed a lush flowering of literature. This was the golden age of Sanskrit, the sacred language of the Brahmans. Knowledge was systematized, and the epic poem, the *Mahabharata,* was recast and put into its present form. A secular literature developed, consisting of lyric poetry, fables, and drama. The Gupta court was the patron of a group of famous writers, most outstanding being Kalidasa, the great master of Sanskrit. A great stir was created in Europe in 1789 when Europeans first learned of Kalidasa's masterpiece, the play *Shakuntala,* through the translation of Sir William Jones. One of the most important contributions of India to world literature has been its great storehouse of fables, fairy stories, and animal tales. Their themes have been borrowed by the writers of many nations, such as Chaucer, Boccaccio, Shakespeare, and Kipling in western Europe. The *Panchatantra,* a collection of animal tales, was carried to the courts of Baghdad, Byzantium, and Cairo and thence to Europe.

In science, scholarship, and industry, Gupta India had few competitors and many imitators. The greatest university, that at Nalanda, attracted students from all over Asia. Eight colleges and three libraries ministered to the needs of the students.

In mathematics the influence of Hindu mathematicians has been profound. The so-called "Arabic numerals," the zero, and the decimal place system all originated in India and were gradually transmitted westward to Europe. Advanced in chemistry and metallurgy, Indian industry was famous for its fine dyes and for the tempering of steel and iron. Above all, India was the home of fine fabrics; the methods of making many of these were taken over by the Arabs and from them by Europeans. The Arabs named one Indian fabric *quittan,* hence the word *cotton. Calico* comes from Calicut in India, and the terms *chintz, cashmere,* and *bandanna* are also Indian.

A famous Indian philosopher has written, "Half the world moves on independent foundations which Hinduism supplied. China and Japan, Tibet and Siam, Burma and Ceylon look to India as their spiritual home." [9] This statement may appear extravagant to people of the West, but what it refers to is India's past dynamic role in Asia, especially at its height during the Gupta period, when its culture spread, its maritime power was evident on many seas, and waves of colonists established numerous overseas kingdoms. Especially did China and India maintain intimate relations, with the former sending constant streams of devout Buddhist pilgrims to the latter's monasteries and to seats of learning like Nalanda. Although many cultural traits were borrowed from India, the Chinese were careful not to be too much influenced by the asceticism of their teacher. Perhaps this feeling was responsible for the following Chinese proverb: "If the government gets hold of you, they'll flog you to death; if the Buddhists get hold of you, they'll starve you to death." [10]

From the first century A.D. colonists from India sailed across the seas to Burma, Malaya, Borneo, Java, Indochina, and Ceylon. Many kingdoms were established in Greater India. One area of Indian colonization was in Kambuja (Cambodia), where several Hindu dynasties rose and fell. One of the most famous was that of the Khmer kings, who, about the year 1100 A.D., built the magnificent temple of Angkor Vat. This edifice, dedicated to Shiva, covered three and a half square miles. With its galleries covered with fine bas-reliefs of scenes from the Hindu epics, it must be acknowledged one of the greatest religious monuments ever constructed by man.

Another famous colonial Indian dynasty was the Sailen-

[9] Sir S. Radhakrishnan, *The Hindu View of Life* (London: George Allen & Unwin, Ltd., 1927), p. 12.
[10] Quoted in Nehru, *The Discovery of India,* p. 193.

dra, which built up a wide-flung empire in Malaya, Siam, Java, and Bali. Followers of Buddhism, the Sailendras built many splendid temples, including the greatest Buddhist shrine in the world at Borobudur in Java.

Referring to the diffusion of Indian culture to Indochina, Malaya, Sumatra, and Java, an Indian historian writes: "Indian religion, Indian culture, Indian laws and Indian government moulded the lives of the more primitive races all over this wide region, and they imbibed a more elevated moral spirit and a higher intellectual taste through the art and literature of India." [11] Toward the end of the Middle Ages, much of the area came into the hands of Muslim invaders, and the Indian kingdoms were destroyed; but remnants of Indian culture survive in dances and legends originally brought from Hindustan and Tamil Land.

After giving northern India political unity and peace for less than two centuries, the Gupta Empire began to decline. Central Asian nomads, the White Huns, began to attack the empire in 455 A.D., and the main Gupta army was defeated. The Huns were finally defeated, but not before they had succeeded in dealing a death blow to the Guptas, whose empire collapsed in 480 A.D.

The curtain comes down on northern India for a hundred years, but out of the wreckage of the Gupta kingdom a powerful but short-lived state emerged. In 606 A.D. a ruler named Harsha came to rule a state located just north of modern Delhi. After much fighting nearly all the lands formerly held by the Guptas came under the control of Harsha. For forty-one years peace and strong government prevailed in north India. From the writings of a Chinese pilgrim we have an intimate picture of Harsha, who undoubtedly must have been a remarkable man. Tolerant of all religions, special patron of Buddhism, friend of poets, and himself no mean literary figure, Harsha stands out with Asoka and Chandragupta II as one of the greatest figures in Indian history.

On the death of this great ruler in 647 A.D., his empire collapsed. This was the last of the great native kingdoms of the north. Indian history again became the story of the rivalry and feuding of petty states, and north India had to wait for five hundred years for another paramount power.

About 1000 A.D., a definite deterioration in Indian strength, morality, and creativeness became apparent. The last great waves of colonization subsided and a spirit of complacency mounted as the invasions from the north ceased. Except for a toehold secured by Muslim Arab invaders in the Sind, there was no serious menace from the outside from the fall of the Guptas to the eleventh century. Contact with China diminished, and the result of this isolation was a spirit of smugness and superiority. A contemporary observer noted:

> The Hindus believe that there is no country but theirs, no nation like theirs, no kings like theirs, no religion like theirs, no sciences like theirs. . . . If they travelled and mixed with other nations they would soon change their mind, for their ancestors were not so narrow-minded as the present generations.[12]

Social organization, and the caste system in particular, became set in a rigid, inflexible mold that was inimical to innovation and progress. Nehru asserts that this led to a "decline all along the line—intellectual, philosophical, political, in techniques and methods of war, in knowledge of and contacts with the outside world." [13] Literature declined, in the arts there was representation of moral perversions, and in religion there came about the growth of such practices as the Devadasi system (generally referred to as temple prostitution). Although in southern India there were some kingdoms that could be called "national," enjoying the support of the people in general, in most of India the governmental structure was weak. The government of Indian kingdoms, in most instances, consisted of a corrupt bureaucracy in which the state was held together by the power of the ruling dynasty, not by the support of its subjects.[14]

All in all, India around the beginning of the eleventh century was hardly in a position to hold off a serious threat from without; but before recounting its conquest at the hands of the Muslim invaders, it will be appropriate to sum up the Hindu period from 3000 B.C. to 1000 A.D. In retrospect, Indian history during this period is largely one of numerous alien streams forcing their way into northern India. In spite of this constant ethnic interruption from without, the invading cultures were absorbed by the dominant racial stocks in India. The essential core was the Aryo-Dravidian Synthesis, and to it such other elements as Greek, Persian, Scythian, and Hun were added and assimilated. Caste played an important role in the process, for it offered a place and a status for any type of culture. The absorptive capacity of Hinduism is also partly explained by its tolerance. "Hindu-

---

[12] Quoted in K. M. Panikkar, *A Survey of Indian History* (London: Meridian Books, Ltd., 1948), p. 130.

[13] Nehru, *The Discovery of India*, p. 221.

[14] Panikkar, *A Survey of Indian History*, p. 137.

ism absorbs everything that enters into it, magic or animism, and raises it to a higher level." [15] Names mean little; Brahma, Vishnu, Kali, Buddha, are used indiscriminately for God the Absolute Reality. Linked to its absorptive capacity was its tenacity. Hinduism weathered many shocks. As we will see shortly, one of the most shattering blows came with the Islamic conquest, but Hinduism, unlike Christianity in the Near East, survived in the land of its birth.

In addition to tenacity and absorptive capacity, religiosity has been another important attribute of Hinduism. From Vedic times there has been preoccupation with the mystery of life. The qualities of mysticism, brooding, and asceticism have been much more pronounced than was the case even in the heyday of monasticism in medieval Europe. Religion dominated thought and art. This was true in the long era from the Vedas to 1000 A.D., and it continued to be true down to modern times. Unlike Europe, India, up to the twentieth century at least, never went through a potent secularizing process.

Another fundamental feature of the Indian traditional culture pattern has been its neglect of what we might call the science of society, and more specifically the art of government. Attention throughout the ages has been centered mainly on otherworldly matters. It is natural that mundane politics would hardly have much appeal in a society whose members considered existence an evil and an illusion, and who were primarily interested in escape from, and not fulfillment in, the world.

It is perhaps this emphasis upon metaphysical matters and the consequent neglect of humanistic values that explain what would seem to be a serious weakness in Indian development. The country has suffered constantly from political fragmentation. Even in those kingdoms that did achieve a modicum of greatness, "the political and administrative unity of the territory achieved spasmodically by able and victorious monarchs," writes A. R. Desai, "was surface unity." [16]

There is a tendency on the part of some Indian authors to make much of the "democratic tradition" of the Indian village, the basic cell of the country. Each of these villages had its little council, the Panchayat, and they have been referred to as "little republics." It should be understood, however, that what self-government existed functioned only within the village. The people never had an opportunity of extending their political activities outside the confines of

15 Radhakrishnan, *op. cit.*, p. 47.
16 A. R. Desai, *Social Background of Indian Nationalism* (Bombay: Oxford University Press, 1949), p. 15.

their local Panchayat. "In spite of Indian claims," asserts an English authority, "hitherto the system of government has had no roots spreading right down among the masses of people." [17] The self-governing village Panchayat was a vigorous and hardy seed of democracy, but it was never nurtured into anything on a provincial or national scale. It has been pointed out that popular parliaments or councils in the upper political brackets are not found in Indian history. These were to come only as a result of the influence of the West in the nineteenth century.

The Impact of the Muslims

Up to 1000 A.D. India had been able to assimilate the numerous invaders who had pushed through the narrow passes of her northern mountain wall. But not long after the death of King Harsha in the seventh century and the collapse of a strong government in the north, a new invasion movement began to take form that would seriously challenge the traditional capacity of Hinduism to absorb alien cultures.

As early as the year 711 Muslim Arabs came in conflict with Indians when an expedition of Arab marauders reached the mouth of the Indus and captured the area of Sind. Further expansion in this region, however, was blocked, and Muslim raids into India were started in earnest from the northwest late in the tenth century. Under the redoubtable Amir Mahmud of Ghazni, an Afghan Turk who began raiding in 998, seventeen looting expeditions were carried out. Few of the previous invaders into India matched the ferocity and ruthlessness of Mahmud's Turks. To his Muslim horsemen, India was a land handed over by Allah for pillage and plunder. Fiercely monotheistic, detesting idolatry, and believing in the equality of man, the Muslims abhorred the "Hindu infidels and unbelievers" with their idols and their caste system.

The Hindus opposed the Muslim invader with desperation, and terrible battles were fought. No quarter was given on either side, thousands were massacred, and the cities and temples of the land were destroyed or despoiled. On occasion, when Hindu defenders of a stronghold realized that further resistance was futile, they carried out the terrible rite Jauhar, in which the men assembled their women and children, placed them on a huge pyre, and then, as the flames extinguished the lives of their families, sallied forth from the gates to die with sword in hand. Although resistance was

[17] Sir George E. Schuster and Guy Wint, *India and Democracy* (London: Macmillan and Co., Ltd., 1941), p. 242.

desperate, the Hindu armies were no match for the invaders. Hindu military tactics were outmoded; their lumbering war elephants could not cope with the fast maneuvers of the horsemen from central Asia. Furthermore, the defenders of India were not united, and they were additionally weakened by the fact that fighting was the traditional duty of only one caste.

A new chapter in Muslim invasion began in 1191 when Mohammed Ghori, an Afghan, not only raided India but began to occupy the country. By 1200 Mohammed Ghori controlled much of northern India, and on his death in 1206 one of his generals established a Muslim kingdom at Delhi. This Delhi Sultanate was in existence from 1206 until 1526. Its heyday was in the first century and a half of its rule, when the sultans re-established political unity in northern India. Military expeditions were also dispatched into the south, and the Hindu kingdoms in the Deccan and Tamil Land were conquered.

After 1388 the Delhi Sultanate weakened. Strong government collapsed amid a welter of warring small states, and in 1398 the dread Amir Timur, the Tamerlane of English literature, invaded India and sacked Delhi. In 1450 the Delhi Sultanate was revived. Its rulers, however, were generally puppets who did not succeed in reuniting the old Delhi Empire. These sultans maintained a precarious existence until 1526, when they too, like their victims before them, fell prey to an invasion from the north.

In 1524 the chieftain Babur, founder of the Mogul dynasty, invaded India. This hard-fighting leader of men, a Turk descended from Timur and Genghis Khan, had started out as the ruler of a small kingdom in what is now Russian Turkestan. In 1504 he captured the important Afghan stronghold of Kabul, and in 1519 he began to move toward India. With a ridiculously small force, only twelve thousand men, Babur pushed into India in 1524 and two years later defeated the forces of the decrepit Delhi Sultanate at the decisive battle of Panipat. Thus the Mogul dynasty ("Mogul" comes from the Arabic word for "Mongol") was established in India and was to be a dominant factor in the country's history from 1526 until 1707, the date of the death of the last great Mogul emperor.

The son of Babur had considerable difficulty in holding his own in northern India, and for a time he was forced to flee the country. His son, Akbar, destined to be the greatest of the Moguls, succeeded to a weak throne in 1556. Though only thirteen years of age, the young ruler defeated a strong Hindu army and then proceeded to control and purge his conniving court. Akbar was resolute, strong, and efficient, and by 1576 he had eliminated all opposition in northern India and ruled over a submissive and dutiful empire stretching from the Himalayas to the Vindhya Mountains.

Akbar had a noble vision: his central purpose was to unite Hindus and Muslims in a common loyalty to the crown. He accordingly abolished the *jizya*, the tax on non-Muslims. Hindus were employed in many branches of the government, and religious toleration was offered to all. In particular, Akbar strove to conciliate the proud and martial Rajput Hindu princes. His policy of toleration was a significant departure from the bigotry of the sultans of Delhi.

Akbar was outstanding as a civil administrator. The empire was organized into a dozen provinces and placed in the hands of a well-paid and competent civil service. Well-educated men from all parts of central Asia flocked into India to become important administrative cogs in the Mogul bureaucracy; about 30 per cent of the officials, mainly in the middle and lower grades, were Hindus. An efficient system of land revenue was organized and a royal mint set up that produced coins not matched at this time, for design, in any other state in the world. The Mogul Empire at the beginning of the seventeenth century was probably the best-organized and most prosperous then existing in the world.[18]

Akbar as a man was an intriguing and appealing character. Though he was not formally educated—and was, in fact, illiterate—he was one of the "best-read" men of his day, for many books were read to him by his scholars. Akbar was a profound thinker and a patron of the arts and of learning. Nothing suited this Grand Mogul so much as to listen in on a brilliant conversation; and so we learn that "Crowds of learned men from all nations, and sages of various religions and sects, came to the court [where] they would talk about profound points of science, the subtleties of revelation, the curiosities of history, and the wonders of nature." [19]

Akbar was at heart a religious mystic who was searching for some eternal verity that somehow he could not find in Islam. The emperor finally founded a new religion consisting, as he thought, of the best in all religions and one that could be accepted by both his Muslim and his Hindu subjects.

Akbar must be considered one of the great figures of world history. In his own day he did not suffer one whit in comparison with such contemporaries as the French Henry

18 Rawlinson, *India: A Short Cultural History*, p. 308.
19 Quoted in Will Durant, *The Story of Civilization* (New York: Simon and Schuster, 1935), I, p. 469.

of Navarre or Elizabeth of England. The successors of the great emperor, however, did not measure up to his greatness. His son Jehangir, who ruled from 1605 to 1627, was an indolent and ineffectual sovereign who ended his days a drunkard. There was little expansion during Jehangir's reign, the one important development being the coming of English merchants to India.

Jehangir's son, Shah Jahan, came to the throne in a welter of blood, and before the fighting was over he had killed most of his male relatives. This reign is supposedly the summit of Mogul power. The wealth of the emperor was enormous, the treasury holding the equivalent of more than a billion dollars. Shah Jahan was a magnificent builder, his masterpiece being the world-famous Taj Mahal, a beautiful white marble tomb built in honor of his favorite wife. This structure, called "the miracle of miracles, the final wonder of the world," employed twenty thousand workers for fifteen years. Underneath the glitter and magnificence of the Mogul court, however, all was not well. The great mass of the people no longer prospered as under Akbar. They were heavily taxed, and, what was worse, Shah Jahan reversed the tolerant policy of his grandfather and set about destroying Hindu temples.

The climax of the empire of the Moguls came during the reign of Aurangzeb (1659-1707). His path to the throne, like that of his father, was drenched with the blood of his victims, mainly his brothers. For the first twenty years of his reign he was occupied almost exclusively with domestic matters. Unfortunately, his object was to free the land of heretics. Muslim apostates were put to death. The poll tax was reimposed on the Hindus, their temples were destroyed, and the ranks of the bureaucracy were purged and cleansed of nonbelievers. The noble ideal of a secular state comprehending men of various religions had been forgotten.

Having sought to restore a pristine orthodoxy to Islam in India, Aurangzeb embarked on his second main objective, the complete political unification of India under Mogul rule. The conquest of central and south India, directed mainly against independent Muslim kingdoms and the proud Hindu hill people, the Mahrattas, began in 1681. By 1690 all effective opposition had been crushed. For the first time in all its history the Indian subcontinent was under one sovereignty. From the Himalayas to Cape Comorin the writ of Aurangzeb was supposedly supreme. But not for long. Revolts broke out in various parts of the empire as its different peoples—Sikhs, Mahrattas, and Rajputs—rose in rebellion. For more than fifteen years Aurangzeb moved his great unwieldy army across the country trying to crush his foes, above all the Mahrattas; in the end he completely failed. Aurangzeb died while in the field at the age of eighty-nine, with the forces of rebellion, whose ranks he had done so much to fill by his bigotry and intolerance, still defiant and undefeated.

The Muslim impact upon the pattern of Indian culture was profound and widespread in its influence. During the first phase of the conquest there was much brutality and even massacre. During this time the religious fanaticism of the victors frequently caused severe suffering among the subject Hindus. But while the rich Hindus saw their goods and land confiscated, the lives of the masses of people in their villages were little touched by the new masters.

After this phase of conquest had been completed, there was a settling-down process. The Muslim rulers had to organize government, collect taxes, and stabilize their position. In the process there was bound to be a mixing of cultures. Hindus were employed in the civil service, especially in the subordinate posts. There was some intermarriage, especially between Turks and Moguls and Hindu women. In order to escape taxation, on occasion to be free from the incubus of caste, or to secure preferment in government, some Hindus were converted to Islam. The number, however, relatively speaking, was remarkably small.

Culture traits passed from one group to the other. The institution of purdah—i.e., the seclusion of women—was copied by the Hindus. Hindi, the Indian vernacular, was adapted by the Muslims as a kind of lingua franca; changed to Urdu by the use of Persian instead of Sanskrit script and by the addition of Persian and Arabic words, this modified Hindi became the common language of the day. Mogul manners were copied throughout the country. Just as the court of Louis XIV was imitated in Europe, the food, manner of dress, and system of etiquette prevailing at the Mogul capital were the models for both Muslim and Hindu princes in India. More fundamentally, Muslim thought, with its emphasis upon monotheism and democracy, made a deep impression upon Hinduism and led to the birth of important new movements that sought to reform and liberalize the native faith.

Culture reached a new height in India under the Moguls. Their courts were famous for their great luxury and for being the center of a galaxy of artists and scholars. Akbar employed many artists, lapidaries, artisans, and architects. While sculpture was neglected, Akbar founded an important school of Indo-Persian painting, which later was influenced by the Italian style. The exquisite work of this Mogul school of art can be seen in most of the great museums of the West. The official court language of the Moguls was Persian, and many important Sanskrit works were translated into this language. While the classical Indian language, Sanskrit, was displaced, there was an important advance in the development of Indian vernaculars, especially in the north. The most famous poet of this new literature was Tulsi Das (1532-1623), often considered the greatest of all Indian poets.

It was in architecture that the Muslims made their greatest achievement, combining Persian and Indian elements into a distinctive new style. Indo-Islamic architecture began with the Delhi sultans, who introduced mosques and tombs and added to Indian forms the arch, dome, and minaret. With the Moguls the Indian influence declined. Their buildings were characterized by the use of the bulbous dome, the cupolas at corners on slender pillars, and lofty vaulted gateways. The city of Fathpur Sikri, built by Akbar, with its glorious mosque, tomb, baths, and palace; the Taj Mahal of Shah Jahan; and this latter emperor's palace at Delhi with its marble and richly inlaid pillars and its Peacock Throne— all attest to the rich architectural contributions of Islam in India.

The Muslim conquest introduced a new kind of invader into India with a culture both proud and militant and with no intention of being assimilated.

By 1707, with the death of Aurangzeb, the Mogul Empire rapidly fell apart. It was an Asiatic despotism, whose cycle can well be described in the words of Edward Gibbon, "one unceasing round of valour, greatness, discord, degeneracy, and decay." [20] Although in theory the Mogul emperors sat on their thrones until 1858, they were increasingly impotent after 1707, *rois fainéants* with hardly anything left but memories of the glorious past. The Mogul cultural contribution remained.

[20] Quoted in Stanley Lane-Poole, *Medieval India Under Mohammedan Rule, 712-1764* (New York: G. P. Putnam's Sons, 1903), p. 34.

East India House

3. The Supremacy and Spirit of British Rule

As THE ONCE ALL-POWERFUL and strongly unified Mogul Empire declined, it left in the wake of its collapse a power vacuum in India. Several promising indigenous powers might well have risen to the challenge of creating again a structure of political unity for the country; but they failed to do so, leaving the European trading companies which were already on hand no other alternative than to intervene. It was out of this background of turmoil, as we shall see in this chapter, that the English East India Company emerged as the political sovereign of India.

The narrative of the Company's conquest is an absorbing and even an amazing story of courage, audacity, and often downright chicanery; but much more important were the effects of Company rule upon Indian life and institutions. In the long chronicle of invasion, with the exception, of course, of the all-important Aryan incursions, no invaders—not even the Muslims—modified, influenced, and even reshaped the pattern of things in India as did the British rulers.

Western rule brought India into contact with the major historical trends—political, economic, scientific, and intellectual—that were agitating and infiuencing the European world. As we shall see in this chapter, these contacts had mixed results, good and bad. The important thing, however, is to see how a new India was created largely as a result of the British impact. This new India was effectively united, politically, for the first time. It began to become conscious of the importance of the humanistic and secular approach to life's problems. Eagerly its leaders imbibed and digested the food of European liberalism, with its emphasis on democracy, that was made available in the school system established by British rule. And in the area of economics, it was jarred out of the old avenues of barter and self-sufficiency into the highways of world markets, international finance, and at least the first stages of industrialization.

The return of the spice-laden ships of Vasco da Gama from Calicut to Lisbon in September 1499 marked the beginning of the European contact with India; from this time on steadily increasing European influence finally became control. Six years later, in 1505, a rapidly expanding trade justified the appointment of Francisco de Almeida as the first Portuguese viceroy, or Governor of the East. Under his direction, control of the Indian Ocean was wrested from the Arabs, and his successor, Alfonse de Albuquerque, established Portuguese settlements at Goa, Malacca, Ormuz, and the island of Socotra off the entrance to the Red Sea.

For roughly a century the Portuguese commercial supremacy, built on the foundation of sea power, remained unchallenged. Tremendous revenues flowed to Goa, the capital of the Portuguese empire, and an immense trade monopoly was established. After 1600, however, the growing sea power of the Dutch and English, and the corruption, religious intolerance, and deterioration of Portuguese officialdom in the East combined to lessen the importance of Portugal as a power in Indian affairs.

By the mid-seventeenth century Portugal had ceased to be a factor in Indian development. Her rule had introduced Catholicism, popularized the use of tobacco, and given many words to Indian languages, but by the twentieth century all that remained of the once mighty Portuguese empire was a few decayed bits of territory on the west coast of India.

Between 1596 and 1602 fifteen Dutch expeditions were sent to the East, and in the latter year the great United Dutch East India Company was organized. These traders were determined to drive the Portuguese out of the Spice Islands and to challenge their trading monopoly in India. After capturing important Portuguese posts in the Spice Islands in the early 1600's, the Dutch expanded their empire, and by 1658 they were firmly established in Java, Goa, Malacca, and Ceylon. Dutch trading posts in India were opened at Surat, Masulipatam, and Pulicat before 1620, and other trading sites were acquired throughout the seventeenth century.

The first Englishman to come to India was Father Thomas Stevens, a refugee Jesuit who landed in Goa in 1579.

As the reign of Queen Elizabeth ended, English interest in the trade of the East mounted rapidly. The leader of the first English traders to the East, Captain Lancaster, returned in 1594 from a three-year trip to Malaya. In 1599 Dutch merchants raised the price of pepper, and a group of English traders, having met in London to determine how they could escape the rising Dutch monopoly in the East, incorporated on December 31, 1600, as "The Governor and Company of Merchants of London trading into the East Indies." One hundred and twenty-five shareholders of the English East India Company subscribed £70,000 and were given exclusive trading rights and other prerogatives in the East for an initial period of fifteen years, after which these privileges were to be periodically renewed.

At the outset the English East India Company was mainly interested in the trading opportunities in Malaya and the East Indies, not those in India. Altogether, between the years 1601 and 1618, nine voyages were made, mainly to the Spice Islands. On the first of these expeditions (1601-1603) Captain Lancaster brought back to England 1 million pounds of pepper. The English, however, encountered the implacable hostility of the Dutch, and a species of undeclared war broke out. The final outcome was the so-called Massacre of Amboina in 1623, in which a small English factory, or trading post, in the Spice Islands was wiped out and its staff tortured and executed. By 1624 the Dutch had driven their competitors completely out of the islands.

Under these circumstances it was natural that the English should turn to the subcontinent of India, where pepper, albeit in smaller quantities, as well as silks, muslins, and calicoes, could be secured. The first landing in India was made by Captain William Hawkins, who disembarked at Surat early in 1609. Making his way to the Mogul emperor's court at Agra, he soon ingratiated himself with the chief officials and earned the favor of the emperor, Jehangir, by participating in his lusty drinking bouts. Hawkins succeeded in obtaining permission for the Company to erect a factory at Surat. In response the Portuguese began strenuously to bar English ships from Indian harbors, but in 1612 a small English naval squadron defeated a much larger flotilla of Portuguese vessels. Again, at the end of 1614, a much more decisive victory was gained by the English squadron over their European rivals.

The English East India Company was now free to proceed with the task of expanding its activities in India. Permission was obtained from the Mogul authorities to set up other factories at Agra, Ahmadabad, Broach, and Masulipatam. Much more important than these early factories was the actual acquisition of land by the Company in three widely separated but strategic spots. In 1639 a factor, Francis Day, secured a lease of land from a local Indian ruler on the Coromandel coast. On this strip of land, on the Cooum River, a fort named St. George was built; it was to grow into the modern city of Madras. In 1660 Bombay with its magnificent harbor came to Charles II as part of the dowry of Catherine of Braganza, when the English monarch married the Portuguese princess. In 1668 Charles handed Bombay over to the English East India Company. Calcutta, which has been described as "the third leg of the tripod on which England has built up its supremacy in India," [1] was founded in 1690 by a Company official named Job Charnock on a desolate and marshy east bank of the Ganges, and nine years later the Mogul government granted a definite lease of the land on which was built Fort William.

Seventeenth-century India

What kind of country did the English find when they arrived in India early in the seventeenth century? In comparison with other countries in this period before the Industrial Revolution it had important industries, active commerce, and a favorable balance of trade. Europe could supply few goods wanted by Indians, and in return for the pepper and textiles so avidly desired by the West her traders had to pay in precious metals, usually silver. Sir Thomas Roe, ambassador of the English East India Company at the Mogul court, referred to the situation when he remarked that "Europe bleedeth to enrich Asia." [2]

The manufacture of cotton cloth was the most important industry, while others of sizable dimensions were silk weaving; shawl and carpet weaving; the production of saltpeter (used in gunpowder); the making of paper, glass, and pottery. There has been a tendency on the part of some modern Indian economists to overemphasize the extent and importance of industry in Mogul India. For example, R. C. Dutt writes, "India in the eighteenth century was a great manufacturing as well as great agricultural country, and the products of the Indian looms supplied the markets of Asia and Europe." [3]

[1] C. M. Cross, *The Development of Self-Government in India, 1858-1914* (Chicago: University of Chicago Press, 1922), p. 2.

[2] Quoted in W. H. Moreland, *From Akbar to Aurangzeb* (New York: The Macmillan Company, 1923), p. 53.

[3] R. C. Dutt, *The Economic History of India under Early British Rule* (2nd ed.; London: Kegan Paul, Trench, Trubner, and Co., Ltd., 1906), p. vii.

The truth of the matter would seem to indicate that the main industries were confined to a few large towns and that their products never enjoyed any wide market among the masses, who could not buy the luxury wares turned out by the urban workshops. Furthermore, the village—the heart of Indian life—was practically self-sufficient and economically isolated from the nearby town. In discussing these matters an Indian economist admits that "India was never a great manufacturing country in any adequate sense of the term." [4] Another index to the extent of Indian trade and manufacturing in the Mogul period has been expressed by the statement that in the time of Akbar a modern cargo ship of 5000 tons, sailing once a month, would have been sufficient to carry India's sea-borne trade.[5]

The social structure of India was bounded by two extremes. At the top there was a small but very wealthy aristocracy living on a palatial scale characterized by extravagance and pomp. The middle class was prosperous but numerically small and relatively unimportant. At the bottom of the social scale were the masses—perhaps more than 90 per cent of the population—whose condition in general was pitiful. The common man lacked adequate clothing, his work was usually not voluntary, and he suffered from the dread visitations of famine. In the seventeenth century, for example, there was an appalling famine in 1630-1631. European travelers have left us harrowing accounts of the misery of the population. There were eight other famines in the same century, and a well-known economic history dealing with this period says, "We must regard it [famine] rather as a spectre in the background, always visible to peasants, labourers and artisans, and coming forward from time to time to wreck the social and economic life of one region or another." [6]

Another aspect of Indian life in the Mogul period—and indeed even before the advent of Babur the Mogul—was the static life of the village in which the great majority of India's 100 million people lived. The village was not only isolated; it was caste-ridden and bound by custom. A modern Indian economist sums up the situation thus:

> The isolation of the village made the villager village-minded. The domination of caste over him in the minutest detail of his life, dictating to him not only what profession he should follow but how he should eat, marry and even die, made him caste conscious. The precarious nature of the

[4] P. Padmanabha Pillai, *Economic Conditions in India* (London: George Routledge and Sons, Ltd., 1925), p. 29.

[5] Sir John Cumming, ed., *Modern India* (London: Oxford University Press, 1932), p. 269.

[6] W. H. Moreland and Atul C. Chatterjee, *A Short History of India* (New York: Longmans, Green and Company, 1945), p. 248.

economic life of the village population struggling against Nature with weak instruments of production and not in co-operation with people outside the village but as a solitary human group, made it defeatist and penetrated with a feeling of helplessness and frustration.[7]

All of this is not to imply that on balance India suffered in any marked degree by comparison with socio-economic conditions in contemporary Europe. After all, the *Travels* of the Englishman Arthur Young add up to a very dismal picture of the state of the countryside in eighteenth-century France. The economic conditions alluded to in Mogul India, however, do tend to correct the roseate picture that some writers have painted of a veritable Utopia existing in pre-British India.

The Fall of the Mogul Power

Whatever prosperity and tranquillity India enjoyed in the sixteenth and seventeenth centuries disappeared early in the eighteenth when the Mogul Empire broke apart. The most immediate cause of this breakdown was the religious intolerance of the Emperor Aurangzeb, which led to open rebellion in many parts of the realm. It was to crush these revolts that the bigot ruler spent many years in the field, with immense armies consuming the revenues of the country and harrying the countryside. There were, however, more deep-seated causes. The corruption of officials, the extravagance of the nobility, and the oppression of the masses steadily drained away the empire's life blood. For some time there had been a noticeable deterioration in the character of the ruling Muslim caste. Wars of succession had wiped out the leading families, and new blood from central Asia was no longer recruited for the higher governmental posts. Finally, the Mogul Empire was an alien regime. It continued to be so after Akbar's policy of conciliation was abandoned, and it wore itself out trying to maintain its power against the ceaseless opposition, only now and then overt but always present, of the discontented Hindus. In summing up the reasons for the decline Vincent Smith writes:

> The Mogul empire, like all Asiatic despotisms, had shallow roots. Its existence depended mainly on the personal character of the reigning autocrat and on the degree of his military power. It lacked popular support, the strength based on patriotic feeling, and on the stability founded upon ancient tradition. . . .[8]

Following the death of Aurangzeb in 1707 the imperial authority became quite ineffectual. While emperors still sat

[7] A. R. Desai, *Social Background of Indian Nationalism* (Bombay: Oxford University Press, 1949), p. 13.
[8] Vincent Smith, *The Oxford History of India* (2d ed.; London: Oxford University Press, 1923), p. 465.

on the throne at Delhi, governors of various provinces declared their own independence and established separate dynasties. In this fashion one of the imperial viceroys became the ruler, or Nizam, of the state of Hyderabad in 1724. The area of Mysore in 1761 fell into the hands of two Muslim soldiers of fortune, Hyder Ali and his son, Tipu Sultan. At the same time both Bengal and Oudh became in effect independent kingdoms.

While members of the Muslim aristocracy were founding their own dynasties, a notable revival had been taking place in Hindu power, especially in the case of the Mahrattas and the Sikhs. The former were a hardy hill people whose home was in the western Ghats. The founder of their power was Sivaji, born in 1627, who became a kind of Robin Hood defying Mogul authority. Under their leader the Mahrattas built up a strong state with its center at the city of Poona. While Aurangzeb succeeded in crippling Mahratta power, he never quite extinguished it, and after his death it quickly revived. New Mahratta leaders carved out their own states, and quickly a great Mahratta confederacy was built up, covering all of the Deccan and extending its influence into north India.

About 1740 the Mahrattas decided to invade north India with the idea of seizing the imperial authority from the weak grasp of the Mogul emperor. Little opposition was met, and Mahratta forces reached the frontiers of Bengal in the east, and in the northwest occupied Delhi and annexed the Punjab. The Mahrattas, however, were not destined to become the heirs of the Moguls and thus unite India again. Their expansion was too rapid and their conquests were mainly predatory. They exacted *chauth,* or blackmail, from the conquered peoples and were continually raiding their neighbors for plunder. In 1761 whatever hope had been entertained by the Mahrattas of uniting Hindustan and the Deccan under their rule was shattered by the battle of Panipat, in which their main army was completely destroyed by Afghan forces that had been carrying out raids into the Punjab.

It was out of this confusion in northwest India that the Sikh power arose. As previously noted in Chapter 1, the origin of Sikhism goes back to the teaching of the holy man Nanak in the fifteenth century. The new sect was persecuted by Jehangir and Aurangzeb, with the Sikhs fighting desperately for their faith. As a result they organized themselves into a kind of warring brotherhood proud of their military prowess. The founder and unifier of the Sikh nation was the famous Ranjit Singh, born in 1780, who united his people in the Punjab, created a splendid army, and established a strong kingdom in northwest India. The Sikhs did not play an important role in eighteenth-century India but waited until the 1840's to try to expand their kingdom into a great empire.

By 1740 the Mogul Empire was in its death agony. Only the year before, the ruler of Persia had invaded India and captured the great imperial city of Delhi. The population was massacred and huge quantities of booty, including all the crown jewels and the famous Peacock Throne, were carted away by the invaders. From 1748 to 1762 there were repeated raids into northwest India. The incessant raids of the Mahrattas, the incursions of Afghans and Persians, and the rivalries of soldier adventurers as they fought among themselves for the tottering thrones brought about a collapse of law, order, and civilization unprecedented in the annals of world history.[9] Trade was disrupted, industry languished, and the condition of the masses in the villages was perhaps worse than it had been for the preceding five hundred years.

In addition to the various new powers that were springing up out of the debris of the Mogul realm there were also present the European trading companies. The Portuguese no longer counted. The Dutch had had brilliant success until 1670, but after that date they began to lag behind the English East India Company. By the closing decades of the eighteenth century the Dutch had virtually been eliminated from India, and today there are no Dutch possessions there; only a few quaint houses with Dutch tiles and carvings remain. There were also companies sent out by Denmark and Sweden, as well as the Austrian Ostend Company, but these had only an ephemeral existence.

The French came relatively late to India, for the French East India Company was not organized until 1664 by Colbert, the brilliant finance minister of Louis XIV. In the 1670's the company became very active and established important and thriving factories at Chandernagore in Bengal and at Pondicherry on the Coromandel coast. Other trading posts were subsequently acquired, such as Mahé, Karikal, and Yanaon, and early in the eighteenth century the French obtained possession of the strategic islands of Bourbon and Mauritius in the Indian Ocean.

Five powers were possible heirs of the Moguls in India— the French, the English, the states of Mysore and Hyderabad, and the Mahratta Confederacy. There were several possibilities: some kind of balance of power or equilibrium between members of the above powers might be achieved, or there might be continuous shifting of combinations and alliances

9 K. M. Panikkar, *A Survey of Indian History* (London: Meridian Books, Ltd., 1948), p. 266.

accompanied by endemic warfare. The last alternative might ultimately result in the unchallenged hegemony of one power that would destroy or assimilate all its rivals. As we will see, this last is what actually happened.

The first elimination took place among the European rivals who at first stood aloof from Indian politics. The various wars between England and France that convulsed eighteenth-century Europe had their repercussions not only in North America but also in India. At the outset, the French company, led by a brilliant leader, Dupleix, seemed on the verge of ousting the English from south India. This prospect was foiled by the audacious Robert Clive, young official of the English East India Company. Following the tragic "Black Hole of Calcutta" incident in which more than a hundred British subjects lost their lives at the hands of the Indian ruler of Bengal, Clive again showed his mettle by defeating a large native army at the decisive battle of Plassey in 1757. And between 1759 and 1760 British forces proceeded to destroy the remnants of French power in South India. By the Treaty of Paris in 1763 France retained only a few insignificant trading posts such as Pondicherry.

Meanwhile, internecine war and predatory raids continued unchecked in India. The strength of the English East India Company, however, grew steadily. The main settlements of the Company were havens of security to which many important Indian traders and bankers made their way. It is estimated that as early as 1744 there were 250,000 Indians living in Madras.

During the American Revolution, British power was challenged not only in the New World but in far-off India, where the British governor-general, Warren Hastings, confronted an alliance of the principal native powers left in India. These were Mysore, Hyderabad, and the Mahratta princes. Only by the most desperate measures did Hastings hold out; but by 1784 the emergency had ended.

The next significant period (1798-1805) is the governor-generalship of Lord Wellesley, older brother of the famous Duke of Wellington and a man of tremendous energy, military skill, and diplomatic astuteness. After Napoleon had landed in Egypt and had made contact with some of Britain's rivals in India, Wellesley destroyed the power of Tipu Sultan, the ruler of Mysore. By 1800 there were only two powers left, the Company and the Mahrattas. Turning against the latter power Wellesley defeated them decisively, but before his work was completed he was recalled by the London authorities. Wellesley not only defeated the Company's rivals on the field of battle but initiated the policy of extending control over the princely states by making them in effect protectorates. This was done by the system of subsidiary alliances by which the Indian princes accepted British garrisons, the cost of which was paid out of the funds of the rulers.

The tenacious power of the Mahrattas was finally crushed by Lord Moira, who was governor-general from 1814 to 1823. At the same time the Company, now dominant in the heart of the subcontinent, reached out to make itself secure

British India under Wellesley, 1799

on the frontiers of India. In campaigns from 1814 to 1818 the doughty mountaineers of Himalayan Nepal—the Gurkhas —were defeated and henceforth fought for British arms. In the northwest, in the Punjab, the proud Sikhs were in an expansionist mood. In the 1840's, after severe fighting, the turbaned Sikh armies were defeated and their lands were annexed by Lord Dalhousie, then the governor-general. The Company was also confronted by danger from the Kingdom of Burma, whose forces moved toward Calcutta. In two wars, in 1823 and again in 1852, British armies were victorious, and a large part of the Burmese Kingdom came under the East India Company.

By the 1840's the entire Indian subcontinent had come under British control, either directly (as in Madras, Bengal, and Bombay) or indirectly by the subsidiary treaties in the case of the protected princely states. British power, exercised through the agency of the East India Company, had fanned out in all directions from the Indus on the west, the Brahmaputra River on the east, the mountain wall of the Himalayas on the north, and Cape Comorin in the far south of Tamil Land.

The narrative in this chapter thus far has dealt largely with diplomatic maneuvering, alliances, wars, and treaties in which a half dozen powers competed against each other for supremacy. In these pages references have been made to the East India Company as the agent of Great Britain, and the terms "Company" and "Britain"—in India—have been used synonymously. What was the position of the Company? Was it a mere agent of the British government, or did it preserve some degree of independence while acting in the name and with the authority of the British crown?

In the following pages the status of the Company *vis-à-vis* the British government will be examined and the steps by which it became endowed with political rights and responsibilities recounted. Furthermore, after studying the rise of British supremacy in India, the logical question to raise is: What was done with this power, and how did it affect the destiny of the country and the lives and institutions of the Indians?

Of all the extraneous influences, none has been as momentous and significant as that of the British, although this contact was only really effective and widespread for a period of a hundred and fifty years, during which time India in whole or in part was under British rule.

Undoubtedly the foundations of modern India are the traditions of the past, going back to the days of the Mauryas and the Guptas, to the thought of the *Upanishads* and the ideals of the great epics; and to these must be added the cultural heritage brought to India during the Mohammedan conquest. All of these elements constitute the ground floor of the Indian structure, but the upper and most modern stories were added during the period of British occupation: the rule of law; parliamentary government and basic democratic freedoms, interest in science and a growing secular spirit; the advance of industrialism and the addition of the technological paraphernalia of posts, telegraphs, railways, and harbors. The remainder of this chapter will recount the history and the nature of the British impact on India in the realm of politics.

After the victory of Plassey in 1757 the East India Company became the *de facto* ruler of rich Bengal. Uncontrolled officials here and in other parts of India feathered their nests at the expense of the people. Puppet rulers also gave large gifts to officials in the Company. After accumulating enormous profits the "nabobs," as the Company officials were called, returned to England to flaunt their wealth in their elegant country houses and their influence in the halls of Parliament.

In 1765 Robert Clive was sent out to Bengal for his second governorship. He made a start in ousting corruption and also got from the Mogul emperor the gift of *diwani*—the right of collecting the Bengal revenues. During the period from 1772 to 1786 Indian affairs were constantly debated in the British Parliament. There was a growing realization that it was incongruous for a commercial company to exercise political power over a people. There was also the rising force of the humanitarian movement, which stressed the view that "all political power which is set over men . . . ought to be some way or other exercised ultimately for their benefit." [10] During this ferment over Indian affairs Clive was cross-examined thoroughly by Parliament and, while exonerated, was reproved by indirection. The British government also passed the Regulating Act in 1773, which was the first step in the direction of the Company becoming the agent of the English state. Finally, William Pitt, the prime minister, placed on the statute books an India Act which sought to give the British government full control over the East India Company. By it a board of control was set up to supervise all civil, military, and revenue matters. This body was made up of a secretary of state, who had a place in the British cabinet; the chancellor of the exchequer; and four privy councillors. The governor-general was the servant of the British government and was appointed by it. All patronage and trading activities were kept by the Company.

Instead of abolishing all political responsibilities of the Company, the British government had in a sense made it its partner. The Company still traded, and its servants and soldiers continued to govern and fight in India, but it acted as the carefully supervised agent of the British government.

A by-product of this interest in Indian affairs was the famous impeachment of Warren Hastings, who, after a protracted trial, was finally acquitted. These proceedings, however, gave warning that all officials in India were responsible to Parliament for their actions.

In the first decades of the nineteenth century a strong

[10] Quoted in *Cambridge History of the British Empire* (Cambridge: Cambridge University Press, 1929), IV, p. 197.

liberal movement manifested itself in Indian government. In 1833, when the charter of the East India Company was renewed for twenty years, the commercial side of the Company was closed down. Henceforth its shareholders were to be paid out of Indian revenues. The Charter Act expressly provided that "no Native of the said (Indian) Territories, nor any natural-born subject of His Majesty resident therein, shall, by reason only of his religion, place of birth, descent, colour, or any of them be disabled from holding any Place, Office, or Employment under the said Company." [11]

The Charter Act was passed during the governor-generalship of Lord William Bentinck (1828-1835), who was perhaps the earliest such official to make reform and the uplift of the Indian people the first charge of his administration. Bentinck was interested, as he expressed it, in founding "British Greatness upon Indian Happiness." [12] There followed much administrative reform, especially in the direction of opening up positions in the subordinate grades of the government service to qualified Indians. Attention was also given to cutting the costs of government. Supervision of the princely states, bound to the British crown by treaty, was also made more strict. In the case of the state of Coorg, the raja was deposed for cruelty, and in the great state of Mysore the Indian government took over the complete administration of the state owing to the evils and excesses of the ruling raja.

Most famous of Bentinck's reforms was his abolition of the practice of suttee (or *suti*), i.e., widow-burning. English missionaries had long been denouncing its inhumanity, and some reform groups in Indian circles likewise were asking the government to interfere. Suttee was a custom of great antiquity in which the widow placed herself on the funeral pyre of her late husband. This was considered to express the highest idealism of Hindu womanhood. The practice was especially prevalent in Bengal, where the average annual number of suttees reported from 1818 to 1826 was six hundred. Against some warnings from his officials that the British government dare not interfere with Hindu custom and religion, Bentinck in the famous Regulation XVII of 1829 declared the practice of suttee to be illegal; the ruling made it murder if the act were involuntary and culpable homicide if otherwise. In the princely states outside British India it was more difficult to get the practice abolished, and as late as 1844 we read of one Sikh chief's funeral in which ten wives and three hundred concubines were burned to death.

---

[11] Quoted in Ramsay Muir, ed., *The Making of British India* (Manchester: Manchester University Press, 1923), p. 304.
[12] *Ibid.*, p. 283.

Another outstanding accomplishment of Bentinck was the suppression of thuggee (or *thagi*), ritual strangling. The thugs were worshipers of the goddess Kali, to whom their victims were dedicated. Gangs of these murderers lurked around the main highways, where they waylaid their victims, murdered them with a noose, and buried the corpses so they could not be traced. The task of hunting down the thugs was given to a capable officer, Major-General Sleeman, and in a few years the secrets of the terror society were discovered, many of the murderers were hanged, and the organization was disbanded. An account of these events may be found in Meadows Taylor's novel, *Confessions of a Thug,* published in 1836.

Bentinck and the governors-general who succeeded him also gave attention to the problem of infanticide. Many girl babies were killed because of the economic burden of securing marriage for them. Often families could not afford to provide the necessary dowries, and, as unmarried women were considered a disgrace, ruthless steps were taken to insure limitation of the number of girls in the family. British officials gradually eliminated female infanticide by giving large presents to tribes that kept their daughters, and also by obtaining funds to supply dowries for marriageable girls.

All of these reforms were outstanding in their own right, but probably the most important of Bentinck's acts, in terms of its influence upon modern India, was his selection of English as the medium of Indian education. The argument for the use of English was presented to the governor-general by his brilliant legal member of the Indian council, Thomas Macaulay, who put forward his case so effectively that Bentinck in 1835 announced that the object of the government should be the promotion of European science and literature in India, to be taught in the English language.

The administration of Lord Bentinck was concerned almost exclusively with the affairs of peace; accent was on reform. He has been called the first of the modern rulers of India, and there are few, either in India or in Britain, who would find fault with the inscription on his statue in Calcutta: "He abolished cruel rites; he effaced humiliating distinctions; he gave liberty to the expression of public opinion; his constant study was to elevate the intellectual and moral character of the nations committed to his charge." [13]

The program of reform and modernization initiated by Bentinck reached its climax in the governor-generalship of

[13] Quoted in Howard Robinson, *The Development of the British Empire* (Boston: Houghton Mifflin Company, rev. ed., 1936), pp. 199-200.

Lord Dalhousie (1848-1856), who had been trained in public affairs under Peel and Gladstone at home and was outstanding for his great ability and energy. Every aspect and department of government was galvanized and improved by his statesmanship. A public works department was set up; great roads such as the Grand Trunk Highway from Peshawar to Calcutta were constructed; new harbors were built; telegraph lines were laid and a postal service introduced; and impressive progress was made in irrigation. Ably supported by the board of control in London, Dalhousie began to build the foundations of a national system of education.

British India in 1856

Dalhousie had little use for the system of subsidiary alliances introduced by Wellesley, whereby the British government guaranteed the native rulers the enjoyment of their thrones without, at the same time, demanding from them suitable guarantees to provide decent and just government for their subjects. In the old pre-British days, at least the people had in the last resort the right of revolution. Under the alliance existing between the Company and the native rulers this was taken away. Dalhousie firmly believed that direct British rule would be a great improvement over raja rule, and he was determined on every occasion to annex states governed by Indian dynasties. His weapon at hand was the doctrine of lapse. Whenever the direct line of succession died out in a state he refused to accept the Hindu practice of adoption of an heir, but added the state to the British holdings. The great states of Nagpur and Oudh were accordingly annexed, together with a number of small states such as Sattara and Jhansi. In the case of Oudh, the ruler had been warned on several occasions that, unless his scandalous misrule ceased, the Company on behalf of the British government would be forced to act. Altogether about 150,000 square miles of territory, heretofore under the rule of Indian potentates and rajas, were annexed to British India.

The conclusion of Dalhousie's administration in 1856 was in a sense the terminal point of a distinct period in Anglo-Indian history characterized by liberalism and reform and by the belief, even the wish, on the part of many eminent British administrators that India someday would ask for self-government. Referring to this possibility, Governor-General Lord Moira declared, "In that hour it will be her greatest boast that she [England] has used her sovereignty towards enlightening her subjects, so as to enable the native communities to walk alone in the paths of justice." [14] And Macaulay, referring to this possibility, announced, "Whenever it comes, it will be the proudest day in English history." [15]

In 1857 there occurred a tragedy that did much to embitter relations between the British and their Indian subjects. This was the Indian Mutiny, a fascinating saga of bitter fighting, heroism, massacre, and brutality. Indian patriots today endeavor to interpret the Mutiny as a national revolt against foreign tyranny. It was rather the confused and unorganized revolt of Indian troops, called sepoys, against their officers. One of the precipitating events was the issuance of the famous "greased cartridges" that offended the religious beliefs of the sepoys.

The revolt lasted little more than a year. The British were at first taken by surprise, but they quickly rallied and took the offensive. There were few outstanding Indian leaders. One of the most colorful was the Mahratta princess, the Rani of Jhansi, who died at the head of her troops. The Mutiny was relatively restricted, being confined in the main to north

[14] Quoted in H. G. Rawlinson, *The British Achievement in India* (London: William Hodge and Co., 1948), p. 151.
[15] Quoted in Sir George Schuster and Guy Wint, *India and Democracy* (London: Macmillan and Co., Ltd., 1941), p. 78.

India. As to its consequences, the first was the end of the East India Company. After 1858 the government of India was a direct responsibility of the British government. A second result was the decline of much of the liberalism that had characterized British Indian administrators since the 1820's. The optimistic view that Indian customs and traditions would be transformed by the impact of Western ideas had been rudely shaken by the horrors of the Mutiny. British policy, henceforth, became much more conservative in spirit. There was more caution about reforms, more concern in maintaining the status quo than zeal in improving and transforming it. This new conservatism was plainly evidenced in Queen Victoria's Royal Proclamation. Issued in 1858, this message pledged Britain not to molest any princely state in the future and not to impose Western convictions and religious beliefs upon the Indian people.

This proclamation was a far cry from Dalhousie's doctrine of lapse, and while its effect politically was to freeze and petrify the India of 1858 in the field of social and religious custom, its consequence was a "hands off" policy on the part of the British government.

The British Framework of Control

Following the end of Company rule, a governmental system was established for India that was to last until after First World War. It was a vast hierarchy with its base in India but its official apex in London in the person of the secretary of state for India. This official, of course, was a member of the British cabinet, and his term of office depended upon the fortunes of party politics.

The Council of India, originally consisting of fifteen members, nine of whom must have lived at least ten years in India, was established in London to advise the secretary; but, although it was originally designed to wield considerable power, its influence waned after 1870. In fact, the position of the secretary of state for India tended to become more and more dominant in relation to other elements in the government of India. Parliament, embroiled in Irish problems, foreign affairs, and domestic issues, had little interest in Indian affairs and generally gave the secretary a free hand.

The head of the British government in India was the governor-general, styled the viceroy when acting as the direct representative of the crown, and usually appointed for a term of five years. This official was assisted by an executive council of five members, none of them Indian until 1909. This council, for the purposes of lawmaking, was expanded by the addition of not less than six nor more than twelve members, at least half of whom were to be non-officials. Although not expressly provided by law, two Indians were appointed to this legislative council.

While the powers of this lawmaking body were very limited and at all times subject to the assent of the governor-general, its creation constituted a landmark in the political development of modern India. It was the first step toward parliamentary government. In addition to these councils of the central government, there were similar bodies in the provinces, all of which were completely subordinated to the control of the center.

For administrative purposes British India was broken up into units called provinces, each under a governor or a lieutenant-governor. These political units in turn were broken into divisions and these in turn into districts. The district was the basic administrative unit in the British scheme of government. Altogether there were 250 of these districts, averaging a little less than 4000 square miles with a population, in the 1890's, of 875,000. The key figure in Indian administration was the district officer, called the magistrate and collector in some provinces and in others merely the collector. This official had to maintain the peace, dispense justice, and collect the revenue.

By no means a desk man, the district officer spent much of his time touring the countryside, checking the crops, investigating crime, helping to fight plague, and always meeting the people.

From 1860 to 1885 the post-Mutiny governmental structure was planned, established, and completed. Old government departments were expanded and new ones introduced. By 1885 a number of highly centralized departments, dealing with education, public works, public health, railways, irrigation, and forests, were in operation.

To run the administrative machine in India the British operated with a small force; there was never the host of minor European officials one found in the French colonies. Writing in the latter part of the nineteenth century, Sir John Strachey pointed out that less than 1000 Englishmen were employed in the civil government of 221 million people and in the partial government of 67 million in the princely states.[16] Another authority, referring to the situation about 1900, says that, counting all types of administrative personnel, excluding the military, there were 4000 British in contrast to 500,000 Indian.[17] The great majority of the latter

16 Sir John Strachey, *India* (London: Kegan Paul, Trench, Trubner and Co., 1894), p. 63.

17 Sir Reginald Coupland, *India: A Restatement* (London: Oxford University Press, 1945), p. 46.

were, of course, in subordinate positions. The creation of a provincial and a subordinate service by the British in 1891 opened up more administrative posts of an intermediate rank to Indians, but the upper echelons of the Indian government were almost exclusively reserved for Britons.

The heart and sinew of the British administration in India was the I.C.S. (Indian civil service). This body of men is considered to be one of the oldest civil services in the world; and this term "civil service," first used by the East India Company to designate its civilian employees, had become current by 1765. As early as 1800 Lord Wellesley established a college at Calcutta to train the Company's civil servants, and in 1805 a college was set up at Haileybury, in England, for the same purpose. After 1853 appointments for the service were taken from the Company and opened to public competition.

The I.C.S. has been well described as a *corps d'élite;* its high standards of admission, excellent remuneration and generous pension allowance, and opportunities for advancement always attracted some of the most capable and brilliant young men in Great Britain. The I.C.S. in 1892 consisted of only 939 officials. Entering the service at an initial salary of £320, they could look forward in twenty-five years to a salary of £2350, with a few top positions paying from £4000 to £6000. Retirement came at a relatively early age, after thirty-five years of service, which usually meant around the age of fifty-five. All officials, regardless of rank, received a pension of £1000. There was, undoubtedly, room for much argument on the ultimate justification of British rule in India; but few would deny that the I.C.S., within the pattern of day-to-day administration carried on by the average official, was a remarkable body of conscientious, hard-working, and incorruptible men. A former I.C.S. officer wrote in the 1950's a noteworthy two-volume study of *The Men Who Ruled India.* In it he likens them to the remarkable ruling caste— the Guardians—described by Plato in his *Republic.*

In the minds of most British Indian officials, the Mutiny was primarily a revolt of the Bengal Sepoy Army. It was natural, therefore, that after 1857 there should be fundamental changes in military organization. There was a drastic reduction in the strength of Indian personnel; artillery and the most important weapons were placed exclusively in British hands; and care was taken to recruit troops from tribes and peoples who could be trusted to maintain the government's authority. The new policy was succinctly expressed in a report of the Indian Army Commission of 1879.

By 1863, British troops numbered 65,000 and the number

of Indian troops had been reduced to 140,000. In 1910 the numbers were 69,000 and 130,000 respectively. It should also be noted that the Indian army was not a "national" force, in the sense of including fairly equal proportions from each section of the country. The army came mainly from the northwest and consisted in great part of Pathans, Sikhs, Punjabi Muslims, and Gurkhas. The military arm of the government, therefore, was a professional rather than a national force. The leadership of this army, as can be expected, was British. No Indian could hold the king's commission. He might become a *risaldar* or *subadar,* but "he was junior to the youngest [British] subaltern." [18]

Another important factor in the British framework of control was the group of princely states, already described in Chapter I. After the Mutiny, the queen's proclamation made it evident that Great Britain would show a new solicitude toward the states and that Lord Dalhousie's doctrine of lapse was repudiated. In the 1860's, "sanads of adoption" were signed with the various native rulers, guaranteeing their thrones and admitting the right to adopt heirs when necessary. Most Indian historians make the point that this post-Mutiny policy toward the princely states was, in effect, an alliance of Britain with the conservative, even reactionary, forces in India.

It should also be pointed out that British concern for the princely states was not to be explained exclusively by reference to self-survival but that there was also another important factor of a less selfish nature. Many British administrators sincerely believed it was desirable to perpetuate the traditional monarchical systems of the princely states as a kind of stabilizing factor, one that would be a bulwark against too rapid changes and insure a proper balance between the old and the new in India.

While the princely states were supposedly sovereign in their domestic affairs, the British exercise of what was known as the principle of paramountcy meant that there was considerable limitation of their powers. No state could participate in foreign relations, for this was the prerogative of the paramount power. Furthermore, all matters between one state and another had to pass through the channels of the viceroy acting for the British government. It was also understood that no state should concern itself with the affairs of British India.

The paramount power, for its part, pledged itself to protect and support the government of the princely states but reserved

18 Edward J. Thompson and G. T. Garratt, *Rise and Fulfilment of British Rule in India* (London: Macmillan and Co., Ltd., 1934), p. 539.

to itself the right to intervene in cases of maladministration and gross injustice.

While democracy, industrialism, Western education, and urbanization throughout the nineteenth century increasingly modified the pattern of life in British India, the princely states in many ways remained isolated from this modernizing impact. Some of the states remained entirely untouched by the spirit of progress. A British Indian official has referred to them as "museum pieces, their political institutions being those of Mogul times." [19]

There was evidence, however, that the princely states did not have to be medieval backwaters. Some of the large states, especially Mysore, Cochin, Baroda, Travancore, and Gwalior, were further advanced than British India in such matters as education, public health, and advancement of women. While politically the princely states were in too many instances seventeenth-century remnants, anachronisms in modern times, yet from the standpoint of Indian culture they were at the same time valuable preservers of much that was distinctive and autochthonous, including many of the beautiful handicrafts of the past, picturesque festivals, colorful costumes, and the pageantry of court durbars.

The Golden Age of the British Raj

The four decades following the Indian Mutiny may be thought of as the golden age of the British bureaucratic machine in India. The comparatively easy defeat of the uprising of 1857 was taken by most Britishers as a justification for their rule. In the 1870's and 1880's came the influence of the new imperialism and with it the halcyon days of the White Man's Burden, a term which implied the conviction that it was the right and the responsibility of Europeans in general, and the British in particular, to extend their rule and culture to the four corners of the earth. Benjamin Disraeli was the prophet of imperialism in Britain in the 1870's, urging Englishmen to "be a great country, an imperial country where your sons, when they rise, rise to paramount positions, and obtain not merely the esteem of their countrymen, but command the respect of the world." [20] It was Disraeli who as prime minister carried through an act in the British Parliament in 1877 proclaiming Victoria Queen Empress of India. This announcement of the imperial title symbolized the rising tide of imperialism in Britain.

The British bureaucracy in India naturally was imbued with

[19] Quoted in Schuster and Wint, *op. cit.,* p. 130.
[20] Quoted in W. F. Moneypenny and G. E. Buckle, *The Life of Benjamin Disraeli* (London: John Murray, rev. ed., 1929), II, p. 536.

this pride of empire. In justification of their rule the members of the Indian civil service could point to a number of indisputable achievements. With British ascendancy had emerged peace for all of India. In the wake of the Mogul Empire's disintegration had come lawlessness and banditry. Millions of adventurers were on the loose, out for all they could get by the sword, and restrained by none. It has been estimated that at the close of the eighteenth century there were two million mercenaries in India. Lacking the protection of effective government, the people obtained arms for themselves and defended their lives and property as well as they could; one authority estimates that as late as 1851 every third man possessed arms. The extirpation of the Pindaris, the freebooters, and the bandits, together with the establishment of law courts backed with adequate force, introduced a new era of peace throughout India. To Indians of the first half of the nineteenth century this was a great boon. Later generations, however, born amid conditions of tranquillity, tended to take the rule of law for granted.

Much could be claimed by the British Indian civil servant for the new system of law accompanying his rule. The old indigenous systems—both Hindu and Muslim—were well developed in the law of family relations, but otherwise there were serious gaps. "There was no definite law of procedure, criminal or civil, no law of torts, no public and constitutional law." [21] The British brought into India a new structure of law, outside Hindu and Muslim personal law, yet based on careful regard for the customs and feelings of the people. The most important legal contribution undoubtedly was the Indian penal code. The result of three years' work, it was written in the concise and beautiful prose of Macaulay, who acted as president of a commission to inquire into the jurisdiction of British India from 1834 to 1837. This draft was not put into effect until 1862, but subsequently it has been widely accepted as almost a model criminal code. While the British system of justice as it has worked in India has had its weakness, it nevertheless brought into the country the great legal principle of equality under the law of all individuals, regardless of their caste status.

Closely connected with the development of a modern judiciary and impartial justice under British auspices was the elimination of slavery. The slave trade was forbidden by Cornwallis as early as 1789. In 1833 the governor-general was empowered to take steps leading to the abolition of slavery, a task involving the emancipation of some 9 million persons. In 1843 the courts were instructed to refuse to recognize the

[21] L. S. S. O'Malley, *Modern India and the West* (New York: Oxford University Press, 1941), p. 110.

status of slave, and the final act in 1860 decreed that the keeping of slaves was a criminal offense.

By the end of the nineteenth century another achievement that could be rightly claimed by British rule in India was the introduction of the first steps toward representative government. Such institutions on a national scale had heretofore been entirely unknown in Asia. The first advance in self-government in local units was the work of Lord Ripon, governor-general from 1880 to 1884. This official has been likened to Bentinck for his interest in social and political reform; he was a real liberal of the Gladstonian type. In sponsoring an advance in local self-government, he issued an important resolution in 1882 in which it was stated: ". . . it is not primarily with a view to improvement in administration that this measure is brought forward. It is chiefly desirable as a measure of political and popular education." [22]

Following this lead, acts were passed in the provinces whereby local elected boards were to be set up beginning with the smallest administrative units and including municipal boards for cities. In addition to this attempt to foster local self-government, there was also a slight liberalization at the highest level in the legislative councils of the various provinces and in the council of the governor-general. After much discussion in the British Parliament, the Indian Councils Act was passed in 1892. This measure enlarged the non-official membership of the provincial councils and provided that they should be nominated by members chosen by such local bodies as district boards, municipal corporations, and universities. In the governor-general's legislative council the non-officials were appointed from the four provincial councils, and one was selected by the Calcutta chamber of commerce. Thus in a very roundabout manner the principle of election was admitted, and these new councils were also granted the new power to discuss budgets and to interpellate the executive officers of government on matters of public policy. While the act of 1892 fell far short of introducing real representative government into India, it was a transition from the purely bureaucratic and paternal government that had prevailed during most of the nineteenth century to the increasingly representative system that was to develop during the first decades of the twentieth. While the advance in 1892 was admittedly small, it "did bring a breath of life and reality into the proceedings of the councils, and quite definitely marked a stage in the development of popular government in India." [23]

[22] Quoted in *Cambridge History of the British Empire* (Cambridge: Cambridge University Press, 1932), V, p. 521.
[23] Sir John Cumming, ed., *Political India, 1832-1932* (London: Oxford University Press, 1932), p. 170.

Throughout the long history of India famine has been a constant menace, bringing death and suffering to millions of people. Rainfall over much of the land depends upon the southwest winds, the monsoons, and their failure spells catastrophe.

Records indicate there were fourteen major famines between 1660 and 1750. In the writings of such European travelers as Van Twist, the Dutch merchant, we have vivid pictures of the misery and death resulting from these famines. This eyewitness observed of a famine that took place in 1630 and 1631:

> As the famine increased, men abandoned towns and villages and wandered helplessly. It was easy to recognize their condition: eyes sunk deep in the head; lips pale and covered with slime; the skin hard, with the bones showing through; the belly nothing but a pouch hanging down empty; knuckles and kneecaps showing prominently. One would cry and howl for hunger, while another lay on the ground dying in misery. Wherever you went, you saw nothing but corpses.[24]

Witnessing another famine in 1670, the Dutch traveler Van Graaf wrote, "We saw nothing but poverty and misery. . . . The people died in heaps and their corpses remained extended on the roads, streets, and market-places. . . ."[25]

It was not until the 1860's that the British government began to study the problem of famine systematically. In 1866–1867 a catastrophe took place in the area of Orissa. The crops failed, and the lack of transport facilities prevented the authorities from sending grain and supplies into the stricken districts. As much as one-quarter of the population may have perished; the death toll was estimated at more than a million.

This Orissa catastrophe marked the turning point in famine administration. A start was made in creating machinery that would go into action as soon as famine threatened in any district. In 1876–1877 an unusually terrible famine raged in south and central India and, although more than 11 million pounds were spent in relief measures, 5 million people lost their lives. Following this holocaust a famine commission was set up under Sir John Strachey. The recommendations of this commission, which were reported in 1880, formed the basis for the famine code adopted in 1883 by the Indian government.

This code, which was continually improved and expanded, was based on the principle that government must provide adequate relief to the needy during times of crop failures. Schemes for employment on public works were prepared and a regular sum was set aside by the government for famine in-

24 Quoted in H. G. Rawlinson, *India: A Short Cultural History* (New York: D. Appleton-Century, 1938), p. 338.
25 Quoted in O'Malley, *op. cit.*, p. 13.

surance. A chain of "protective railways" was built to insure the delivery of adequate stocks of food in any part of the country that might be threatened by famine. Great irrigation projects were also completed, so that by 1900 India could claim to have the greatest irrigation system in the world, serving some 14 million acres.

A heavy strain was placed on famine-prevention machinery during the four years' drought that affected India from 1896 to 1900. Despite herculean efforts and the saving of millions of lives, the loss of life was still heavy. Improvements, therefore, continued to be made in the famine code, and in the next major emergency in 1907-1908 the relief measures proved to be very effective.

It is this progressive improvement of famine-prevention machinery, together with the elimination of civil wars and banditry, that accounts for the rapid increase of the Indian population. The population in the seventeenth century has been estimated at 100 million; for 1850 the figure was 150 million; for 1881, 250 million; and for 1901, 283 million. In the first half of the twentieth century the increase was maintained and even accelerated, so that by 1945 the population was 400 million.

The establishment of peace and equality under the law, the elimination of slavery, the introduction of semirepresentative government, and the first systematic attack against the age-old problem of famine were important accomplishments of British rule; the most significant, however, was the realization of political unity for India. In the past the country had enjoyed a common socioreligious way of life and culture. "But political activities meant little to the Hindu; dynasties came into power and fell from power, empires arose and broke up, yet history leaves them unrecorded and they never affected India's real life and her profounder unity." [26]

For the first time in its history, India under British rule was unified under the same government, since the princely states in the last analysis were subordinate to the paramount power—Britain. Furthermore, as we shall see in the next chapter, under British auspices the country was drawn together by a network of modern transportation and communication facilities and, in the upper levels, by a common form of education given in the English language. In ancient and medieval India, even in the days of the Guptas or those of the Mogul Empire, there had been no administrative unity in all the country by which an integrated and continuous chain of allegiance and authority proceeded from the king

[26] Hans Kohn, *A History of Nationalism in the East* (London: George Routledge, 1929), p. 350.

or emperor down to the lowliest ryot. In consequence of British rule this lack was filled. "The Indian people, for the first time," writes an Indian historian, "found a substantial sector of their economic and social life coming under the governance of a universally and equally operating system of law." [27]

In summary, under the new dispensation of the British raj the individual enjoyed liberty—if not self-government—under a unified government whose law offered him the enjoyment of freedom of religion, freedom from arbitrary arrest, and much freedom of speech.

In the nineteenth century the defense of India's frontiers and its sea approaches was the foremost military problem of the British Empire. To the north of the Himalayas and the strategic mountain passes was a restless, expansionist Russia, and Britain's foremost aim, like that of the United States in the twentieth century, was to contain the Russian Bear. In this rivalry Afghanistan was a pivotal buffer state; and on two occasions—in 1839 and again 1879—British forces waged war on its amir. This intervention was costly, however, and finally Britain wisely recognized Afghan independence. A subsidy was granted, and the amir gave Britain the right to control his country's foreign relations.

Another important buffer state guarding the northern passes to India was Tibet. Rumors of Russian interference caused Lord Curzon, the governor-general, in 1904 to send an expedition to the Tibetan capital. An agreement followed whereby Tibet agreed not to admit any foreign agents. In another area the remnant of the kingdom of Burma guarded the southeastern approaches to India. Following the refusal of its government at Mandalay to accept British advice on foreign affairs, war followed and what was left of independent Burma was annexed to India.

Less weighted with international complications but equally important to the defense of India was the northwest frontier area. Located on the southern slopes of the Hindu Kush mountains, and populated by warlike Pathan tribes who were constantly fighting each other or raiding Indian territory, this Northwest region was a perpetual source of anxiety to the military authorities in India. It has been estimated that fifty-four British expeditions had to be sent into this area from 1848 to 1898 to punish the mountaineers for their looting expeditions. Their practice of going in and burning the Pathan villages and then retreating was called the policy of "butcher and bolt."

In 1893, by an agreement with the Amir of Afghanistan,

[27] Desai, *op. cit.,* p. 154.

the Durand Line was laid down to indicate the political boundary, while some thirty miles to the east was the administrative line of British India. Close control ended at the latter, leaving a sort of no man's land between it and the Durand Line. It was the policy of Lord Curzon to pay subsidies to the tribes in this buffer "unorganized area." In addition, the government of India supported tribal forces called Khassadars, who where paid to support some semblance of law and order. No British troops were stationed west of the administrative boundary. The frontier system of Lord Curzon was, on the whole, an improvement over the policy that had preceded it, but tribal raids were not eliminated. No matter what group governs India, whether the alien British or the native Indians, the existence on its borders of a people forced, without raiding and looting, to scrape a bare pittance from the barren mountains, usually occupied with blood feuds, and always ready to listen to the voice of the mullah (holy man) calling them to a jihad (holy war), will constantly be a source of danger to the more wealthy and less martial people living on the plains at the foot of the mountains. This problem of the northwest frontier will be referred to again in the discussion of political developments in India after Britain's withdrawal in 1947.

In retrospect, the *Pax Britannica* ensured that the Indian Ocean was a British lake and the land frontiers were held as effectively as were those of Rome when her legions were at the height of their power. Mistakes, of course, were made by the Indian government. Looking back, it would seem that Britain was unduly alarmed over the Russian menace and that both Afghan wars were unnecessary. Curzon's Tibetan expedition also would come in this category. Despite these errors, however, India enjoyed such a peace as had never been known before in its history.

British Rule Evaluated

British rule, as we have seen, had its positive side, but at the same time there were a number of serious defects. In this chapter reference will be made only to the political shortcomings, while the economic results will be analyzed in the following chapter and referred to again briefly later.

Three defects may be commented upon. In the early days of Company rule there had been close contact between the ruler and the ruled. There was no rigid machine of administration with rules to cover all exigencies, but rather improvisation and individual responsibility on the part of the Indian civil servant were expected to get his day's work done in a satisfactory manner. After the Mutiny, however, a rigid administrative machine was built up in which there was too much routine and too much departmentalism. An English historian has written, "For these reasons the system of Indian government was becoming not merely more efficient and punctiliously exact, it was becoming gradually more mechanical, more formal, and more impersonal." [28]

The impersonal nature of the official machine and its lack of contact with the people it ruled was a serious weakness of the post-Mutiny British bureaucracy. Another, and a closely allied defect, was that British administrators had little concern with the ultimate results, goals, or purposes of their rule in India. Day-to-day efficiency rather than the preparation of the people of India for some objective, such as self-rule, was the hallmark of the Indian civil service. This was completely unlike the liberal attitude expressed in the 1820's and 1830's by British Indian officials, who gave much thought to why Britain was in India and what, in the long run, she should make of her responsibility. The following statement well describes the attitude of British officials in the second half of the nineteenth century: "In India . . . during the greater part of this period they are merely governing. Their rule, if often aloof and unimaginative, is superbly incorruptible and highly efficient and it achieves many prodigious results, yet does not seem to contain within it . . . the impulse of organic growth." [29]

In keeping with the day-to-day philosophy of the British Indian bureaucracy and its disregard of the ultimate aims of administration, there existed opposition to reforms in government and a strong reluctance to open the upper brackets of public service to Indians. There had been too little progress made in alleviating the attitudes which as early as 1818 had caused Sir Thomas Munro to remark:

> "Foreign conquerors have treated the native with violence and often with great cruelty, but none have treated them with so much scorn as we; none has stigmatized the whole people as unworthy of trust, as incapable of honesty, and as fit to be employed only where we cannot do without them." [30]

There was a lack of sympathy on the part of British officials with the scheme for local self-government introduced by Lord Ripon, and two English historians of India assert that the

[28] Ramsay Muir, *A Short History of the British Commonwealth* (New York: World Book Company, 1923), II, p. 557.

[29] Lord G. Elton, *Imperial Commonwealth* (New York: Reynal and Hitchcock, 1946), p. 459.

[30] G. R. Gleig, *The Life of Sir Thomas Munro*, 1, pp. 518-519, quoted in Raleigh Parkin, *India Today* (New York: John Day Co., rev. ed., 1946), p. 178.

rural boards were allowed by the officials to "function in an almost farcical manner." [31] This explanation, however, was not the whole story, as other authorities have pointed out that Indian politicians tended to disdain the humble apprenticeship of local government and that the peasants were often apathetic.

Less open to debate than this question of the failure of the plan to develop local self-government was the determination of the British officials to monopolize the highest posts and not to share with Indians the formulation of public policy. The appointment of Indians to the highest posts had been legalized in the Charter Act of 1833 and in Queen Victoria's proclamation in 1858, in which it was promised ". . . that, as far as may be, our subjects, of whatever race or creed, be freely and impartially admitted to office in our service." [32] This promise, however, was not carried out. Examinations for the Indian civil service, which monopolized all high positions, were held in England, and Indians were practically debarred from the I.C.S. when the maximum age for taking the examination was reduced from twenty-one to nineteen. In 1870 there were only seven Indian candidates and in 1880 only two. By 1892, out of 939 members in the I.C.S. only 21 were Indians; and in 1913 out of 2501 administrative officers with salaries of 800 rupees ($266) a month or more, only 242, less than 10 per cent, were Indians. Among the educated Indians who were ambitious to rise in the ranks of the public service there was naturally much resentment against the I.C.S., "the practical owners of India, irremovable, irresponsible, and amenable to no authority but that of their fellow members." [33] The passage of the Indian Councils Act of 1892, with its hesitant acceptance of the principle of election, marked the end of bureaucratic paternalism.

[31] Thompson and Garratt, *op. cit.*, p. 536.
[32] *A Collection of Extracts from Royal Proclamations, Official Reports and Speeches* (New Delhi: Government of India Printing Office, no date), p. 7.
[33] W. W. Blunt, *India under Ripon* (London: T. F. Unwin, 1909), p. 313.

4. The Hindu Revival
and the Growth of Nationalism

ON THE EVE OF BRITISH CONQUEST Indian civilization had reached a low ebb. While strong and centralized monarchies developed in much of western Europe, in India the fatal weakness of political fragmentation and instability brought turmoil and widespread disorder to the unhappy land. While the western Europeans were rapidly forging ahead with the development of modern science, seeking to discover and control the secrets of nature for the happiness of man, and beginning at the same time to interest themselves in the problems of government and economics, the Indians exhibited little creative thought, contenting themselves with a culture that had become both stagnant and esoteric.

As we have seen in the preceding chapter, British rule brought about a revolution in India in the realm of law and government. It was also the vehicle for the impact of Western culture, causing significant economic and intellectual changes in the pattern of Indian life. This impact of the West largely explains the all-important Hindu revival, or recovery, that got well under way shortly after the mid-point of the nineteenth century.

Furthermore, while the status of the great mass of the people in the villages was changed with the commercialization of agriculture and the passing of a subsistence economy, in the cities a relatively new class—the *bourgeoisie* —emerged. Along with the economic influences came new intellectual forces. The city people were exposed to Western science and nineteenth-century liberal thought. And Western education, established by the British, exposed the eager Indian students to the democratic and nationalistic currents that were agitating the stream of European history. Out of this Western impact, with all its complexities and ramifications, came the Hindu revival and the genesis of modern nationalism in India as both a reaction to and an emulation of the West.

An economic transformation, more thorough and basic than any that had taken place in India in its entire history, followed upon the conquest of the country by Great Britain. In the early days of its activities the English East India Company was interested mainly in securing cheap Indian goods for export, chiefly to England and the Continent. This trade, especially in cotton and silk goods, reached its height about the year 1700. In the following decades, as English manufacturing began to grow, especially in the field of textiles, there was a demand for protection against Indian goods. And in accordance with the mercantile philosophy of the day, which foolishly preferred to have many exports and few imports, various duties and prohibitions were placed on the imported goods from India. The East India Company, however, managed to sell a large volume of them as re-exports from England to the Continent. This re-export trade suffered severely during the Napoleonic wars, when the European market practically ceased to exist. In 1813 the Company lost its monopoly of trade in India, and the field was opened to all comers. After this date, because of the rapid development of the Industrial Revolution in England, most businessmen desired to sell their manufactured wares in the Indian market. No longer able to compete against the machine-made fabrics of England, the native textile industry declined, and a large number of weavers and other workers lost their traditional employment. At the same time, however, India greatly increased her export trade, for she still enjoyed a comparative economic advantage in the production of certain raw materials, such as indigo, cotton, tea, jute, wheat, oilseeds, hides, and linseed oil.

After the mid-point of the nineteenth century, when British control was completely established, India had a moderate tariff rate. In 1882 the tariff was lowered still further, and for the next twelve years the country enjoyed practically free trade. Then, in 1894, a general import duty was imposed ranging from 5 to 15 per cent—with the exception of English cotton imports, which were taxed at the rate of only 3.5 per cent. Even this lower rate, however, led the English textile manufacturers to protest, and a countervailing excise was levied against domestic cotton production, placing English and Indian mills on the same level of competition. Except for this cotton excise tax, no preferential treatment was enjoyed by British goods at the expense of either Indian producers or Britain's foreign competitors for the Indian market.

Nearly all the socio-economic evils from which modern India suffers today are attributed by most Indian historians to the decline of native industry. An American writer supporting this view states: "India was thus rapidly transformed from a country of combined agriculture and handicrafts into a purely agricultural colony of British industry, resulting in the severe overpressure on agriculture which has remained one of the most critical problems of modern India." [1]

Accompanying the decline of industry came fundamental changes in the status of the Indian village. For hundreds of years, while dynasty succeeded dynasty in India, the village had remained changeless. It was little affected by the outside world and was practically self-sufficient. Its members had a primitive form of self-rule, and usually land was held as communal property. The impact of the new economic forces that entered India with British rule upset this ancient village way of life.

Early in the nineteenth century railroads were built and began to crisscross the countryside. The old roads were also improved and made usable through the rainy season. These changes gradually opened up the villages to the outside world. Cash could be obtained by the peasants from the sale of their produce in the nearby markets. Agriculture consequently became commercialized. Before the British conquest farm products had to be sold in each local area. A good crop meant merely a local glut, as the surplus could not be transported elsewhere. There were also wide variations in prices, which would be low in one area and excessively high in another. The opening of the village now brought it into contact with the Indian market, and, in the case of certain products such as wheat or tea, with the world market.

Cash crops meant that the villager could buy the enticing English manufactured goods. As a result, many of the village handicrafts declined. The introduction of enameled ironware hurt the village potter. The village oil man felt the competition of the new kerosene, and, as carcasses went now to the tanning industry, the village tanner had less call for his services. Another change in the village was the increased mobility of its members. Although the great majority of Indian villagers still are born and die in the same rural area, the advent of better communications gave the more ambitious the chance to "try their luck elsewhere," sometimes in a less densely populated district or perhaps in a large city.

[1] Kate Mitchell, *India without Fable* (New York: Alfred A. Knopf, 1942), p. 121.

New concepts of property also exerted their influence in village life. From time immemorial the rulers of India had obtained the bulk of their revenue from the land. In an attempt to regularize the system in Bengal, just acquired by the East India Company, Governor-General Lord Cornwallis in 1790 made what is known as the Permanent Revenue Settlement. By this action the old tax collectors, the zamindars of the Mogul Empire, were recognized as private landlords. These landlords were expected to turn over to the government a permanent annual sum, taken from the rents they collected. Unfortunately, as land values increased, the government by its own arrangement got no part of the increased rents. The peasants, in spite of efforts made to protect them in the late nineteenth century, were increasingly overcharged and exploited.

In large parts of Bombay and Madras a different approach was made to the land-revenue problem. Here the government dealt directly with the peasants, collecting the rent, or taxes, from the villagers. Unlike those under the zamindari system of Bengal, the cultivators in the ryotwari settlement were recognized as the owners of the land, endowed with the rights of private property and privileged to sell, lease, or mortgage their land. Unfortunately, the peasants were not adequately prepared for this transfer from village ownership to individually held land. In times of prosperity they tended to be extravagant, and "improvident borrowing and unscrupulous lending" [2] became all too common. When the monsoon failed and crops were nonexistent, the peasants were unable to pay off their debts to the moneylender. The result was heavier and heavier indebtedness.

In explaining what has become a major agrarian problem of modern India, rural indebtedness, some writers tend to stress what they believe is the heavy and inelastic land taxation in relation to peasant income. Other authorities point out the effect of certain social and religious customs, such as the high expense of marriage. It is charged that moneylenders (the banias) and the Brahmans frequently conspired in insisting upon expensive purifications after certain diseases.

Thus, as the village was swept into the stream of world economic forces, the villager was not prepared to stand alone and take care of his property, and the results in all too many instances were tragic. It can be argued, however, that the change from self-subsistence and isolation was necessary before India could begin to approach a modern economy. The important question involved is whether the economic status

2 Edward J. Thompson and G. T. Garratt, *Rise and Fulfilment of British Rule in India* (London: Macmillan and Co., Ltd., 1934), p. 485.

of the village could have been transformed with less human dislocation and suffering.

In commenting on this situation an Indian economic historian has observed:

> But the fact remains that the village life was poor in cultural quality, on a narrow village scale, unprogressive, and passive. If the Indian people were to advance to higher forms of social existence such as nationhood, economic unity and intellectual progress, the self-sufficient village had to leave the stage of history.[3]

The negative aspects of the economic effects of the West were in some instances counterbalanced by compensatory effects. While some classes suffered economically, others prospered and gained materially in wealth. One of the most important results of the new economics in India was the rise of a well-educated, dynamic, and ambitious middle class, numerically small in proportion to the total population (perhaps totaling 5 million), but influential. Opportunities for expanding trade and better protection for property brought about the development of a wealthy banking and commercial class. To its ranks were added the new professional men, especially the educators, journalists, and lawyers. Under the Moguls the middle class had been insignificant and inconsequential; now, for the first time, a bourgeois element emerged which was to have a major role in shaping the new India.

Continuing the discussion of the positive effects of British economic influence, special attention should be paid to the creation of a modern business structure in India, mainly by foreign capital. The period from 1858 to 1900 may be called the "opening-up period" of Indian economic history. It was during this time that India received her railroads, mails and telegraphs, modern roads, banks, and harbors. Before the British period only a few roads had existed, connecting the main centers of population, and even these had been only fair-weather facilities.

The first railroad dates from 1853; by 1869, there were 4000 miles of railroads open to traffic; and by the 1890's the mileage had reached 24,000. "Railways," wrote Sir Edward Arnold, "may do for India what dynasties have never done . . . they may make India a nation." [4] The consequences of the new railroads were manifold. They helped materially in combating famine; they facilitated religious pilgrimages from one part of the country to the other and thus assisted the move-

[3] A. R. Desai, *Social Background of Indian Nationalism* (Bombay: Oxford University Press, 1949), p. 39.

[4] Quoted in L. S. S. O'Malley, *Modern India and the West* (New York: Oxford University Press, 1941), p. 241.

ment—discussed later in this chapter—for the revival of Hinduism. Finally, they helped to open up areas of land heretofore inaccessible. In this last case the underdeveloped section of Assam is a good example.

Following the Mutiny, British capital flowed into India in huge amounts, financing the railroads and the plantations producing indigo, jute, and tea. By 1911 these investments were in the neighborhood of 4 billion dollars. India's foreign trade reflected the modernization of her economic structure:

	EXPORTS	IMPORTS
	(in millions of pounds)	(in millions of pounds)
1834	8	4.5
1870	53	33.5
1910	137	86

There was little rapid development of industry in the nineteenth century. Only three kinds of industrial activity were of any importance: cotton mills, which increased from 58 in 1880 to 264 in 1914; jute mills, which increased in number from 22 to 64 in the same period; and coal mines, which increased their yield from 1,294,000 tons in 1885 to 15,738,000 tons in 1914.

Only the more obvious results of the economic effect of British control on India have been indicated. It is difficult to strike a judicious balance, not only because the problem is so complex but because much more research will have to be done to secure the necessary facts.

On this matter of the pros and cons of the economic consequences of alien rule in India, the fundamental question is whether she would have been any better off without foreign control. In such an event, political stability would have been an essential prerequisite for the attainment of economic well-being, and no one can hazard how long it would have taken India to build up an effective system of government, law, and order on the debris of the Mogul Empire. And even if one grants the possible rapid achievement of political stability, would India have been able to create a modern structure of business? Above all, would she have been able to build up her own industries? Certainly the task would have been extremely difficult, for India in the nineteenth century lacked the necessary technological knowledge. Furthermore, she lacked capital, a condition explained by the age-old propensity of her people to hoard precious metals instead of using them for productive purposes. There would have been not only the difficulty of procuring capital, but also the problem of interesting most of the upper-class Indians in business enterprise. As an American economist has observed, "Anything that savored of material productivity or of trading for gain was strictly tabooed by these 'twice born.' " [5]

The Intellectual Impact of the West

The introduction of Western thought and education was as significant for India as the economic transformation. The missionaries were the pioneers in introducing European culture into India. First the Portuguese in the sixteenth century, then Italians in the seventeenth, and Danes in the early eighteenth century set up their missions. These early missionaries carried on important linguistic studies and prepared grammars in various native languages. British missionaries were at first excluded by the East India Company, but they managed to establish themselves on Danish territory not far from Calcutta. Here, at Serampore, in 1801 William Carey, a Baptist missionary, and his colleagues set up a printing press and began the publication of books in the Indian vernaculars, grammars and dictionaries, and works in the English language.

Up to this time, with the exception of the printing presses brought in by European trading companies and used for official purposes, no presses existed in India, and only the very wealthy possessed written works in their libraries in the form of manuscripts. The Serampore press soon had many imitators, and by 1838 printing was a widespread industry. The first Indian newspaper was issued in 1816, followed by another published at Serampore two years later. By 1823 there were four Indian newspapers in Calcutta alone. The product of these presses brought out a flood of new ideas which were eagerly absorbed by the small but influential group of literate Indians.

In the early days of the English East India Company most of the officials were pro-Orientalists; that is, they favored the encouragement of the classical languages, Persian and Sanskrit, used by the governing class and the scholars. At this time the vernacular languages were in low esteem, lacking grammars and models of good literary style. Thus it was that Warren Hastings sponsored a Muslim college in 1780, and in 1792 Lord Cornwallis set up a comparable college for the study of Sanskrit at Benares.

Early in the nineteenth century both Indian intellectuals and Englishmen began to look favorably on the establishment of Western education in India. In 1817 the Hindu College

[5] D. H. Buchanan, *The Development of Capitalistic Enterprise in India* (New York: The Macmillan Company, 1934), p. 458.

for the study of English was set up at Calcutta through the efforts of David Hare, an English watchmaker in Calcutta, and Ram Mohan Roy, an Indian admirer of European culture. The following year saw a mission college started by William Carey at Serampore. In the Charter Act of 1813 the Company was authorized to make an annual grant of £10,000 for education, to be used for the teaching of Arabic and Sanskrit. Meanwhile, however, the ranks of the Anglicists, as they were called, were increasing, and the government of India in 1829 announced its intention of making English the official language.

Thomas Babington Macaulay, member of the governor-general's executive council, issued his famous *Education Minute* in February 1835. In it he showed a lack of appreciation of Hindu culture and a cocksure confidence in the superiority of European thought. "I have never found one [of the Orientalists]," declared Macaulay, "who would deny that a single shelf of a good European library was worth the whole native literature of India and Arabia." [6] Such rhetoric was unnecessary; but Macaulay's basic recommendation, that English be the medium and English literature and science the material of instruction in the advanced schools, was cogently argued, and was accepted not only by the Indian government but by many influential Indians. The decision to base higher education in India upon the English language and on Western culture was announced by Bentinck in March 1835. Behind the *Minute* was the belief of English officials that Western education was the best medium for "modernizing" India, the recognition that Britain needed a Western-educated class to help in the administration of the country, and also the understanding that Western education *might* lead to the demand for Indian self-government. But such a possibility did not worry the liberally inclined British administrators of the early nineteenth century. It was only after the Mutiny of 1857 and the consequent growth of the imperialistic spirit that British officials failed to see the inconsistency of teaching Indians Western history and ideals and at the same time scoffing at their desire to rule themselves.

In 1853 the British Parliament for the first time thoroughly investigated Indian education. In consequence a famous dispatch was issued in 1854 by Sir Charles Wood, who stated that its aim should be the extension of European knowledge among all classes in India. In accordance with the instructions of the dispatch, the governor-general, Lord Dalhousie, in the 1850's began laying the foundation of a national system of education. The dispatch called for the setting up of universities,

6 Quoted in Ramsay Muir, ed., *The Making of British India, 1756-1858* (Manchester: Manchester University Press, 1923), p. 299.

the establishment of training colleges for teachers, expansion of the government colleges and high schools, and the extension of vernacular elementary schools designed for the masses.

By 1885 this educational system was well established; the number of students in colleges and universities increased between 1885 and 1900 from 11,000 to 23,000, and those in secondary schools from 429,000 to 633,000. It was this system of education that was the vehicle of Western culture and brought about a veritable revolution in the thought-climate of India.

The new Western learning dispensed in the English high schools and colleges exerted tremendous influence. By it the Indian recovery, soon to be traced, became possible; by it India became part of a world community, sharing in the rich legacy of science and rational thought that was the product of the nineteenth century. A new generation of Indian intellectuals was produced who looked to Europe for their inspiration. The number of these Western-educated Indians has never been large; in the 1920's it was estimated that 2.5 million persons were literate in English. One Englishman wrote:

> Familiarly acquainted with us by means of our literature, the Indian youth almost cease to regard us as foreigners. They speak of our great men with the same enthusiasm as we do. Educated in the same way, interested in the same subjects, engaged in the same pursuits with ourselves, they become more English than Hindus, just as the Roman provincials became more Roman than Gauls or Italians.[7]

Nehru in describing them has written: "The British had created a new caste or class in India, the English-educated class, which lived in a world of its own, cut off from the mass of the population, and looked always, even when protesting, toward their rulers."[8] This evaluation is hardly tenable, since traditionally the upper classes throughout Indian history have shown little interest in and solicitude for the masses, while, in fact, it has been among these very Western-educated Indians, trained in liberal and rationalist thought, that the main reform movements for uplifting the masses have arisen. Nehru himself is an outstanding example!

The best early example of the product of Western education was Ram Mohan Roy (1772-1833). A member of a Brahman family in Bengal, he broke with his parents over the spectacle of his sister's torture on the funeral pyre of her husband. Ram Mohan Roy then traveled widely in India and entered the service of the British government. Learning English, studying

[7] Quoted in O'Malley, *op. cit.*, p. 92.

[8] Jawaharlal Nehru, *The Discovery of India* (New York: John Day Co., 1946), p. 412.

Greek and Hebrew, he became fascinated by Western thought and deeply interested in all religions. He translated some of the *Upanishads* into English and also published a book of extracts from and commentaries on the New Testament, called *The Precepts of Jesus, A Guide to Peace and Happiness*. As a reformer he supported the introduction of English education and the elimination of barbarous customs such as suttee. While championing reform and admiring European thought, he was nevertheless interested in preserving the best in Hindu culture.

In 1828 Ram Mohan Roy founded his society, the Brahma Samaj, which sought to purge Hinduism of such practices as purdah and child marriage. The society also rejected polytheism and image worship. While Hindu in its orientation, the Brahma Samaj contained Christian and humanistic elements. It was open to all comers regardless of creed or race, and was strongly reminiscent of the credo of the European deists of the eighteenth century.

The society never reached the masses, but it had widespread influence among the middle-class intelligentsia.

The Origin of Nationalism and the Founding of the Congress

Modern nationalism was imported into India from Europe. Most authorities agree that there is nothing to indicate the existence of any genuine nationalist sentiment until at least two decades after the Mutiny of 1857. Before India could be truly nationalistic it had to be united; and, furthermore, it needed the inspiration so abundantly provided by the various nationalistic movements that sprinkled the pages of European history from 1500 on. The story of the national unification of France and England, the patriotic crusade of subjugated Europeans against the imperialistic tyranny of Napoleon, the struggle of the Greeks against the Turks for their national independence, and the achievements of Bismarck and Cavour in creating united and independent motherlands for their peoples—all these helped to kindle the nationalistic fire in India. In addition to the political unification brought about by the British conquest, the use of English as the lingua franca made it possible for men all over the country to exchange views and compare opinions. Cheap postage and the printing press were indispensable agencies working for a sense of unity that had never existed before in India. The railroads also assisted in the process, mainly by facilitating travel all over the country.

The education provided in the schools was a rich well

from which young middle-class Indians drank deeply. They read of the political philosophy of John Locke, of his social contract theory justifying revolution. They studied the lives of Charles Stewart Parnell, the Irish patriot; Giuseppe Mazzini, the inspirer of Italian youth; and Louis Kossuth, fighter for a lost cause in Hungary. This type of instruction inevitably caused Indians to consider their own case and claim the liberties and rights which had been acquired by other peoples, including the English who ruled them. This first generation of Indian nationalists followed the tradition of Ram Mohan Roy. They were liberals and had an abiding faith in parliamentary institutions; and, while awakening to the thrill of nationhood, they were in no sense anti-English, for they confidently expected the "Mother of Parliaments" to grant them self-government without too much delay.

In addition to the stimulating shock of Western ideas, Indian nationalism was also nourished by the recovery of India's past, which, before the opening of the nineteenth century, was almost a blank page as far as the pre-Mogul period is concerned. A number of enthusiastic Europeans, many of them scholar-administrators, carried out historical, archeological, and linguistic researches of inestimable value. Societies like the Asiatic Society of Bengal did much to recover the glories of India's past. India owes a great debt to such scholars as Charles Wilkins, Sir William Jones, Henry Thomas Colebrooke, James Prinsep, and Alexander Cunningham. This debt is thus graciously recognized by an Indian historian: "Today when we talk of the Mauryas, the Guptas, the Chalukyas and the Pallavas, let it be remembered that the story of these great ages of Indian history was recovered to us by the devoted labours of European scholars in the service of the British Government in India." [9]

A sense of nationalism hesitatingly made itself evident in the 1860's, but in the next decade, during the viceroyalty of Lord Lytton (1876-1880), it grew rapidly. This British official was the spokesman for the rising tide of jingoism and imperialism that was sweeping Britain under the leadership of Prime Minister Benjamin Disraeli. It was the flood of this new spirit, fortified by the fear complex engendered by the Mutiny, that completely inundated the liberal and reformist attitude so characteristic of British Indian officials from 1820 to 1850. During Lytton's administration, therefore, little concern was manifested for the national susceptibilities of Her Majesty's Indian subjects. A vernacular press act was passed, giving the government better control over Indian newspapers. People

9 K. M. Panikkar, *A Survey of Indian History* (London: Meridian Books, Ltd., 1948), pp. 264-265.

were also restricted from carrying firearms by the enactment of an arms act. Another action, this time by the government in London, aroused much resentment. Official statements and royal proclamations had been made, promising Indians equal opportunities in the government service. Yet the I.C.S., the top-level branch of the administration, was kept practically a closed preserve to Indians. Whatever feeble intentions the home government might have entertained in the direction of widening the opportunities in the administrative services were stymied by the opposition of the British bureaucracy in India. One of its members, Sir John Strachey, frankly wrote: ". . . let there be no hypocrisy about our intention to keep in the hands of our own people those executive posts . . . on which, and on our political and military power, our actual hold of the country depends." [10]

In 1877 the age beyond which candidates for the I.C.S. could not sit for the examinations in England was reduced from twenty-one to nineteen years. This act stirred up considerable indignation in India. An Indian eyewitness of these reactions wrote, "Throughout India, this was regarded as a deliberate attempt to blast the prospect of Indian candidates for the Indian Civil Service." [11] Even when Indians were successful in the examinations, they experienced difficulty in securing posts in the I.C.S.

This was true in the case of Surendranath Banerjea, who was finally admitted only to be dismissed from the I.C.S. on a minor charge. Frustrated in his ambition for a government career, Banerjea turned to politics, and in 1876 founded the Indian Association of Calcutta with branches in the main cities of north India. This organization was definitely nationalistic in inspiration and had as its objective a united India strong enough to secure concessions from Great Britain. In 1877, following the reduction in age for the I.C.S. examinations, Banerjea used the Indian Association for a whirlwind campaign against the action of the British government. As a result an All-India Memorial was sent without success to the British House of Commons, asking that the examination age be raised. There can be no doubt that this civil service agitation played an important part in the story of the origin of nationalism in India.

Another factor that helped to bring nationalistic feelings to a head was the widening gulf in race relations between the British and Indians. English writers point out the un-

[10] Sir John Strachey, *India* (London: Kegan Paul, Trench, Trubner and Co., 1894), p. 390.

[11] Sir Surendranath Banerjea, *A Nation in the Making* (London: H. Milford Co., 1925), p. 44.

fortunate consequences of the influx into India in the 1860's of a stream of British planters and businessmen who were inclined to be raucous and superior and who looked down upon, and sometimes despised, all Indians. Undoubtedly the Mutiny had much to do with this feeling. In India this group constantly exacerbated the already difficult relations between Europeans and Indians by their noisy determination to uphold the prestige and superiority of the "white man."

Lord Ripon, the governor-general following Lytton, was a Victorian liberal, and during his administration (1880-1884) sincere attempts were made to liberalize the government. One of the measures was the Ilbert Bill, introduced in 1883 and designed to remove the privilege heretofore enjoyed by Europeans by which they were guaranteed a British judge in case of trial. As Indians were now moving up into the higher brackets of the judiciary, Ripon saw no reason why these well-qualified public servants could not preside at any trial regardless of the birthplace of the defendant. This Ilbert Bill, however, provoked a tempestuous explosion among the members of the European community, who started a Defence Association and carried on a noisy and violent agitation against the measure. Consequently the bill was emasculated and toned down. The European community had won its point, but, at the same time, it had given Indians a good object lesson in the value of organization and agitation. The European explosion over the Ilbert Bill also exposed to sensitive Indian nationalists the racial arrogance of many Englishmen in their country. Indian vernacular newspapers assumed a new tone in attacking the government—and the press had by this time become an influential factor in molding public opinion, as there were twenty newspapers published in English and some two hundred in Indian languages.

It was during the agitation over the Ilbert Bill that Indian spokesmen for the nationalist movement responded by organizing the Indian National Conference. Led by Surendranath Banerjea, it met in Calcutta in 1883 with representatives from all parts of India. The following year the growing national spirit was reflected in a meeting held at Madras under the aegis of the Theosophical Society, whose importance will be shortly discussed.

Meanwhile, the initiative was taken by Allan Octavian Hume, a retired civil servant, who, after thirty years in the Indian government, occupied himself in studying the country's problems. Hume believed that British rule had given the land he had come to love peace and political stability, but that much more had to be done to raise the standard of living of the people. Hume believed too that the British bureaucracy was out of touch with the people and maintained it was "of paramount importance to find an overt and constitutional channel for discharge of the increasing ferment which had resulted from western ideas and education." [12]

Acting upon this belief, Hume sent out in 1883 a letter to the graduates of Calcutta University urging them to form an association for the mental, moral, and political regeneration of India. Following a meeting held at Madras in December 1884, attended by such representative Indians as S. S. Iyer, Surendranath Banerjea, and Dadabhai Naoroji, a circular was sent out the following March inviting attendance at a meeting to be held in Poona, December 25 to 31, 1885. The objective of the meeting was outlined thus: "Indirectly this Conference will form the germ of a Native Parliament and . . . will constitute in a few years an unanswerable reply to the assertion that India is still wholly unfit for any form of representative institutions." [13]

The first meeting of what came to be known as the Indian National Congress duly convened in December at Poona. There were seventy delegates, mostly Hindu lawyers, educators, and journalists, with only two Muslims among them. The Congress carried on its deliberations in English, and the tone was loyal and moderate. In the first presidential address by W. C. Bonerji, parliamentary government was declared to be the goal, but it was claimed that this was in no way incompatible with loyalty to England. The President further declared:

> I ask whether in the most glorious days of Hindu rule you could imagine the possibility of a meeting of this kind. . . . Would it have been possible even in the days of Akbar for a meeting like this to assemble, composed of all classes and communities, all speaking one language . . . ? It is under the civilized rule of the Queen and the people of England that we meet here together, hindered by none, freely allowed to speak our minds without the least fear or hesitation. Such a thing is possible under British rule, and under British rule only.[14]

Resolutions were passed asking for a royal commission to investigate the workings of Indian administration; for the abolition of the Council of India in London; for the right to have the government budgets presented to the legislative

[12] Quoted in Sir H. Verney Lovett, *A History of the Indian Nationalist Movement* (London: John Murray, 1920), p. 34.

[13] Quoted in Annie Besant, *How India Wrought for Freedom* (Adyar, India: Theosophical Publishing House, 1915), p. 4.

[14] Quoted in Sir Reginald Coupland, *India: A Restatement* (London: Oxford University Press, 1945), p. 89.

councils for examination; and for the creation of a standing committee in the British House of Commons to consider formal protests from the Indian members of the legislative councils.

Each year after 1885 the National Congress met in December in a different city of India. In 1888 the Congress carried out extensive publicity, distributing thousands of pamphlets and arranging for hundreds of lectures. In 1894, at Madras, the ranks of the annual Congress meeting swelled to fifteen hundred delegates and three thousand visitors. The delegates in the annual meetings discussed various problems connected with British rule and passed resolutions urging the spread of education, the reduction of military expenditures, wider government employment for Indians, the improvement of the status of Indian nationals in South Africa, and the abolition of the countervailing excise of 3.5 per cent on domestic cotton goods.

The Indian National Congress during this period was controlled and directed by what we may refer to as the first generation of nationalists—men like G. K. Gokhale, Surendranath Banerjea, Pherozeshah Mehta, and Dadabhai Naoroji. These leaders championed a Western and a liberal view. They admired Great Britain and were apostles of cooperation. Gokhale was the outstanding Indian political leader up to the First World War. Born a Brahman in Bombay Presidency, he received an excellent education and became a professor of law at Ferguson College. Entering politics in 1899, he became a member of the Bombay legislative council and from 1902 to 1915 was a member of the Indian imperial legislative council. Gokhale served as president of the National Congress in 1905. As an orator and debater he had no superiors in India, and in his speeches he advocated self-government for India within the Empire and compulsory education. In 1905 Gokhale founded the Servants of India Society, an idea derived from the Jesuit Order. Its purpose was "to train men prepared to devote their lives to the cause of the country." [15] The members had to spend five years as initiates, during which time they could not marry and were not supposed to earn more than £4 a month. The society interested itself in social reform, such questions as improving the status of women and raising the level of the Depressed Classes (i.e., the Untouchables).

As we have already mentioned, there were other great moderate leaders, but Gokhale towers above them all. "Gokhale was perhaps the finest character that India has produced,"

[15] Hans Kohn, *A History of Nationalism in the East* (London: George Routledge, 1929), p. 369.

wrote one English observer, "blending accurate knowledge of Western history and Western thought with a profound understanding of the Indian mentality and of the ancient civilization that has moulded it." [16]

And what of the attitude of British officials to the Congress? At first the government of India was friendly to the new movement. Officials attended the Congress, and governors in the various provinces arranged official receptions and garden parties for the members. This sympathy, however, soon waned, and the viceroy, Lord Dufferin (1884-1888), rather contemptuously referred to Congress membership as a "microscopic minority."

Denied recognition from officialdom, the National Congress received valuable support from unofficial British circles. Allan Hume was known as the "Father of Congress," and until 1907 he was—at times with others—in charge of the general Congress secretariat. Visiting England, Hume solicited and secured the support of John Bright and Charles Bradlaugh. Before the First World War, Britishers were frequently elected presidents of the Congress. Sir William Wedderburn received this honor in 1889 and 1910, Sir Henry Cotton in 1904, and David Yule in 1888. A group friendly to the cause of Congress also carried on work in England. Known as the British Committee for Representative Government, founded in 1888, this agency published a journal and subsidized the distribution of pamphlets and the giving of lectures. Each annual Congress expressed its "thanks to the British Committee."

The Hindu Renaissance

The first reaction to the impact of the West in India had been the growth of an influential class of liberals who looked to Europe as an intellectual home. They were critical of many elements in their own culture pattern, and their ideal was the rationalization and modernization of Indian life, to be best achieved by a harmonious blend between East and West. This sometimes uncritical admiration and imitation of things European came to be challenged by a new movement that emerged in the 1870's and reached full tide in the closing years of the century. Often referred to as the Hindu Renaissance or Recovery, this movement regarded Western culture as soulless and materialistic. At the same time, the culture and the past of India were idealized, some thinkers going so far as to assert that all modern inventions could be found

[16] Sir Valentine Chirol, *India* (London: Ernest Benn, Ltd., 1926), p. 108.

in germ in the ancient Vedas. There was a poetic and emotional glow in the references to India's past golden age.

> We had corn in our granaries; our tanks supplied us with fish and the eye was soothed and refreshed with the limpid blue of the sky and green foliage of the trees. All day long the peasant toiled in the field; and at eve, returning to his lamp-lit home, he sang the song of his heart.[17]

Above all, the Hindu Renaissance, as a new manifestation of nationalism, was suffused with religion. Nationalism was deified as the manifestation and voice of God. This idea was made possible by the fact that Hinduism had long taught that God reincarnates himself from time to time for the saving of the world, and now God had appeared in the form of Mother India. An Indian newspaper in 1919 asserted: "This motherland . . . is the symbol of our nation-idea . . . the Divine Idea, the Logos, which has been revealing itself through the entire course of our past historic evolution. The Motherland is really the synthesis of all the goddesses that have been, and are still being, worshipped by Hindus." [18]

The religious motivation of the Hindu Renaissance gave it a fervor and an emotional strength comparable to what religion gave to Elizabethan England in its struggle against Spain. But this religious tinge to nationalism meant that the movement was to lose some of its early catholicity; that the Indian revival was going to be prevented from being truly national. As a European observer pointed out in the early 1900's, "The National party really replaces true Indian patriotism by a Hindu nationalism in which Musalmans and Buddhists could not join without very considerable reserves." [19]

Swami Dayanand Saraswati is usually regarded as the founder of the new nationalism and the Hindu Recovery. Although his family was well-to-do, Saraswati eschewed an English education, left home, and became a homeless ascetic. In 1860 he began his teaching. To his mind everything foreign was bad. Attacking modern Hinduism as corrupt, he exhorted the people to go back to the Vedas, in which there was no justification for caste, images, or polytheism. In 1875 this teacher established the Arya Samaj, the antithesis of the previously founded liberal-rational Brahma Samaj. The Arya Samaj was intensely nationalistic, opposing both Islam and Christianity. Its motto could be said to be "India for

[17] Earl of Ronaldshay, *The Heart of Aryavarta* (London: Constable and Co., 1925), p. 93.

[18] Quoted in Ramsay MacDonald, *The Awakening of India* (London: Hodder and Stoughton, 1910), p. 187.

[19] Quoted in Joseph Chailley, *Administrative Problems of British India* (London: Macmillan and Co., Ltd., 1910), p. 164.

the Hindus." While it preached a primitive and purified form of Hinduism, the society was not unmindful of the evils in contemporary Hindu life. It therefore opposed child marriage, proposed reforms in the caste system, and carried on extensive educational operations. The Arya Samaj became very influential in the Punjab.

Another apostle of the superiority and self-sufficiency of Hindu culture was the Swami Vivekananda, of whom it has been said, "The call to reform, restore and revive India, to help India in every way possible for human effort, was essentially Vivekananda's call, and of all the makers of modern India, his was the most classless and purely patriotic voice." [20] Born into a high-caste Bengali family, Vivekananda received a thorough education, impressing his English teachers by his brilliance and his remarkable memory. Becoming interested in spiritual problems, he turned in 1882 to the teacher Ramakrishna, a famous ascetic. After the death of his *guru* (teacher) in 1886, Vivekananda carried out various pilgrimages and in 1893 was sent by his supporters and friends to the Parliament of Religions, meeting in Chicago.

On September 11, 1893, Vivekananda made before the parliament a famous speech which created a tremendous impression. The young Hindu declared he spoke for "the Mother of Religions, a religion which has taught the world both tolerance and universal acceptance." Disclaiming any narrow denominationalism, however, he went on to proclaim the basic oneness and universality of all religions, using as his text these lines from an ancient Vedic hymn: "As the different streams having their sources in different places all mingle their water in the sea, so, O Lord, the different paths which men take through different tendencies, various though they appear, crooked or straight, all lead to Thee." [21]

He became famous, not only in the United States, but all over the world, and for three years he remained in America and Europe lecturing and founding his missions. In January 1897, Vivekananda returned to India and was welcomed as a national hero, for he was the first Indian in modern times to become a world figure. To this teacher all religions were true and good, but the noblest and most venerable was Hinduism. His was the voice of militant nationalism blending political aspirations with religious exhortation. After his return from abroad he gave this message to the Hindus:

Once more the world must be conquered by India. This is the great ideal before us. Let them come and flood the land with their armies, never mind. Up, India, and conquer the world with

[20] Vincent Sheean, *Lead, Kindly Light* (New York: Random House, 1949), p. 354.
[21] Quoted in *ibid.*, pp. 341-342.

your spirituality! Spirituality must conquer the West. Where are the men ready to go out to every country in the world with the messages of the great sages of India? There is no other alternative, we must do it or die. The only condition of national life, once more vigorous national life, is the conquest of the world by Indian thought.[22]

Vivekananda founded his Ramakrishna Order to propagate his beliefs, and it continued after his death in 1902 to do valiant work in the regeneration of Indian life. Today there are some three dozen monasteries and sixty-six missions run by the Ramakrishna Order, plus a number of schools and colleges.

There were other manifestations of the Hindu Revival, chief of which was the work of the Theosophical Society. Founded by Madame H. P. Blavatsky and Colonel H. S. Olcott in New York in 1875, the organization came to India in 1879 and established its headquarters at Adyar in Madras. Distinctive features of the society were its championship of Hindu ideals and practices, its acceptance of the doctrines of Karma and transmigration, and the idealization of India's past. The society also evinced a critical attitude toward Christianity.

The importance of the Theosophical Society really began with the leadership of Annie Besant, a remarkable woman whose career was varied and tempestuous. Born in 1847 the daughter of a London doctor, Mrs. Besant married early in her life, her chosen husband being a minister. She soon left him, however, after repudiating Christianity, and for some years was a follower of Charles Bradlaugh, the English freethinker and reformer. Mrs. Besant championed such un-Victorian causes as birth control and atheism; in the mid-1880's she came under the spell of Bernard Shaw and was converted to socialism. In 1889 she became a theosophist and four years later went to India, where she became the spokesman of the Theosophical Society. In 1898, with Olcott and others, she founded the Central Hindu College, which ultimately became the Hindu University at Benares. From the beginning of her sojourn in India, Mrs. Besant allied herself with the Hindu Renaissance. In her autobiography she wrote:

> The Indian work is, first of all, the revival, strengthening, and uplifting of the ancient religions. This act brought with it a new self-respect, a pride in the past, a belief in the future, and, as an inevitable result, a great wave of patriotic life, the beginning of the rebuilding of a nation.[23]

[22] Quoted in J. F. C. Fuller, *India in Revolt* (London: Eyre and Spottiswoode, 1931), p. 76.
[23] Quoted in R. C. Majumdar, H. C. Raychaudhuri, and K. Datta, *An Advanced History of India* (London: Macmillan and Co., Ltd., 1946), p. 886.

The Muslim Reaction

In contrast to the stirrings that activated the Hindu community after the Mutiny, the Muslims lacked any animation. The British conquest of the Mogul Empire had removed the upper-class Muslims from the status of the elite governing class. After the Mutiny the Muslim community passed under a dark cloud, as it was saddled with most of the responsibility for the outbreak of 1857. While many Hindus took advantage of the commercial opportunities that came in the nineteenth century with the growth of trade in India, the Muslims lagged behind economically, showing little aptitude for business. Furthermore, their Koran forbade them the practice of usury. And while the new schools were filled to capacity with Hindu youths eager for the new Western learning, the leaders of the Muslim community urged their people to have nothing to do with it. In consequence, the professions of law, medicine, teaching, and journalism were closed to the Muslims, and, most important, they could not compete with the Hindu candidates for positions in the government service. "While Bengali Hindus, Madrasis, and Marathas inspired by the arts and sciences of Europe were experiencing an intellectual and moral renaissance, the Muslims all over India were falling into a state of material indigence and intellectual decay." [24]

It was from this melancholy state that the Muslims were elevated through the vision of a remarkable leader, Sir Seyed Ahmad Khan (1817-1898). Born in Delhi of an old Muslim family, Sir Seyed entered the service of the British government in India at the age of twenty-one. During the Mutiny he supported the cause of the British, and after its conclusion concentrated on two objectives: (1) to achieve better understanding between his coreligionists and the viceroy's government and (2) to arouse his fellow Muslims from the torpor and stagnation that had been retarding their progress.

In the 1860's Sir Seyed Ahmad Khan busied himself with these two tasks; a visit to Europe in 1869 convinced him that his community must adopt certain aspects of Western culture. His letters written in Europe are full of astonishment and admiration for the wonders he encountered on his tour. He was especially impressed with what he saw in England, and in referring to the differences between conditions in Great Britain and India he wrote:

> I am not thinking about those things in which, owing to the specialities of our respective countries, we and the English dif-

[24] Sir John Cumming, ed., *Political India, 1832-1932* (London: Oxford University Press, 1932), p. 87.

fer. I only remark on politeness, knowledge, good faith, clean-
liness, skilled workmanship, accomplishments, and thoroughness,
which are the results of education and civilization. All good
things, spiritual and worldly, which should be found in man,
have been bestowed by the Almighty on Europe, and especially
on England.[25]

The message of Sir Seyed to his fellow Muslims was to
lay aside their old superstitions and bigotries. He argued
that the Muslim way of life must be regenerated, and that
this end could only be achieved through Western education.
Such a course was not contrary to the teachings of Islam,
and Sir Seyed reminded his people of the Prophet's words,
"Go even to the walls of China for the sake of learning." As
a result of this reformer's efforts the Aligarh Anglo-Oriental
College was founded in 1877. This institution was pro-British and was modeled after Oxford and Cambridge. The
opening prospectus declared that its object was "to establish
a College in which Musalmans may acquire an English
education without prejudice to their religion." The college at
Aligarh, later to become a university, became the heart of
the Muslim reform movement, winning a considerable body
of Sir Seyed Ahmad Khan's community to Western education and ideas.

From the very inception of the National Congress Sir
Seyed perceived in it a potential danger to the Muslims. He
was bitterly opposed to the extension of the representative
principle because he saw in it the device which would rele-
gate the Muslims into the status of a permanent minority.
In 1883 Sir Seyed made this quite clear when he said:

For socio-political purposes the whole of the population of
England forms but one community. It is obvious that the same
cannot be said of India. The system of representation by election means the representation of the views and interests of the
majority of the population, and in countries where the population is composed of one race and one creed, it is, no doubt, the
best system that can be adopted. But in a country like India,
where caste distinctions still flourish, where there is no fusion
of the various races, where religious distinctions are still violent,
where education in its modern sense has not made an equal
or proportionate progress among all sections of the population
. . . the system of election, pure and simple, cannot safely be
adopted. The larger community would totally override the interests of the smaller community.[26]

[25] Quoted in Raja Rao and Iqbal Singh, ed., *Changing India*
(London: George Allen and Unwin, 1939), pp. 51-52.
[26] From "Proceedings of the Council of the Governor-General of
India, 1883," quoted in Coupland, *India: A Restatement*, p. 93.

If Sir Seyed was concerned about the ultimate results of the program outlined by the Indian liberals who initiated the Congress movement, he was, with his followers, more and more alarmed over the Hindu bias of the new wave of nationalism that obtained its inspiration from Vivekananda and Saraswati. And in the late 1890's, as we will note shortly, new militant nationalists, such as B. G. Tilak, sponsored "cow-protection societies" definitely aimed against the Muslims. Tilak referred to the Muslims as foreigners and glorified the famous Hindu patriot, Sivaji, for his exploits in the seventeenth century against Muslim oppressors. As a result of Sir Seyed Ahmad Khan's influence, the Muslims had little to do with the National Congress. In 1885 only two Muslim delegates attended the first meeting of the Congress; the next year there were 33 out of a total attendance of 440; in 1890 there were 156 Muslims out of a total of 702. After this date there was a rapid decline, and in 1905 only 17 Muslim delegates attended out of a Congress membership of 756.

In 1906, the Muslims launched their own All-India Muslim League, mainly through the activities of the Aga Khan and the two brothers, Mohammed and Shaukat Ali, who had assumed the direction of the Muslim movement after the death of Sir Seyed Ahmad Khan. The first meeting of the League was held at Dacca; in 1907 it met at Karachi and in 1908 at Aligarh.

Much has been written to the effect that it was the British authorities who originated this artificial Muslim-Hindu dichotomy in Indian politics. Undoubtedly, when its existence was presented to them, the British understandably welcomed the Muslim League as a make-weight against the Congress. In this stage of Muslim-Hindu relations the dominant factor was not the policy of the British government but rather the Hindu bias of the Congress movement. This fact is supported by the statement of R. P. Dutt, who wrote:

> The insistence on orthodox religion as the heart of the national movement, and the proclamation of the supposed spiritual superiority of the ancient Hindu civilization to modern "Western" civilization . . . inevitably retarded and weakened the real advance of the national movement and of political consciousness, while the emphasis on Hinduism must bear a share of the responsibility for the alienation of wide sections of Moslem opinion from the national movement. . . .[27]

The same author went on to say that it was the militant Indian national leaders who "sought to build on a basis of Hindu religion for their agitation and to identify the national

[27] Quoted in Desai, *op. cit.*, p. 303.

awakening with a revival of Hinduism. By this act they cut off the Moslem masses from the national movement and opened the way to the Government's astute counter-move with the formation of the Moslem League in 1906." [28] Rather than the British officials, it was the Indians themselves who, while Indian nationalism was still in its formative period, held the initiative in determining the nature of the movement. While recourse to religion, that is, Hinduism, is understandable, it is apparent that the Hindu leaders did not appreciate the implications of transforming the nationalist movement from a purely secular to a politico-religious one. And, when there was the inevitable Muslim reaction, most members of the Congress made a serious error in refusing to admit the existence and validity of Muslim nationalism.

Lord Curzon and the End of an Epoch

After 1890 there was a basic change in the Indian situation. The epoch of complacency on the part of the British bureaucracy came to a slow end, and at the same time the heretofore liberal and constitutional Indian nationalist movement was challenged by a militant wing of nationalists who sought their inspiration in the ancient Vedas rather than in European thought and who condoned and even supported the use of violence in attaining their ends.

By 1895 what came to be known as "the Indian problem" had emerged. The stars in their courses seemed to conspire against British authority in India as plague, drought, famine, unrest along the northwest frontier, and political terrorism descended on the land. "The Government of India," two British historians wrote, "never regained the aloofness, conscious rectitude, and confidence of the 'eighties and early 'nineties." [29]

The transformation to militant nationalism was mainly the work of Bal Gangadhar Tilak (1856-1920), who is referred to by British historians as the "father of Indian unrest." Tilak came from the Mahratta country, where his father was a school inspector at Poona. An excellent student, Tilak not only received a good Western education but seriously studied both Sanskrit and Marathi. At the age of twenty he received a college degree with honors and until 1890 taught law at Ferguson College, which he had helped to establish.

In 1880 Tilak began the publication of two newspapers,

[28] Quoted in *ibid.*, p. 304.
[29] Thompson and Garratt, *op. cit.*, p. 527.

one in English and one, the *Kesari* ("Lion"), in the vernacular. Becoming editor of these publications in 1890, he at once initiated a campaign of militant nationalism. The secular counterpart of Saraswati and Vivekananda, Tilak stoutly defended Hindu orthodoxy. In 1890, for example, he entered politics by roundly condemning the Age of Consent Bill, by which the government hoped to lessen the evil of child marriage. To Tilak everything indigenous was sacred. A fierce opponent of Western culture, he denounced the Brahma Samaj and had little use for moderates, like Gokhale, who admired European institutions. Tilak sought to resurrect what he believed was the former martial prowess and manliness of a past Hindu age, symbolized by the courage of the great Mahratta leader Sivaji, who had assassinated a Muslim general. Gymnastic societies were founded by Tilak, with members drawn especially from the ranks of college students. Sivaji was revered as a great hero, and festivals were held in honor of Ganesh, the elephant-headed god of the Hindus. Tilak's nationalism was exclusively Hindu, and in this connection he founded a cow-protection society that was aimed against the Muslims.

In June 1897 Tilak in his *Kesari* justified the use of force in defense of national ideals and used Sivaji's deed as an example. Shortly afterwards two British officials who had been active in plague-prevention measures, such as the disinfection and evacuation of houses, were murdered by youthful nationalists. As Tilak had accused the plague commissioner and his assistants of tyranny in carrying out their prevention measures, he was sentenced to prison for one year.

While Tilak was beating the drums of militant nationalism, other factors were helping to strengthen his cause. There is little doubt that the India Councils Act, passed in 1892, disappointed many moderate nationalists. It was too cautious an advance toward representative government, and one wonders what might have been the course of politics in India had British statesmen been more courageous in their constitutional reforms.

Famine and plague in the 1890's caused much suffering and added to the general sense of grievance in India. Plague was first detected in Bombay in 1896, and within two years the recorded deaths from this scourge reached 173,000. The monsoon was deficient in 1895 and almost failed in 1896, and the rains failed again in 1899. This brought about the worst drought in two hundred years. The total area affected was 475,000 square miles with a population of 60 millions. Six million people were placed on government relief and

25 million dollars were spent in relief measures. Despite all this, the death toll was tremendous.

Outside of India the trend of events also worked to strengthen the cause of nationalism. Heretofore, European supremacy had been unchallenged. At the end of the nineteenth century, however, a number of happenings seemed to indicate that this uncontested leadership was waning. In 1896 an Italian army was completely defeated in Abyssinia by the African warriors of King Menelik. The Indians were also amazed at the stout resistance of the Boer farmers, as they inflicted resounding defeats upon the best soldiers Britain could send to South Africa. Though ultimately victorious, British arms lost much of their luster in the Boer War (1899-1902). Above all, the rise of Japan electrified the Indian nationalists, who in 1905 saw this Asiatic power, so small compared to her opponent, defeat the Russian Empire, which had so long been described by British officials as a dread and powerful foe of their empire. Describing the effect of the Japanese victory, Mr. C. F. Andrews wrote:

> A stir of excitement passed over the North of India. Even the remote villages talked over the victories of Japan as they sat in their circles and passed round the *huqqa* at night. A Turkish consul of long experience in Western Asia told me "that in the interior you could see everywhere the most ignorant peasants tingling with the news." Asia was moved from one end to the other, and the sleep of the centuries was finally broken.[30]

The slogan of "Asia for the Asiatics" now became the rallying cry of young nationalists in China, Burma, and the Dutch East Indies as well as in India.

It was an unkind trick of fate from the British point of view that the period which witnessed such an increase in nationalistic fervor should also coincide with the viceroyalty of Lord Curzon, who—while desiring to rule the country with what he considered to be the best traditions of enlightened bureaucratic despotism—would brook no criticism of his policies and had little regard for the likes or dislikes of his Indian subjects. His one aim was to rule India efficiently, and he felt that the government of India, of which he was the head, was alone qualified to decide how this could best be done.

No viceroy had ever been so well prepared for his duties. A product of Eton and of Balliol College, Oxford, he had been elected to the House of Commons in 1886; he had been appointed undersecretary of state for India in 1891 and undersecretary for foreign affairs in 1895. At the same

[30] Quoted in Fuller, *op. cit.*, p. 91.

time he was an inveterate traveler, and during the period 1883 to 1895, with the exception of one year, he visited some foreign country annually. Persia, central Asia, India, and the Far East were of greatest interest to him. Before he was made viceroy in 1899 he had visited India four times and was personally acquainted with such rulers as the Amir of Afganistan, the Shah of Persia, the Emperor of Annam, and most of the Indian princes. In addition to his travels, Curzon had written several scholarly books on such subjects as Persia, Japan and Korea, and Russia in central Asia; furthermore, he had received the gold medal of the Royal Geographical Society for discovering the source of the Oxus River.

As for the character of Curzon, this indefatigable student and globe-trotter was thoroughly honest and unusually hardworking and competent. He was also, be it said, completely convinced of his own unusual powers, and one member of the House of Commons once remarked, "When I say that Mr. Curzon is about one-tenth as clever as he thinks himself I am paying him a very high compliment indeed." [31] Closely tied in with this self-confidence, which some might label simple egotism, was a certain aloofness and hauteur that seriously detracted from his other great qualities.

Immediately upon his arrival in India, Curzon set about with feverish energy to tackle the country's problems. It is difficult to catalogue all of his activities or credit him with all of his achievements. He strove to make the land revenue system more elastic and equitable and to protect the peasant from the moneylender. He initiated rural banks and the system of cooperative credit for the farmers. Under his direction the agricultural department was reorganized and scientific research undertaken. Fresh impetus was given to railroad building and to irrigation projects. An ardent student of Indian history and a keen admirer of India's ancient culture and monuments, Curzon was instrumental in passing the Ancient Monuments Act of 1904. No man has done more to preserve and also to unearth the precious relics of early India. He also introduced a new policy along the northwest frontier, and waged an energetic foreign policy in defense of British imperial interests in the Persian Gulf, Tibet, and central Asia.

In the early years of his viceroyalty Curzon was popular with the Indian people. On several occasions he took severe measures against British soldiers who had abused Indians yet had been protected by army authorities. After three

[31] Quoted in Earl of Ronaldshay, *The Life of Lord Curzon* (London: Benn and Co., 1928), I, p. 187.

years, however, his popularity waned; then it completely disappeared and was superseded by hostility and even hatred. Curzon's fundamental lack of sympathy with Indian aspirations alienated even the moderate leaders like Gokhale. "The Congress," wrote the viceroy, "is tottering to its fall, and one of my great ambitions while in India is to assist it to a peaceful demise." [32]

While failing to appreciate the growing national sentiment, Curzon also initiated two reforms that did more to arouse hostility and misunderstanding against the British regime in India than perhaps any act of a previous viceroy. The first measure concerned the reform of education, which was in an unsatisfactory condition. Though elementary education was neglected, the universities were overcrowded. Bengal had as many college students as Great Britain, with perhaps one-tenth of the opportunities for employment. In many educational institutions the discipline was poor and the teachers inefficient, and the main effort was on drilling the students to pass examinations. Of these institutions Curzon wrote that they constituted "a huge system of active but often misdirected effort, over which, like some evil phantom, seemed to hover the monstrous and maleficent spirit of Cram." [33] After two years of investigation the Universities Act of 1904 was passed. By this act, which sought to eliminate the more serious abuses, government control was made much more effective and the examination system was revised.

The act kindled the wrath of Indian leaders, who saw in it the desire of the government to curb and even throttle higher education; an Indian observer wrote of the report of the Universities Commission upon which the act was based that it "convulsed educated India from one end of the country to another." [34] While this reform was justified from many angles, it had been imposed in such a fashion as to infuriate the very people whom it was designed to benefit.

The second Curzon measure to intensify Indian nationalism was the partition of Bengal. This province covered a huge area of 189,000 square miles with a population of 78 million. Because of this huge mass of people the provincial administration was overburdened, and, in particular, the area of the province east of the Ganges was neglected. While Indian writers usually saddle Curzon with all the responsibility for the partition measure, in reality the viceroy

[32] Earl of Ronaldshay, *The Life of Lord Curzon,* II, p. 33.
[33] Quoted in O'Malley, *op. cit.,* p. 167.
[34] Banerjea, *op. cit.,* p. 175.

himself did not originate it. For more than a year the partition was discussed by various officials without Curzon's knowledge. Finally, the file of correspondence reached the viceroy.

Having once studied the partition proposal, Curzon was completely convinced of its worth. It would lighten the burden of administration in western Bengal, would help to rectify the previous neglect of eastern Bengal, and would give Assam a much-needed seaport. The partition was administratively justified, and that was sufficient for the viceroy, who could not appreciate the fact that Bengal more than any other section of India had developed a local patriotism. Here the Hindu Renaissance of which we have already spoken had been particularly active, not only in a religious revival, but in the development of a rich literature using the Bengali language as the medium of expression. The Hindu Bengalis thought of themselves as one nation, and many interpreted the proposed partition as a British plot to enfeeble their nationalistic movement. There were other motives, too, less ingenuous. Lawyers in Calcutta feared the competition of the new law courts to be set up in Dacca, and businessmen also disliked the prospect of competition from new enterprises that might spring up in the new province.

Despite widespread opposition among the Hindus of Bengal—not the Muslims—the scheme was passed in June 1905. East Bengal was created a province inhabited by 18 million Muslims and 12 million Hindus and with a new capital at Dacca, while the new Bengal contained 42 million Hindus and 12 million Muslims with the capital at Calcutta. After the passage of this partition act Hindu resentment reached unprecedented heights. On August 7, 1905, a vast multitude congregated in Calcutta to protest against the partition. An annual day of mourning was planned, and at the same time the Swadeshi movement, the boycott against English goods which was later to be such a feature of Gandhi's program, was initiated for the first time. The vernacular press created a wide feeling of emotional excitement among the public. A feature of the rising nationalistic fervor was the resurrection of an old folk song, *Bande Mataram* ("Hail to thee, My Mother") "as the Marseillaise that was to carry young Bengal to the storming of the British Bastile." [35]

While anti-partition agitation raged, Curzon resigned following a disagreement with Lord Kitchener, the military commander-in-chief in India. In spite of his herculean efforts, Curzon was a failure in India because, with all his many accomplishments, he failed in the most important

[35] Chirol, *op. cit.*, p. 118.

task—the true appreciation of the temper of the Indian people.

The Indian national movement might have been something different from what it was in the first decade of the twentieth century if Curzon had been more sympathetic and tactful. Rabindranath Tagore said the last word about this viceroy's efficient and impersonal administration when, likening it to the claim of a new-fangled bakery in Calcutta, he declared it was "untouched by hand." [36]

Bombs and Boons, 1905 to 1914

When Lord Curzon departed, he left behind him an indignant and vociferous national movement which demanded more self-government than that afforded by the cautious constitutional reform of 1892. Lord Minto, the new governor-general who arrived in India in November 1905, soon admitted, "The Government of India cannot shut our eyes to present conditions. The political atmosphere is full of change; questions are before us which we cannot afford to ignore, and which we must attempt to answer." [37]

For some time the moderate leaders of the National Congress had been dissatisfied at the lack of response of the British government to their suggestions for a constitutional advance. Various schemes had been offered, such as the one in 1895 proposing the inclusion of six Indian representatives in the House of Commons so that this body could be kept informed of Indian public opinion. In 1905 the National Congress adopted a more uncompromising tone. Referring to the partition of Bengal, the moderate leader Gokhale indicted the government for "its utter contempt of public opinion, its reckless disregard of the most cherished feelings of the people." [38] And for the first time the Congress came out for self-government (*swaraj*) in a form similar to that existing in the self-governing colonies of the British Empire, such as Canada.

While the tone of moderate nationalists was hardening, Bengal had become the center of a militant movement elements of which were quite ready to use violence to achieve their ends. Getting under way in 1902, and strongly influenced by the tactics of Tilak in Bombay, the extremists (that

36 Quoted in H. C. E. Zacharias, *Renascent India* (London: George Allen and Unwin, 1933), p. 132.

37 *Report on Indian Constitutional Reforms* (The Montagu-Chelmsford Report), Cd. 9109 (London: His Majesty's Stationery Office, 1918), p. 63.

38 *Report of the Twenty-first Indian National Congress, 1906* (Calcutta, 1907), p. 8.

is, the wing of the national movement whose ideas were "extreme" compared to those of the moderates) borrowed many techniques and objectives from abroad. They studied the use of the boycott by the Irish nationalists, and the operations of the Nihilists in Russia were carefully followed. At the same time, the story of the Italian *Risorgimento* and the work of Louis Kossuth in Hungary were studied. Turning to America's past, the extremists borrowed the term "War of Independence."

This Bengal movement was suffused with religion. Indian nationalism was personified in the form of a goddess. B. C. Chatterji, in a famous novel written in 1882, had interpreted the motherland by using the goddess Kali as a national symbol. This Black Goddess was the deity of destruction and death, and was worshiped as the symbol of creative power by her monks, who sang the sacred hymn *Bande Mataram* in a temple near Calcutta (from "Kalighat"). Kali now became the religious token for Bengali nationalism. The ultra-nationalist newspaper, *Yugantar* ("New Era"), advocated that young men be trained in secret bands, that weapons be made, and that money for the cause be obtained by any method. In one of its issues of May 1908, this paper declared, "The mother is thirsty and is pointing out to her sons the only thing that can quench that thirst. Nothing less than human blood and decapitated heads will satisfy her. . . ." [39]

The party of direct action in Bengal first inaugurated a policy of terrorism through the use of bombs in 1906. On December 6, 1907, a train carrying the lieutenant-governor of Bengal was bombed and derailed. The first bombs used were not very effective, and the revolutionary party sent one of its number to Paris to learn the intricacies of bomb making. Returning in 1908, this postgraduate in explosives helped to set up a bomb factory in the suburbs of Calcutta. Several serious outrages followed. In one of these a bomb was thrown into the wrong carriage, and two Englishwomen were killed. A few days later the bomb factory was raided and a large number of suspects were arrested. The desperate nature of violent nationalism in Bengal is seen in the reprisals inflicted upon persons connected with this case. A member of the group who turned informer was shot in prison; later an Indian police officer was killed in the streets of Calcutta, and another who had taken a prominent role in investigating the case was actually shot and killed in the High Court of Calcutta.

While popular unrest, of both a constitutional and a ter-

[39] Quoted in Cumming, ed., *Political India, 1832-1932*, pp. 228-229.

roristic nature, was mounting in Bengal, the same phenomenon appeared in the Punjab. Sporadic violence broke out, numerous arrests were made, and two leaders—Lala Lajpat Rai and Ajit Singh—were deported. The former was one of the most influential nationalists in India at this time. He was an ardent member of the militant Arya Samaj and helped found the important Anglo-Vedic College at Lahore. Lajpat Rai went to the United States just before the First World War, and while there carried on ceaseless work for the cause of Indian freedom and wrote the important work *Young India.* He was the author of many books and exerted tremendous influence because of his attainments as an orator and an author and because of his simple, austere life.

It is interesting that much of the pre-1914 revolutionary movement in India and many of the instances of terrorism were stimulated and directed from centers outside the country. A group of enthusiastic young nationalists was established at India House in London in 1905 and carried on active propaganda in the newspaper, the *Indian Sociologist.* The intrigues of India House unfortunately culminated in the outrage of July 1, 1909, when one of its members slipped into a gala reception being held at the Imperial Institute and shot to death Dr. Lalkaka and Sir William Curzon Wyllie. The latter had been an official at the India Office and had been active in the welfare of young Indian students in London.

There were other foreign centers of undercover movements, notably San Francisco and Paris. The former will be discussed in connection with the First World War in the following chapter when the famous *Ghadr* Conspiracy will be related. In Paris the schemes of a nationalistic group were under the direction of Madame Cama, a Parsi who edited the paper *Bande Mataram.* This group assisted in smuggling arms into India before the First World War.

While the extremist wing of the Indian national movement was becoming active, and in Bengal alone, between 1906 and 1917, was responsible for 168 outrages which took the lives of 61 persons, the moderates led by Gokhale denounced terrorism and believed in resort only to constitutional methods. Gokhale declared that the aim of the extremist faction was "to stir up disorder and have recourse to every practicable form of violence because it regards any disorder or misery, or even anarchy itself, as preferable to the presence of the foreigner in the land." [40]

The alarming growth of terrorism and the rising dissatis-

40 Quoted in O'Malley, *op. cit.,* p. 96.

faction of even the moderate majority in the National Congress convinced the British government that some advance would have to be made to satisfy Indian national aspirations. The time was propitious, because at the end of 1905 in Britain the Conservative party had fallen from power and had been succeeded by a Liberal cabinet much more inclined to be sympathetic to the cause of Indian reform. Visiting London at the end of 1905, representatives of the Congress reported that "narrow and aggressive imperialism" was declining and that the new Liberal government was definitely friendly. In particular, Indian nationalists expected much from the Liberals because of their new secretary of state for India, John Morley. Famous as a historian and the biographer of William Gladstone, editor of the *Fortnightly Review,* a lifelong liberal and champion of freedom, Lord Morley was looked to by India with hope and expectancy as a British official who would be likely to concede a generous advance in the direction of self-government.

Between the years 1907 and 1909, therefore, Morley and the governor-general in India, Lord Minto, sought to satisfy the growing demands of Indian nationalism by liberalizing what had been up to this time an almost completely bureaucratic system of government. In 1907 two Indian representatives were appointed to the advisory India Council in London. During this same year Lord Minto canvassed many sections of public opinion in India to determine views on constitutional reform. The Muslim community made it plain that they feared the introduction of the representative principle, which could only mean their relegation to the position of a permanent and impotent minority. The Muslims pointed out that heretofore in one area, the United Provinces, with 14 per cent of the population, they had not secured a single representative in the provincial council.

On November 1, 1908, the fiftieth anniversary of the assumption of direct responsibility for the government of India by the British crown, a message from the king-emperor to the people of India announced the extension of representative government. The details of the new scheme, commonly known as the Morley-Minto Reforms, were made known shortly afterwards and were enacted into law in 1909 by the British Parliament.

The Indian Councils Act increased the membership of the provincial legislative councils and also provided for a majority of non-official members in contrast to the official members, who represented and were nominated by the British government and who, in turn, were bound to support its decisions and measures on all occasions. Election to these provincial councils was voted by certain bodies, such as district and municipal boards, landowners, chambers of commerce, universities, and the Muslim community. Voters representing these agencies were very few, the largest constituency numbering less than seven hundred. In the central legislature the membership was raised to 60, of whom 27 were elected—7 by landowners, 5 by Muslims, 2 by chambers of commerce, and the remainder by legislatures in the provinces. Another important feature of the Morley-Minto Reforms was the appointment of an Indian member to the executive council of the governors in both Bombay and Madras and, most important, to the executive council of the viceroy. For the first time an Indian had been admitted to the inner sanctum of the central government of India where fundamental decisions were made and policies discussed.

The Indian members of the new councils were given much greater latitude in criticizing the policies of the government. On all matters of public interest—save those affecting the princely states—discussion was allowed and resolutions could be made.

A study of the Morley-Minto Reforms makes it apparent that they in no sense introduced responsible government into India. In the last analysis, even where an unofficial majority existed, as in the provincial councils, the British governor was fully prepared to override any opposition. In essence, therefore, in the words of a famous British report on Indian affairs, "They [the reforms] were based on the fundamental principle that the executive government should retain the final decision on all questions, although some degree of popular control over legislation was established in the provinces by providing small non-official majorities." [41] The desire of the British government to introduce an element of representative government while, at the same time, maintaining complete control over all policy made the reforms a contradiction within themselves. They attempted to blend the past autocracy of traditional Hindu monarchy and that of the Mogul emperors with the representative principle derived from Great Britain. The result was a kind of "constitutional autocracy."

The most controversial feature of the reforms was that providing communal electorates for the Muslim community. By this feature the Muslims were guaranteed a certain number of seats in the new councils, and these representatives could be elected only by voters on the Muslim communal roll. Furthermore, Muslim representation was weighted—

[41] *Report on Indian Constitutional Reforms,* Cd. 9109, p. 7.

that is, their numbers were in excess of those that would be computed if only the exact proportion of Muslims to the entire Indian community were taken into consideration. Apparently Lord Morley was against the idea of separate electorates for the Muslims, but reluctantly gave up his opposition after hearing the arguments of a deputation sent to England by the Muslim League. It is also asserted by the Muslims that the eminent Hindu nationalist, Gokhale, supported their claim. Mohammed Ali Jinnah, the leader of Muslim separatism in the 1930's and 1940's and founder of Pakistan, maintained in one of his speeches that in 1907 Gokhale had declared:

> Confronted by an overwhelming Hindu majority, Muslims are naturally afraid that release from the British yoke might in their case mean enslavement to the Hindus. Were the Hindus similarly situated as are the Muslims in regard to numbers . . . we would undoubtedly have felt the same fear and adopted the identical policy which the Muslims are adopting to-day.[42]

When the Muslim-Hindu feud began to mount to serious proportions in the late 1920's, most Hindu publicists took the view that the gulf between the two communities was a result of British "divide and rule" technique initiated by the foreign ruler in 1909 with the policy of communal electorates. British authorities indignantly deny this charge, maintaining that the policy of separate electorates for the Muslim community was only the expression in the field of government of the fundamental facts already existing in the socioreligious sphere. On this whole moot question, Mohammed Ali, a prominent Muslim leader, declared: "It is the old maxim of 'divide and rule' but there is a division of labour here. We divide and you rule." [43]

During the gestation and enactment of the Morley-Minto Reforms, important events had been taking place in the National Congress. In its annual meeting in 1906 at Calcutta, the left-wing group led by Tilak, forming what we might think of as the new party, clashed headlong and bitterly with the moderates led by Gokhale. Some semblance of harmony was retained only through the mediating efforts of the venerable leader, Dadabhai Naoroji, India's "Grand Old Man." The showdown occurred the following year, when the National Congress convened at Surat. The left-wing element tried to secure the presidency for Lala Lajpat Rai,

[42] Jamil-ud-Din Ahmad, ed., *Some Recent Speeches . . . of Mr. Jinnah* (Lahore, Pakistan: Muhammad Ashraf, 1943), I, pp. 455-456.
[43] Quoted in Sir Reginald Coupland, *The Indian Problem* (London: Oxford University Press, 1944), Part I, p. 36.

the Punjab nationalist leader recently deported by the government. When a motion of Tilak's, designed to pave the way for this result, was declared out of order by the presiding officer, delegates swinging *lathis* (weighted clubs) stormed the platform and the meeting broke up in a riot. An eyewitness who was present has described the scene for us:

> Chairs flew through the air, like shells discharged at a venture. Long sticks clashed and shivered. Blood flowed from broken heads. It was a confused and difficult conflict—ten thousand men crowded together among ten thousand chairs; no uniform, no distinction, nothing to mark off Extremist from Moderate except the facial expression of temperament.[44]

The following day the moderates met and a new constitution for the Congress was drawn up. Article 1 of this document called for a system of government for India similar to that existing in the self-governing members of the British Empire, such as Canada, and declared that this object was to be achieved by constitutional means through the process of steady reform. As for the extremists, they remained outside the fold of Congress, a faction without much following until 1916.

Following the announcement of the Morley-Minto Reforms, Congress, dominated in 1908 by the moderates, expressed "its deep and general satisfaction at the Reform proposals." Gokhale and his followers, however, had hoped for more than had been received from Lord Morley, who had not lived up to his reputation as a progressive liberal. Nevertheless, Congress accepted the reforms while hoping for further advances in the not too distant future.

Between 1910 and 1914 a more tranquil spirit seemed to pervade the Indian political atmosphere. For one thing, the more militant extremists were either imprisoned or deported, and the government passed new acts controlling seditious meetings, the purchase of explosives, and the use of the press, all of which restricted the more militant variety of nationalism. In 1911 the British government decided to "play the king and take the trick." For the first time the king and queen, George V and Mary, were crowned in a Grand Durbar at Delhi. This ceremony, with its pomp and circumstance, sought to strengthen the ties between the British crown and the Indian people. Under a resplendent canopy surrounded by Indian princes and with a great concourse of India's crack regiments, the king-emperor in a royal message announced the imminence of a number of boons for his Indian subjects.

[44] Quoted in Edward Thompson, *Reconstructing India* (New York: The Dial Press, 1930), p. 97.

As later announced by the governor-general, these included: (1) the annulment of the unpopular partition of Bengal, a gesture to Hindu sentiment; (2) transfer of the capital of India from Calcutta to the ancient seat of Mogul power at Delhi, a concession to Muslim feeling; (3) the release of certain political prisoners; and (4) the setting aside of a substantial sum of money for the advancement of education.

Despite these coronation boons and the Morley-Minto Reforms, political extremism continued to exist as an undercover movement. In December 1912, Lord Hardinge, the viceroy, was seriously wounded by a bomb while making a state entrance into Delhi. And scattered incidents of violence occurred in various parts of the country.

The National Congress, however, controlled by such moderates as Gokhale, Malaviya, Mehta, and S. Banerjea, was convinced that constitutional and evolutionary methods formed the only appropriate path leading to self-government for Indians to take. In a famous speech delivered at Poona in July 1909, Gokhale summed up the philosophy of the Indian moderate's creed, declaring:

> Our public life was based on frank and loyal acceptance of British rule, due to a recognition of the fact that it alone could secure to the country the peace and order which were necessary for slowly evolving a nation out of the heterogeneous elements of which India was composed. . . . We have to realise that British rule, in spite of its inevitable drawbacks as a foreign rule, has been on the whole a great instrument of progress for our people. Its continuance means the continuance of that peace and order which it alone can maintain. . . . Our rulers stand pledged to extend to us equality of treatment with themselves. This equality is to be sought in two fields: equality for individual Indians with individual Englishmen and equality in regard to the form of government which Englishmen enjoy in other parts of the Empire.[45]

With the year 1914, the first great phase in the history of modern Indian nationalism was coming to an end. The new sense of the unity of India and the desire for representative institutions had come, as we have seen, mainly from the impact of the West through the medium of British rule. During the period from 1880 to 1914 both the Hindu and the Muslim community had experienced a revival comparable to the *Risorgimento* in nineteenth-century Italy. While this new nationalism expressed itself in certain quarters by acts of violence, in the main it was a constitutional movement guided

[45] Quoted in *Cambridge History of the British Empire* (Cambridge: Cambridge University Press, 1932), V, pp. 557-558.

by moderates who were essentially nineteenth-century liberals who admired British institutions and had faith in British intentions.

In the quarter of a century since its establishment in 1885, the National Congress had grown until its membership covered all parts of British India. It was, however, almost exclusively a middle-class movement dominated by lawyers, journalists, and merchants, who were concerned only with political freedom and had little appreciation of the economic misery of the masses. These politically ambitious members of the Indian bourgeoisie conducted their proceedings in English and sprinkled their speeches with references to Magna Carta, Hilton, Gibbon, Spencer, and Darwin. Congress before 1914 was definitely a minority urban movement. The great masses of people were little affected by its gospel except when some specific and tangible grievance—such as the partition of Bengal—could be exploited and dramatized. Congress did not become a mass movement until after World War I and the appearance of Mohandas K. Gandhi.

5. World War
and the Advent of the Mahatma

NOT LONG AFTER Big Ben, the Empire's symbolic timepiece in London, had struck midnight, on August 4, 1914, and given notice that a state of war existed between Great Britain and Germany, many eyes were turned in the direction of India. Now that Britain and her Empire were engaged in a desperate struggle, what would be the course of events in this great dependency? Would India, especially its more militant and revolutionary nationalists, see in 1914 a golden opportunity to throw off the yoke of the British raj?

Such a course had been predicted by many writers, mainly German—but they were mistaken. The various German-inspired plots against British rule in India were foiled, and the great bulk of Indians supported the Allied cause. Indian troops fought in many theaters all over the world: in Europe, the Near East, Africa, and Asia.

Even more important than the military repercussions was the effect of the war upon Indian nationalism. Aspirations for self-government were accelerated, but, unfortunately, Britain did not appreciate the strength of the new nationalism. Out of this failure plus the frustrations and tensions of the postwar period, when the Indian masses felt the shock of high prices, and scarcity of goods, and the ravages of a deadly epidemic, there emerged the figure of Mohandas K. Gandhi, the leader who was to take his people into their promised land and who was to dominate the course of Indian politics for three decades.

When the British Empire went to war against the Central Powers led by Germany, in August 1914, Britain feared and her foes hoped that a period of unprecedented turmoil and disorder would follow in India. To the world's astonishment, the Indian people—including moderate and extremist nationalists—in both British India and the states of the Indian princes immediately pledged their full support in the struggle against Germany. There were some revolutionary conspiracies and intrigues with German agents; but, considering the extent of the unrest of prewar days, these outbursts were few and were easily controlled. India remained loyal because the moderates, still in control of the Congress, believed that self-government would soon be granted by Britain. Furthermore, there is little question that the invasion of Belgium by German armies shocked liberal opinion in India and led it to believe that Britain was defending the cause of justice. As for the Indian Princes, their support of Britain came primarily from self-interest. These potentates regarded Britain as the guardian of their thrones and as an ally to be assisted against its enemies, even in distant Europe.

Many of the princes immediately volunteered for active duty. One, the regent of Jodhpur, was seventy years of age, yet he insisted upon going with his young ward, the sixteen-year-old maharaja, to the battle front in France. The twenty-seven larger princely states, which maintained forces known as the Imperial Service Troops, placed them at the disposal of the Indian government; and from twelve other states the viceroy accepted contingents of infantry and cavalry. On September 9, 1914, the secretary of state for India, speaking in the House of Commons, paid tribute to the loyalty and support of the crown's Indian subjects. At this time mention was made of the gift of a hospital ship by a number of princes; of the Maharaja of Mysore's gift of $1,600,000 to help defray the expenses of the Indian expeditionary force; of the large donations of horses and camels from many princes; and of the little mountain state of Nepal placing all its troops at the government's disposal. Somewhat later came the gift of £400,000 from the Nizam of Hyderabad, together with an offer to pay the entire expense of two of his regiments while they were fighting overseas.

In British India the legislative council, meeting in Simla on September 8, 1914, passed a resolution which expressed the members' "feelings of unswerving loyalty and enthusiastic devotion to the King-Emperor and an assurance of their unflinching support to the British Government. They desire at the same time to express the opinion that the people of India, in addition to the military assistance now being afforded by India to the Empire, would wish to share in the heavy financial burden now imposed on the United Kingdom." [1] Letters and telegrams pledging loyalty streamed into the offices of the

[1] *India and the War*, a collection of documents, introduction by Lord Sydenham (London: Hodder and Stoughton, 1915), pp. 51-52.

provincial governments and were also received by the viceroy.

Not to be outdone by the patriotic manifestations of the Indian legislative council and by the princes, the Indian press was almost unanimous in its declarations of support.

India was remote from the main theaters of the conflict, and her masses had little idea of what was taking place. The wildest rumors were spread. At night planets were mistaken for German airships; German battleships were reported off the coast; and the raids of the cruiser *Emden* in the Bay of Bengal, and especially its bombardment of Madras, created widespread alarm. There were also considerable disturbance of trade and fluctuations in prices in the first months of the war. Money became scarce, and heavy withdrawals from the banks took place. After a few months, however, confidence returned, trade improved, and there was considerable expansion in industry.

From the standpoint of trained men, India in 1914 was far better prepared than any other part of the Empire. The Indian army was designed to take care of two responsibilities: defense of the frontier and the maintenance of internal order. In 1913, a committee appointed to study the status of the army officially reported that "while India should provide for her own defense against local aggression and, if necessary, for an attack on the Indian Empire by a great power until reinforcements can come from home, she is not called upon to maintain troops for the specific purpose of placing them at the disposal of the Home Government for wars outside the Indian sphere." [2]

Notwithstanding this agreed policy, the situation in France in the early months of the war was so serious and the demand for reinforcements so urgent that the British government felt it had no alternative but to utilize the Indian army for service overseas. Therefore, in the early days of September 1914, within a few weeks after the outbreak of war, an expeditionary force was organized and sent from Bombay and Karachi. The country was practically denuded of troops. For a few weeks, before British territorial troops arrived to take the place of the departed regulars, there were only 15,000 British troops in all India. It was what one writer has called India's "rare chivalry" in not taking advantage of the Empire's danger that permitted the withdrawal of so many British regiments. [3]

The Indian expeditionary force sent to France under the

[2] *Cambridge History of the British Empire* (Cambridge: Cambridge University Press, 1932), V, p. 342.
[3] H. N. Brailsford, "Indian Question," *Encyclopedia of the Social Sciences* (New York: The Macmillan Company, 1932), VII, p. 667.

command of General Sir James Willcocks consisted of 44,000 men from all parts of India in two divisions. These Indian divisions were hurriedly sent to Flanders, where they distinguished themselves in the first battle of Ypres. According to General Willcocks, they "arrived in the very nick of time and took their place in the sadly reduced battle line." [4] During the difficult winter of 1914-1915 the Indian expeditionary force helped hold the Allied line in Flanders. The cold was intense, and many of the troops, accustomed only to subtropical weather, suffered severely. The losses of the Indian Corps in France in killed, wounded, and prisoners were 34,250. Recognition for their services was generously given by Britain.

Apart from the invaluable aid of the Indian expeditionary force in France, in November 1914 a contingent from India was sent to German East Africa. During October and November two divisions of Indian infantry and one brigade of cavalry were sent to Egypt; and in November 1914 Indian troops assisted Japanese forces in capturing the great German fortress of Kiaochow on the Shantung peninsula, in China. It is estimated that, in the first few months of the First World War, 80,000 British and 210,000 Indian troops were sent overseas from India. Well might a German writer in *Der Tag* early in the war ruefully admit: "We have been mistaken in so many of our calculations! We expected that the whole of India would revolt at the first sound of the guns in Europe; but, behold, thousands and tens of thousands of Indians are fighting with the British against us." [5]

Within a few months after the outbreak of war, in order to relieve the serious shortage of munitions, India from her own supplies furnished to England 70 million rounds of ammunition, 60,000 modern rifles, and 500 pieces of artillery. During the course of the First World War Indian troops fought in France, Belgium, Gallipoli, Salonika, Palestine, Egypt, the Cameroons, German East Africa, Persia, Kurdistan, North China, Mesopotamia, and the northwest frontier in India.

Participation on so many fronts was made possible only by the strenuous mobilization of manpower in India. During the more than four years of the First World War, over 800,000 soldiers and more than 400,000 noncombatants were recruited. The greatest war effort was made by the province of the Punjab, the home of the Sikhs, which provided half of all the

[4] "The Indian Army Corps in France," *Blackwoods*, CCII (July 1917), p. 8.

[5] Quoted in A. L. Cross, *A Shorter History of England and Greater Britain* (3rd ed.; New York: The Macmillan Company, 1939), p. 798.

soldiers recruited in India. The war memorial arch at Delhi and monuments at Gallipoli, in Palestine, Persia, East Africa, and France are reminders that more than 26,000 Indians were killed and 70,000 wounded in that war. Commenting on this fact an English historian muses: ". . . it must be the first time in the world's history that so many thousands from a subject race willingly offered themselves, in a war dreadful beyond all precedent and to support a quarrel which was none of their bringing about and cannot have seemed any of their business." [6]

The invaluable service of the Indian people to Great Britain and the Allied cause did not end with the recruiting of thousands of men. Almost as significant was the achievement of supplying the Allied war effort with badly needed strategic materials and foodstuffs. In 1917 the Indian Munitions Board was established to develop local industries and to centralize their direction so that India could become, in large measure, the arsenal for the Allies in the Near East. This board had under its direction munitions works; the tanning of hides; the supply of railway track; the production of textiles, clothing, boots, tents, and jute goods; and the shipping of timber. Under its direction India contributed vast supplies of war material. The wolfram mines were developed until they produced one-third of the world's supply, and the Tata Iron and Steel Works, established a few years before the outbreak of war, supplied the steel rails so essential for the transport of troops and equipment in Mesopotamia, Egypt, Palestine, and East Africa. India's cotton and jute mills turned out enormous quantities of material, and immense supplies of petroleum, mica, rubber, and tea—to mention only a few commodities— were shipped abroad. It is estimated that the total value of materials exported overseas to troops dependent on India for supplies reached the sum of £34,408,000. Finally, India supplied the British wheat pool with some 5 million tons of this cereal.

The creation of large armies and the production of huge quantities of war materials obviously necessitate the expenditure of large sums of money. India, therefore, made heavy financial sacrifices during the war years. The government was compelled to raise a great deal of money in spite of the fact that India is a relatively poor country and cannot stand a high rate of taxation. Normally, when Indian troops served abroad, it was understood that the British imperial exchequer would defray their expenses; but during the First World War, at the suggestion of the Indian government, India undertook to pay

[6] Edward Thompson, *Reconstructing India* (New York: The Dial Press, 1930), p. 116.

the cost of maintaining her troops regardless of the place of service. This obligation cost between 20 and 30 million pounds sterling a year at a time when the total revenue of the central government was only £100,000,000. In September 1918 it was voted in the Indian legislative council that India would defray the cost of an additional 100,000 troops. India's greatest single financial contribution was a free gift of £100,000,000, a sum that added 30 per cent to its national debt. As a result of these extraordinary financial efforts, India experienced grave difficulties with its currency system, which in 1917-1918 nearly collapsed. Even when India sold goods to Great Britain, it had to act as the latter's banker. Owing to the difficulty of transferring funds to Delhi, payment was made in London; but payment had first to be made in India. This placed a staggering burden upon the monetary reserves of the country.

Wartime Plots and Conspiracies

It must not be thought, of course, that India was perfectly tranquil under British rule during the period 1914-1918. Naturally, attempts were made by German agents to enlist the help of Indian nationalists in the war against Britain. On the whole, however, the plots were remarkably few. The most serious was the so-called *Ghadr* conspiracy, which had two centers, one in the Punjab and the other in the western United States and Canada. The founder was Har Dayal, a former native of Delhi who had been granted a government scholarship to Oxford and had made a brilliant record at that university. On his return from England, Dayal came in contact with such nationalists as Lajpat Rai, prominent in the Arya Samaj, and henceforth became an ardent advocate of Indian independence.

The year 1914 found Har Dayal in Berkeley, California, where he carried on an active anti-British campaign among the students attending the state university. Contact was also made with many Indians, chiefly Sikhs, who had settled in British Columbia and in western states of the United States. Several anti-British newspapers were set up and distributed up and down the coast, the most important being the *Ghadr* ("Mutiny"), established in San Francisco by Har Dayal in November 1913. In a mock advertisement this newspaper in its first issue announced: "Wanted: Brave soldiers to stir up *Ghadr* in India; Pay—death; prize—martyrdom; pension—liberty; field of battle—India." [7]

Har Dayal for a time served as a lecturer on Indian phi-

7 Quoted in William Roy Smith, *Nationalism and Reform in India* (New Haven: Yale University Press, 1938), p. 78.

losophy at Stanford University, but was discharged from this post because of his propagandist activities. Under his direction the *Ghadr* group in the San Francisco Bay region was very active. Pamphlets were distributed and many meetings held. In December 1912 a jubilation meeting was called to celebrate the attack on the life of the viceroy, Lord Hardinge; and in December 1913, in a meeting at Sacramento, Har Dayal told his audience that it was time to get ready to go to India for the coming revolution.[8]

It became more and more evident that the United States was being utilized as a base for stirring up revolution in India, and in March 1914 the United States government arrested Har Dayal as an undesirable alien. Released on bail, which he forfeited, he made his way to Geneva, Switzerland, leaving a trusted lieutenant in the United States to continue the *Ghadr*. It is probable that all this time Har Dayal was in contact with German agents. At any rate, we know that when the First World War broke out he and a group of Indian revolutionists were in Berlin. Har Dayal and his colleagues were attached to the Indian section of the German General Staff and assigned the work of fomenting revolt in India. Aiding in this was the German Oriental Bureau, which translated into Indian languages pamphlets that were distributed among the Indian prisoners of war and letters that were smuggled into India.

In the early months of 1914, the British secret police had notified the Indian government that thousands of Indians, mainly Sikhs, were planning on returning to India to spearhead a revolution against British authority. In January 1914 a large meeting of the *Ghadr* group had met in Stockton, California, and volunteers enrolled for the prospective mutiny. To meet this situation, the government in India passed an emergency act regulating the entry of suspicious Indians from abroad.

About this time occurred the *Komagata Maru* incident, which added further fuel to the *Ghadr* movement. This Japanese vessel was chartered by a Sikh to collect several hundred Indians from various parts of the Far East and to convey them to Vancouver. When the steamer arrived in port the Canadian authorities refused to admit them. Returning to the Far East, the *Komagata Maru* was not permitted to land its passengers at either Shanghai or Hongkong, but had to proceed to Calcutta. Here, on September 27, 1914, the Indians were disembarked and, as most of them came from the Punjab, trains were waiting to return them, under police supervision, to their homes. Apparently the majority of these

[8] Sir Michael O'Dwyer, *India as I Knew It, 1885-1925* (London: Constable and Company, 1925), p. 187.

Indians had been indoctrinated with *Ghadr* ideology. Only a few consented to enter the trains, and over three hundred started to march into the city, where they were met by a force of soldiers. Shots were fired on both sides, and the Indian rioters fled and scattered over the countryside. In a few days, however, most of them had been rounded up.

Meanwhile, ship after ship began to return Indians at such ports as Madras, Calcutta, and Colombo. Machinery for supervising their entry was at this time entirely inadequate, and many hundreds of ardent revolutionists, members of the *Ghadr* movement, slipped into the interior. It is estimated that as many as eight thousand Indians returned to India as a result of *Ghadr* propaganda. As a great majority were Sikhs, they made their way to the Punjab, where they launched a widespread revolutionary movement that called for a revolt during February 1915. Fortunately for the British, the plot was uncovered, the revolutionary headquarters in Lahore were raided, and by the summer of 1915 the conspiracy was completely quashed.

Back in the United States the successors of Har Dayal were busily engaged in various conspiracies that read now like a cloak-and-dagger mystery with such elements as codes, an underground movement, the smuggling of arms, and the secret rendezvous. By means of large sums of money provided by German agents, an underground movement was built by which converts to revolution were sent to Shanghai, thence to Swatow, and finally to Siam, from which country the Indians were smuggled into India. The most ambitious plot concocted by the *Ghadr* group in the United States was a plan to land enough arms and ammunition on the Indian coast to equip a revolutionary army of ten thousand men. Active in this conspiracy was Captain Franz von Papen, the German military attaché in Washington. Sixteen carloads of arms were obtained and paid for by German agents and sent to San Diego, California. From this port two vessels were to be used to carry the arms through the British blockade to India.

This plot did not succeed, and during the months of March and April, 1917, numerous arrests of Indian agents were carried out in the United States. The trial of the main Indian leaders and their accomplices in a federal court in San Francisco aroused much interest in the American press. As if to supply the newspapers with a smashing climax, on the last day of the trial one of the Indian defendants, apparently suspicious of his leader, Ram Chandra, shot him dead in the courtroom with a pistol he had managed to conceal on his person. While spectators dashed for cover, a United States marshal shot and killed the murderer.

From time to time, as the war progressed, other plots were unearthed in India and sporadic outrages continued, but these were minor compared to the *Ghadr* conspiracy. One serious outbreak did take place at Singapore in February 1915, when an Indian regiment, the Fifth Bengali Light Infantry, revolted and terrorized the city. Marines from anchored war craft in the harbor quelled the uprising, but not before some fifty persons had been killed.

Apart from the *Ghadr* conspiracy the most serious menace to British authority during the war emanated from the area of the northwest frontier, inhabited by fanatical Muslim hill tribes. A Pan-Islamic movement on the part of certain Mohammedan groups in India, designed to bring about closer cooperation with Turkey and the weakening of British rule, was already under way before 1914. The entrance of Turkey on the side of Germany accelerated this movement, for it seemed that Britain had now become the enemy of the sultan, who was the caliph and as such the head of Islam and the protector of all Mohammedan holy places. In February 1915 a number of young Muslims left college at Lahore and crossed the border into the chaotic territory of the northwest frontier. Here they joined with fanatical tribesmen who were intent on launching a jihad (a holy war) against the British in India. The persistent hostility of these frontier tribesmen made it necessary for the British to send several expeditions against them. That more serious revolts did not take place along the border was due largely to the role played by the Amir Habibullah of Afghanistan, who "despite all difficulties and dangers, kept his turbulent people to strict neutrality and threw the whole of his great influence into the task of tranquillising the border." [9] An interesting episode along the northwest frontier was the mission of Mahendra Pratap. This Indian at the outset of the war made his way to Switzerland and then to Berlin. An interveiw with the Kaiser was obtained, and as a result a Turco-German mission, with Pratap as one of the leaders, was sent to Afghanistan, but it was unable to dissuade the amir from his position of benevolent neutrality toward Great Britain. [10]

Nationalist Politics Revive

For almost two years following the outbreak of war there was little agitation for political concessions. In the imperial legislative council, the appeal of the viceroy to cease controversy of any sort was heeded and no attempt was made to

[9] *Cambridge History of the British Empire*, V, p. 485.
[10] See Mahendra Pratap, "My German Mission to High Asia," *Asia*, XXV (May 1925).

harass the government. In the late months of 1914, the radical nationalist Tilak, who had been expelled from the ranks of Congress in 1907, was released from prison and then tried to re-enter the Congress in order to obstruct the government in any manner possible within the law, so that Great Britain would be forced to grant *swaraj* (home rule). But Tilak's trumpet call fell mainly upon deaf ears, for the moderates were still in control of the Indian nationalist movement.

Throughout the year 1915 politics in India continued serene. The only disquieting event was the untimely death of G. K. Gokhale, who in the decade before the war had been both the heart and the spirit of the Indian National Congress. So long as he lived it followed the path of conciliation and moderation. The Congress held its anual meeting in Bombay in December 1915, and was presided over by the moderate and colleague of Gokhale, S. P. Sinha, who delivered a momentous presidential address. He argued in this message that Britain should announce a definite goal or objective for India in order to satisfy the rising generation of young Indians and thus check anarchistic tendencies kindled by frustration. It was also stressed by Sinha that this goal, which should be democracy pure and simple, could only be achieved by gradual advances, for India was not as yet prepared for full self-government. He paid tribute to the spirit and work of the British government in India, but he insisted firmly that good government was no substitute for self-government.

Sinha also declared that the fullest Indian patriotism could be reconciled with the idea of remaining part of the British Empire. Although there was little evidence at this Congress meeting of 1915 to indicate the almost complete transformation that was to take place in the Indian nationalist movement during the next two years, it was prophetic that changes were made in the rules of the Congress that would permit the return of ousted extremists like Tilak. Looking back, it can be seen that Sinha's address constituted the swan song of the old liberal and moderate leaders. A new generation was about to take over.

During the course of the year 1916 it became apparent that the war was quickening and sharpening Indian nationalism. A new group of young nationalists was just coming of age. They were excited at the news of the Irish Revolt of 1916 and read with intense interest accounts of the eloquent speech made by its leader, Sir Roger Casement, at his trial. Speaking of the nationalist revival, Nehru writes in his autobiography, "The atmosphere became electric, and most of us young men felt exhilarated and expected big things in the near future." [11]

[11] Jawaharlal Nehru, *Toward Freedom* (New York: John Day Company, 1941), p. 44.

These young nationalists noted that for two years Britain and her allies had been continually reiterating the idea that they were fighting for the principle of the self-determination of nations. Later this aim was given even more advertisement by President Woodrow Wilson's Fourteen Points. Wide publicity was also given in India in the early months of the war to speeches made by British officials in which they promised generous measures of constitutional reform for India. In particular, Prime Minister Asquith had declared that henceforth Indian questions would have to be approached from a different angle of vision.[12]

Apart from the effect of the Allies' war aims and the promises of British statesmen, another factor explaining the rapid advance of Indian nationalism in 1916 was the failure of Great Britain to utilize adequately the loyalty and support for the war manifested by all classes in 1914 and 1915. After being assured that there was little danger of serious revolt, the Indian government went its own way. Consequently, somewhat rebuffed and with little to do, the educated classes turned back to politics.

By the middle of 1916 there was a definite undercurrent of unrest. Nothing had been done about the pledges of reform. The British government was too preoccupied with the problems of the war, and maintained an enigmatic silence on the question of Indian constitutional reform. Furthermore, war weariness began to manifest itself in India as in other parts of the world. The war was too long. Many Indians could not understand why the powerful British armies could not secure speedy victory. Casualty lists, return of the wounded, and rumors of bad management at the battle fronts all helped to spread the spirit of disillusionment. In the spring of 1916 came the surprising news of a British disaster when Turkish forces compelled the surrender of General Townshend's army at Kut-el-Amara in the British attempt to conquer Mesopotamia.

In this atmosphere of disillusionment and mounting political consciousness, Mrs. Annie Besant and Lokamanya Tilak stepped forward to lead a vigorous campaign for home rule for India. Somewhat repulsed by the extremes of Bengali nationalism in the anti-partition controversy of Lord Curzon's day, Mrs. Besant had stood aside until 1913, when she actively entered politics. In 1914 she started two newspapers to publicize her ideas and was recognized as one of the leaders of the National Congress. Early in the war Mrs. Besant began her campaign for home rule, and at the same time Tilak

12 Quoted in Sir Valentine Chirol, *India* (London: Ernest Benn, Ltd., 1926), p. 160.

began a similar movement. In the Congress meeting of December 1915, Mrs. Besant tried unsuccessfully to enlist its support for her movement. Thereupon she carried out a whirlwind campaign, formally establishing her Home Rule League in September 1916 and setting up some fifty branches of the organization in different parts of the country. September 14 was celebrated by these branches as Home Rule Day.

In October 1916 an important memorandum was presented to the government by nineteen elected members of the imperial legislative council. This document was the work of balanced and moderate nationalist leaders, who declared that India's loyalty entitled her to a position of comradeship, not subordination. In essence the document asked for responsible government for India.

Momentous developments in the Indian national movement took place in the closing months of 1916. Hindu-Muslim enmity had been an unfortunate but nevertheless basic feature of Indian history for many years, and the Muslim League since its establishment in 1906 had consistently maintained an attitude of both aloofness and suspicion toward the National Congress. In November 1916, however, representatives of the Congress and the League met in Calcutta. Differences were patched up and both agreed to support Mrs. Besant's Home Rule League. This *rapprochement* between Hindu and Muslim was hailed as signifying the end of controversy between these two great religious groups and the birth of an undivided nation.

This amicable Congress-League agreement is explained largely by a few significant developments. First, the younger intellectuals in both the Muslim community and Congress were becoming much more nationalistic than their older leaders. In 1913 the Muslim League for the first time came out definitely for the goal of Indian self-government while maintaining its continued loyalty to the British crown. This statement caused much controversy in the ranks of the League and led the Aga Khan, who tended to be conservative and very pro-British, to resign his presidency of the League. Second, a considerable section of the Muslim community became anti-British because of Great Britain's policy toward Turkey. Active war was waged by Britain against this Mohammedan power, and further, as in the case of the revolt of Sharif Hussein of Mecca, leader of the Arabs, the British subsidized the enemies of the Sultan and seemed bent on the destruction of his spiritual authority in the Mohammedan world. The unhappy position of many Muslims was underlined by a resolution passed at the League's session in 1915, at which time it was stated: "It is a sore point with us that the Government of our Caliph should be at war with the Government of our King-Emperor."[13] The predominantly Hindu Congress had always maintained that this body was truly national and secular. As the majority group in India, the Hindus had nothing to fear and everything to gain by accepting the support of the Muslim minority.

The Congress and the League both held their annual meetings in Lucknow the last week of December 1916. Leaders of both organizations came out for home rule and joined in supporting the recommendations of the "Memorandum of the Nineteen," which they made the basis for the so-called Congress-League Plan. This scheme demanded that India be granted immediately the status of a self-governing entity within the British Empire. While under the Congress-League Plan the British government would have control of military matters and foreign affairs, Indian members of the government would have fairly complete control over legislation as far as the central government was concerned and full control over all matters in the provincial governments. As part of this scheme, Muslims and Hindus joined in the Lucknow Pact, in which it was agreed that the members of the former community were to elect their representatives by means of special Muslim electorates—as had been granted in the Morley-Minto Reforms—and were to be guaranteed a specific number of representatives in both provincial and central legislatures.

The Congress-League Plan is a landmark in Indian history, and equally important were the developments within the ranks of the National Congress. Since 1907 the so-called extremists had been debarred from membership, but a change in the rules made in 1915 allowed the prodigal radicals to re-enter the fold. This they did, and when Tilak mounted the platform he was given a tumultuous ovation. Not only were the extremists permitted to rejoin the Congress, but it was evident that they had actually won over most of its members to their militant views.

An enthusiastic campaign soliciting support for the Congress-League scheme was carried out during the first six months of 1917. Mrs. Besant was in the van of this movement, and her articles in the newspaper *New India* spread the gospel of home rule. In June the Indian government ordered the internment of Mrs. Besant, prohibiting her from speaking in public or writing for publication. This action resulted in an angry volume of protests from all over India. It became increasingly clear that some positive action should be taken in order to appease Indian national sentiment. Yet no move was made by the British government in London, "until the Government of

13 Sir Verney Lovett, *A History of the Indian Nationalist Movement* (London: John Murray, 1920), p. 101.

India implored it to put war-maps aside for a moment and make some definite pronouncement that should stem the rising tide of political unrest in India." [14]

Britain Turns to Reform

The British government, which on the surface seemed oblivious to the rising chorus of discontent in India, had not been wholly idle. Shortly after Lord Chelmsford had become the new viceroy in April 1916, this official presented two basic questions at the first meeting of his executive council. These were: "What is the goal of British rule in India and what are the steps on the road to that goal?" [15] In 1917 Chelmsford in a dispatch to London recommended a greater measure of Indian self-government.

It was the disaster of the Kut-el-Amara surrender, already referred to, that stepped up the growing demand for Indian constitutional reform. The surrender was a grievous blow to British prestige. Ugly rumors and biting criticism spread concerning the management of the campaign, and public opinion in Britain demanded that the matter be investigated. A special commission, therefore, was appointed in August 1916 to investigate the Mesopotamian campaign.

Its report accused the government of India, which had directed the venture, of fatal inaction and lack of vision. The bureaucratic system in India was castigated in such phrases as "intense isolation and centralization," and "cumbrous and inept." [16] One of the commissioners in a minority report declared:

My last recommendation is that we should no longer deny to Indians the full privileges of citizenship, but should allow them a large share in the government of their own country and in the control of that Bureaucracy which in this War, uncontrolled by public opinion, has failed to rise to British standards.[17]

The Mesopotamian Report, submitted in June 1917, was vigorously debated in Parliament. In spite of the plea of Austen Chamberlain, the secretary of state for India, that only injury could come from mixing up a debate over alleged military mismanagement with the question of the political future of India, the discussion resolved itself into an attack upon the bureaucratic and outmoded structure of Indian administration.

[14] Chirol, *India*, p. 163.
[15] *Cambridge History of the British Empire*, V, p. 587.
[16] H. C. E. Zacharias, *Renascent India* (London: George Allen and Unwin, 1933), p. 171.
[17] *Ibid.*, p. 172.

Edwin Samuel Montagu, a former undersecretary of state for India, was foremost in criticism. Speaking in the House of Commons, July 11, 1917, he characterized the existing Indian system of government as "too wooden, too iron, too inelastic, too antediluvian to be of any use for modern purposes." He further demanded that the whole system of Indian government be explored in the light of the Mesopotamian Report.[18]

One result of these debates was that Sir Austen Chamberlain resigned, but more important was the fact that while Indian nationalists were demanding governmental reform, coincidentally a similar demand was being made in the British Parliament. Meanwhile, Mr. Montagu had become the new secretary of state for India and immediately set to work formulating a pronouncement clearly stating the direction and goal of Indian constitutional evolution. As we have already noted, the British government and the viceroy had been paving the way for such action as far back as the spring of 1916. A draft was prepared by Montagu, submitted to the British cabinet, and reshaped, mainly at the hands of the former viceroy, Lord Curzon. It was a fateful and dramatic moment in British imperial history when Samuel Montagu on August 20, 1917, announced in the House of Commons Britain's long-term objective in India. The announcement in part declared:

> The policy of His Majesty's Government, with which the Government of India are in complete accord, is that of the increasing association of Indians in every branch of the administration and the gradual development of self-governing institutions with a view to the progressive realisation of responsible government as an integral part of the British Empire.

.   .   .   .   .

> I would add that progress in this policy can only be achieved by successive stages. The British Government and the Government of India, on whom the responsibility lies for the welfare and advancement of the Indian peoples, must be judges of the time and measure of each advance, and they must be guided by the co-operation received from those upon whom new opportunities of service will thus be conferred and by the extent to which it is found that confidence can be reposed in their sense of responsibility.[19]

While making his historic announcement in the House of Commons, Montagu also stated that substantial steps toward more self-government in India should be taken as soon as possible and that he was proceeding shortly to India to confer with the viceroy, Lord Chelmsford, and to study conditions at

18 Quoted in Nihal Singh, "Constitutional Reforms for British India," *Fortnightly Review*, CIII (1918), p. 775.

19 Quoted in *Report of the Indian Statutory Commission*, I, Cmd. 3568 (London: His Majesty's Stationery Office, 1930), p. 2.

first hand. The secretary of state for India and his deputation arrived in India in November 1917 and at once began their investigations. Preliminary conferences were held with the viceroy and the heads of the provincial governments. Then, accompanied by Lord Chelmsford, the deputation visited Calcutta, Madras, and Bombay. Mr. Montagu's tour attracted wide interest. Everyone felt that the old order of things was doomed, and all were anxious to present arguments before the investigators. At every place visited by the secretary, members of Congress, Muslims, Sikhs, Eurasians, Untouchables, and others appeared to press their claims.

The investigation was completed by the end of April 1918, and the deputation returned to England to formulate its report, published on July 8. Signed by both the viceroy and the secretary of state for India, this document is usually referred to as the Montagu-Chelmsford Report. At the time it was written it was undoubtedly one of the most penetrating and valuable studies of constitutional problems in India, and it has been called "the first authoritative survey of the state of India since the Mutiny." [20]

The Montagu-Chelmsford Report was liberal in its approach and sympathetic to Indian aspirations. Montagu, in particular, was occasionally irked by the attitude of British civil servants in India, and in *An Indian Diary* he wrote, "I wish I could get the damned Bureaucracy to realize that we are sitting on an earthquake." [21] The report made it quite plain that the Morley-Minto scheme of government no longer met the needs of the times, that the World War had accelerated political aspirations in India, and that the desire for self-government was the natural outcome of British rule and the impact of liberal Western thought.

The nature and functioning of the scheme of government established in India in 1919, and based on the Montagu-Chelmsford proposals, will be discussed in the next chapter. It may be noted that the changes proposed constituted a great advance over the system set up before the war by the Morley-Minto Reforms. In short, the bloc of British officials constituting a majority was abolished in the central legislature at Delhi, although in emergencies the governor-general was given power to override the Indian majority. As for the provincial governments, the first elements of responsible government were introduced and Indian ministers were given complete charge of such departments as education and public works.

These reform proposals received wide publicity, and liberals

[20] Sir Valentine Chirol, *India Old and New* (New York: The Macmillan Company, 1921), p. 151.
[21] Quoted in Zacharias, *op. cit.*, p. 173.

all over the world regarded them as a valuable contribution to the problem of colonial self-government. Opinion in India, however, was sharply divided. Nationalist leaders like Tilak and Mrs. Besant considered the report a sham and in no way a fulfillment of the pledge made in the House of Commons in August 1917. Mrs. Besant in her newspaper, *New India*, declared: "The scheme is unworthy to be offered by England or to be accepted by India." [22] And at a special session of the Madras Provincial Congress she characterized the reforms as "leading to a line beyond which its authors cannot go—a perpetual slavery which can only be broken by revolution." [23]

The most important immediate result of the projected reforms was a schism between the moderate and radical elements in the Indian National Congress. In contrast to the intransigence of the radicals, the so-called moderate nationalists, though disappointed that no major reforms were to be made in the Indian central government, regarded the Montagu-Chelmsford Report as a substantial advance toward Indian autonomy and were prepared to pledge their support. This moderate faction believed that the difference between itself and the militant group—which had completely dominated the Congress in 1917—was fundamental, and therefore absented itself from the special session of the National Congress held in August 1918. In the following November the secessionists met at Bombay and organized the Liberal party. Immediately after this conference came the news of the armistice, and the First World War came to an end.

The Aftermath of War

During the last six months of the war, despite the dissatisfaction on the part of the Indian Congress with the Montagu-Chelmsford Report and the agitation of the Home Rule League, India was at the height of its war effort. In March 1918 had come word of the disastrous British reverses in France, and, following an urgent appeal from the British prime minister, a great war conference was held in Delhi, in April, to determine what could be done to provide additional assistance in men, money, and supplies. The majority of the delegates expressed willingness to cooperate wholeheartedly in bringing the war to a successful termination. The only hint of dissent was an attempt by one delegate to introduce a resolution into the conference requesting the British government immediately to bring before Parliament

[22] Sir Surendranath Banerjea, *A Nation in the Making* (London: H. Milford Co., 1925), p. 305.
[23] Quoted in Lovett, *op. cit.*, p. 168.

a bill "meeting the demands of the people to establish a responsible government in India within a reasonable and specified period." [24] In contrast, it is interesting to note that on April 29 another member of the conference, Mohandas Karamchand Gandhi, spoke eloquently in support of a resolution requesting the viceroy to dispatch a message to the king-emperor pledging India's full support and loyalty in the prosecution of the war.

The armistice, then, found the politically minded classes in India united in their war efforts but split into contending factions on the merits of the Montagu-Chelmsford reforms. Purged of its moderate members, the Congress held its annual meeting at Delhi in December 1918. It was the feeling of many of its members that India had contributed generously to victory and Great Britain, therefore, should immediately demonstrate her appreciation by instituting sweeping reforms. In this spirit the Congress assembled and demanded the application of the principle of national self-determination to India, the release of political prisoners, and the introduction of complete self-government in the provinces. It was also stated that the Montagu declaration of August 1917 was cautious and cold and that the proposed reforms were inadequate. The Congress further branded the recommendations of the Rowlatt Sedition Committee, shortly to be discussed, a violation of the basic liberties of the people. Coincidentally the Muslim League also met and passed resolutions (1) urging Britain not to interfere with the Sultan of Turkey as the true Khalifa (Protector, Caliph) of the Muslim Holy Places and (2) supporting the goal of self-determination.

Leaving for the moment the constitutional demands of the politically conscious Indians, what was the temper of the people when peace again returned to their land? Peace was acclaimed not so much with relief as with expectancy. A widespread publicity campaign had spread roseate accounts of the war aims of Britain and her allies. The masses had been willing to endure high prices, aggressive recruiting campaigns, stringent restrictions upon personal liberty, and other abnormal conditions because it was believed that the inauguration of a golden age, almost a Utopia, was bound up with the victory of the Allies. The "war to end wars" had created similar hopes among the masses in Europe, particularly in Italy.

However, the months after the armistice brought no surcease from the existing hardships and restraints, but rather accentuated them. Following the failure of the monsoon in 1918, famine conditions existed in many parts of India. A

[24] Quoted in Lovett, *op. cit.,* p. 153.

serious epidemic of bubonic plague had ravaged the country in 1917, but this was nothing compared to the horrors of the influenza epidemic of 1918-1919, which caused the deaths of 13 million people—more than the number who had died on the battlefields of the late war. Prices showed no decline. The cost of living was still mounting in 1919, "and the few cotton rags worn by a peasant became almost unpurchasable." [25] Transportation and railway service were still disorganized as a result of war demands, and this contributed to the general chaos. And, although the war had brought great riches to a few, the rural population had suffered severely. Such conditions were especially onerous in view of the visions of an era of plenty that had been expected to follow the victory of Great Britain. Widespread dissatisfaction grew into active discontent and resentment.

This Indian discontent was directionless in itself, but was to achieve much under a leader, Mohandas K. Gandhi, who stimulated and directed it into a constructive channel of protest of his own creation. He created a movement to throw off the foreign yoke combined with an attempt to regenerate the social, economic, and religious elements of Indian society. It was one of those unusual coincidences of history that there was available at the crucial moment a man like Gandhi, who blended in his make-up the traits of a religious saint, a Mahatma, which gave him irresistible power over the masses, and the shrewdness of a practical politician, which enabled him to use his great influence to embarrass and weaken the authority of British rule.

The Emergence of Gandhi

As Gandhi's entrance into the Indian limelight was precipitated largely by the government's enactment of the Rowlatt Acts, it will be necessary to discuss their origin and purpose before taking up the career of this great Indian nationalist.

Revolutionary terrorist crime, frequently in the form of assassinations, had, as we have seen, first begun in India in 1897; but it was in 1906 that there began a long series of outrages which were deplored by the moderate leaders of the National Congress but with which the government seemed powerless to cope. The ordinary machinery of justice could do little in the face of various kinds of intimidation, and even murder, practiced on witnesses or jurors who aided the government in the prosecution of terrorism.

No changes, however, were made in legal procedure until

25 Chirol, *India*, p. 184.

the First World War, when, as a counterpart to the Defence of the Realm Act in Great Britain, the Defence of India Act was passed by the Indian legislature. This act, by means of special tribunals and special wartime powers, enabled the executive branch of the government to curb espionage and revolutionary activities.

The act was destined to come to an end six months after the end of the war, and British officials began to consider what, if anything, should take its place when the struggle ended. Their perturbation was increased at the prospect of the release of many Indian extremists, regarded as dangerous revolutionists from the English point of view, who were being held in prison under the terms of the Defence of India Act.

Sir Sidney Rowlatt, judge of the Court of the King's Bench in England, was, therefore, sent to India to preside over a committee appointed in December 1917 to study the situation. This body heard testimony and drafted a report which showed how terroristic outrages, on the increase, were beyond ordinary legal procedure. Witnesses were intimidated and juries refused to serve. Two bills were, therefore, recommended. These Rowlatt measures gave the government, in cases of emergency, the right to judge cases without trial. Furthermore, suspected terrorists could be interned. A storm of protest followed the publication of the proposed Bills in January 1919. In spite of a rising volume of criticism from Indian nationalist circles, one of the Rowlatt bills—with the above provisions—was passed, but its life was restricted to three years.

In view of the fateful repercussions soon to follow, was the nationalist denunciation deserved? The answer that may be given is that the government did not intend the Rowlatt Acts to serve any despotic purpose, but only to act as a legitimate safeguard against anticipated terrorist and subversive activities. And, in understanding the Indian reaction to the bills, it should be kept in mind that Indian national pride and sensitivity—as well as aspirations for the future—had been greatly heightened by the war. India in 1919 was not thinking in terms of any abridgment of her liberties but rather of their rapid expansion.

"The Rowlatt Act," says Sir Surendranath Banerjea, "was the parent of the Non-Co-Operation Movement." [26] It was this act more than anything else that brought Mahatma Gandhi to the center of the Indian political scene. It is a truism that no adequate explanation of modern India can be made without reference to the influence, activities, and ideals

[26] Banerjea, *op. cit.*, p. 300.

of this enigmatic leader about whom have raged such storms of controversy. To some a "supreme humbug," a "madman," a "half-naked fakir," a "self-deluded visionary," to others Gandhi has been the Holy One, and to Rabindranath Tagore, who by no means agreed with all of his teachings, he was not only the greatest man in India, but the greatest on earth.

The fascinating story of Gandhi's life may be read in his remarkable autobiography, *The Story of My Experiments with Truth,* which was dictated by Gandhi to one of his fellow-prisoners during a period of imprisonment in the years 1922-1924. Originally published in two large volumes in India, both in Gujarati and in English, the work was published in abridged form by C. F. Andrews, an English missionary and long the friend and intimate confidant of Gandhi. This story has been likened to the *Confessions* of St. Augustine and of Rousseau. It is above all self-revealing in its frankness, for Gandhi does not spare himself as he digs into his past and describes his sins, mistakes, and frailties of character.

Born in 1869 at Porbandar, the capital of an Indian princely state situated in the Kathiawar peninsula northwest of Bombay, Mohandas Gandhi was the son of respectable middle-class parents. The family belonged to the Vaisya caste and was very religious, especially the mother, who followed the dictates of the strictest Hindu orthodoxy. The future Mahatma was reared according to the Hindu traditions of his parents. It is not surprising that, although he did not exhibit unusual intellectual prowess in the classroom, Gandhi from the very first manifested a tendency to introspection, a love of truth, and a sensitive conscience. The *Autobiography* relates, almost as if it were a heinous crime, how the young boy became the friend of a youth who had no compunctions about breaking the Hindu code. Gandhi's acquaintance quoted the following doggerel:

> Behold the mighty Englishman;
> He rules the Indian small,
> Because, being a meat-eater,
> He is five cubits tall.

This persuaded Gandhi to eat meat, but he was overcome with remorse and confessed the deception to his father with great sorrow.

The first great decision in his life, and one that was to have momentous effects upon his destiny, was that made at a family conference following his father's death to send Gandhi to London to study law. There was some fear expressed that the young student might fall prey to the wicked practices of the foreign city. Thereupon a friend of the family advised that the boy should take three vows: "He administered the oath and I vowed to live a celibate life in England and never to touch wine or meat. This done, my mother gave her permission and her blessing." [27]

London in 1888 proved to be very strange and disquieting to the bewildered youth. Ignorance of English customs constantly proved a source of embarrassment to his sensitive nature. One of his new-found Indian friends ridiculed his determination to abstain from meat, and for a time he nearly starved amid an abundance of good English beef, until one day by chance he ran across a good vegetarian restaurant. "There I had my first hearty meal since my arrival. God had come to my aid." [28] For a few months Gandhi tried to emulate the sophisticated young Englishmen he met, taking elocution and dancing lessons and wearing clothes of the most rakish cut. This phase soon passed, however, and the young student settled down to live frugally and to concentrate on his legal studies.

In the second year of his sojourn in London he made several contacts that helped to stimulate and shape his philosophical bent and his religious point of view. Two members of the Theosophical Society interested him in the *Bhagavad-Gita,* the great Hindu epic poem, and also Sir Edward Arnold's *The Light of Asia.* About this time he purchased a Bible from a Christian friend and was especially delighted with the message of the New Testament, which "went straight to my heart." [29]

The law examinations were finally taken and passed, and in 1891 the young lawyer, proud of his success, sailed for home. These three years in London had brought him into contact with the forces of nationalism, democracy, and Christianity, while his study of the *Gita,* the New Testament, and other similar books had kindled within him the fire of ascetic self-renunciation and service.

In 1893, after little success in India in the practice of law, Gandhi accepted a commission to represent a large Indian firm involved in an important legal suit in Pretoria, South Africa. This was the beginning of a career in which Gandhi first achieved great success, building up a practice paying as much as £3000 a year. This was to be followed by a period of self-renunciation in which he courageously and unselfishly fought for the removal of inhuman legal disabilities imposed

[27] C. F. Andrews, ed., *Mahatma Gandi: His Own Story* (London: George Allen and Unwin, 1930), pp. 77-78.
[28] *Ibid.,* p. 83.
[29] *Ibid.,* p. 93.

by the South African government upon his countrymen. It was in this struggle that he was imprisoned four times, beaten by a mob, and once left for dead.

Gandhi soon became the champion of the thousands of Hindus who had been brought out to South Africa as indentured laborers. In the courts he was a constant defender of their rights, and he was also instrumental in starting a newspaper to publicize the wrongs of the Indians. At this time the Indian "coolies," as they were called, were treated with equal injustice in the Boer Republic and the English South African colonies. But when the Boer War broke out in 1899, Gandhi persuaded his countrymen to offer their services to England. The war offered the despised "coolies" an opportunity to show their loyalty as British subjects, to render good for evil. Perhaps after the victory of British arms, thought Gandhi, something might be done for the Indian cause. An ambulance corps was therefore organized, whose members received official commendation for their bravery under fire.

Victory for Great Britain did little, however, to ease the disabilities of the Indians. In fact, after the Boer and the English population came together to form the Union of South Africa, the burdens of the Indians became heavier. Especially galling was the Asiatic Registration Act of 1906, which fingerprinted Indians; the $15 poll tax on Indians in the province of Natal; and the decision of the Cape province that all marriages performed under Hindu rites were illegal. And in addition to these and other legal disabilities there was a whole pattern of Jim Crowism that placed the South African Indians in a subordinate status, somewhere midway between the European at the top and the black Kafirs at the bottom.

For eight years, from 1906 to 1914, Gandhi carried on the fight, rousing to action the Indian laborers and instilling into them the precepts and techniques of non-violence. From the time of his early days in London, Gandhi had been studying and familiarizing himself with the traditional Hindu belief of *Ahimsa*, or non-violence, and the possibility of using it as a technique to rectify injustice. This idea was not entirely unknown to the Western world in the form of passive resistance, but Gandhi preferred to coin a new term for his weapon against injustice, which he named *Satyagraha*, or Truth Force. Without violence the object was to win over your opponent by "sympathy, patience, and self-suffering." [30] Resorting to *Satyagraha*, no force should be used, but this

[30] R. R. Diwakar, *Satyagraha, The Power of Truth* (Hinsdale, Illinois: Henry Regnery Co., 1948), p. 5.

fact, according to Gandhi, did not imply weakness or cowardliness but rather the positive and courageous action of moral character. "I cultivate," said Gandhi, "the quiet courage of dying without killing." [31]

Under the leadership of Gandhi a series of hunger strikes, public demonstrations, strikes in mines, and mass marches of protest followed. Arrest was welcomed, martyrdom gloried in, and prison embraced by thousands. The courage of the "passive resisters" under all kinds of physical intimidation aroused public opinion in both India and Great Britain. Lord Hardinge, the British viceroy, openly criticized the South African authorities, who, it must be remembered, were enjoying self-government from Britain after 1909. In a speech given at Madras in November 1913, Hardinge expressed "the sympathy of India, deep and burning, and not only of India but of all lovers of India like myself for their compatriots in South Africa in their resistance to insidious and unjust laws." [32] This protest carried much weight and was supported by pressure exerted by London. The result was the enactment of legislation in South Africa in the summer of 1914 that removed the most vexatious legal injustices.

The victory now won, Gandhi left South Africa in the summer of 1914 for a visit to England, arriving in London on August 6, just two days after Britain had declared war against Germany. Gandhi immediately urged all Indians in England to render all possible service to the Empire. His plea was that the best method to improve the status of Indians in the Empire was by unselfish service and love. Gandhi himself started to serve in ambulance work in England, but a serious illness forced him to return in December 1914 to the milder climate of India. Back in his native land he rendered valuable service to the British cause, publicly denouncing revolutionary conspiracies and assassinations, going on recruiting tours, and from time to time being consulted by the viceroy on important problems. Not long after his return to India, Gandhi was given the Kaiser-i-Hind Gold Medal by the government of India for distinguished humanitarian service in the Empire.

Gandhi was forty-five when the triumph of non-violent passive resistance in South Africa made him the Mahatma, the Holy One or Great Teacher, in India, and earned him respect and admiration throughout the British Empire. In May 1915, he established his Ashram, or seminary, with twenty-five of his disciples from South Africa, near Ahmadabad in order to teach his ideas to the Indian masses. Even at

31 *Ibid.*, p. 26.
32 Chirol, *India*, p. 202.

this time, because of his work in South Africa, the Indian crowds reverently paid him homage when they caught a glimpse of his slight figure passing by. Gandhi had promised G. K. Gokhale, the noted Indian leader, not to enter politics for a year after his return while he became acquainted with conditions in India. The returned native son, however, was eager to use *Satyagraha* for the redress of injustice in India should the need arise. The opportunity was soon to come.

In addition to his war services from 1915 to 1918 in India, Gandhi felt constrained to intervene as the champion of justice on several occasions. There was his investigation of the exploitation of the peasants of northern Bihar by the indigo planters, and the encouragement of the peasants in the Kaira district of Gujarat to take up passive resistance against the government in response to unjust taxation. Gandhi intervened in several other instances where he believed injustice was being committed. Most of these affairs were not of any great significance, and were settled merely by the threat of a *Satyagraha*. These tentative beginnings of passive resistance in India, however, were given much publicity by the nationalist press and thus educated public opinion for the more ambitious program of *Satyagraha* later to be undertaken by Gandhi.

Gandhi's First Challenge

There may be differences of opinion as to the degree of provocation presented to Indians by the Rowlatt Act, but it is a plain fact that, justified or not, this was the first of several actions of the Indian government that changed Gandhi from a friend to a foe of British rule. Up to 1918 he believed in the basic justice of Britain, but "the first shock," wrote Gandhi, "came with the Rowlatt Act, a law designed to rob the people of all freedom." [33] While the Rowlatt Bill was being debated in the Indian legislature, Gandhi urged the viceroy to drop the measure, and warned that if the government proceeded there was no other course left except resort to *Satyagraha*.

On February 23, 1919, a meeting of the Ahmadabad branch of the Home Rule League was held to protest against the Rowlatt Bill. This event may be regarded as the beginning of Gandhi's first nation-wide campaign against British rule in India. The following day a similar meeting was held at Gandhi's Ashram and was attended by nationalist leaders from Bombay. At this time a manifesto was drawn up in-

[33] Quoted in Sir John Cumming, ed., *Modern India* (London: Oxford University Press, 1932), p. 49.

augurating passive resistance if the Rowlatt Bill became law. In part this declaration announced: "We shall refuse civilly to obey these laws and such other laws as a committee to be hereafter appointed may think fit, and we further affirm that in this struggle we will faithfully follow truth and refrain from violence to life, person, or property." [34]

Upon receiving the news of the passage of one of the Rowlatt Acts, Gandhi appealed dramatically to his countrymen to observe a hartal, a day of national humiliation and prayer. This was to be a time of self-purification, the inauguration of *Satyagraha,* a sacred fight. All the people, therefore, were to close their shops, cease their work, and observe the day by means of fasting and prayer. The day of the hartal was first set for March 30 and then changed to April 6. Word did not reach Delhi of the change in date until too late, and on Sunday, March 30, Gandhi's non-violent hartal was observed. It soon ceased to be non-violent, however, when vendors of food at the railway station refused to close their shops in deference to the hartal. A large mob stormed the station. Police were called to disperse the throng, and, finally, troops had to be called in to restore order, which they succeeded in doing only after they fired on the rioters, killing eight and wounding many more. Minor disturbances continued in Delhi for the next two weeks.

In the meantime, Gandhi had decided to visit Delhi and Amritsar in the Punjab. Fearing the spread of rioting, the British authorities arrested Gandhi and returned him to Bombay, where he was shortly released. The news of the arrest was the signal for serious riots in Bombay, Ahmadabad, and all over the Punjab. At Virmagam, in Gujarat, an Indian magistrate who opposed a mob was seized and beaten; kerosene was poured over him, and he was burned to death. A British troop train was also derailed, but no lives were lost in the accident.

Deeply crushed by the failure of his followers to maintain their campaign on a non-violent plane, Gandhi in a great public meeting at Ahmadabad bitterly reproached them for using force.

The disturbances thus far were nothing compared to the terrible holocaust which broke out in the Punjab and had its main storm center at Amritsar, a city of some 150,000. For some weeks there had been rumblings of revolt. Those killed at Delhi in the rioting had been glorified as martyrs, and posters had mysteriously appeared warning the government that there would be a great *Ghadr.* The British authorities

[34] *Report of the Disorders Inquiry Commission* (The Hunter Report) (London: His Majesty's Stationery Office, 1920), p. 61.

tried to counteract the agitation by spreading thousands of leaflets explaining the purposes of tthe Rowlatt Act. The unrest, however, mounted, and the news of Gandhi's arrest and the deportation of two militant nationalists from the Punjab precipitated the bloodiest incidents since the Mutiny of 1857.

Rioting began in Amritsar the morning of April 9, and troops were called out to fire on the milling crowds. Outbreaks occurred all over the city. Several Europeans were murdered, and banks, churches, and railway stations were burned. Meanwhile, in the city of Lahore, in the Punjab, the European residential section was barely saved from attack by the arrival of a detachment of troops. On April 12 a serious riot took place at Kasur, forty miles from Amritsar, in which two British officers were taken from their train compartment and beaten to death. There were numerous other scattered incidents of violence, and all telegraph connection between Amritsar and the outside world was cut off.

The situation in this city was still serious when a British officer, General Dyer, arrived with a force of about a thousand soldiers. On April 12 he arrested some men regarded as the leaders of the outbreaks and the next morning issued a proclamation, by beat of the drum, warning that no public meetings were henceforth to be held and that if this order was disobeyed the troops would use their rifles.

On the following day word was received by Dyer that a great crowd was collecting in the Jallianwalla Bagh, a low cleared space enclosed on all sides by mud walls with a few narrow entrances. What followed was a terrible and excessive retribution for the recent acts of violence of the Indian mobs. General Dyer marched about fifty Gurkha soldiers to the Bagh, where he saw a large throng of people, most of them listening to speeches. Without warning, he opened fire and did not cease until the ammunition was nearly exhausted. The crowd was in a cul-de-sac and vainly tried to escape, but did not succeed before some four hundred had been killed and more than a thousand wounded.

For a week after this terrible scene isolated outrages continued. Trains were derailed, telegraph lines were cut, and the movement of railway freight was practically paralyzed. Sir Michael O'Dwyer, then governor of the Punjab, maintains that news of General Dyer's stern action spread rapidly and was responsible for the prevention of further serious outbreaks. Whether or not the disorders would have gradually died down in the face of less stringent measures was an issue which later led to bitter controversy. By the end of April the Punjab was tranquil again. A new threat, however, materialized from Afghanistan, where a new amir, bitterly hostile to

Britain, began moving his troops to the attack and actually attempted in May an invasion of northern India. The Afghans proved to be no match for the British Indian army. Airplanes bombed the Afghan capital, and by June 2 the amir's forces had been badly beaten. Peace was signed in August, but the northwest frontier continued to prove troublesome, and for a year expeditions had to be sent to subdue various marauding tribes.

Gandhi, the mystic and idealist, was shocked over the blood shed both by the British authorities and by his followers. After Amritsar and the riots in other parts of India he suspended passive resistance. In a speech the Mahatma declared that his followers had not been sufficiently educated and disciplined to carry out *Satyagraha*, and that resort to what he had hoped would be non-violence was a "Himalayan miscalculation."

And so Gandhi's first campaign against British authority came to what seemed to be a sorry and inconclusive end. As for his future plans, the Mahatma in the summer of 1919 said little and seemed to be following a policy of "wait and see." There were some indications, however, that Gandhi might still cooperate with the government to some extent in trying out the new postwar governmental reforms—based on the Montagu-Chelmsford Report—recently passed by the British Parliament.

6. Toward Independence and Division

INDIA IN THE 1920's EXPERIENCED LITTLE TRANQUILLITY, while the world watched with keen interest the growing intransigence of Indian nationalism and the increasing discomfiture of British rule, as it sought to convince the people of its good intentions and of the urgent necessity of cooperation between them and the British in progressing toward self-government. There was an element of the unreal and make-believe in the Indian scene in this decade. The machinery of administration was ostensibly designed to give experience in the art of self-government, but the dominant national party, led by Gandhi, would not cooperate. This attitude ruled out any possibility of evolutionary and harmonious development toward freedom. As we will see, Britain temporized, cajoled, and reflected upon new schemes of government. In essence, however, she had only two alternatives: either to get out of India or to govern the country in her own way and according to her own principles. What actually happened? Britain followed neither course but hopelessly confused the situation by following a line made up of elements taken simultaneously from both alternatives. And, meanwhile, the Indian nationalists became more frustrated and irresponsible, glossing over basic problems inherent in their society and blaming all ills upon the alien ruler.

While India seethed with indignation over the Rowlatt Acts and the tragedy of Amritsar, the British government proceeded with the task of carrying out the recommendations of the Montagu-Chelmsford Report. The problem was turned over to a joint select committee of both houses of Parliament. This body had its first meeting on July 16, 1919,

148

and sat continuously, hearing evidence, for a period of six months. All shades of British and Indian opinion were heard, and its report was finally presented to Parliament on November 17, 1919. The joint committee made a few minor amendments to the India Bill that had been prepared by the government. These were accepted by the coalition ministry of Lloyd George, and the bill became law, December 23, 1919.

During the debate in the House of Commons, the secretary of state for India, Edwin Samuel Montagu, was eloquent and convincing in his defense of the reforms. Outlining the goal of a free India, Montagu declared:

> I implore this House to show to India to-day that Parliament is receptive of the case for self-government and only seeks an opportunity of completing it by the demonstrable realisation of the success of its stages. . . . Here is a country desirous of achieving nationality. . . . Let us pass this Bill and start it, under the aegis of the British flag, on the road which we ourselves have travelled.[1]

Other supporters of the India Bill, especially Lord Sinha, who was an outstanding Indian nationalist, an ex-president of the Congress, and a leader of the Indian moderates, cogently argued that the bill was not aimed at setting up a final constitution for India. It was intended to provide a bridge of transition whereby India could pass from a bureaucratic form of control to a government in which she would determine her own destinies.

The Indian Governmental Reforms of 1919

The new act had a twofold purpose: to initiate the first step in the direction of self-government and, at the same time, to give to Indians the opportunity of responsibility and experience in democratic government. The field primarily selected for this opportunity was in the provincial governments. Here, in the provinces, an ingenious device or mechanism in self-government was provided. Each province was to be allowed a legislature in which 70 per cent of the members were elected by voters in urban and rural constituencies. The governmental administration of the province was to be of a dual nature, in which the departments were classified as either "reserved" or transferred." In the former category were such departments as justice, famine relief, irrigation, police, and prisons. These were under the exclusive

[1] Quoted in Sir George E. Schuster and Guy Wint, *India and Democracy* (London: Macmillan and Co., Ltd., 1941), p. 79.

control of a British governor, assisted by a small executive council, and acting independently of the will of the provincial legislature.

The transferred departments, such as education, local government, sanitation, health, and agriculture, were turned over to Indian ministers, who in turn were responsible to the provincial legislature. While unchecked by the legislature in the field of reserved powers, the provincial governor was expected to accept the advice of his ministers in the area of transferred government. This bifurcation of governmental administration into two halves—one responsible and the other bureaucratic—was termed dyarchy.

The Act of 1919 for the first time divided the functions of government in India between the provinces and the central government. To the latter went such powers as customs, military and foreign affairs, and relations with the Indian states; to the former (i.e., the provinces) went such functions as police, justice, education, and public works. The old unitary form of government was thus discarded, and in effect a quasi-federal system was established. This action was taken in the belief that the ultimate form of government in India, one uniting both the British provinces and the princely states into one integrated political pattern, must be some type of federation.

In the central government of British India, the Act of 1919 established a bicameral legislature, consisting of the council of state and the assembly, in which the unofficial element (that is, elected members) were in a majority over those official members who were expected to support the views of the British government. Voters on a restricted franchise selected their representatives for the central legislature, while the official members were designated by a section in the Indian constitution. In the last analysis, however, the governor-general could override the will of the elected majority by the power of "certification." The governor-general was able to certify any bill which in his opinion might endanger the general safety and tranquillity of the country, and thus prevent its enactment. He could also certify a bill as essential, and thus enact it into law without the consent of the legislature. Also, in the budget of the central government a number of items, relating to salaries of officials, to the military establishment, and to other matters, were not votable. The governors in the provinces were also endowed with the certifying power, and were able to block legislation even in the transferred field of government if the British executive thought it essential to do so.

Despite the certifying power possessed by both governor-general and the provincial governors, the Act of 1919 constituted a major constitutional advance toward ultimate Indian self-government. Before 1919 the franchise was enjoyed by a microscopic minority, only 33,000 voters, but after the act the vote was given to 5,179,000 males. The usual requirement for the franchise was the payment of a small amount of land tax or municipal rates. All who paid income tax and all former soldiers in the Indian army were also given the vote. Even with what might be thought to be a very moderate extension of the franchise, many of the voters were illiterate, and special devices at the polls were necessary to facilitate elections. On the ballots, for example, candidates were given symbols rather than names, such devices as the tiger, elephant, flag, and sword being used. Women did not receive the right to vote in 1919. The various legislatures, however, were given power to confer female franchise. Madras led the way in 1921, and by 1928 practically all constituencies had women voters. Also, in seven out of the nine provinces of British India and in the assembly of the central legislature women could be members by 1928.

A feature quite distinct from customary democratic practice was the provision of communal electorates in the voting machinery set up in India in 1919. Apparently the Montagu-Chelmsford investigators held an adverse opinion of the system as it had been first applied by the Morley-Minto Reforms, but the various minorities—especially the Muslims —demanded guaranteed representation in separate or communal electorates, and Mr. Montagu was reluctantly forced to concur. In voting for the central legislature, therefore, separate electorates were set up for the Muslims, Sikhs, and Landholders, and for Indian commerce as well as the electorate termed Non-Muslim, which presumably would be overwhelmingly Hindu. In the voting for the provincial legislatures additional electorates were created to represent Anglo-Indians, Indian Christians, and representatives of universities.

Such was the system of government introduced in India by the Act of 1919, which was opposed both by the National Congress in India and by the imperialistic diehards in Britain. From many quarters came criticism and skepticism concerning the practicality of dyarchy, or divided government. The Calcutta *Statesman*, for example, asserted that the newfangled device of dyarchy "can result only in an irritating form of association and a profitless semblance of responsibility."[2] A die-hard British newspaper, the *Morning Post*, satirized the origin of dyarchy in a conversation between Montagu and Chelmsford: "The latter says, 'How can we ever come to an agreement since I believe in a Trinity and you believe in

2 Quoted in *Literary Digest*, LXVIII (December 20, 1919), p. 23.

a Unity?' Montagu replies, 'Let us split the difference,' and the worship of the great God Dyarchy is forthwith inaugurated."[3]

Despite a heavy volume of censure, however, the Indian moderate faction, which had bolted the Congress, and most liberal opinion in Great Britain stuck to their guns in defense of the new scheme of political reform. And in February 1921 the reforms were officially initiated when the Duke of Connaught formally presided at the opening of the new Indian legislature at Delhi. The ceremony was impressive, with troops in full-dress uniform, and the princes attending in their colorful costumes. A message of good will was read from the king-emperor, who sent his assurances that Indians on this day were witnessing the beginings of self-government within the Empire.

Undoubtedly with Amritsar in his mind, the Duke of Connaught made a strong appeal for cooperation in making dyarchy work. Said he:

My experience tells me that misunderstanding usually means mistakes on either side. As an old friend of India, I appeal to you all—British and Indians—to bury along with the dead past the mistakes and misunderstandings of the past, to forgive where you have to forgive, and to join hands and to work together to realise the hopes that arise from to-day.[4]

The inauguration of the new scheme of Indian government, however, coincided with a great mass movement of Hindus and Muslims, led by Mohandas Gandhi, in which the declared object was the boycotting of the reforms and the achievement of complete self-government, *swaraj*, for India.

Non-cooperation and the Khilafat Movement

In order to understand how this mass boycott of British rule came to be launched, it is necessary to retrace our steps a little, back to the closing months of 1919. At this time Gandhi, notwithstanding the Amritsar incident, was apparently inclined to cooperate with the government in working the reformed Indian constitution. In his newspaper *Young India* he wrote, "Our duty is not to subject the Reforms to carping criticism, but to settle down quietly to work so as to make them a success."[5] The Congress met at Amritsar in December

[3] Quoted in H. E. A. Cotton, "Constitution-Making for India," *Contemporary Review*, CXVII (1920), p. 69.

[4] *India in 1920* (Calcutta: Superintendent Government Printing, 1921), p. 21.

[5] Quoted in Kate Mitchell, *India without Fable* (New York: Alfred A. Knopf, 1942), p. 160.

1919, and here the Mahatma urged the gathering to give the reforms a fair trial. This 1919 conclave may be regarded as the first Gandhi Congress. Gandhi was rapidly becoming the idol of the young nationalists and a veritable god to the masses. From now on in the Congress the cry "Mahatma Gandhi Ki jai" was heard more and more frequently.

Only six months after the Amritsar Congress, Gandhi was spurning the reforms and calling for a mass movement against a government he termed "Satanic." Said the Mahatma, "It is better to die in the way of God than to live in the way of Satan. Therefore, whoever is satisfied that this Government represents the activity of Satan has no choice left to him but to dissociate himself from it." [6]

Why this Gandhian *volte-face?* The answer is easily found in what the Mahatma maintained were the broken pledges and insincerity of the British government manifested in the "whitewashing" of the culprits of Amritsar and in another injustice imposed upon Indian Muslims, the Khilafat grievance.

As the facts of the disturbances in the Punjab, and especially the details of the Amritsar outbreak, became fully known in the late spring and summer of 1919, Indian public opinion loosed a storm of denunciation against the ruthless tactics of the British officials involved. Seeking to mollify aroused Indian sentiment, the British governor-general appointed a special committee under the chairmanship of Lord Hunter to investigate the disturbances in Bombay, Delhi, and the Punjab. Coincidentally, the Congress had appointed its own special committee to secure the facts on the "Punjab wrong."

In March 1920 the report of the Congress committee was published, and it contained a scathing attack against the measures resorted to by British officials in coping with the Punjab disturbances of the spring of 1919. The official Hunter Commission in the meantime heard evidence in four Indian cities. In defending his actions, General Dyer maintained that law and order had been menaced and were in the balance at Amritsar, and said that if this challenge had not been met, open and bloody rebellion would have broken out. Said Dyer, "It only struck me at the time it was my duty to do this [i.e., fire on the assembled crowd], and that it was a horrible duty." [7] Nevertheless, the commission in its report published in May 1919 censured Dyer for firing without notice and continuing to fire after it was evident that the situation was well in

6 Quoted in Glorney Bolton, *The Tragedy of Gandhi* (London: George Allen and Unwin, 1934), p. 156.
7 Quoted in H. G. Rawlinson, *The British Achievement in India* (London: William Hodge, 1948), p. 202.

hand. A minority report, signed by the three Indian members of the commission, went much further than the majority report (signed by the five British members) in condemning the brutality and inhuman treatment meted out to Indians at Amritsar. On receipt of the Hunter Report the government of India, summing up its final view, declared that Dyer's action was "dictated by a stern though misconceived sense of duty. . . ." It added, "We can arrive at no other conclusion than that General Dyer acted beyond the necessity of the case, beyond what any reasonable man could have thought to be necessary, and he did not act with as much humanity as the case permitted." [8]

Accordingly, Dyer was deprived of his command and censured, actions that were fully discussed and approved in a decisive debate carried on in the House of Commons. So far so good, from the Indian standpoint, but the conciliatory gestures of the Indian government and the Commons were undone by the action of the House of Lords, which dissented from the lower house and vigorously supported Dyer. At the same time, the British die-hard press launched a shrill campaign in favor of Dyer, a campaign which included sponsoring a fund for the aggrieved officer.

These events opened up anew the Amritsar wound. Tagore, the great Indian poet, astounded by some of the speeches in Parliament in defense of Dyer, wrote that "the unashamed condonation of brutality expressed in their speeches . . . is ugly in its frightfulness." [9] Anti-imperialists in other parts of the world joined in the chorus of denunciation. In rebuttal British writers pointed out that the very torrent of criticism against what had happened in the Punjab was evidence that such occurrences were rare under British rule, and that nothing like Amritsar had happened since the days of the Indian Mutiny in 1857.

While the report of the Hunter Commission and the debates on Amritsar in the British Parliament were adding fuel to the fires of nationalism in India, the Khilafat (or caliphate) controversy was turning many Indian Muslims against British rule. All Mohammedans in India looked to Turkey as the greatest Muslim power. Furthermore, the Turkish Sultan was the Caliph of Islam and as such the spiritual head of Mohammedanism. During the First World War it was a source of great embarrassment to Britain that she was at war with Turkey, a state whose ruler was revered by so many millions of her subjects in India. In January 1918 the British prime

[8] *India in 1920*, p. 238.
[9] Quoted in C. H. Van Tyne, *India in Ferment* (New York: D. Appleton and Co., 1923), p. 144.

minister, Lloyd George, had declared that Turkey was not to be deprived of its capital or the lands of Thrace and Asia Minor, which were predominantly Turkish. At the conclusion of the war, however, there were rumors of secret treaties made by Britain and France for the division of the Ottoman Empire. Constantinople was seized by Allied troops, and in the spring of 1919 Greek forces landed in Smyrna with the encouragement of the British government.

In May 1920 the draft treaty of Sèvres was published. This document imposed a severe peace upon Turkey, internationalizing the Straits; depriving her of all rights in Egypt, Tripolitania, Morocco, and Tunisia; and taking away the territories of Arabia, Palestine, Mesopotamia, and Syria. In addition, Greece was temporarily to administer Smyrna and southwestern Asia Minor, and to add eastern Thrace to her realm.

Such terms were regarded by Muslims, especially in India, as unnecessarily severe, and the cry of "Islam is in danger" was raised. In vain did British statesmen try to point out that Britain herself could not undo the Treaty of Sèvres, that Britain had commitments to France, that the Allied world supported the design of a Zionist National Home in Palestine, and that a soft peace for Turkey—after the long history of Turkish misrule and atrocities—was out of the question.

Despite these arguments, Indian Muslims proceeded to organized their Khilafat movement to force the British government to amend the Sèvres Treaty on the side of leniency. In November 1919 a Khilafat conference was held in Delhi. Gandhi attended and suggested the possibility of all Indians, Muslim and Hindu, joining in a boycott of the government. In the spring of 1920 the Khilafat movement rapidly gained momentum. In March a Muslim delegation was sent to London to demand revision of the Sèvres Treaty, and March 19 was proclaimed as a national day of fasting for Turkey by Indian Muslims.

At this juncture Gandhi stepped forward as the Khilafat champion. He warned the government that if justice were not done to Turkey he would launch a great Hindu-Muslim non-cooperation movement. In his *Open Letter to All Englishmen in India*, Gandhi accused Lloyd George of treachery and declared that the Khilafat wrong and the British whitewashing of Amritsar had completely shattered his faith in the good intentions of Britain. In August Gandhi returned to the viceroy various medals and decorations he had received from the British government for his services during the Boer War and the First World War. Following this action, the leaders of the Khilafat movement, Mohammed Ali and his brother Shaukat Ali, proclaimed a Hindu-Muslim entente and toured India with Gandhi appealing for support.

The National Congress convened in special session at Calcutta in September 1920. This meeting was dominated by Gandhi, who made a powerful speech in favor of "progressive non-violent non-co-operation" to be used as a weapon in support of the Khilafat movement and also to force the British government to grant India self-rule "within the British Empire if possible, without if necessary." [10] The Congress accepted Gandhi's non-cooperation program, which called for the following measures: (1) the surrender of all British titles; (2) refusal to attend any government functions; (3) the withdrawal of all students from schools and colleges; (4) the boycott of courts; (5) no service by Indians in the British army in Iraq; and (6) absolutely no cooperation with the new governmental reforms, either as candidates for office or as voters in elections. A few months later, the regular annual session of the Congress, meeting at Nagpur, enthusiastically endorsed the non-cooperation movement. And so it was that Gandhi completely repudiated his position, taken just a year before in 1919 at the Amritsar Congress, in support of the new governmental reforms.

This *volte-face* was a decisive event destined to shape the course of India's history from 1920 through the next two decades. Gandhi was not perhaps greatly motivated by an appreciation of any deep injustice to his Muslim colleagues inflicted by the Sèvres Treaty or even by the "condoning" of Amritsar, but rather by the fact that an unusual opportunity had been offered him of uniting all Indians—Muslim and Hindu—and thus of accelerating the pace toward national independence. As Gandhi declared, it was "such an opportunity of uniting Hindus and Mohammedans as would not arise in a hundred years." [11] Yet there was something incongruous in this union of soul-force and militant Islam. Perhaps Gandhi had rationalized his advocacy of the Khilafat cause until he came to believe in its inherent justice, but actually it would seem that this alliance sprang primarily from political expediency.

In initiating his non-cooperation movement, Gandhi was not concerned exclusively with the rectification of the Khilafat injustice or the realization of self-rule *(swaraj)*. His campaign also became the vehicle for spreading his way of life, for securing certain moral and social objectives. To Gandhi's mind Western civilization, with its science, industry, and cities, was a soul-destroying curse. Gandhi, Rousseau-like, espoused the simple and the uncluttered life. In his view,

[10] Post Wheeler, *India against the Storm* (New York: E. P. Dutton, 1944), p. 177.
[11] Edward J. Thompson, *Reconstructing India* (New York: Dial Press, 1930), p. 127.

India's salvation consists in unlearning what she has learned during the last fifty years. The railways, telegraphs, hospitals, lawyers, doctors and suchlike have all to go; and the so-called upper classes have to learn consciously, religiously, and deliberately the simple peasant life. . . . Every time I get into a railway car or use a motor bus I know that I am doing violence to my sense of what is right.[12]

To Gandhi, India was happy and free wherever the curse of modern civilization had not reached. The simple and unspoiled village life, therefore, must be resurrected. As part of his non-cooperation movement Gandhi consequently preached the boycott of all foreign manufactured goods, especially cloth. He urged the use of the spinning wheel, the charkha, for the production of homespun cloth, khaddar. To cleanse India of another evil excrescence of modern civilization, Gandhi also championed the temperance movement. He detested liquor as a root cause of poverty and moral depravity. Liquor shops were boycotted, and the American prohibition leader "Pussyfoot" Johnson was invited from the United States to give advice to Gandhi and his Congress leaders.

The non-cooperation campaign reached a climax in 1921. Symbolic burnings of foreign cloth were carried out, some of which were attended by multitudes of more than 100,000 people. An eyewitness of one of these burnings of a great pyramid of cloth gives the following vivid description: "The Mahatma lighted the heap of foreign clothing. The sight was extremely impressive; the vast audience, the burning clothes, and the passionate speakers, under God's sky in the growing night." [13] It should be kept in mind that this attack on foreign goods was an expression of nationalist demands for economic independence as well as political *swaraj*.

In parts of India college and secondary education was seriously disrupted. Calcutta University reported that four thousand students had dropped out of Bengal's colleges, and the loss of students in this province's secondary schools ran to about 40 per cent.

While Gandhi exhorted his followers to practice non-violence scrupulously, his movement became increasingly marred by incidents of bloodshed and force. Strikes, riots, and raids on property became more and more common. The Khilafat movement was also getting out of hand. Aroused by religious fanaticism, many Muslims had preached a *Hijrat*, that is, a mass exodus, enabling true believers to escape from

[12] Quoted in Jawaharlal Nehru, *Toward Freedom* (New York: John Day Company, 1942), p. 314.
[13] Gertrude Emerson, "Non-Violent Non-Cooperation in India," *Asia*, XXII (August 1922), p. 610.

the pollution of British rule. Accordingly, a great mass emigration got under way in the latter part of 1920, and at one time some eighteen thousand people were on the move through the Khyber Pass en route to Afghanistan. This country at first gave the Muslim pilgrims a friendly asylum but later closed the frontier. Thousands of emigrants were stranded, and the road from Kabul to Peshawar became dotted with the graves of homeless refugees.

Along the Malabar coast of India in the province of Madras a group of Muslim people, the Moplahs, inflamed by the Khilafat propaganda, rose in rebellion and turned against their Hindu neighbors. Hundreds of Hindus were murdered and their temples defaced. At least two thousand Moplahs were killed by troops striving to restore order, and martial law was in force for seven months. It was this bloody outbreak that terminated the brief Hindu-Muslim entente, and the president of the All-India Muslim League announced the withdrawal of his organization from the Congress campaign of non-cooperation. A year later events took place in Turkey which completely shattered the Khilafat agitation. In 1922 the sultanate was abolished. Mohammed VI was deposed but remained as the caliph; however, in 1923, when the Turkish Republic was proclaimed, steps were taken to abolish completely the institution of the caliphate, which was ended in March 1924.

Despite these setbacks, Congress and its leader were still confident of success. Perhaps the surrender of Lloyd George to the demands of the Irish Sinn Fein leaders, Michael Collins and David Griffiths, with the consequent creation of a self-governing Irish Free State, was a straw in the wind indicating Great Britain's growing willingness to admit the validity of nationalistic aspirations in her Empire. Accordingly at the Ahmadabad Congress in December 1922, Gandhi asked for and was given authority to initiate a campaign of mass civil disobedience. Heretofore, non-cooperation of schools, political offices, and courts had only touched the upper classes; now Gandhi was about to appeal to the common people to refuse to pay taxes and to "non-cooperate" against the government in every possible manner. On February 1, 1922, Gandhi addressed to the viceroy, Lord Reading, a letter demanding a complete change of heart on the part of the government within the space of a week. If Congress demands were not met by this time, civil disobedience would be introduced in the district of Bardoli, in Gujarat.

Three days later, however, a mob of Congress volunteers attacked a police station at Chauri Chaura, set it afire, and burned twenty-one policemen to death. Following the receipt of this news, Gandhi with his Congress Working Committee suddenly suspended his whole program of non-cooperation and civil disobedience. Gandhi deplored the bloodshed at Chauri Chaura; insisted that all defiance of authority should cease; declared that the withholding of taxes and rent payments was contrary to the interest of Congress; and, most significantly perhaps, assured the landlords that the Congress movement in no way intended to attack the rights of private property.

The news of the suspension of non-cooperation was received with dismay by many members of Congress. Nehru, a young and ardent nationalist destined for leadership, observed:

> Suddenly, early in February 1922, the whole scene shifted, and we in prison learned, to our amazement and consternation, that Gandhiji had stopped the aggressive aspects of our struggle, that he had suspended civil resistance. . . . We were angry when we learned of this stoppage of our struggle at a time when we seemed to be consolidating our position and advancing on all fronts.[14]

There has been much conjecture about the motive behind this cancellation of the Congress campaign against British authority. Was it because Gandhi, as a pacifist and a believer in non-violence, refused any longer to tolerate bloodshed? Undoubtedly this explanation has relevance, but there are some authorities who find the solution in the bourgeois character of the Congress. The middle-class leaders of the nationalist movement, including wealthy landowners and industrialists, were fearful of a genuine popular movement that might become an attack on all property, privilege, and power —Indian as well as British. More and more in the 1920's funds flowed from Indian capitalists into the coffers of Congress. Apart from purely patriotic motives, the millionaires could hardly be blamed for trying to hurry the day when their own national government would adjust Indian tariffs to suit their interests.

After the Bardoli retreat, Gandhi's bolt seemed to have been shot. His promise of *swaraj* "within a year" had not been realized, and a growing number of critics questioned the utility of non-cooperation and boycott of the new legislatures. Mrs. Besant had assailed Gandhi's tactics and had taken refuge in the ranks of the Liberal party, a group that had bolted from the Congress. Even Tagore, ardent nationalist that he was, averred:

> The idea of non-co-operation is political asceticism. Our students (kept out of colleges) are bringing their offerings of sacrifices to what? Not to a fuller education, but to a non-education.

[14] Nehru, *Toward Freedom*, p. 79.

It has at its back a fierce joy of annihilation which at its best is asceticism, and at its worst is that orgy of frightfulness in which the human nature . . . finds a disinterested delight in an unmeaning devastation. The anarchy of mere emptiness never tempts me.[15]

Gandhi was arrested on March 10, 1922, and brought to trial by the British authorities. The courtroom proceedings made excellent copy in the newspapers of the world. Mrs. Sarojini Naidu, poetess and nationalist, likened the trial to that of Jesus, with the British magistrate cast in the role of Pontius Pilate. Gandhi and his judge outdid themselves in trying to be polite. The former declared he was here "to invite and submit cheerfully to the highest penalty," [16] and the latter, after sentencing the prisoner to six years, added that no one would be more pleased than he if circumstances in India might make it possible for the government later to reduce the period of imprisonment.

On the surface the non-cooperation campaign had seemingly failed, but Gandhi had succeeded in making an all-important contribution to the Indian nationalist movement. He was the first national leader not only to secure the support of the Indian intelligentsia and the middle classes, but also to stir and attract the loyalty of the untold masses in the countless villages of India. No better evaluation of Gandhi's significance in the 1920's can be found than the following passage written by an eyewitness of non-cooperation just a few months after the Bardoli surrender:

Gandhi has, I believe, done his work. He has made India self-conscious. He has given India a new sense of self-respect. His program has been characterized by many negative features. . . . It has never put forward even a suggestive outline of the government it would substitute for the one it would tear down. . . . But Gandhi has given a moral basis and a spiritual standing to India's revolution.[17]

Politics in the Uneasy 1920's

At the end of 1920, when Gandhi and the Congress had decided to inaugurate "non-violent non-cooperation," elections had just been held for the first time under the new Government of India Act. The new legislature was severely handicapped by the Congress boycott. Notwithstanding this burden, the government under the leadership of the Liberal party

[15] Quoted in Van Tyne, op. cit., pp. 134-135.
[16] Quoted in Roy Walker, Sword of Gold (London: Indian Independence Union, 1945), p. 88.
[17] Emerson, op. cit., p. 674.

carried out a progressive program. India obtained practical control of her tariffs, repealed the Rowlatt Act, agitated for more rapid Indianization of the civil service and the Indian Army, and enacted important measures in labor legislation. In the transferred areas in the provinces, British officials worked harmoniously under Indian ministers and numerous measures were passed in the fields of local government, education, and health.

Despite this encouraging record, it was evident by 1926 that dyarchy and the reforms of 1919 were breaking down.

Buoying up and supporting the rapid advance of Indian nationalism in 1926 and 1927 was a new generation of young nationalists more dynamic and radical than their elders. Gandhi had been imprisoned in 1922 and remained in jail until early in 1924, when he was released by the government. For the next four years he remained out of the field of political agitation, contenting himself with working for the removal of Untouchability, better relations between the Hindu and Muslim communities, and the development of his hand-spinning program. During this interregnum, first Das and then Motilal Nehru had assumed leadership of the nationalists. A new group of more ardent and radical nationalists, however, was emerging, including Jawaharlal Nehru, the son of Motilal, and Subhas Chandra Bose.

Up to this time the Congress movement had been mainly bourgeois and upper-class in its leadership and policies. By 1925 it began to reflect the growth of socialist and workers' groups in India. The first socialist weekly had been founded in 1923 and the first Workers' and Peasants' party set up in Bengal in 1926, while a Communist movement was also growing. Thus it was that there developed in Congress a left wing whose members sponsored a student and youth movement and an All-India Independence League. The objective of the latter was not only the complete cutting of the painter connecting India with the British ship of state, but also the amelioration of the condition of the masses, the liquidation of the parasitic zamindars (landlords), and the introduction of a socialist state. Jawaharlal Nehru was the president of this league, and its appearance signalized the fact that in addition to political independence there was crystallizing another objective—complete socio-economic revolution.

Nehru, the leader destined to take his country eventually into the promised land of independence, came from a Brahman family of ancient lineage which had migrated from the state of Kashmir. His father, Motilal Nehru, first a prominent and wealthy lawyer and a lukewarm nationalist, had after 1919 thrown himself wholeheartedly behind Gandhi and had even adopted his ascetic way of life. The son, Jawaharlal, had all the advantages of wealth. He was sent to the English public school of Harrow and later to Trinity College, Cambridge, where he obtained his B.A. in 1910; he was admitted to the bar in 1912.

Upon his return to India, Nehru showed little interest in the law and gradually became interested and then completely absorbed in his country's fight for freedom. While a great admirer of Gandhi, Nehru could not agree with the Mahatma's asceticism and mysticism, or with his antagonism toward Western industrialism. At heart this Brahman is a rationalist, a believer in science, and a foe of all supernaturalism. Above all, he is a blend of the cultures of the East and West, with the latter perhaps predominating. As he himself has said: "I have become a queer mixture of the East and the West, out of place everywhere, at home nowhere. Perhaps my thoughts and approach to life are more akin to what is called Western than Eastern, but India clings to me." [18] As a rationalist, a humanitarian, and an implacable foe of the exploitation of his fellow men, Nehru found it logical to support socialism, which he believed could be made compatible with democratic political freedoms.

By the end of 1927 the tide of nationalism was rapidly mounting. At the annual meeting of Congress held at Madras, Nehru—just recently returned from a visit to Europe, including Russia—persuaded the meeting to pass a resolution declaring complete independence to be India's goal.

Some response to this challenge had to be fashioned by the viceroy Lord Irwin, who, ever since the day he arrived in India, while sympathizing with nationalistic aspirations, had sought to divert them into constitutional and evolutionary channels. As we will see in the next chapter, the viceroy made every attempt to encourage Hindu-Muslim amity. But anti-British feeling grew rather than diminished. The Liberal party continued to lose followers, while the more radical Congress became more impatient in its demands and also more popular and influential.

The year 1928 was a turbulent one. When the Simon Commission, a body named to study Indian political conditions, landed in Bombay in February, it was greeted by a huge hostile demonstration displaying the slogan, "Go back, Simon!"

Lord Birkenhead, the secretary of state for India, who was not too sympathetic with Indian nationalism, introduced another complication into Indian politics when he more or less challenged the various Indian parties to get together and produce a scheme of government agreeable to all. The various groups, Congress, Muslim League, and Liberals, proceeded

[18] Nehru, *Toward Freedom*, p. 353.

to set up a committee for this purpose under the chairman-ship of Motilal Nehru. In August 1928 the Nehru Report was published. This document (discussed more fully in the next chapter) was in some ways a courageous attempt to draft a new constitution granting dominion status and one that would satisfy the various political groupings. The net result, however, was violent disagreement between the Muslim League and the Congress.

Meanwhile, Congress was rent with personal rivalries and divided by exponents of differing programs of action. Only one man could get it out of this impasse, and this was Gandhi, who returned to active political life in December 1928. At Calcutta the Mahatma succeeded in getting the Congress to accept a compromise which satisfied both the radical and conservative wings. A resolution was passed demanding that Britain should accept the Nehru Report; and, as one British historian has pointed out with much justification, the Congress "ordered Government to accept what they could not persuade their own communities to accept." [19] This acceptance, more-over, was to be an accomplished fact within one year. If it were not forthcoming, a campaign of non-violent non-coopera-tion would be initiated against the government.

Events were now rapidly moving in the direction of a de-cisive showdown.

The very next month the Conservatives under Stanley Baldwin were turned out of office in Britain; their successors were the representatives of the Labour party under Ramsay MacDonald. The British Labour party since its inception had consistently attacked imperialism and expressed its impatience at the slow pace of democratization in India.

In June 1929 Lord Irwin returned to England to discuss the serious deterioration of affairs in India. Supported by the Labour government, he and Captain Wedgwood Benn, sec-retary of state at the India Office, decided that the time had come for a bold gesture in Indian affairs. On October 25 the viceroy returned to Delhi, and six days later he issued his momentous statement on Indian affairs. In part this statement declared:

> In view of the doubts which have been expressed both in Great Britain and India regarding the interpretation to be placed on the intentions of the British Government in enacting the Statute of 1919, I am authorized on behalf of His Majesty's Gov-ernment to state clearly that in their judgment it is implicit in the declaration of 1917 that the natural issue of India's constitu-tional progress . . . is the attainment of Dominion status.[20]

[19] Thompson, *op. cit.*, p. 164.
[20] *India in 1929-1930* (Calcutta: Superintendent Government Print-ing, 1931), p. 468.

Furthermore, it was also announced that as soon as possible a round-table conference, with British and Indian representatives, would be called to take up the Indian problem—presumably to draft a new constitution.

The period from 1930 to 1939 was a fateful decade in Indian history. During these ten years India more than ever before was placed in the limelight, with the press of the world giving lengthy coverage to its problems, its leaders, and its intermittent crises. There was much for the journalists to describe. Gandhi launched a great civil disobedience movement designed to achieve complete independence for his homeland. London witnessed the coming and going of many dignitaries, both British and Indian, as constitutional reform was debated in three separate round-table conferences. And in the British Parliament for many months both houses engaged in long and often acrimonious debates over the political future of India. Finally, in August 1935, a new act designed to carry India toward the goal of dominion status became law.

India at the begining of the 1930's was essentially in a fluid situation. British statesmen and Indian patriots could in large measure determine what the course of events was to be. As one looks back on this decade, however, it is apparent that something went wrong, that neither the British nor the Indian leaders measured up to their grave responsibilities and opportunities.

The most tragic happening of all was the failure of the Indians themselves to maintain a united front in their national movement. Bitterness and rancor rapidly widened the gulf between the Hindu and Muslim communities. In the late 1930's the Muslim League, spokesman of the latter and led by Mohammed Ali Jinnah, began to envisage Indian independence in terms of a separate nation for the followers of Allah.

Lord Irwin's announcement of October 1929, that dominion status was definitely the goal for India, and that a round table would soon be convened to study the problem, was a praiseworthy attempt to convince the Congress party that Britain was ready and willing to stand by the promise made by Montagu in 1917.

The first reaction to the viceroy's invitation to a round-table conference had been encouraging. A group of Indian leaders, representing all parties, accepted with some reservations. But after the debate in Parliament the Congress attitude hardened, and Gandhi, in a meeting with the viceroy, announced that the Congress would not attend the round-table conference unless it should be clearly understood that its purpose was the drawing up of a scheme of full dominion status, to be put into effect immediately. This meeting was attended by representatives of the Indian Liberal party and the Muslim League, who were keenly disappointed that Congress would not accept the round-table invitation. Shortly afterwards, the Indian Liberals in annual conference at Madras passed a resolution calling for dominion status in as short a time as possible, but accepting the offer of the round-table meeting.

The Congress met at the close of 1929 in an intransigent and confident mood. A great city of tents was set up for the delegates at Lahore for their annual meeting, which has been described as "part gipsy encampment, part football match, part parish bazaar." [21] There was much excitement and activity, with great parades, the adulation of Gandhi, and the hoisting of the flag of independence. And everywhere there were correspondents, Indian, British, and especially American, for India had become front-page news.

An unsuccessful attempt had been made to assassinate Lord Irwin just before the Congress met, and one of its first acts—on the insistence of Gandhi—was the adoption of a resolution congratulating him on his escape; this passed, after much debate, by a vote of 935 to 897. Within the higher circles of the Congress there was an inside struggle on the issue of whether Irwin's offer of a round table should be accepted. Gandhi, supported by the two Nehrus, had his way, and on December 31, 1929, Congress adopted his pledge of complete independence, which was to be taken by all Congress members on the following January 26, a date to be observed as Independence Day. This pledge undoubtedly obtained much inspiration from some of the great revolutionary declarations of the past, especially the French Declaration of the Rights of Man and the American Declaration of Independence. In part it read:

> We believe that it is the inalienable right of the Indian people, as of any other people, to have freedom and to enjoy the fruits of their toil and have the necessities of life, so that they may have full opportunities of growth. We believe also that if any government deprives a people of these rights and oppresses them the people have a further right to alter it or abolish it. The British Government in India has not only deprived the Indian people of their freedom but has based itself on the exploitation of the masses, and has ruined India economically, politically, culturally, and spiritually. We believe, therefore, that India must sever the British connection and attain Purna Swaraj, or complete independence. . . . We will therefore prepare ourselves by withdrawing, so far as we can, all voluntary association from the British Government, and will prepare for civil disobedience, including non-payment of taxes. [22]

21 Schuster and Wint, *op. cit.*, p. 166.
22 Quoted in Nehru, *Toward Freedom*, pp. 388-389.

In other words, the one-year period of grace granted to the British at Calcutta to accept the Nehru Report had lapsed. Gandhi was empowered to initiate civil disobedience at his own discretion, and, as a preliminary move, Congress declared a boycott on all the legislatures and directed its followers who were members of them to resign immediately. On January 26, 1930, thousands of people signed the pledge of independence and witnessed the raising of the Congress tricolor flag.

For a few months after the Lahore Congress there was some sparring between Gandhi and Lord Irwin. The former presented the viceroy with a number of demands which, if met, would mean the cancellation of the forthcoming civil disobedience movement. Among the demands were: (1) total prohibition, (2) halving the land tax, (3) abolition of the salt tax, (4) a 50 per cent cut in the military budget, (5) the scaling down of the salaries of the higher officials, (6) an amnesty for political prisoners, and (7) the reservation of coastal shipping for Indians. Certain of these demands, notably the first four, were drastic ones, and it is debatable whether any independent Indian government could have carried them out. Irwin accordingly turned them down and on March 2 received a letter from Gandhi, addressed to "Dear Friend," announcing that civil disobedience would begin on March 12 and would be initiated by a pilgrimage to defy the salt tax.

On March 12 Gandhi was given a great ovation by thousands of his followers and, with 79 disciples, commenced a hike to the sea, 170 miles away. The march lasted three weeks and made headlines in most of the newspapers of the world. On April 6 Gandhi reached the sea at Dandi on the Gujarat coast and waded into the surf as his followers cried, "Hail, Deliverer!" Sea water was then dipped up and placed on a fire, and the symbolic act of manufacturing salt was carried out in defiance of the government's monopoly. The defiance of the salt laws was a shrewd move by Gandhi, because this tax fell on every family and was universally disliked.

The salt march was the signal for full-fledged civil disobedience. Officials resigned, tax collection was resisted, railway employees quit, liquor shops and foreign businesses were boycotted. The full weight of the Congress was thrown into the fight to paralyze the government. The mounting effects of the world depression had done much to increase unemployment and lower the already atrociously debased Indian standard of living. In 1930 India lost nearly one-fourth of its foreign trade. Congress, therefore, in its civil disobedience campaign received the support of a mass of disgruntled and often hungry workers and peasants; and, at the other economic extreme, the Congress received the enthusiastic support of Indian business, especially the cotton-mill owners, who saw in the boycott of foreign goods an excellent opportunity to drive out their British and Japanese competitors. It has been estimated that several hundred thousand rupees were donated every month to Congress by Indian business. This financial support enabled the nationalist organization to enroll large numbers of Congress volunteers and give them food and a daily wage. As the civil disobedience movement got under way, its exponents were motivated by a complex pattern of profits, patriotism, and piety.

In the spring of 1930 the flags and colors of the Congress were everywhere. Large crowds of youths paraded the streets of the main cities singing and shouting nationalist slogans. For the first time women were enlisted in large numbers in the Congress ranks. The nationalists had their own uniformed volunteers who patrolled the bazaars, allowing no carts to proceed without the driver presenting his certificate of "No British goods." Many European businessmen were ruined, and imports of Lancashire cotton cloth declined precipitously. At the same time tax strikes reduced Indian government revenues. Salaries of civil servants, budgets, and social services all had to be cut, and on several occasions loans had to be raised in London to meet deficits. While ostensibly non-violent, civil disobedience soon resulted in widespread disorders in which officials were murdered and salt depots of the government raided. Rioting broke out in the large cities.

In April 1930 an armory was raided and six government employees killed; riots took place in Peshawar, where the mob had control of the city for several days, and serious disturbances took place in Madras, Karachi, and Calcutta. There were also tensions between Muslims and Hindus, as the former refused to support the Congress campaign. It was natural that mass demonstrations, business boycotts, and from time to time outright terrorism should lead to clashes between the police and soldiery, on the one hand, and the followers of civil disobedience on the other. Frequently the police dispersed crowds of pickets by *lathi* charges, the *lathi* being a long, weighted club. Indian nationalists have heatedly charged the police with excessive brutality, and undoubtedly, in the confusion and turmoil of the moment, the police were unnecessarily severe. On the other hand, there is much evidence to show that soldiers and police acted with great patience and forbearance during the long months of the civil disobedience when nerves and tempers were at the breaking point.

Lord Irwin during these hectic days held out the olive branch to Congress, welcoming its participation in the round-table conference scheduled to be held in London in November, but demanding that civil disobedience cease and that laws be obeyed. Declaring that civil disobedience had degenerated into violent rebellion, Irwin had a number of special ordinances passed to strengthen the hand of the government. In May Gandhi was arrested and imprisoned, and soon the jails were filled with thousands of prisoners. The disorders reached their climax in the midsummer of 1930, when perhaps 60,000 members of Congress were in prison. Yet, at the height of civil disobedience Lord Irwin in a speech to European businessmen at Calcutta declared: "We should, I am satisfied, make a profound mistake if we underestimate the genuine and powerful feeling of nationalism that is today animating much of Indian thought. And for this no simple, complete or permanent cure ever has been or ever will be found in strong action by Government." [23]

Late in the spring of 1930, during the turmoil of civil disobedience, the Simon Commission released its report. This document was out of date as soon as it fell from the government presses. In the main it was an ultra-cautious and conservative analysis of the Indian problem, and it stressed the difficulties and obstacles lying in the way of self-government.

During the summer of 1930 Lord Irwin encouraged the efforts of the Liberal party leaders to persuade the Nehrus and Gandhi to call off the civil disobedience campaign. Gandhi, however, refused to withdraw the demands he had served on the government just prior to launching civil disobedience. The peak of the movement was reached in August, and in September it began to subside. Meanwhile, delegates representing all views and parties in India, except the Congress, were assembling in London for the round-table conference which convened in November. This body, as will be shown shortly, made remarkable progress and continued in session until the middle of January 1931. Its activities and those of the second round table will be analyzed together a little later (see pp. 172 ff.). At the end of the conference, the British prime minister, Ramsay MacDonald, announced an amnesty for all political prisoners in India, including Gandhi. It was the hope of both the Labour government and its viceroy that Congress might still be induced to come into

[23] Quoted in Alan Campbell Johnson, *Viscount Halifax* (New York: Ives Washburn, Inc., 1941), p. 284.

the fold of the round-table discussions and that a new constitution might be devised, one which would enjoy the support of all Indian parties.

The release order for political prisoners was announced by Lord Irwin on January 25, 1931, and the leaders, including Gandhi, were set free immediately, with the rank and file to be released later. The country by this time was sick of civil disobedience. In many cities business was at a standstill and trade disrupted. Gandhi, because of urgent appeals by Indian representatives who had attended the round-table conference to open negotiations with the viceroy, and because of the evident desire of Irwin for such a move, proceeded to Delhi to see the head of the government. Gandhi wrote to Irwin asking to see him "not as a viceroy but as a man." The first personal meeting took place on February 17, and in the next four weeks eight additional conversations took place. There was much criticism of Irwin's conciliatory policy from die-hard circles in Britain. Lord Rothermere in the *Daily Mail* attacked the viceroy as a "weak and sentimental man," who has "humiliated himself and lowered the prestige of his country on which British rule in India entirely depends." [24] Churchill, doughty defender of the Empire, naturally was aroused at the news that the leader of civil disobedience had been received with courtesy by Irwin. Churchill was "nauseated," he declared, "to see Mr. Gandhi, an Inner Temple lawyer, now become a seditious fakir of a type well known in the East, striding half-naked up the steps of the Viceregal Palace while he was still organizing and conducting a defiant campaign of civil disobedience, to parley on equal terms with the representative of the King-Emperor." [25]

Notwithstanding attacks from extremists in both India and Britain, Irwin persevered in his conversations with Gandhi. Finally, an agreement was drawn up on March 5, known as the Delhi Pact, bringing an end to civil disobedience and providing for Congress participation in the next session of the round-table conference. Although the salt tax was not abolished, there were to be some concessions in areas where people were especially poor. The boycott of foreign goods for political purposes was halted, but Irwin recognized the right of peaceful propaganda in behalf of domestic industries. All special ordinances of government aimed against civil disobedience were to be ended, and all persons in prison were

[24] Quoted in *ibid.*, p. 281.
[25] Great Britain, *Parliamentary Debates* (5th series), House of Commons, Vol. 247, column 755.

to be released, unless they had committed crimes of violence.

In most circles, in India as well as in Britain, there was complete satisfaction when the news of the Delhi Pact was released. A month after the document had been initialed Lord Irwin left India and was succeeded by Lord Willingdon as viceroy. Irwin, or Lord Halifax, to give him his later title, was to assume high office in the British cabinet later in the 1930's. He was to serve as the foreign secretary during the lamentable days of appeasement under Neville Chamberlain, and thus his policies, both at home and abroad, were on occasion harshly criticized. For his Indian record, however, there was warm praise, and the verdict was that he was not only one of the greatest of Britain's viceroys but, what was more important, one of the best loved by Indians. One great English liberal newspaper declared:

> For a Viceroy to be attacked by the fanatic nationalists of both countries is not to his discredit. . . . He will be remembered in India not because he came there as the representative of a Great Power, but because in the discharge of his duties as a Viceroy he exemplified all that was best in the civilisation to which he belonged and in the religion he followed.[26]

The Argument over British Rule

In a sense, the high point of the Congress nationalist movement was reached in 1930. There was a buoyant spirit of optimism and confidence, oversimplification of the obstacles barring the path to independent nationhood, and a tendency to hold British rule responsible for all India's problems, which would somehow be removed almost automatically by the magic solvent of independence. During the next two decades, and particularly after the achievement of independence in 1947, a sobering realization of the complexity of India's situation gradually dawned upon the more realistic nationalist circles. In 1930, however, the nationalist indictment of British rule was unequivocal and uncluttered by any qualifications.

It was charged that the widespread poverty in India was primarily attributable to British policy. Sixty per cent of the Indian budget was spent on the army, allowing Britain to train thousands of her own troops and make India foot the bill. Besides this, the best positions in the Indian civil service were earmarked for Englishmen, who were paid unnecessarily high salaries. In addition, these favored alien bureaucrats were also given fat pensions on retirement. Every year, it was claimed, a large portion of India's wealth, usually referred

[26] *Manchester Guardian*, April 24, 1931.

to as the "drain," had to be sent to England in the form of
pensions and interest payments on the huge amounts of British
capital invested in India. The British capitalists got the profits
but Indians did the work. Britain kept India a free-trade
country, discouraging industrialization and thus maintaining
it as a convenient market for British manufactured goods.
Indians desired tariff protection. It was also charged that the
Indian people, especially the impoverished peasants, were
bowed down by a crushing burden of taxation imposed by the
British regime.

In the political realm, it was asserted that Britain had
followed a policy of divide and rule, supporting and coddling
the medieval autocratic princely states and encouraging fac-
tionalism in India, especially in the case of the rivalry between
the Hindus and Muslims. On this last point an Indian writer
asserted in 1933:

> The so-called Mohammedan leaders . . . are mere creatures
> of the government, without standing in India and without in-
> fluence there except in the direction of working mischief. Hindus
> and Mohammedans could reach agreement tomorrow were it
> not for the continuous wire-pulling of those in authority who
> expect to benefit by keeping them divided.[27]

The neglect of health and medical services, as proved by
the high death rate, and the prevailing mass illiteracy were
also blamed on the British. Finally, the Indian indictment
asserted that British rule was autocratic and would continue
so, clumsily camouflaged by such devices as dyarchy without
real self-government and vague promises of ultimate dominion
status.

On the other side of the balance sheet, British publicists
called attention to the safety afforded India by the British
fleet, and pointed out that army expenditures for the defense
of India were very reasonable compared with the burden
carried by other nations. It was true that Englishmen in the
Indian civil service were paid generously and retired hand-
somely, but the standards of admission were so high that only
men of the highest caliber were selected, whose incorruptibility
and efficiency had more than given back to India the value
of their salaries. The argument of the "drain" was countered
by the assertion that much of the money sent to Britain from
Indian sources represented interest—and a very low rate
usually—paid on capital which had helped build railroads,
telegraphs, canals, and great irrigation projects. Furthermore,
these modern facilities earned enough not only to pay the

27 D. N. Bannerjea, "India's Case for Independence," *Current History*, XXXVIII (May 1933), p. 173.

interest charges due in London but to leave a surplus besides.

British officials in India also pointed out, in answer to the charge of overtaxation, that the items most criticized, land and salt revenue, were taken over from the Mogul regime and that the amount collected under British rule was substantially less than it had been under the Mogul emperors. Widespread poverty had little connection, the British claimed, with politics and the kind of government ruling India. Rather, this condition was the result of factors within the Indian culture pattern: the caste system and its resultant social stratification, excessive spending on religious and marriage ceremonies, the despotism of the moneylender, and "the sacred cow, an undue regard for mere life as opposed to good life." [28] It was stressed that, because of the sanctity of all life in India, the ravages of rats alone cost each year more than the sum spent on the army and that the annual loss incurred by maintaining old cattle ran to 1,760,000,000 rupees, four times the land revenue obtained by the government.

Round Tables in London

In the spring of 1931 the National Congress approved Gandhi's attendance at the second round-table conference in London. After some sparring with the viceroy, Lord Willingdon, less patient than Irwin, Gandhi proceeded to Europe.

Gandhi's steamer passed through the Suez Canal into the Mediterranean and headed toward the shores of France. It is well to point out here that Gandhi was not going to London to start negotiations with the British government on a new Indian constitution, for such a task had already been undertaken by the first round table, which must now be described.

The first round-table conference proper was in session from November 1930 to January 1931, and was made up of some of the foremost leaders in Indian public life. There were fifty-seven of them, representing various parties, including the Sikhs, Untouchables, Muslims, Christians, and the Liberal party in British India. In this group Dr. Bhimrao Ramji Ambedkhar represented the Untouchables, Mohammed Ali Jinnah and the Aga Khan the Muslims, and Sapru and Sastri the Liberals.

In his early days Jinnah had been a nationalist pure and simple, working with any Indian—Muslim or Hindu—for

[28] Vera Anstey, "Population, Poverty, and the Drain," in *Modern India,* ed. by Sir John Cumming (London: Oxford University Press, 1932), p. 267.

self-government. Thus it was that Nehru once wrote of Jinnah as "the ambassador of Hindu-Moslem unity," and the Indian poetess and patriot, Mrs. Sarojini Naidu, wrote a eulogistic biography of Jinnah in 1918. Born in Bombay in 1876, he had received a legal education in England, and on his return to India had built up a wide and extremely lucrative practice. Before the First World War he was an outstanding member of Congress, but when the Gandhian period began, he resigned from the organization. In the 1920's Jinnah became increasingly antagonistic to what he regarded as the Hindu nationalistic tendency of Congress. In all aspects of his character Jinnah was a striking contrast to Gandhi. "He lived in stately mansions, was tall and elegantly groomed, with a distinguished presence and fastidious tastes. In his fast-greying hair a white lock stood aggressively like a plume." [29] Jinnah had none of the mysticism, pacifism, or philosophical subtleties of Gandhi. He was a fighter, believed himself to be a realist, and defended his position by cold, clear, lawyer-like logic.

This first conference, with the agreement of representatives from the princely states, had approved the principle of a federal government for India. The new structure would embrace both British India and that of the princes. In addition there was to be an end of dyarchy in the provinces, where responsible government under Indian ministers would be introduced. At New Delhi the national government would have extensive powers, with the British retaining control over defense and foreign affairs, and, finally, the interests of British business and investment were to be protected. Furthermore, in the event of any emergency the British governors in the provinces and the viceroy in New Delhi were endowed with special safeguards to maintain the peace.

Though the above general principles were adopted at the first round-table conference, little progres was made at the second, attended by Gandhi, in translating them into specifics. In the name of Congress, Gandhi balked at many proposals, especially the rights of the minority groups for special consideration in the form of separate electorates. While this second conference was in session, widespread disorders broke out again in India. Willingdon, the governor-general, acted promptly and sternly in meeting this challenge. On his return from London, Gandhi revived civil disobedience, and he, together with many other Congress leaders, was sent to prison.

Amid civil disobedience and communal rivalries in India the third round-table conference convened in London on November 17, 1932, and continued in session until December 24. The Congress was not represented, and neither was the

[29] *The Times* (London), September 13, 1948, p. 7.

British Labour party. The purpose of the meeting was to fill in the final details of the new Indian governmental structure. After the conference had concluded, the British government took over its proposals and from them drafted a proposed constitution for India. This draft was the famous White Paper of March 1933.

With this document in hand Parliament in the spring of 1933 proceeded to set up a Joint Committee on Indian Constitutional Reform to study the White Paper and make its recommendations. Composed of thirty-one members, three of whom were ex-viceroys and three former secretaries of state for India, and representing the three political parties in Britain, the joint committee spoke with much authority. Its report, issued in November 1934, was used as the basis for the British national government's India Bill, which was introduced into Parliament in January 1935.

Notwithstanding strong opposition, the India Bill had the support of a good majority in Parliament, and in the most crucial vote it was carried 404 to 133 in the House of Commons and 236 to 55 in the Lords. On August 4, 1935, the bill received the royal assent and thus became law. In the main, public opinion in Great Britain warmly commended the act. The London *Times*, for example, commenting on the legislation, editorialized: "A great constructive measure, the greatest indeed that a British Government has taken in hand in this century, has passed from project to enactment." [30]

Laboratory of Freedom

The new constitution for India was a complex and voluminous document, running to 451 clauses and 323 printed pages. As far as territorial changes were concerned, it provided for the separation of Burma from India. With an area of 262,000 square miles and a population of 17 million, Burma had been part of India only by reason of the accident of conquest. Its people differed from those of India in race and culture, and they had come to resent being tied to what they considered an alien country. During the 1920's nationalism in Burma kept pace with that in British India in demanding more self-government. Accordingly, while the round tables on India were being held in London, a separate Burma round table was convened in December 1931. The following year a general election was held by the Burmese in which they voted to separate from India.

In 1937 Burma was given a new government which made it more autonomous than any other British colonial area and

[30] *The Times* (London), August 3, 1935.

placed it in status just below that of an independent British dominion. While the British governor still had control of defense, foreign relations, and monetary policy, and also over the tribal areas where such non-Burmese as the Shans and Karens lived, the Burmese people had a substantial area of government in which they enjoyed complete autonomy.

In India's new constitution, the governor's provinces of British India, of which there were eleven, were given a new and separate legal status. Except under certain emergencies they were independent of the central government and untrammeled in their exercise of those powers designated in the constitution as "provincial." The old form of divided government, or dyarchy, disappeared, and responsible government took its place. All the departments of government in a province were now under the direction of Indian ministers, who, in turn, were responsible to the elected members of the provincial legislature. The British, however, had tempered responsible government with certain safeguards. Each provincial governor was endowed with seven special responsibilities over which he could exercise his individual judgment without reference to the will of the legislature. Two of the most important of these special powers were the safeguarding of the legitimate interests of minorities and the prevention of any grave menace to the peace or tranquillity of a province. In addition, in case of the breakdown of government, the governor could take over the administration of his province.

Within the provincial franchise a complex system of separate electorates was introduced. Under this system of voting there were separate electorates for the Sikhs, Backward Tribes, Labor, the Universities, Landholders, Commerce and Industry, the Indian Christians, Europeans, and Muslims, and an electorate termed the General Population, which would usually be predominantly Hindu. And within this scheme seats were reserved for the Untouchables and for women. Altogether, the franchise was extended to some 30 million voters in British India.

The federal part of the Government of India Act established a bicameral legislature: the council of states and the assembly. The powers which these lawmaking bodies could exercise were carefully listed, together with those powers that came solely within the purview of the provincial legislatures. While dyarchy had been eliminated in the provinces, it reappeared in the federal government, for here the governor-general had full authority in the fields of defense and foreign affairs. In the other departments of government, the governor-general was normally expected to defer to the wishes of the Indian ministers and the legislature. As to finance, such items as the salaries of judges and the governor-general, the pay of the Indian civil service, and the cost of the two reserved departments were excluded from the vote of the legislature. The governor-general was to be appointed by the British government, and, like the provincial governors, he was endowed with a number of special responsibilities, among them the power to prevent any discrimination of an economic nature against British subjects and goods. He could also suspend the constitution, prorogue the assembly, veto its acts, and certify legislation which it refused to pass.

The Constitution of 1935 provided for the union of British India and the princely states into a federal structure. The exact terms on which a princely state was to come into the federation were to be matters of negotiation between Britain and each ruler concerned, who would indicate what powers he would be willing to turn over to the federal government. Federation was not to be established until rulers representing 50 per cent of the population of the states and half of the states' representation in the council of state had signified their intention of joining. Pending agreement with this required number of princely states, the central government was to remain unchanged under the provisions laid down in the Act of 1919.

Most politically conscious Indians from all parties were disappointed with this new constitution. The Liberal party, the most moderate and most inclined to follow the path of cooperation with Britain, was irked at the act's failure to mention dominion status specifically, and also it considered the safeguards too numerous. The Liberals, nevertheless, reluctantly decided to accept the act. The Muslims and other minorities in British India also considered the act as falling short of what had been promised in self-government in 1930. They were gratified, however, by the provision of separate electorates in both the provincial and federal legislatures and by those safeguards designed to protect the interests of the minorities. Muslim opinion, therefore, was in the main ready to try the act. Only the Congress turned the act down as completely unacceptable.

The political atmosphere in India was one of exhaustion and uncertainty. While the India Bill was passing through Parliament the civil disobedience movement faltered and then flickered out. The ranks of Congress declined to little more than half a million members; the people were tired and discouraged. Gandhi and other leaders were released from prison in 1933. Nehru writes of this period, "India was numbed by the violence and harshness of repression. The nervous energy of the nation as a whole was for the moment exhausted and it was not being recharged." [31] In May 1934, Congress called

31 Nehru, *Toward Freedom*, p. 224.

off the civil disobedience campaign, and in the following months the government's ban on this body was lifted. The failure of civil disobedience had cost Gandhi some of his popularity. There were questioning and uncertainty among the Congress leaders; finally, in the fall of the year, Gandhi announced that, because of the growing difference between himself and some Congressmen, he was retiring from politics and henceforth would occupy himself with social reform, working to aid the Untouchables and to support the movement for village industries.

Congress quickly revived. In the elections of 1935, held under the old Constitution of 1919, this party showed remarkable recuperative strength and the old Liberal party practically disappeared. Meanwhile, the native princes met in Bombay and raised a number of objections to the federal scheme proposed in the India Act of 1935. Preparations, therefore, were made by the viceroy for introducing responsible government only in the provinces of British India. In the spring of 1936, at a conference held at Lucknow, Congress decided to contest the forthcoming elections. The following August it issued an important manifesto assailing the new constitution, declaring its aim still to be complete independence, and asserting that entry into the legislatures was not to cooperate with the act "but to combat it and seek the end of it . . . to carry out the Congress policy of the rejection of the Act and resist British imperialism." [32] A new orientation in policy is discernible in the manifesto, which laid stress upon social and economic reform, asserting the determination of Congress to reduce poverty and unemployment and to reform such institutions of exploitation as the privileged position of the landholders.

This growing concern of Congress with the economic amelioration of the masses as well as with political independence was primarily the achievement of Jawaharlal Nehru, who in the mid-1930's became the outspoken advocate of socialism. Eloquently he declared:

> Socialism is thus for me not merely an economic doctrine which I favor; it is a vital creed which I hold with all my head and heart. I work for Indian independence because the nationalist in me cannot tolerate alien domination; I work for it even more because for me it is the inevitable step to social and economic change. [33]

Disregarding the pros and cons of the particular means advocated by Nehru, his realization that political independence was not enough, that there was much work of a socio-economic reformist nature that Indians must do for themselves, was a healthy sign.

[32] Quoted in the *Round Table,* London (December 1936), p. 142.
[33] Nehru, *Toward Freedom,* p. 401.

In December 1936, at the Faizpur Congress, Nehru gave a stirring address in which he castigated imperialism and fascism and also urged the necessity of economic reforms. He referred to the new act as a "new charter of slavery," and warned the British that Congress was not going to the legislatures to follow the path of constitutionalism. With enthusiasm and confidence the National Congress entered the elections for the new provincial legislatures, held early in 1937. During the past two decades of agitation this organization had built up a nation-wide system which, starting with the humblest members in the villages, had a disciplined hierarchy culminating in the All-India Congress Committee, and in the president of the Congress with his cabinet of fourteen, called the Working Committee.

Congress demonstrated its strength in the elections by winning 711 seats out of a total of 1585 in the provincial lower houses. In five of the eleven provinces Congress had a clear majority, and in two others it was the dominant party. "This general success," wrote a British correspondent, "was largely due to sentimental regard felt for a movement which has focussed and fostered the national aims, to an intensive and thorough party organization, and to the obvious dissatisfaction of the poorer voters and the unemployed." [34] Congress membership climbed steeply at this time. It was 3 million in 1937, and by 1939 it had reached 5 million. This revitalization of Congress was aided materially by more interest in and dependence upon the masses. The party was losing its once almost exclusively middle-class character and turning more and more to workers and peasants.

Provincial responsible government came into force in April 1937. While Congress controlled seven provincial governments, it held to its pre-election promise not to cooperate with the new reforms. Nehru and what might be called the left wing of the Congress were against taking office and were for resorting to any kind of obstruction to discredit the new legislatures. A partial retreat from this extreme position was made when Congress offered to allow its members to take their offices and form provincial ministries, if each British governor would promise not to use his special powers. Some months of bargaining ensued. Interim governments were installed, however, in the provinces; and, finally, when the viceroy, Lord Linlithgow, made a conciliatory gesture, Gandhi emerged from retirement and used his great prestige to avert the deadlock. The viceroy gave assurances that only under the most extreme provocation would the safeguards be resorted to. Members of Congress then took office and formed ministries in seven provinces.

[34] *The Sunday Times* (London), April 30, 1937.

It was soon apparent that provincial self-government was a success. British civil servants carried out the policies of Indian ministers, and the governors remained in the background, giving Indians a free field. In only four instances in all the provinces were bills passed by legislatures vetoed. The provincial governments, and especially those controlled by Congress, during the brief period from 1937 to 1939 made a commendable record in social reform. In two provinces attempts were made to lower the rents charged by the landholders. Acts were passed designed to reduce the power of the moneylenders and to help the peasants get out of debt. Measures were also enacted for better famine relief and for providing improved market facilities for the peasants. A bold attempt was made to carry through prohibition, but this reform involved such a huge loss of revenue that it was made effective in only a few districts.

Some attention was given by the provincial governments to economic planning, and in the field of education substantial progress was made. The governments supported Gandhi's Wardha Scheme, which sponsored what was called "basic education." Children were "to make things," and to work in the fields as well as to be given training in the three *R*'s, while the products they made and grew were to be sold to help support the new schools. Some attention was also given to the problem of mass illiteracy. Altogether, the expenditure on the social services increased 14 per cent from 1937 to 1939. These socio-economic reforms have been evaluated by a British historian thus: "All in all, the agrarian legislation of the Congress Ministries, boldly conceived and swiftly carried through, was a notable achievement." [35]

Congress participation in the new provincial legislatures was to last for only two years, from 1937 to 1939. During this brief period three significant trends deserve comment. The first was the fading away of the possibility of federation. During 1936-1937 Linlithgow as viceroy had sent his emissaries to visit the princely states with the purpose of ironing out problems raised by the princes. Nothing came of this attempt, however, and in June 1939 the princes definitely turned down federation. Had they but known, this action was a fateful decision and, from the point of view of the princes' interests, an act of suicide. Had they entered the federation, the course of events in 1947-1948, which practically obliterated what had been the princely states, might have been different. From the point of view of national unity, however, the action of the princes in turning down federation was extremely fortunate.

An important factor explaining the princely states' refusal to

[35] Sir Reginald Coupland, *India: A Restatement* (London: Oxford University Press, 1945), p. 159.

federate was the princes' growing fear and resentment of Congress. At first this body had followed a policy of noninterference in the states. In 1927 the states' Peoples Conference had been organized, with the aid of Congress, to carry on agitation for democratic government in the states. In the mid-thirties, however, Congress began to assume a bolder policy, and in 1938 it declared: "The Purna Swaraj or complete independence which is the objective of Congress is for the whole of India, inclusive of the States." [36] Gandhi warned the rulers to cultivate friendly relations with Congress. Between 1937 and 1939 Congress intervened in several states, such as Mysore and Rajkot, and demanded political reforms. Its prestige and influence were such that it gained partial victories in both cases. Agitation was also carried on in Kashmir, Travancore, and Hyderabad. Nehru was particularly embittered by what he regarded as the medieval autocracy of the states, referring to them as "sinks of reaction and incompetence." [37]

The second trend was the rapid growth of the leftist wing in Congress and an increasing emphasis upon social revolution. This shift from the pure politics of national independence to social reform and, in some instances, even to the class war of Karl Marx, was illustrated by new interest on the part of Congress in such problems as rural indebtedness, agricultural debt and the moneylender, unsanitary conditions in factories, and mass illiteracy. At the same time, the threat of a schism between its right and left wings appeared in Congress. It was claimed by the latter wing that the Congress provincial governments were becoming increasingly conservative. Their reforms were considered too limited. Governmental responsibility had brought a sobering experience to Congress statesmen as they sought to restrain extremists, collect taxes, and discourage strikes. Labor troubles, lawlessness, and tax strikes were met by stern measures on the part of the ministries, who were acting, to all intents and purposes, just the same as British officials in the old days. Radicals of all kinds began to charge that the Congress governments were backsliding, that the sweet fruits of office were turning them into imitators of the British.

The spring of 1939 saw a serious crisis in Congress ranks. Subhas Chandra Bose, long a stormy petrel, a Socialist, and an uncompromising nationalist, had been elected Congress president in 1938. As election for a new president approached, Bose charged that the conservative elements had made a deal with Britain, and that they were selling out. Bose ran against

[36] Mitchell, op. cit., p. 210.
[37] Jawaharlal Nehru, The Unity of India, Collected Writings 1937-1940 (London: Lindsay Drummond, 1941), p. 30.

a presidential candidate sponsored by Gandhi and was victorious by a narrow margin. There was now a serious split in the Congress membership, as Bose and his adherents believed Gandhi was an incurable medieval mystic. The latter was of a mind that Bose was skirting close to revolution and could not be trusted. As in so many crises in the past in Congress, when Gandhi appealed for support he received it, and the party closed its ranks. Bose was forced to resign and did so in high dudgeon, proceeding to organize his own party, which he called the Forward Block.

It is extremely important, in view of recent developments, to understand that both Gandhi and Nehru were now coming to be regarded as old-fashioned by the younger leftist elements in the Congress. Nehru, a Fabian or evolutionary socialist, eschewed violence and intemperate extremism. He criticized attempts to embarrass the provincial ministries by strikes and demonstrations; he criticized the rowdies who joined peasant and workers' parties the better to fill their own purses rather than to aid their fellow men; and he attacked the forces of what he called "indiscipline and chaos."

If war had not broken out in 1939 it is probable that the feud in Congress between right and left might have exploded. The same trend could be observed in China. As we will see in a later chapter, war and the achievement of independence interrupted the growth of a schism along economic lines in Congress. A new phase in this economic rivalry was to begin just as soon as the British left India.

The third and last trend during the period of provincial self-government, 1937-1939, was the mounting tension between the Muslim and Hindu communities; or, to put it specifically, between the Muslim League and the National Congress. In those provinces controlled by Congress ministries there were fifty-seven serious communal outbreaks in two years, with some 1700 persons injured and 130 killed. Communal strife was becoming a frightening menace; the dark shadow of partition—what Gandhi called "the vivisection of India"—was appearing over the land.

Portents of Partition

In explaining the division of India into two parts—one the predominantly Hindu Indian Union, the other strongly Mohammedan Pakistan—the American journalist Margaret Bourke-White points a dramatic finger at one man, as if he alone created the conditions and conjured up the forces essential for the bifurcation of India. She says:

> . . . the decision was made in Bombay. It was a one-man decision, and the man who made it [Mohammed Ali Jinnah] was cool, calculating, unreligious. This determination to establish a separate Islamic state came not . . . from some Muslim divine in archaic robes and flowing beard, but from a thoroughly Westernized, English-educated attorney-at-law with a clean-shaven face and razor-sharp mind.[38]

The great-man theory of history is perhaps the easiest for most people to comprehend, for it conveniently concentrates a complex of historical forces in the soul and mind of a single individual. That Jinnah had much to do with the creation of Pakistan will be made clear in the following pages; that he only directed and took advantage of forces and ideals already in existence will be equally manifest.

In earlier chapters we have already seen that the Muslims were once a ruling caste in India but that they lagged behind the Hindus in commerce and education following the British conquest. We saw, however, that an Islamic revival took place under the leadership of Sir Seyed Ahmad Khan; and we noted how, as a result, the Muslims developed the University of Aligarh as a cultural center, revived in memory the glories of their past, and encouraged the flowering of Muslim thought in their language, Urdu. In consequence, the Muslims developed a new sense of their cultural distinctiveness and a feeling of destiny. Early in the twentieth century it became evident, in the face of the increasingly Hindu outlook of the Congress party, that this destiny must be political as well as religious and cultural. The growing self-identification of the Muslims as a group which should have a special political place in India led to the establishment of the All-India Muslim League in 1906. The League secured political recognition when the British government granted it separate electorates under the Morley-Minto Reforms of 1909.

During the First World War a Hindu-Muslim entente was realized in the Lucknow Pact of 1916, in which Congress recognized the League as the spokesman for the Muslim community and, in addition, accepted the principle of separate electorates. For the next five years both communities were actuated primarily by nationalism. The common foe was Britain, the one all-important objective self-government. In this phase of Hindu-Muslim relations apparently little attention was paid to the problem of what would happen after independence had been secured; how would the fruits of office and political power be distributed between Muslims and Hindus? This all-important question seemed of little moment as Hindu and Muslim nationalists joined in the Khilafat move-

[38] Margaret Bourke-White, *Halfway to Freedom* (New York: Simon & Schuster, 1949), p. 13.

ment and in non-violent non-cooperation. This entente, however, rested on insecure foundations and in 1922, following the horrors inflicted upon hundreds of Hindus in the Moplah outbreak, the alliance broke down completely.

A tragic feature of the history of the 1920's in India was the mounting incidence of violent outbreaks between the Muslim and Hindu communities. The first serious clash took place in the Punjab in the fall of 1922, and in the following year violence continued to rise. By 1924 it was apparent that Hindu-Muslim antipathy was assuming menacing proportions, for during this year there were eighteen serious outbreaks, the worst at Kohat, where 36 people were killed and 145 wounded. It was in protest against communal fanaticism that Gandhi undertook a famous three-week fast, and in consequence a unity conference of all creeds was called to discuss the problem. As a result of this action there was some improvement in 1925, but in 1926 communal tension again increased, with a total of 36 outbreaks and some two thousand casualties. The most serious occurred in Calcutta, where the shrill music of a Hindu procession disturbed and angered the Muslim worshipers in a mosque. The result was a total of fourteen hundred dead or injured, two hundred shops gutted, and twelve churches wrecked.

Now the question of what would happen after the exodus of the British was being raised. "Behind the façade of a united nationalist campaign against the British Raj, a struggle had already begun for the heritage of place and power it would some day leave behind it." [39] By 1927 the toll of victims in the preceding four years had reached five hundred dead and five thousand injured in communal violence. It was in this atmosphere of tension that Lord Irwin arrived in India in 1926 as governor-general. This official made a commendable but fruitless effort to bring the Hindu and Muslim communities closer together.

In the mid-twenties several events took place which seriously exacerbated communal tension. In December 1926 a prominent Hindu of the Punjab, Swami Shaddhanand, who was active in the movement to reconvert former Hindus who had turned Muslim, was assassinated by a Muslim fanatic. Then there was the uproar over the *Rangila Rasa* case. A Hindu bookseller of Lahore published a book in 1924 titled *Rangila Rasa (The Debauched Prophet)*, which was a scurrilous attack on Mohammed. The bookseller was prosecuted in court but was not convicted, much to the anger of the Muslims; a few years later, however, he was murdered in his shop. The founding of the Hindu Mahasabha must also be regarded as

39 Coupland, *India: A Restatement,* p. 123.

an important factor in the worsening of communal relations. This organization was set up in 1923 at Benares under the leadership of Pandit Malaviya, and soon became the agency of militant Hinduism. Among its purposes were the reconversion of Hindus who had become Muslims; the Shuddhi movement, the encouragement of physical fitness among young Hindus; and the protection of the rights of Hinduism in any controversy with other communal groups. Its slogan was said to be "India belongs to the Hindus and is nobody else's patrimony." The Muslim reaction to the militant Mahasabha is seen in this statement: "A new ideology was envolved, namely that India was the Holy Land of the Hindus, that the Hindus were a nation in their own right in which Muslims, Christians, and Parsis had no place, and that the political goal of the Hindus was Hindu Raj." [40]

Some of the outstanding Hindus in Congress emphatically excoriated the Mahasabha for its intemperateness, but the damage was done. In response the Muslims became more anti-Hindu and organized their own Tanzim movement for the conversion of Hindus to Allah. And in 1924 the Muslim League, which had been moribund during the Khilafat period, was revived by a leader destined to become famous in Indian history, Mohammed Ali Jinnah.

In 1928 the so-called Nehru Report had decisive influence upon the communal problem. In May of this year an All-Parties Conference met in Bombay to try to agree upon some pattern of government for a self-governing India that would be acceptable to all, especially to Hindus and Muslims. A committee headed by Motilal Nehru was set up to draft such a document, and in three months a report was submitted. This plan called for the Muslims to give up separate electorates, and proposed a federal plan of government in which the provincial units would have little autonomy. The Muslim community reacted strongly; and when the All-Parties Conference met at Calcutta, December 22, 1928, to discuss the Nehru Report, Mohammed Ali Jinnah and his supporters attended and proposed a number of amendments, which were voted down. There was bitter debate, during which the Muslims left the conference.

For some time the Muslims had been divided politically into a number of factions. The Nehru Report, however, tended to throw them together, and in the last week of December 1928 a great unity meeting was held at Delhi under the chairmanship of the Aga Khan. This conclave was the most representative meeting the Muslims had held up to this time,

[40] F. K. Khan Durrani, *The Meaning of Pakistan* (Lahore, Pakistan: Sh. Muhammad Ashraf, 1944), p. 93.

and it drew up a number of demands which would have to be met in any new constitution. Among the more important were: (1) Provinces in any federation must have complete autonomy. (2) In any legislature, provincial or federal, all legislation affecting communal relations can be blocked by the opposition of three-quarters of the votes of a community. (3) There must be separate electorates. (4) Muslims must be given fair representation in all cabinets. (5) They shall be given an adequate share of posts in the governmental services. (6) Muslim culture is to receive its rightful share of public funds, so that its schools and other institutions are not neglected.

The upshot of the Nehru Report was that it intensified communalism. Muslims such as Mohammed Ali, who had been an enthusiastic coadjutor of Gandhi's from 1920 to 1922, now attacked the Congress and the Hindus with vehemence; and in the spring of 1929 twenty-three prominent Muslims issued a manifesto against the Nehru Report and its supporters. From now on the Congress was for all purposes a Hindu organization. The Muslim community, however, found it difficult to present a united political front. Jinnah drafted a platform, later famous as his Fourteen Points and modeled somewhat upon that adopted at Delhi's unity meeting, which was designed to unite all Muslim groups. But this endeavor failed, and one faction of Muslims, led by A. K. Azad and Dr. M. A. Ansari, joined the Congress, maintaining that it was a secular all-India party. And outside the Congress there were the All-India Muslim Conference and the All-India Muslim League. It was this last organization which was destined to unite the great majority of Muslims under the leadership of Jinnah.

The decade of the 1920's ended with Gandhi taking the Congress into civil disobedience. Although there were some outstanding Muslims in Congress, the majority held aloof and refused to have anything to do with Gandhi's campaign. This led to serious communal riots. At Cawnpore, in March 1931, members of Congress tried to enforce a day of mourning in commemoration of a young terrorist who had been executed for killing a British police officer. The Muslims would not close their shops, and fighting broke out. The most terrible atrocities occurred, and in the course of three days more than four hundred people were killed and hundreds wounded. The exact casualties will never be known, since many bodies were dumped into the city's drains. Again, in 1932, there was a serious communal outbreak at Bombay caused by the refusal of non-Congress members, especially Muslims, to honor the boycott of foreign goods.

Communal tension spread far to the north, to the remote state of Kashmir. This native state was ruled by a Hindu maharaja and a small Hindu governing caste, but the population was nearly 80 per cent Muslim. The mass of people had long been discontented with their rulers, and in 1931 communal feeling from other parts of India fed their smoldering resentment. There were outbreaks in the summer which were successfully controlled. The news of the severity of repression spread, and by the end of the year bands of Muslims were trying to cross the border into Kashmir to help their co-religionists. Only the existence of British troops saved the government and prevented civil war. Kashmir was to serve again in 1947 as the arena for communal strife, but this time for two nations—Pakistan and the Union of India.

The round-table conferences held in London between 1930 and 1932 did little to minimize communal rivalries; on the contrary, they tended to inflame them. The Muslim League signified its intention of supporting the proposed federation of India, but only if adequate safeguards were granted to the Muslim community, and in June 1931 the president of the League declared, "Moslems would rather die fighting for preservation of their rights than to accept slavery at the hands of the infidels." [41] The communal problem overshadowed all other issues and difficulties at the second round-table conference, where Gandhi refused to recognize the right of any party or group other than Congress to speak on Indian affairs. This claim was heatedly refuted by all the minorities, especially by Dr. Bhimrao Ramji Ambedkhar, leader of the Untouchables, and by the leaders of the Muslim delegation. As we have noted above in this chapter, there was complete deadlock among the Indian representatives on whether, how, and how far the minorities were to be protected by special safeguards. The impasse was cleared away only by the Communal Award worked out by MacDonald and his advisers, which laid down the scheme of representation of the various communities and interests in the provincial councils.

While the Muslim community, like the Congress, was disappointed by the limits on complete independence which were presented by the India Act of 1935, they were content and reassured by the special rights and protection which it vouchsafed to minorities by means of the safeguards. Because of this feeling of safety there were indications in 1926 that Jinnah, now president of the Muslim League, was willing to revive the Hindu-Muslim entente of 1916. Events from 1937 to 1939 completely shattered this promising prospect.

When provincial self-government was inaugurated in 1937, Congress members were able to form ministries in seven of the eleven provinces. Bitter feelings among the Muslims were

41 *New York Times*, June 2, 1931.

quickly aroused when Congress refused to admit any Muslim into a provincial ministry unless he became a member of the Congress and gave up allegiance to the League. Resentment ran especially high in such provinces as Bihar and the United Provinces, where strong Muslim minorities existed. The Muslims were quick to call this action a breach of faith, pointing out that at the round-table conference it was agreed that cabinets should include representatives of minorities and that this principle had accordingly been included in the instructions of each provincial governor. Ambedkhar, the scholarly leader of the Scheduled Classes, was quite forthright in his denunciation of Congress policy, and wrote that it was "indeed a covert attempt to break all other parties in the country and make the Congress the only political party. The demand for signing the Congress pledge can have no other intention. This attempt to establish a totalitarian state may be welcome to the Hindus. But it means the political death of the Muslims as a free people." [42]

During the next two years the gulf of misunderstanding and acrimony between the Congress and the League continued to widen. It soon appeared that the Congress cabinets were not responsible to their respective legislatures but rather to the high command in Congress. Nehru frankly declared that "the ministers were the spokesmen of a mighty national movement of India and were under the discipline of their party, and directly controlled by the Congress Working Committee." [43] It was as though in the United States the National Committee of the Republican party laid down all the policies to be followed by all state governors who were Republicans. The Muslims believed that Congress policy was authoritarian and rendered provincial autonomy quite illusory.

There were other aspects of the Congress governments in the provinces that irritated and alarmed the Muslims. When the new provincial governments came in, the Congress tricolor was raised over the public buildings, and when the legislatures convened they were opened by the singing of the Hindu nationalist song, *Bande Mataram*. Further, it was claimed that in appointments to public offices members of Congress obtained nearly all of the positions and that in the realm of education Congress governments were determined to make Hindi the legal language of the educated at the expense of other languages such as the Muslim Urdu. Finally, Congress initiated a mass movement to wean Muslims away from their organizations and into the party of Nehru and Gandhi. As it turned out, these Congress policies were very ill-advised, but

[42] Quoted in Durrani, *op. cit.*, p. 128.
[43] Nehru, *The Unity of India*, p. 429.

at the time it was natural that the party should assume it was the only political group that really mattered. As yet the Muslims were divided, there being no single, all-inclusive organization to represent their interests. As late as 1937 the Muslim League was not well organized or supported. Its finances were inadequate, and only one English daily espoused the League cause in India.

Division and weakness in Muslim ranks were more apparent than real, however, for in two short years they were superseded by a new strength and unity that violently challenged Congress policies. While there was a strong foundation, as we shall see shortly, upon which to build a dynamic Muslim nationalism, the one single person responsible for the transformation was Mohammed Ali Jinnah. Up to 1937 Jinnah was not especially popular in Muslim circles. He still bore the stigma of being too friendly to Congress, of not being quite fully dedicated to the cause of Islam. In less than a year, however, Jinnah began to forge to the front as the *Quaid-i-Azam*, the Leader, of the united Muslim community. A master of invective, he lashed out in a number of speeches against Congress. His main thesis he expressed as follows: "Since the inauguration of the new provincial constitutions, it has been established beyond doubt that the sole aim and object of the Congress is to annihilate every other organisation in the country, and to set itself up as a fascist and authoritarian organisation of the worst type." [44]

Jinnah's leadership soon produced results; all over India there was an upsurge of Muslim League strength. Between 1937 and 1943, sixty-one elections were held for Muslim seats in the legislatures, and of these the League won forty-seven, independent Muslim candidates ten, and the Muslims sponsored by Congress only four. As 1937 drew to a close, 170 new branches of the League were established and in one province alone 100,000 new members were recruited. At a League Conference held in October 1937, Jinnah declared that Muslims could not expect fair play under Congress government.

Meanwhile, Nehru and his colleagues were becoming genuinely concerned over the League revival and what they regarded as the intransigence of its tone. In consequence the Congress Working Committee passed a resolution assuring all minorities that their rights would be scrupulously respected. And in the spring of 1938 Jinnah and Nehru exchanged correspondence in which the former demanded that the League be recognized as the sole organization representing the Indian

[44] *Some Recent Speeches . . . of Mr. Jinnah*, collected and edited by Jamil-ud-Din Ahmad (Lahore: Sh. Muhammad Ashraf, 1943), p. 86.

Muslim community. There was no agreement, however, and in December 1938, at the annual meeting of the League, Jinnah declared that all hope of communal peace had been wrecked "on the rocks of Congress Fascism." [45]

In order to strengthen its case the League published several reports enumerating and describing various grievances and even atrocities suffered by Muslims in the Congress-ruled provinces. These documents (the Pirpur Report and the Shareef Report) undoubtedly contained charges that were greatly exaggerated. There was really no Congress plot against Muslim rights as such, but the seven provincial governments controlled by Congress continually neglected to appreciate the sensitivities and fears of a cultural minority. And in many instances irresponsible persons who thought of themselves as the agents of Congress aroused the fears of Muslims. That there was a genuine anxiety as to the future of their distinctive culture is witnessed by the report of the Kamal Yar Jung Education Committee, drafted by a group of outstanding Muslim educators. This report lamented the low percentage of Muslim students in colleges and universities; underlined the lack of attention paid in university research to Muslim studies; and drew attention to the decline of separate Muslim schools on the elementary level. The upshot, according to the report, was that the Muslim "hardly has any opportunity to know anything about his Prophet, the Caliphs, the saints, the scholars, the philosophers, the poets or the heroes of Islam." [46]

It was in this atmosphere of mounting Muslim fear and resentment that a fundamental change took place in the policy of the League. Originally this organization had supported the new Government of India Act of 1935, but by the end of 1938 Jinnah was declaring that no democratic system of government by merely counting heads could work in India, and that the new act had failed to protect the legitimate interests of the Muslim minority. The Muslims were now beginning to think of Indian independence in terms of self-determination for their own community.

In December 1938, at the Patna meeting of the Muslim League, a special committee, headed by Jinnah, was created "to examine various schemes already propounded and those that may be submitted to the President." A movement had now begun the goal of which was to obtain some kind of territorial autonomy for Muslims. This was ultimately to result in a separate state for the followers of Mohammed, in the partition of India and the creation of Pakistan.

[45] Sir Reginald Coupland, *The Indian Problem* (London: Oxford University Press, 1944), Part II, p. 184.
[46] *Ibid.*, p. 192.

As one looks back on the all-important developments in Indian affairs from 1937 to 1939, when the Muslim-Hindu gulf was irreparably widened, it is valuable to reflect upon the fundamental factors that made this tragic situation possible. There are many observers who emphasize economics as the basic cause of Hindu-Muslim rivalry. Nehru once said that all communal claims go back to the contest for jobs, and to a large extent he was right. Generally speaking, the Muslims were "have-nots" in comparison with the Hindus, who had the lead in education, the professions, the government service, and finance. The Muslim in the village was usually the debtor, the Hindu the moneylender.

Economic rivalries, while important, were distinctly secondary to the fact that Muslim and Hindu cultures in many ways constituted two distinct, and frequently antagonistic, ways of life. This dichotomy was strikingly expressed by Jinnah in an interview with a French author and journalist, Eve Curie, in the following words:

> How can you even dream of Hindu-Moslem unity? Everything pulls us apart: We have no intermarriages. We have not the same calendar. The Moslems believe in a single God, and the Hindus are idolatrous. Like the Christians, the Moslems believe in an equalitarian society, whereas the Hindus maintain the iniquitous system of castes and leave heartlessly fifty million Untouchables to their tragic fate, at the bottom of the social ladder. Now again, the Hindus worship animals. They consider cows sacred. We, the Moslems, think it is nonsense. We want to kill the cows. We want to eat them. Another thing: no Hindu will take food from a Moslem. No orthodox Hindu will even touch *Hindu* food if the shadow of a Moslem or the shadow of a Hindu of a lower caste has polluted the bowl.[47]

What Hindu leaders in Congress apparently failed to understand was the strength of Muslim revivalism. Hindu publicists claimed that a religious group, such as the Muslims, did not constitute a political entity and that there was really no such thing as a distinctive Muslim culture in India. It was true, nevertheless, that beginning late in the nineteenth century there had been the rediscovery of the greatness of the Muslim period, especially that of the Moguls, in Indian history. And following the First World War there had developed a feeling of self-identification, of participation in a pan-Islamic movement with the renascent Muslim states—such as Turkey, Egypt, Iraq, and Iran—which were assuming new dignity and influence in the family of nations. The importance of these developments can hardly be exaggerated.

[47] Eve Curie, *Journey among Warriors* (New York: Doubleday, Doran, 1943), p. 463.

7. War, Independence, and Partition

As THE SHADOWS OF WAR began to lengthen in the spring of 1939, the National Congress warned that it would not fight in other people's wars and that, in its view, the present world tension was nothing more than a struggle between Fascism and imperialism. As early as 1936, the Congress in an election manifesto had declared its implacable "opposition to the participation of India in an imperialist war."[1] During 1938, in the heyday of the Chamberlain appeasement, Congress leaders, and Nehru in particular, excoriated British foreign policy as a betrayal of democracy. In April 1939, Great Britain began to undertake precautionary military measures. Indian troops were sent to reinforce the garrison at Aden, and the British Parliament passed a bill giving the governor-general and the central government in India complete power over the provincial administrations in case of a grave emergency. Replying to these British measures, the Congress charged that a war dictatorship was in the making and Nehru again warned that "it was for the people of India to determine whether India would join a war or not, and any decision imposed on us by Britain would be resisted."[2] In the summer of 1939 additional Indian troops were sent to Singapore and Egypt, and Congress countered by ordering its members not to attend the central legislature.

On September 3 Great Britain declared war against the German Reich, and on the same day the viceroy, Lord Linlithgow, proclaimed India to be at war with Germany. In the central legislature the viceroy addressed the members, ex-

[1] Jawaharlal Nehru, *The Unity of India: Collected Writings 1937-1940* (London: Lindsay Drummond, 1941), p. 401.

[2] Quoted in Raleigh Parkin, *India Today* (New York: John Day Co., 1946), p. 199.

India about 1940

plaining the situation, and a Defence of India Bill was introduced and passed with no opposition. To be sure, Congress members were absent and thus were not able to express their opposition. While they and their colleagues bitterly protested against India's being dragged into the war, it should be noted that the provincial premiers of Bengal, Punjab, and Sind, representing 90 million people, pledged their support of the war effort. Furthermore, all political parties other than Congress took the same stand. The Liberals declared that this was no time for bargaining and that India should support the democratic powers. In the princely states the princes promised "every possible assistance in men, money, and materials." [3] The Muslim League, interestingly enough, made its promise of support contingent upon Britain's guaranteeing the Muslims "justice and fair treatment in the Congress provinces" and promising not to make any constitutional changes in India without the consent of the League.

Two days after India became involved in the war, the vice-

[3] Sir Reginald Coupland, *The Indian Problem* (London: Oxford University Press, 1944), Part II, p. 213.

roy called Gandhi for a conference. After the meeting, the Mahatma announced in his newspaper *Harijan* that he had told Linlithgow he could not, as a pacifist, support the war, but his sympathies were with England and France "from the purely humanitarian viewpoint." Midway in September the Working Committee of the National Congress, led by Nehru, drafted a statement in which it was stressed that the "declared wishes of the Indian people . . . have been deliberately ignored by the British Government," and while the committee "unhesitatingly condemn the latest aggression of the Nazi government in Germany against Poland . . . the issue of war and peace for India must be decided by the Indian people." [4] The statement went on to denounce Britain for its past record of conniving at aggression in Manchuria and its acquiescence in Italian conquest in Abyssinia. Furthermore, the committee let it be known that, if this war was really being fought against aggression and for democracy, India would fight with other free nations, but she must be free herself. And, it was averred, this freedom should be achieved by the Indian people's drafting their own constitution in a constituent assembly. The document closed by requesting Great Britain to declare in unequivocal terms its war aims "in regard to democracy and imperialism."

Meanwhile, the viceroy had been interviewing all the important Indian leaders, some fifty in number, with the view of rallying public opinion to the side of Great Britain. On October 17 the viceroy made an offer to the Indian people. His statement reiterated British aims of ultimate dominion status for India; recognized that after the war the system of government laid down by the Government of India Act of 1935 would have to be reconsidered; and stated that the British government would be ready "to enter into consultation with representatives of the several communities" in order to frame a new scheme of government. It was made clear that the rights of minority groups, such as the Muslims, would be safeguarded in any new constitution. While the viceroy offered at once to form a consultative group, made up of representatives of all parties, to associate public opinion with the conduct of the war, he curtly replied to the Congress demand for immediate self-government:

> The situation must be faced in terms of world politics and of political realities in this country . . . progress must be conditioned by practical considerations . . . there is nothing to be gained by phrases which . . . contemplate a state of things which is unlikely at the present point of political development to stand the test of practical application. . . . [5]

[4] Quoted in Jawaharlal Nehru, *Toward Freedom* (New York: John Day Co., 1941), p. 432.
[5] Quoted in Parkin, *op. cit.*, p. 204.

Early in November the viceroy's offer was further extended to include the temporary expansion of his executive council and thus to associate Indians more closely in the management of the war effort.

The Congress reaction was completely hostile. Gandhi let it be known that in his opinion the government might just as well have made no declaration, while the Working Committee condemned the declaration outright and called upon its Congress ministries in the provinces to resign. Consequently, on November 8 the eight Congress governments gave up their authority. In response Jinnah called upon Indian Muslims to celebrate December 22 as "Deliverance Day" from Congress rule.

From that time to the end of the war the most powerful nationalist political organization in India refused to take office and boycotted the war effort. It was a complete stalemate and one that weakened the ability of the British Empire to stand up against the might of Hitlerite Germany. Opponents of Axis totalitarianism, not only in Britain and France, but all over the world, were deeply disappointed that the parties to the controversy, the British government and the Congress, had been unable to accommodate their different views. The Congress leaders continued to declare that the only solution was a constituent assembly called to draft a constitution for an independent India and that the mention by the British of minority interests in the October Declaration made by the viceroy was completely irrelevant. Jinnah, the Muslim League leader, referred to the constituent assembly demanded by Congress as "a packed body, manoeuvred and managed by a Congress caucus." [6]

For the first nine months most people in India gave little thought to the conflict. During this period of the "phony war" India breathed easily behind the guard and shield of British sea power. As in 1914 the Indian army, consisting of some 160,000 Indian and 50,000 British troops, constituted a valuable pool of trained and seasoned soldiers. In the first months of the war some 60,000 were sent overseas, to Malaya, Aden, and the Army of the Middle East. No one as yet had any notion of the terrible crisis that lay ahead for British arms, from both the German and Japanese armies. The program of recruiting in India, therefore, was taken quite casually during the early stages of the war. Recruits were taken in at the rate of from ten to fifteen thousand per month, and by May 1940 some 53,000 men had been recruited for the Indian army.

In the months following the outbreak of the Second World

[6] *The News Chronicle* (London), December 11, 1939.

War, the Muslim League under the leadership of Mohammed Ali Jinnah became more aggressive, more the single representative of Muslim public opinion, and more determined to challenge the claims of the National Congress to speak for all elements and creeds in India. In particular, as a Muslim author has said, it was at this time that "Mohammed Ali Jinnah became the living symbol of Muslim Unity." [7] It will be recalled that, following the controversy between the League and Congress over the Nehru Report in 1928, the Muslim League under the leadership of Jinnah had formulated the famous Fourteen Points (see p. 185). They were irreducible safeguards demanded by the Muslim League in any new constitution and for a decade formed the political platform around which the Muslims increasingly rallied. But just before the outbreak of war and immediately afterward, a more radical and ambitious program began to crystallize, the plan for Pakistan.

In the spring of 1939 a special committee headed by Jinnah was set up by the Muslim League to examine various schemes that had already been advanced to insure the rights of the Muslim minority in India. One of the first of these had been tentatively sketched by the great Muslim poet, Sir Muhammad Iqbal, in his presidential address before the League in 1930. He advocated a single Muslim state in northwest India, a state to be endowed with extensive autonomy but forming one of the constituent elements of a greater all-India federation. The next development was much more ambitious. In 1933 a group of young Indian Muslims, led by Chaudhuri Rahmat Ali at Cambridge University in England, circulated a four-page leaflet calling for the creation of a new state in India, to be called Pakistan. The authors declared that "India is not the name of one single country, nor the home of one single nation," and called for the establishment of a Muslim national state in northwest India. To form the name of this new state, *P* was taken from Punjab; *A* from Afghan, a term representing the North-West Frontier Province; *K* from Kashmir; *S* from Sind; and *Tan* from the last syllable of Baluchistan.

Several alternatives to Pakistan were subsequently brought forward. For example, Dr. Syed Abdul Latif in 1938-1939 advanced in various publications his Culture Zone Plan. He argued that India was not a single nation, that the crude imposition of "Hindu nationalism" upon the subcontinent would inevitably result in war, but that the solution was not to be found in Pakistan, or partition. A free India should consist of a number of autonomous nationalities, each in its ge-

[7] Matlubul Hasan, *M. A. Jinnah: A Political Study* (Lahore: Sh. Muhammad Ashraf, no date), p. 679.

ographical home, and each forming part of a loose federal government. There were to be four Muslim and eleven Hindu zones, and the princely states were gradually to attach themselves to appropriate zones. Other similar plans were formulated, all endeavoring to recognize the cultural distinctiveness of the Muslims and to give them a wide area of complete political autonomy and yet, at the same time, to dovetail the Muslim zones or states into some kind of larger Indian federation. Thus the unity of India would be preserved.

The response of the National Congress was not sympathetic —in fact it was derisive. This body refused to admit the existence of a distinct Muslim nation and held to the program of calling a national constitutional assembly that would frame a constitution for all India. In the face of this attitude, and particularly during the period of the Congress ministries from 1937 to 1939, the policy of the Muslim League hardened. In September 1939, the Working Committee of the League stated that Muslim India was "irrevocably opposed to any federal objective which must necessarily result in a majority-community rule under the guise of democracy and a parliamentary system of government." [8] In the spring of 1940 Jinnah told the press that the Muslims were not a minority but a distinct nation. Jinnah asserted:

> We are a nation of a hundred million, and what is more we are a nation with our own distinctive culture and civilization, language and literature, art and architecture, . . . customs and calendar, history and tradition, aptitudes and ambitions. In short we have our own distinctive outlook on life and of life.[9]

It was in a mood of expectancy and excitement that the Muslim League met at Lahore in March 1940 to hear Mr. Jinnah declare in his presidential address that Muslims "must have their homelands, their territory and their State." [10] The following day a historic resolution was passed calling for the creation of autonomous and sovereign Muslim states in areas "in which the Muslims are numerically in the majority, as in the north-western and eastern zones of India." [11] Although this declaration was couched in vague terms, it seemed that the League did not view the new Muslim states as belonging to any larger political grouping, such as a federation. Partition could not be reconciled with the political unity of India.

[8] *The Indian Annual Register,* 1939 (Calcutta: The Annual Register Office, no date), II, p. 351.
[9] Quoted in Sir Frederick Puckle, "The Pakistan Doctrine: Its Origins and Power," *Foreign Affairs,* XXIV (April 1946), p. 535.
[10] A. C. Banerjee, ed., *Indian Constitutional Documents* (Calcutta: A. Mukherjee and Co., 1946), II, p. 408.
[11] *Ibid.,* p. 409.

Not long after these deliberations at Lahore the full fury of the Nazi blitzkrieg was unleashed in western Europe. Norway and Denmark were overrun in April 1940, Belgium and Holland in May. France surrendered to Hitler on June 22. As the news of the French debacle reached India, there came with it a recognition of the serious state of Great Britain, and the Congress attitude softened somewhat. On July 27, 1940, the All-India Congress Committee repudiated the Gandhian policy of non-violence and with it the policy of boycotting the war effort. This was a victory for the moderate and realistic elements in the Congress, which was now prepared to support the war at a price. Britain was asked to make a declaration of India's independence, and, as an initial step, to create a provisional national government. In the face of this Congress gesture Jinnah, backed up by the Muslim League, declared that no new constitution during the war period or after should be set up without the approval of Muslim India.

In the midst of the war crisis and the imminent prospect of German invasion of the British Isles, Gandhi persisted in his pacifism and praised Pétain's armistice and France's surrender to Germany. He declared that India could only be defended "non-violently," and called upon every Briton "to accept the method of non-violence." Specifically, Gandhi wrote in his newspaper:

> I do not want Britain to be defeated, nor do I want her to be victorious in a trial of brute strength, whether expressed through the muscle or the brain. I venture to present you with a nobler and a braver way, worthy of the bravest soldier. I want you to fight Nazism without arms. . . . You will invite Herr Hitler and Signor Mussolini to take what they want of the countries you call your possessions. Let them take possession of your beautiful island. . . . If these gentlemen choose to occupy your homes, you will vacate them. If they do not give you free passage out, you will allow yourself, man, woman and child, to be slaughtered, but you will refuse to owe allegiance to them.[12]

Just before the Battle of Britain began, with the German *Luftwaffe* striving mightily to gain control of the air over England and pave the way for a cross-Channel invasion, the British government, seeking to end the political deadlock in India, made its significant August 1940 offer. In a statement issued from New Delhi the viceroy recalled that the previous October the British government had made it quite clear that dominion status was its objective in India and that this goal meant "free and equal partnership in the British Com-

[12] T. A. Raman, *What Does Gandhi Want?* (New York: Oxford University Press, 1945), pp. 24-25.

monwealth." In order to allay and mollify the fears of the Muslim League, the announcement declared that "full weight should be given to the views of the minorities." And, while ruling out the possibility of fundamental constitutional changes during the war, the viceroy announced: "His Majesty's Government authorize me to declare that they will most readily assent to the setting up after the conclusion of the war . . . of a body representative of the principal elements in India's national life in order to devise the framework of the new constitution." [13] The viceroy also stated that the expansion of his executive council by the addition of representatives of various Indian political parties should not be postponed and that the war advisory council suggested by the government in November 1939 should also be constituted without delay.

This "August Offer" utterly failed to eliminate the political deadlock, and President Rajendra Prasad of Congress announced it was "totally at variance" with his party's policy. Other Congress officials declared that the minority problem referred to in the declaration was being made into an insuperable obstacle to Indian progress. Feeling rebuffed, and unable to secure an independent Indian provisional government as a condition to its full support of the British war effort, the National Congress turned back again to Gandhi and gave him its backing in a campaign of non-violent civil disobedience, to be waged as a protest against the war. The movement got under way in October 1940, and members of Congress were selected to give anti-war speeches, including the slogan: "It is wrong to help the British war effort with men or money: the only worthy effort is to resist all war with non-violent resistance." [14] In all parts of India the police arrested members of the Congress as they delivered anti-war speeches, and at one time more than fourteen thousand were in prison.

The reaction to this Gandhian civil disobedience campaign among the Indians themselves served to demonstrate how confused and divided were the various groups on basic issues such as the war. Jinnah and his League denounced the Congress anti-war campaign, not so much because it might hinder the war effort as because in their view it was a kind of political blackmail for putting pressure on the British government to insure the realization of Congress objectives. The small but brilliantly led Liberal party deplored any action that might weaken the resistance of the British Empire against Germany. The famous Muslim prime minister of Punjab Province, Sir

---

[13] *Indian Annual Register, 1940,* II, pp. 372-373.
[14] Sir Reginald Coupland, *India: A Restatement* (London: Oxford University Press, 1942), p. 205.

Sikander Hyat Khan, said that Gandhi's campaign meant "that while Britain is engaged in a life-and-death struggle, he should be given the freedom to stab her in the back. That the stabbing is to be non-violent makes no difference." [15]

During the summer of 1941, the viceroy proceeded to carry through the expansion of his executive council and the creation of a special war advisory council. Five distinguished Indians were added to the executive council, making a total of eight Indian and five British members. A new national war council of thirty-one members was set up, twenty-two from the provinces of British India and nine from the princely states; and in this membership only one was a European. In addition to these gestures, the British secretary of state for India in London, Mr. L. S. Amery, made a number of important speeches endeavoring to convince Indians of Britain's good faith as far as their country's right to self-government was concerned. Mr. Amery specifically promised India after the war "full and equal partnership in the British Commonwealth." The secretary also argued that the main obstacle to a free India was communal rivalry, which could only be eliminated by the Indians themselves. While endeavoring to point out to Indians the seriousness of the Hindu-Muslim problem, Amery at the same time indicated that partition as advocated by Jinnah's League was no solution. Referring to the doctrine of Pakistan, he declared, "It is a counsel of despair and, I believe, of wholly unnecessary despair." [16] The Secretary's emphasis upon the communal problem touched off angry retorts in Congress ranks. Gandhi replied, "It is the British statesmen who are responsible for the divisions in India's ranks." [17]

Despite the general atmosphere of political frustration and suspicion which was widespread in India in 1941 and which, of course, was strongest in Congress ranks, the country since the war crisis of Dunkirk in the spring of 1940 had continued to make tremendous strides in the war effort. Following the defeat of France and the entrance of Italy into the war, the Mediterranean was closed to British shipping for all practical purposes. As British industries were working night and day for home defense needs, industrial production had to be stimulated east of Suez, so that the part of the Near East and North Africa held by Britain, together with other parts of the Empire ringed around the Indian Ocean, could be made as self-sufficient as possible. In the fall of 1940 a mission under Sir Alexander Roger came to India and remained there

[15] Quoted in *ibid.*, p. 206.

[16] L. S. Amery, *India and Freedom* (London: Oxford University Press, 1942), p. 87.

[17] *Indian Annual Register, 1941*, I, p. 327.

for six months to mobilize the country's economic resources for the war. While this mission was in India, the Eastern Group Conference met at Delhi in October 1940. Delegations arrived from New Zealand, South Africa, Burma, Ceylon, Southern Rhodesia, East Africa, Hongkong, Malaya, and Palestine. As a result, the Eastern Group Supply Council was established in February 1941, to coordinate supply and plan production in the vast area represented by these countries with a total population of nearly 500 million.

By the end of 1941 war production in India had made considerable progress. Pig-iron production increased from 1,600,000 to 2,000,000 tons and finished-steel production grew from 867,000 to 1,250,000 tons, while armor plate began to be produced for the first time in India. Government ordnance factories were expanded to produce field guns, machine guns, bombs, depth charges, and other weapons; and 600,000 shells and 150,000,000 rounds of small-arms ammunition were sent overseas. In trying to put its war effort in high gear India was badly handicapped by the lack of trained men, the scarcity of machine tools, and the lack of electric power. A plan was put into effect to meet the manpower shortage by training 10,000 specialists in technical schools and factories.

In the actual field of combat and military effort a new program of recruitment was initiated in June 1940; a call went out for 100,000 men to volunteer for the fighting forces, with an ultimate aim of an army of 500,000 men. Up to this time the process of "Indianization" of the officer ranks had been slow and halting; but now measures for training thousands of Indian officers were formulated.

While the British Isles fought off the efforts of the *Luftwaffe* to force surrender, the main peril to the British Empire in the fall of 1940 was in North and East Africa, where well-equipped Italian Fascist armies threatened to overwhelm Egypt, the Sudan, Uganda, and Kenya. In brilliant campaigns directed by General Sir Archibald Wavell, outnumbered British divisions scored a complete victory over the Italian army in North Africa. Taking the offensive in East Africa against Mussolini's empire, British troops in the spring of 1941 freed British Somaliland and captured Eritrea, Abyssinia, and Italian Somaliland. In all these actions Indian troops, especially the famous Fourth and Fifth Divisions, played a prominent part.

Cripps and Crisis

During the summer and early fall of 1941 the British Empire's prospect appeared much brighter than the year before. The Axis threat to the homeland had been thwarted;

the imperial communications in North Africa had been successfully defended against Fascist attack; and, most important, Britain was no longer fighting alone with her Empire. Russia, erstwhile ally of Nazi Germany, was now feeling the full might of Hitler's Panzer divisions. And from across the Atlantic there was now coming—both to Britain and to Russia—a vast cargo of American lend-lease material. The auguries seemed favorable.

During the last month of 1941, however, the entire prospect changed. The rapid conquests of Japan reversed for a time the balance of power in the Pacific; threatened to take over the vast British, French, Dutch, and American possessions in Southeast Asia; and even extended their menace toward Australia and New Zealand. On December 7 the Japanese attacked Pearl Harbor, Manila, Hongkong, and Malaya. The following day the United States and Great Britain declared war on Japan, and British troops, together with Indian forces, had their first engagement against Japanese forces landing on the coast of northern Malaya. A catastrophic blow was dealt to the successful defense of Malaya and its great naval base, Singapore, when the British battleships *Prince of Wales* and *Repulse* were sunk by hostile aircraft while endeavoring to intercept Japanese troop transports. Outnumbered and outmaneuvered by troops who had been specially trained for jungle warfare, the British forces were pushed down the Malayan peninsula and then cooped up on the island of Singapore. The end came in the middle of February 1942, with the surrender of the hapless British army defending this great and supposedly impregnable naval base. The tide of the Japanese conquest now lapped over into Burma.

The Japanese crossed the southeastern frontier of Burma from Siam with an excellent army of 60,000 men; against it could be pitted only some 20,000 Indian and 7,000 British troops and in north Burma several divisions of Chinese troops under General Joseph Stilwell. The Allied forces lacked air power, transport, radios, and anti-aircraft guns. On December 23, 1941, Rangoon had been bombed and upwards of 100,000 people fled from the city. Burma is surrounded by a horseshoe of mountains with her roads and railways following the narrow valleys, which run north and south. By March 10 the Japanese controlled Rangoon, through which they could funnel reinforcements to the north, where they soon pinned the Allied forces against the mountains. Only 12,000 Indo-British troops were able to escape by crossing the mountains and getting back to India. General Stilwell led the remnants of his Chinese forces through 140 miles of jungle into India.

By May 1942 all of Burma was in Japanese hands. Valuable

oil fields had had to be destroyed, and the Burma Road to China had been cut. The significance of the victory of Japan was that Burma could now be used as a shield along the west to protect the vast new Nipponese empire to Southeast Asia. Burma was also a wedge, for its conquest had isolated China and made it less defensible against Japanese aggression. Most important, Burma could be a springboard for the Japanese conquest of India and resulting Japanese union with German forces in Iran, for in the spring of 1942 General Rommel with his *Afrika Korps* was poised in the Libyan desert ready to strike for the Nile and the Near East.

In a few weeks the war status of India had been changed from that of a rather complacent and somewhat unwilling ally of Britain, remote from the enemy, to one that was on the front line directly in the path of the rapidly approaching enemy, Japan. There was great astonishment in India over the Japanese victories in the Philippines, the East Indies, and Malaya; there was also growing fear, and some people began to flee from Calcutta as they realized that the Japanese were now in control of the waters of the Bay of Bengal. All the while Japan carried on a barrage of radio propaganda, stressing its cultural ties with India, and stating that it was coming as a deliverer to oust the British imperialists.

Within Congress there was some jockeying and maneuvering between various factions as a realization of India's danger became evident. As in the spring of 1940, after Dunkirk, there was another repudiation of Gandhi's pacifism. By this time the civil disobedience campaign had worn itself out. In fact, the government had released all imprisoned members of Congress, including such leaders as Nehru and Azad, just before Pearl Harbor. Having decided to support the war against Japan, however, Congress divided into those who were willing to do so on the basis of reasonable British concessions and those, led by Nehru, who would accept only complete independence. Among the former was the prime minister of Madras, Chakravarti Rajagopalacharia (usually—and understandably—referred to in India simply as "C.R."), who was an outstanding member of Congress and a statesman of exceptional talents. "C.R." toured his province rousing his people to be ready to fight invasion. While urging the British to make some constitutional concessions, such as the grant of some kind of national government, he also called for Hindu-Muslim reconciliation and recognized that the League was one of the two dominant political bodies in India. "C.R." was aided by another Congressman, K. M. Munshi, who, in January 1942, appealed for political unity, declaring, "The dangers of the hour must awaken the wisdom of all communities and interests and ought to make us realize that we should not allow future ambitions to frustrate a program of present safety." [18]

As we will see, the appeals of men like "C.R." had little influence upon Congress policy, and the League seemed oblivious to the menace just beyond the borders of India. On the day Singapore fell the most important organ of the League, *The Dawn,* published the following statement:

> Pakistan is our deliverance, defense, destiny. . . . No amount of threats or intimidation will ever deter us from the chosen path. Hints about a "long period of civil war" we will brush aside with contempt. . . . Pakistan is our only demand . . . and, by God, we will have it. [19]

Tension mounted rapidly in India. Early in January 1942 the leaders of the moderate Liberal party, always ready to lead the way to reconciliation, cabled Winston Churchill urging him to recognize India's national status and to form a new national government that would hold itself morally responsible to the country. In effect the latter proposal would mean an all-Indian executive council at New Delhi.

The month of February was a time of rumor and anxiety in India. In the British Parliament it was evident there was strong feeling that something should be done, and at once, to rally India to the cause of the Empire and the United Nations. On March 10 the leader of the House of Commons, Sir Stafford Cripps, announced that the prime minister would make a declaration on India at the next sitting of Commons. At the same time the viceroy at Delhi issued a message to all the Indian people, regardless of their politics or religion, saying: "You will be invited during the next few weeks to enroll yourselves in the national war front. The land we live in is threatened with danger. . . . I confide in your courage." [20]

On March 11, 1942, Churchill made his statement on India, announcing that Sir Stafford Cripps, Lord Privy Seal and leader of the House of Commons, was to go to India immediately. The prime minister explained that the crisis in India demanded that all must be done to guard this land from invasion.

The appointment of Cripps for this difficult mission was a happy and a logical choice. Reputed to have one of the most brilliant minds in Parliament, Sir Stafford was a prominent English Socialist who had long championed the cause of India's freedom. In December 1939 he had visited India and discussed its problems with many of its leaders; in the spring

[18] *Indian Annual Register, 1942,* I, p. 40.
[19] Coupland, *The Indian Problem,* II, p. 267.
[20] *Indian Annual Register, 1942,* I, p. 55.

of 1940 he went to Moscow as British ambassador, and in February 1942 he was made a member of the British war cabinet. There could be no doubt that the British government was sending to New Delhi a man who was an ardent sympathizer with Indian aspirations.

Sir Stafford Cripps arrived by air at Delhi on March 22 and immediately called a press conference, where in an informal and friendly fashion he explained the purpose of his mission. During the next three days Sir Stafford met various British officials and showed them the draft declaration he had brought to India, containing the proposals which had been approved by the British war cabinet. Then he began a series of discussions with the leaders of the various Indian parties. The League was represented by Mr. Jinnah, the Congress by Nehru and Azad, and the Indian rulers also sent their representatives. During these interviews Sir Stafford showed the Indian leaders the draft declaration, but for the time being they were pledged to secrecy.

Finally, on March 29 Cripps held a large press conference attended by some two hundred journalists. At this historic meeting copies of the draft declaration were distributed for publication. This declaration admitted there were anxieties in India as to the fulfillment of past British promises. It had been decided, therefore, that the steps by which self-government was to be realized should now be laid down in the most precise and clear terms. The aim was the creation of a new Indian Union, "which shall constitute a Dominion, associated with the United Kingdom and the other Dominions by a common allegiance to the Crown, but equal to them in every respect, in no way subordinate in any aspect of its domestic or external affairs." [21]

The new constitution would be drafted by an Indian body in which the princely states were to be represented, following the conclusion of hostilities. A basic feature of the draft declaration was provision for any province of British India to remain out of the proposed Indian Union with the right of formulating its own independent government. This right of "non-accession" was specifically aimed at mollifying Muslim League separatism. The declaration also stated that there should be a treaty negotiated between Britain and the Indian constitution-making body respecting the protection of religious and racial minorities. This treaty, however, would in no way restrict the power of the Indian Union "to decide in the future its relationship to the other Member States of the British Commonwealth." [22]

[21] *Statement and Draft Declaration by H. M. Government,* Cmd. 6350 (London: His Majesty's Stationery Office, 1942), p. 4.
[22] *Ibid.,* p. 5.

The British proposal ruled out any major alteration in India's constitutional position during the war, specifically stating that during the critical period of the conflict the British government must "inevitably bear the responsibility for and retain control and direction of the defence of India." [23] While Britain must be the ultimate authority in India, every effort would be made to associate its people in the counsels of their country and in the war effort. The journalists at Cripps' press conference were given the opportunity to quiz Sir Stafford on every phase of the war cabinet's proposals. In his answers it was made unequivocally plain that, following the establishment of the new Indian Union, India could secede from the Commonwealth; that no British troops would be left in the country except upon request; that all British authority would be removed immediately upon the framing of the constitution; and that there would be no insistence upon special safeguards for British investments or trade in India.

Outside of India, particularly in Great Britain and the United States, the draft declaration was welcomed as a "fair and practicable compromise." [24] Inside India, however, Sir Stafford found the waters of Indian politics more stormy than he had anticipated. From March 29 to April 9 he held numerous conversations with representatives of the Muslim League, Congress, the Sikhs, the Depressed Classes, Anglo-Indians, and the Indian states. By the latter date it seemed as if agreement could be reached, but on the following day, April 10, the Congress leaders rejected the draft declaration and demanded that a free national government should be set up with full power immediately. This would have amounted to a fundamental alteration of the Indian constitution before the end of the war, an event that had been specifically denied by the draft declaration. In order to meet the demand of Congress at least halfway, however, Sir Stafford Cripps did offer to establish a new executive council in which all members should be Indians, except the viceroy and the commander-in-chief. Further, this council should proceed to appoint a member to the British war cabinet and to the Pacific war council. Under this new arrangement practically all the day-to-day details and administration of government would have been in Indian hands. Only in the actual military phases of the war would the British commander-in-chief have had complete authority, and in theory the viceroy, if an emergency should arise, could have overridden the decisions of the council.

On April 11 the Congress by formal resolution turned down the Cripps proposals because they failed to give India full

---

[23] *Ibid.*

[24] Margaret LaFoy, "India's Role in the World Conflict," *Foreign Policy Reports*, XVIII (May 1, 1942), p. 42.

independence immediately, because they contained "the novel principle of . . . non-accession for a Province [which] is a severe blow to the conception of Indian unity," [25] and because defense was not sufficiently turned over to Indian control.

Once Congress had turned down the proposals, other political groups followed suit. The League argued that the terms of non-accession were too indefinite and went on to say:

> So far as the Muslim League is concerned, it has finally decided that the only solution of India's constitutional problem is the partition of India into independent zones: and it will therefore be unfair to the Muslims to compel them to enter such a constitution-making body whose main object is the creation of a new Indian Union. [26]

The Mahasabha party, on the other hand, representing Hindu fundamentalism, argued that its basic principle was that India was one and indivisible. The reaction of the Untouchables was expressed by Dr. Ambedkhar in a letter to Cripps: "We are all of us absolutely convinced that the proposals are calculated to do the greatest harm to the Depressed Classes and are sure to place them under an unmitigated system of Hindu rule." [27] As to the Sikhs of the Punjab, these redoubtable warriors saw the possibility of their homeland, in which the Muslims were in a majority, being cut off from the Indian Union. In their memorandum to Sir Stafford Cripps, therefore, the Sikhs declared: "We shall resist by all possible means separation of the Punjab from the All-India Union. We shall never permit our Motherland to be at the mercy of those who disown it [i.e., the Muslim majority]." [28] The sole exception to this wholesale repudiation of the draft declaration was the Liberal party, which gave it a qualified approval.

On April 11 Sir Stafford Cripps made a farewell broadcast to the people of India and expressed, without any rancor, his extreme disappointment that no agreement had been reached between the British government on the one hand and the various Indian parties on the other. He explained that the real and decisive cause of the breakdown had been the Congress demand for a new national government untrammeled by any control by the viceroy or the British government. Sir Stafford pointed out that "it is easy to understand that great minorities in India would never accept such a suggestion." [29]

[25] "The Cripps Mission to India," *International Conciliation*, Vol. 381 (New York: Carnegie Endowment for International Peace, June 1942), p. 340.

[26] Quoted in *ibid.*, p. 342.

[27] *Ibid.*, p. 347.

[28] *Ibid.*, p. 352.

[29] *Ibid.*, p. 334.

Having turned down the proposals brought to India by Cripps, Congress gave up all thought of actively engaging in the war effort and again turned to Gandhi and his policy of non-violence and civil disobedience. Following the departure of Sir Stafford, Gandhi gradually came to the view that Japan was going to win and would invade India; that British and American troops were an ineffectual shield; that as such they were only a bait inviting Japanese aggression; and that the Allied forces should get out of India. Then, reasoned Gandhi, an independent India, unimpaired by any connection with the Allies, could come to terms with Japan. If Japan should invade India after the departure of the Allied forces, then Gandhi proposed that non-violence be used as a defense. All would be well after the exit of the alien imperialists, the British. Gandhi said, "Leave India in God's hands, or in modern parlance, to anarchy. Then all parties will fight one another like dogs or will, when real responsibility faces them, come to a reasonable agreement." [30]

Gandhi was now in complete control of Congress, which on July 14, 1942, passed a resolution demanding that British rule in India cease immediately. If this were not done, a campaign of mass non-violent civil disobedience under the leadership of Gandhi would be initiated. There was widespread opposition to this resolution.

On August 8 the All-India Congress Committee endorsed the "Quit India Resolution" that had been passed by the Working Committee on July 14. This latest statement was carefully worded and indicated some retreat from Gandhi's pacifism, because it came out strongly for armed resistance, in cooperation with Allied powers, against Japanese invasion. This aid, however, was made contingent on the immediate grant of independence.

Sir Stafford Cripps in London declared that a complete change in government at this time was impossible. Other British critics pointed out that there was no guarantee that the Congress would be able to secure the cooperation of other Indian parties in establishing a stable government. Indeed, all the evidence seemed to point to the fact that the most serious differences would develop between the Congress and the League.

Before the Congress could carry out its campaign of mass civil disobedience, the government of India acted and all Congress leaders—including Nehru, Gandhi, and Azad—were arrested on August 9. Immediately serious and widespread disorders broke out, first in Bombay, then in the United Provinces, Bihar, and Madras. Telegraph wires were cut, installations on flying fields destroyed, railway lines torn up,

[30] Coupland, *India: A Restatement*, p. 220.

and post offices and railway stations burned. By September the "Congress Rebellion," as it was dubbed by British writers, was practically over, its strength spent; but not before 750 persons had been killed and 1200 injured.

The breakdown of the Cripps proposals and the consequent Quit India movement of the Congress with the imprisonment of its leaders seriously threatened the war effort in India. The British were gravely concerned, as was the United States, which regarded India as one of the important links in the chain of victory for the United Nations. It was natural, therefore, that the United States should fashion new ties with India in 1942 and interest itself in trying, as a friendly third party, to help the British and Indians resolve their differences.

Martial India

Notwithstanding the serious disagreements between the various parties, India did make a noteworthy contribution to the United Nations. In particular, the part it played in the defeat of the Japanese armies in Burma was certainly a significant one.

As we have already seen, mobilization for all-out war proceeded slowly in India. For the first eight months the pace was leisurely, but after the fall of France and the Italian Fascist threat in North Africa there was an acceleration of military activity in India. The Indian army was rapidly expanded without the use of the draft. The average number of men recruited was 50,000 monthly, and the peak was reached in July 1942, when 75,000 volunteered. Altogether more than 2 million men were taken into the Indian army.

All branches of the Indian army were expanded. Before 1939 there were less than two hundred commissioned Indian officers; by the end of the war there were more than ten thousand, including one hundred with the rank of colonel, two brigadiers, and one major general. The Air Force was expanded and a training scheme was instituted at five universities. The personnel of the Royal Indian Navy increased from twelve hundred officers and men to more than thirty thousand. The Indian Navy specialized in escort vessels, minesweepers, and submarine chasers. Ten thousand young women were recruited for a Women's Auxiliary Corps.

Of outstanding importance was the tremendous mass of raw materials and industrial supplies that came from Indian mines, factories, and plantations for the war uses of the United Nations. During the North Africa campaign India was the main supplier of bulk stores. In the year 1944 alone she supplied the armed forces of the United States with 78 million yards of cotton cloth, and she was the third largest consigner of war supplies to Australia.

The Indian government built new ordnance factories, which employed 100,000 men in contrast to the prewar figure of 15,000. These and other factories that were converted to war use increased from ten to fifty times the production of such items as rifles, bayonets, guns and gun carriages, grenades, mines, and bombs. Of the forty thousand articles that are needed for the equipment of a modern army, India managed to produce three-fourths. Auto-assembly plants were set up to manufacture chassis, which then were sent to factories to be armor-plated. The manufacture of such chemicals as soda ash, chlorine, and caustic soda was increased; steel production was stepped up in 1943 by 50 per cent; and the shipbuilding and ship-repair industries were so expanded that three hundred vessels were launched in a single year. In addition to munitions, India exported a large and immensely important volume of such raw materials as oil seeds, timber, mica, manganese, tea and coffee, and jute.

One of the most decisive long-range results of this vast war effort was the transformation of India from a debtor to a creditor nation, with Britain's extensive investments in this country practically canceled out. Early in the war an agreement was worked out between the British and Indian governments whereby the former accepted responsibility for financing a large measure of the Indian war effort.

In 1938 the sterling debt of the government of India was equivalent to about 1500 million dollars. During the war, from 1942 to 1945, the Indian defense expenditure was 6756 million dollars, and of this sum Britain accepted responsibility for 3624 million dollars. Thus it was that India was able to pay off the government's debt to Britain. In speaking of this accomplishment the Indian finance minister declared: "India has completed the transition from a debtor to a creditor country, and extinguished within the space of about three years accumulations over decades of its public indebtedness to the United Kingdom." [31] By the end of the war the Indian government not only had managed to pay off its public indebtedness to Britain but had built up in London an enormous amount of sterling credits, to the extent of 5 billion dollars. These were "blocked" by the British treasury, to be gradually released at the conclusion of the war in stipulated annual amounts to the credit of the Indian government.

On the battle fronts, the spring of 1942, immediately after

[31] Geoffrey Tyson, *India Arms for Victory* (Allahabad, India: Kitabistan Company, 1943), p. 267.

the failure of the Cripps Mission, was the time of greatest peril to India. The ineffectual armies of Italy in North Africa had been replaced by those of the German General Rommel, the "Desert Fox." In June the *Afrika Korps* won a decisive battle against British forces defending Egypt, and the German forces plunged ahead, only to be halted by a desperate stand of the British at El Alamein. Here the British army stood firm and in October 1942 launched an attack that routed the *Afrika Korps* and paved the way for the combined British-American drive which ended in the final defeat of the German and Italian divisions in North Africa. In this campaign Indian troops figured prominently, and later they participated in the bitter fighting in Italy.

While the North African campaign was being fought, the British Empire, and India in particular, faced another menace in Burma. The Japanese armies, after overrunning Burma, had blocked land communications via the Burma Road to China and threatened the borders of India. The battle for Burma was one of the hardest-fought of the entire war. In November 1942 Indian forces carried out their first offensive against the Japanese in Burma but were repulsed with heavy losses.

At the Quebec Conference, in August 1943, a new phase of the Burma campaign was planned when Prime Minister Churchill and President Roosevelt appointed Admiral Lord Louis Mountbatten as supreme commander of the Southeast Asia theater. Air power, supplies, and troops were built up in India, and, after the repulse of a last desperate Japanese attack in the direction of Bengal and Assam, the British Fourteenth Army began its victory drive in the fall of 1944. This force was made up of a million men, more than 60 per cent of whom came from India. In March 1945 Mandalay, the capital, was lost by the Japanese, and the Burmese campaign was practically over except for mopping-up operations. Burma had been reconquered by an international army in which the great preponderance of manpower came from India. In a sense, this war theater was always a sideshow, having to give precedence to other Allied requirements in western Europe and the Pacific. Yet Burma was vitally important, for it controlled in large part the fate of both China and India.

In their invasion of India the Japanese had been joined by a small force known as the Indian National Army. Its story largely concerns the activities of Subhas Chandra Bose, a left-wing leader of the National Congress who was mentioned in the preceding chapter. On the eve of the Second World War Bose had been arrested and imprisoned by the Indian government, but in December 1940 he had been released for reasons of health. The following January he secretly fled from India and in March was in Moscow. The end of March saw Bose in

Berlin, where he had conferences with both von Ribbentrop and Hitler.

Bose followed carefully the capture of Malaya by the Japanese and was aware that in March 1942 an Indian good-will mission, made up of representatives from various parts of Southeast Asia, had been received in Tokyo to start an Indian independence movement with the assistance of the Japanese. The following June a conference was held at Bangkok, where a hundred Indian delegates gathered from Japan, Manchukuo, Hongkong, Java, Malaya, and the Indian army which had been captured at Singapore. As a result of this conclave an Independence League was established with headquarters at Singapore. Relations with the Japanese authorities, however, did not run smoothly, and in July 1943 Bose arrived in Singapore as the new leader.

Training camps for the Indian National Army were immediately opened up and a provisional government of Azad Hind (Free India) was established. In Subhas Bose's first proclamation of the provisional government it was declared:

> It will be the task of the Provisional Government to launch and to conduct the struggle that will bring about the expulsion of the British and their allies from the soil of India. . . . We hereby pledge our lives and the lives of our comrades-in-arms to the cause of her freedom, of her welfare and her exaltation among the nations of the world.[32]

This statement was issued on October 21, 1943, and two days later the provisional government declared war on the United States and Britain.

When the Japanese attack on Imphal and Kohima was opened, the Indian National Army took part in the offensive. Following the collapse of this attack the "I.N.A." practically disappeared, and many of its officers deserted to the British-Indian Fourteenth Army. In April Bose fled from Rangoon to Singapore, and in August he moved to Saigon, where he took a plane for Japan. Before the aircraft reached its destination, it crashed, and Bose was killed.

While undoubtedly a sincere patriot, Bose must have caused men such as Nehru acute embarrassment by his pro-Axis sympathies. There were in Bose elements of instability and incipient Fascism which had disturbed leaders in Congress even before the outbreak of war.

The death of Bose did not conclude his striking story, which was renewed with dramatic consequences after the end of the war when certain of his officers in the I.N.A. were placed on trial for treason in Delhi's Red Fort.

[32] Hemendranath Das Gupta, *Subhas Chandra* (Calcutta: Jyoti Prokasalaya Co., 1946), p. 222.

The Home Front: 1942-1945

While Indian armies had been helping to reclaim both Italy and Burma from the invader, India itself from the latter part of 1942 to the end of the war in 1945 was being internally buffeted and changed by the impact of total war. Thousands of foreign soldiers, many of them American, were quartered in the land, and they brought strange and exciting ways from the outside world. War brought a tremendous upsurge of business activity, as new factories for the war effort were built and others were set up to supply the goods for domestic consumption formerly imported from Britain and other countries. The Indian maufacturing and trading classes made enormous profits from war contracts. On the other hand, the life of the masses was seriously disturbed by the economic dislocations of war. There was a serious shortage of goods, prices in some cases increased 300 per cent, and food supplies especially were insufficient. As a result the middle class and white-collar groups suffered a lowering in standards of living and the real wages of the factory laborers decreased.

A tragic reflection of this economic disequilibrium occurred in Bengal, a province with a population of 60 million, where thousands died from famine.

British policy from 1942 to the war's end was to reiterate that the Cripps proposals still stood, but it was made clear that the Congress leaders responsible for the Quit India Resolution of 1942 would not be released from prison until they changed their demands. Amery, the British secretary of state for India, in 1944 stated in the House of Commons that the Cripps offerings remained open "in all their generous amplitude," and "we shall stand by them in the hour of victory as we did in days of adversity." [33]

At the same time Indian leaders of moderate propensities worked to find a way out of the political impasse. They asked the British government to release its Congress prisoners. Rajagopalacharia, himself a Congressman, made many speeches urging a reorientation in his party's policy. In his pamphlet *The Way Out*, he urged that the Cripps proposals be revived, declaring they were "a bonafide gesture by the British Government to the people of India and not a measure of mere expediency or appeasement." [34] Nothing, however, came of these well-intended efforts, and the Congress leaders remained adamant, and also out of circulation, in prison.

[33] *Great Britain, Parliamentary Debates*, 5th Series, House of Commons, Vol. 302, p. 1106.
[34] Coupland, *India: A Restatement*, p. 231.

The sterilization of Congress gave Jinnah and his Muslim League a heaven-sent opportunity to make up for lost time and to rectify the balance between his organization and Congress. Jinnah would have nothing to do with the Quit India campaign, regarding it as a kind of blackmail directed against the hard-pressed British to force them to agree to a Hindu raj. During the period from 1943 to the conclusion of hostilities, Jinnah worked like a man possessed, motivated by one objective: the achievement of Pakistan. His statements to the press and his speeches were many, and they continued to win converts among the Muslims and to make the League the unquestioned spokesman for the Muslim community in India. Speaking before a group of students in 1941, Jinnah declared:

> It is as clear as daylight that we are not a minority. We are a nation. And a nation must have territory. What is the use of merely saying that we are a nation? A nation does not live in the air. It lives on the land, it must govern land, and it must have a territorial state and that is what you want to get.[35]

The Muslim League, under Jinnah's direction, now imitated the tactics of the National Congress. It refused to recognize the right of any other organization to represent Muslims. Jinnah and the League high command formulated basic policies and then demanded that they be implicitly obeyed by all the provincial governments controlled by the League. The League assumed a position of domination in the governments of Bengal, Sind, Assam, and the North-West Frontier Province; and the government of the Punjab, while a coalition, had a majority of members who belonged to the Muslim League. And in 1942 for the first time Jinnah defined the exact geographical boundaries of his proposed Pakistan, for, in the name of the League, he laid claim to five provinces—Bengal, Assam, Punjab, Sind, and the North-West Frontier Province— and also to the administrative district of Baluchistan.

Back in Great Britain, the final months of the Second World War found the Labour party extremely critical of the coalition government's India policy and its inability to end the political stalemate in this great dependency. In December 1944, the Labour party conference had passed a resolution urging the resumption of negotiations with the Congress leaders, with the object of securing as quickly as possible a place for India as a self-governing member of the British Commonwealth. Lord Wavell, the viceroy, spent March of 1945 in London discussing with Churchill and his cabinet how best the deadlock could be ended in India.

[35] Jamil-ud-Din Ahmad, ed., *Some Recent Speeches . . . of Mr. Jinnah* (Lahore: Sh. Muhammad Ashraf, 1943), I, p. 213.

After his return to India, on June 14, 1945, Lord Wavell broadcast a new British offer to the Indian people. In this message it was affirmed that, whatever new constitution should be drawn up, it was to be the work of the Indian people themselves. Furthermore, the offer made in 1942 by Sir Stafford Cripps still remained open. As an immediate step, the viceroy announced that he was prepared to make at once important changes in his executive council, whereby all the members except the commander-in-chief were to be Indian. These new members would be selected from among the Indian leaders "in proportions which would give a balanced representation of the main communities, including equal proportions of Moslems and Caste Hindus." [36]

This British offer of June 1945 was designed to demonstrate the good will of the government in London in conceding a generous measure of representative government within the framework of the existing Indian constitution. However, in the legal sense the viceroy still retained ultimate control if he chose to wield it. In return for this gesture, the British government appealed to Indians to extend their full support in the war against Japan, while in the House of Commons the Indian Secretary, Amery, announced that imprisoned Congress leaders were to be released.

In order to create the new executive council, Lord Wavell invited twenty-two representatives of the various Indian groups to a conference at Simla. At this meeting Wavell appealed for confidence in his good offices, telling the assembled representatives: "You must accept my leadership for the present. Until there is some agreed change in the constitution, I am responsible to His Majesty's Government for the good government and welfare of India. I ask you to believe in me as a sincere friend of India." [37] The viceroy asked the main Indian parties each to present its list of nominees from which he could select members for the reconstituted executive council. All parties except the Muslim League complied. Jinnah, however, rejected this procedure because he demanded that all Muslims appointed to the council should be members of his League, while Congress insisted on nominating two of its Muslim members and placing them on its list. Jinnah maintained further that Muslim-Hindu parity was not enough, his view being that other minority nominees on occasion would vote with the caste Hindus and thus place the League nominees in the minority. Finally, Jinnah contended that the principle of Pakistan should be recognized, for if the League

---

[36] *Statement of the Policy of His Majesty's Government,* Cmd. 6652, June 14, 1945 (London: His Majesty's Stationery Office, 1945), p. 3.
[37] *The Times* (London), June 26, 1945.

accepted the Wavell Plan "the Pakistan issue will be shelved and put in cold storage indefinitely." [38] The Simla Conference dragged on until the middle of July, when Wavell reluctantly announced its breakdown. It was now manifest that the basic issue holding up constitutional advances in India was not the question of how much power was to be transferred to Indian hands but, rather, what Indian hands were to get this power.

In the meantime, a national election had been held in Great Britain in July 1945, and Winston Churchill, the Conservative leader, had been displaced as prime minister by Clement Attlee. The coming to power of the Labour party with a decisive majority was a good augury for the cause of Indian independence. The party of Harold Laski, Stafford Cripps, and Ramsay MacDonald had long been the traditional champion of Indian freedom. In 1929, for example, the election pledge of the Labourites had stood for "the recognition of the right of the Indian people to self-government and self-determination, and the admission of India to the British Commonwealth of Nations on an equal footing with the self-governing Dominions." [39] During the election campaign of July 1945 the Labour party came out specifically for the grant of self-government to India in friendly association with Great Britain. When the new Parliament opened in August, the king's speech outlining the program of the Labour government specifically promised the "early realization of full self-government in India."

Prime Minister Attlee's government announced on August 21 that the viceroy was coming to London for fresh discussions. Upon his return to India, after his conversations in London, the viceroy announced that the British government was now resolved to push forward with plans for the attainment of Indian self-government; that, as soon as possible, a constitution-making body would be convened; and that, as a preliminary step, elections would shortly be held for the central and provincial legislatures. The viceroy also stated his intention of conferring after the elections with the newly elected representatives, to determine whether the proposals brought to India by Cripps in 1942 were still acceptable or whether some other procedure was desired and could be agreed upon. Wavell further stated his intention of making another attempt to reconstitute his executive council. Underlining the British government's desire to know the true situation in India was the announcement made in London on December 4, 1945, that a parliamentary delegation—made up of repre-

[38] Quoted in Parkin, *op. cit.*, p. 310.
[39] Quoted in W. Y. Elliott, *The New British Empire* (New York: McGraw-Hill Book Co., 1932), p. 400.

sentatives of the three British parties—was to leave for India at once in order to study the situation at first hand and report back to Parliament.

The Labour government had now made it quite clear that Indian independence was no longer an issue between Britain and the Indian people. For too long, however, Indian nationalism had felt itself frustrated and the advance toward self-government in the past too slow and halting. Consequently, Congress and its leaders found it difficult to realize that victory had been won against Britain on one battlefield and that it was now imperative to transfer attention to problems in another field of controversy that had to be resolved before India could expect to enjoy the full fruits of independence. This problem was the conflict between the Muslim League and the National Congress, and more specifically the demand of the former for partition and Pakistan.

Instead of devoting complete attention to the Pakistan issue, the National Congress proceeded to expend its energy in waging a battle that had already been won and continued to ignore, or at least to underestimate, serious divisive rivalries among the Indian people themselves that threatened the peace and the unity of their native land. In the elections for the central legislative assembly, carried out in December, and in those for the provincial legislatures held early in the spring of 1946, Great Britain was singled out as the enemy. In the Congress election manifestoes reference was made to the Gandhian Quit India Resolution of 1942, and it was declared: "By its demand and challenge the Congress stands today. It is on the basis of this resolution and with its battle-cry that the Congress faces the election." [40]

Such a rallying cry found a response. The end of the Second World War saw nationalism rampant and impatient in India. The conflict had brought in its wake inflated prices, shortages of goods, and even famine. The masses at war's end were restless and disillusioned. To this ferment were added the new ways and attitudes that had been picked up by thousands of men as a result of their service in the Indian army. For the first time many Indians traveled to distant lands. Masses of men were trained to handle machinery, and officers were educated to be alert and self-reliant. The result of all this was that men in the Indian army "recognized and felt the new trends sweeping across India." [41] Nationalistic susceptibilities were also shocked by the trial of the officers of Bose's Indian National Army in the closing weeks of 1945 in the Red Fort

[40] Indian Annual Register, 1945, II, p. 110.
[41] Phillips Talbot, "The Independence of India," Foreign Policy Reports, XXIII (June 15, 1947), p. 77.

at Delhi. Feeling in India rose to a danger pitch, and Subhas Chandra Bose became canonized as a great national hero. The important thing in the minds of Indian nationalists was not that Bose had cooperated with the Japanese in trying to invade India but that his main purpose had been to drive British authority from India. For this his followers should not be punished. As 1945 ended, the country became more and more tense. Irate mobs periodically paraded in the streets of the large cities insulting all Westerners, and Britishers in particular. In Calcutta there were serious and widespread student demonstrations against the Indian National Army trials.

Early in 1946 strikes, outbreaks of violence, and demonstrations became more frequent and menacing. In February serious disorders broke out in Calcutta over the Indian National Army trials. Many fires were started, and rioting continued for five days. More serious was the mutiny of the sailors of the Indian navy at Bombay. Sailors clashed with the police, and several hundred invaded the European business district, where they smashed windows and beat Europeans. A mob also milled around the United States Information Service office, where they tore down the American flag and burned it in the street. This last incident would seem to show there was a general anti-Western sentiment prevailing, as well as a specific grudge against Great Britain. The naval strike spread to other port cities, such as Karachi, and in addition the police of several cities went on strike. India seemed on the verge of rebellion.

The League-Congress controversy was also building up to a dangerous pitch. The elections to the central legislative assembly and those for the provincial legislatures had shown that there were now only two major parties in India. In the provinces, for example, the League had gained 425 of the available 441 Muslim seats, and in the central assembly the League had won all the Muslim seats. There could be no doubt that Jinnah's organization was the mouthpiece for India's Muslim population. It was at the new session of the legislative assembly that Jinnah delivered an intransigent fighting speech threatening civil war, declaring that partition was the only issue and that both Britain and Congress must concede Pakistan before anything else. Jinnah warned, "Only over the dead bodies of Muslims will the Congress party flag fly in the Northern Provinces." [42]

Up to the end of 1945, during the first half-year of its power, the British Labour government had taken the view that the transfer of power in India could be an orderly and deliberate operation. In its long history of criticizing imperialism,

[42] Quoted in Robert A. Smith, *Divided India* (New York: McGraw-Hill Book Co., 1947), p. 169.

the Labour party had taken the position that the Indian problem was a fairly simple one. All that was needed was the straightforward offer of independence. The events of January and February 1946, however, shocked the Labour government into the realization that the march of events in India was getting out of hand. There was need of a dramatic and resolute move, and one was made when Clement Attlee announced in the House of Commons on February 19 that a Cabinet Mission would shortly leave for India to assist the Indian leaders in drawing up a method of framing a new constitution. At the same time, as an interim measure Indians would be given *de facto* responsibility for their own rule by the creation of a new executive council representing the main Indian parties. Three weeks later Attlee, on the eve of the departure of the Cabinet Mission, made it clear in the House of Commons that his government wanted India to be completely free and that it fully appreciated the strength of nationalistic aspirations among its people. Attlee declared: "India herself must choose what will be her future constitution; what will be her position in the world. I hope that the Indian people may elect to remain within the British Commonwealth. . . . But if [they] so elect, it must be by [their] own free will." [43]

This unequivocal statement and the arrival of the Cabinet Mission in India on March 24 halted the trend toward rebellion and induced the main political parties to use constitutional methods as they worked with the British cabinet members who composed the personnel of the Cabinet Mission: Lord Pethick-Lawrence, the secretary of state for India; Sir Stafford Cripps, then president of the Board of Trade; and A. V. Alexander, the First Lord of the Admiralty.

It was appropriate and logical that a Labour government had taken the decision to give India unfettered freedom. It is doubtful, however, whether any other British government would have made a different decision. The determination of Mr. Attlee's government to give India her freedom is to be explained not only by the traditional belief of his party that this great dependency should be freed but also by the inexorable realities of 1946. The plain truth was that Britain could no longer rule India against the wishes of its people, that Britons indeed had little desire to do so, and that there was hardly any economic justification for their doing so. From an administrative point of view, the government of India had already passed into the hands of the Indian people. Recruitment of British personnel for the all-important Indian civil

[43] Quoted in *The Cabinet Mission in India*, compiled by A. C. Banerjee and D. R. Bose (Calcutta: A. Mukherjee and Co., 1946), pp. 17-18.

service had been stopped during the war, and by 1946 there were only 520 British officers in the I.C.S. out of a total strength of 1060. At the same time there were some 150 British members of the I.C.S. who were eligible for retirement. Practically the entire personnel of the much larger subordinate services, which during the war had assumed more and more administrative responsibilities, was Indian. These Indian civil servants, together with the host of petty local officials and the police, had become very sensitive to the aspirations of the nationalistic movement.

In the 1930's, and even in 1942, the Viceroy and the British governors of provinces could enforce a policy which the major political parties opposed. That such a course would be practically impossible now was admitted in January [1946] by the British governor of one Congress-controlled province, and it is reported that the Viceroy advised London to the same effect.[44]

An important factor in Britain's decision to quit India was her weariness of the burdens of an imperialist power, especially in India, where nationalism was so intransigent and at the same time so confused and divided. The average man in Britain was getting "fed up" with the Empire, and during the war British soldiers frequently showed little enthusiasm for fighting for the sake of India. The sacrifices of the Second World War had left Great Britain tired and impoverished, and there was in England "an incredible weariness widely exhibited over the Indian problem."[45]

And from the view of pounds, shillings, and pence, Britain no longer had any reason to stay in India. During the course of the war, as we have already noted in this chapter, India was able to pay off her huge public debt to Great Britain. She was able not only to do this but to accumulate sterling credits in London to the sum of 5 billion dollars. All that was left in India of the once imposing British financial stake was the equivalent of a few hundred million dollars of private investment, which as early in the war as 1943 was estimated to be no more than what British capital had invested in Argentine railways.

Independence with Partition

The Cabinet Mission was engaged for three months, from the last week of March to the end of June 1946, in continuous conversations with various Indian leaders. An important press conference was held on March 25 in which Lord Pethick-Lawrence again made it clear that the object was to give India

[44] Talbot, *op. cit.,* p. 76.
[45] *Ibid.,* p. 75.

complete, unfettered freedom—inside or outside the British Commonwealth—and that the aim of the Mission was to help Indians to establish a constitutional structure including the provinces of British India and the princely states. During April the Cabinet Mission conferred with the viceroy and leading British officials and then with the Indian leaders. On May 5 the so-called Tripartite Conference was opened at Simla, where representatives of the Congress and the League conferred with the three British ministers on how British authority could best be wound up in India. The two main Indian parties were violently opposed. Congress, as can be seen from its published correspondence with the Cabinet Mission, insisted upon a strong central government. It also asked for the immediate relinquishment of all authority by Great Britain and its transference to a sovereign interim Indian government. Congress further maintained that the constituent assembly, when it met to frame India's new government, must have perfect freedom to draft the constitution and should not be bound by any previous arrangements. [46]

Jinnah and the League insisted upon a federal system in which the central government would have minimum powers as compared with those exercised by the federated units. There would have to be prior agreement as to the basic features of the new constitution, and presumably Britain would stay in India as the ultimate authority until an acceptable constitution was drafted. Jinnah had tersely expressed the League's position to Britain in the slogan "You divide and then quit," whereas the Congress said in effect to Britain, "You quit and then we will divide." There could be no reconciliation, no accommodation, between these two views, and on May 12 the announcement was made of the failure of the Tripartite Conference.

Confronted with the inability of the two main Indian political parties to agree on any plan, the Cabinet Mission drafted a scheme of its own which was announced on May 16. The cabinet statement, while agreeing that there was a genuine anxiety among the Muslims "lest they should find themselves subjected to a perpetual Hindu-majority rule," came out strongly against Jinnah's claim for partition based upon a Pakistan of six provinces. Statistics were cited to show that the non-Muslim population would be 48.31 per cent of the total population in the northeast area and 37.93 per cent in the northwest area of the proposed Pakistan. In the remainder of British India left outside Pakistan there would be a Muslim minority of 20 million amid a total population of 188 million.

Obviously the six-province area of Pakistan as envisaged by

[46] See the letters of Maulana Azad in *The Cabinet Mission in India*.

the League would not solve the religious-minority problem, and this fact was strongly underlined by the statement of the Cabinet Mission. In addition it was pointed out that the transportation, postal, and telegraph system had been planned and constructed by the British on the basis of a united India. Furthermore, the Indian armed forces had been built up and trained for the defense of the subcontinent as a whole. A final point made was that the two halves of Pakistan, one in the northwest and the other in the northeast, would be separated from each other by seven hundred miles. For these reasons the Cabinet Mission strongly recommended that India should not be divided into two sovereign states.

Having ruled out the practicability of Pakistan, the Cabinet Mission presented an ingenious scheme which retained the unity of India and at the same time made some substantial concessions in the direction of recognizing the League's desire for autonomy for the Muslim-majority provinces. The plan envisaged a "Union of India" made up of the provinces of British India together with the princely states. There was to be a central government endowed with authority in the fields of foreign affairs, defense, and communications. All other powers were to rest with the component parts of the Union— the provinces and the states. In the Union legislature, as a safeguard for minorities, no communal matters were to be acted upon save by a majority vote of each major community —i.e., the Muslim and the Hindu.

Thus far the Cabinet Mission's plan called for a Union at the top tier, so to speak, of the governmental structure and a group of provinces and states at the bottom tier. Midway between the Union and the bottom tier were to be three groups of provinces: one predominantly Hindu India and the other two the Muslim majority provinces in the northwest and northeast of India. The latter groups would consist of the Punjab, North-west Frontier Province, and Sind on the one hand, and Bengal and Assam on the other. Each of these three groups was to draw up its own regional constitution.

It can be seen that the Cabinet Mission's plan for grouping was an attempt to satisfy in some degree the Muslim demand for Pakistan. Given the limited powers of the proposed Union government, the Muslims could feel reasonably secure in the enjoyment of a wide degree of autonomy in each of their group areas. While the Congress might protest that Assam with its non-Muslim majority should not be joined to Bengal, the Cabinet Mission could point out that there would be some 20 million Muslims in predominantly Hindu India. This figure was in contrast to 47 million non-Muslims in the two "Pakistan areas." In short, the scheme, while not achieving a clear-cut grouping on the basis of religion, did constitute a nicely balanced plan aimed at securing Muslim-Hindu amity in India. The reasonable treatment of non-Muslims in the two Pakistan areas would call for a similar respect for the rights of the Muslim minority elsewhere in India.

A few additional details of the Cabinet Mission's proposals should be noted. A constituent assembly was proposed, to be made up of 292 members from the provinces of British India and 93 from the states. The legislative assembly of each province was to elect its representatives on the basis of one for each million of population. Following the convening of the constituent assembly at New Delhi the representatives of each of the three groups envisaged by the Cabinet Mission were to meet separately and then decide the nature of their group constitutions. After this action the group representatives were to reassemble in a single body for the drafting of the Union constitution. The Cabinet Mission further recommended that any province after a period of ten years could call for a reconsideration of the terms of the constitution and that after the new constitutional arrangements had come into operation it should be possible for any province to elect to move out of any group in which it had been placed. Finally, the constituent assembly was asked to negotiate a treaty with Great Britain "to provide for certain matters arising out of the transfer of power." In closing its proposals the Cabinet Mission appealed to the Indian people for good will and mutual accommodation in this supreme moment in Indian history.

On May 25, the Cabinet Mission issued a clarifying statement on its proposals. It was intended that there should be immediately set up an interim government, and in this new viceroy's executive council all members were to be Indian. Until the new Indian constitution was adopted the present constitution was to remain in force, and during this time British troops would remain in India, as Great Britain was responsible for the ultimate security of the country until the actual transfer of authority had taken place.

The reception of the Cabinet Mission plan was none too encouraging. While it cleared the air by demonstrating that Great Britain was completely serious in her intention of quitting India, it seemed only to exacerbate the existing rivalry between League and Congress. For the next nine months there was a continuous jockeying for position, party maneuvering, and acrimonious debate, with the Congress-League deadlock getting more and more ominous. After some delay the Congress accepted the long-range plan of the Cabinet Mission with some reservations, but refused to accept the conditions laid down for the entrance of its representatives into an all-Indian executive council. The Muslim League, on the other hand, had finally accepted the conditions for participating in an interim government and in the constituent assembly. At the same time the election had taken place for this latter constitution-making body, and the contest had given the Congress 97 per cent of all the general seats—i.e., all but 7 out of 210 seats—and the League all but 5 of the 78 set aside for the Muslims. There could be no shadow of doubt as to the right of the League to speak for the Muslim community of India, and, equally, no doubt that the Congress represented the remainder of public opinion.

In spite of the confusing barrage of criticisms, proposals, and counter-proposals that had emanated from the League and Congress headquarters following the announcement of the Cabinet Mission plan, the last week of June 1946 was a brief period of high hope for the success of the cabinet plan and for the preservation of the unity of India. With both the League and Congress accepting the long-range plan—i.e., the three-tier system of government and the constituent assembly that was to blueprint its form—the British Cabinet Mission felt its work was done, and accordingly left for England.

The rising confidence of the closing days of June, however, was soon succeeded by the grim despair and deadlock of mid-July 1946. During this time Jinnah and his League made a clear turnabout and repudiated the Mission proposals, lock, stock, and barrel. It is difficult to assess blame for this grievous disappointment, but it would seem that a strong case can be made out for blaming the intemperate remarks of Congress leaders, especially Pandit Nehru. As the spokesmen for the overwhelming majority party in India these leaders, one would think, would have been particularly careful not to excite the already strong fears of the minority party of the League.

On July 6, 1946, Pandit Nehru was inducted as president of the National Congress, and as its spokesman he proceeded to make a number of statements defining the position of Congress in the plans for the taking over of authority in India. On July 7, before the All-India Congress Committee, Nehru stated:

> There is a good deal of talk of the Cabinet Mission's long-term and short-term plan. So far as I can see, it is not a question of our accepting any plan long or short. It is only a question of our agreeing to go into the Constituent Assembly. We will remain in the Assembly so long as we think it is good to India. We are not bound by a single thing except that we have decided for the moment to go into the Constituent Assembly.[47]

Three days later Nehru had declared at a press conference that, as far as the constitution-making body was concerned, *"What we do there, we are entirely and absolutely free to*

[47] *The Cabinet Mission in India,* pp. 312-313.

determine. We have committed ourselves on no single matter to anybody." [48] Another Congress leader, Maulana Azad, had also declared in a speech that when the constituent assembly met it would have the "unfettered right to make a constitution; it would be sovereign; and would legislate for a united, not a divided India." [49]

Such utterances completely doomed the Cabinet Mission proposals. The worst fears of Jinnah were realized. To his mind, once the League went into the constituent assembly the overwhelming majority of Congress would scrap the scheme formulated by the Cabinet Mission and then proceed to set up just the kind of government they desired, one in which there would be little guarantee of Muslim rights.

A few days after Nehru's statements, Jinnah reacted strongly, declaring that the Congress leader's interpretation of the constituent assembly was a complete repudiation of the long-term scheme of the Cabinet Mission. On July 27 the League Council met in Bombay. Amid tumultuous scenes it reversed its acceptance of the Cabinet Mission plan and announced that the time had come to resort to direct action to achieve Pakistan. August 16 was announced as Direct Action Day, when a Muslim hartal, or general strike, was to be observed against both Congress and Britain, who were accused of trying to trick the League. Jinnah, amid cheers, defiantly declared, "Today we bid good-bye to constitutional methods. Today we have also forged a pistol and are in a position to use it." [50]

The inflammatory result of such exhortations soon became tragically evident. On August 16 the Muslims observed their Direct Action Day. In Calcutta riots broke out, and for four days frenzied mobs milled in the streets. This was the bloodiest communal outbreak in modern Indian history. In what was called "the Great Calcutta Killing," there were 4700 deaths, 15,000 injured, and 150,000 refugees fleeing the city. This Muslim-Hindu affray was just the beginning. Rioting spread to various other areas—to east Bengal, to Bihar, and early in 1947 to Punjab—with a total loss of life from August to February of 12,000.

Meanwhile, in September Lord Wavell had succeeded in getting Nehru to form an interim government. The viceroy's executive council at last was all Indian, but Jinnah and the League refused to come in. Finally, at the end of October Wavell succeeded in getting Jinnah and four colleagues to enter the government. The members of the interim govern-

[48] *Ibid.*, p. 315. The italics are mine.
[49] *The Constituent Assembly of India*, compiled by A. C. Banerjee (Calcutta: A. Mukherjee and Co., 1947), p. 105.
[50] *The Cabinet Mission in India*, p. 363.

ment, however, were just as much divided among themselves as before. The crux of the matter was that Jinnah refused to have anything to do with the constituent assembly scheduled to convene in December. In desperation Prime Minister Attlee called for Congress and the League each to send two representatives to London, and the Sikhs one, for a conference. The meeting was fruitless, however, and when the constituent assembly opened on December 9, no League representatives attended. As the troubled new year began, the breach between the two main parties remained as wide as ever. It was not now a question of rebellion against the British raj; the country teetered on the brink of civil war.

It was at this critical point that Mr. Attlee grasped the nettle. On February 20, 1947, speaking in the House of Commons, the prime minister stated that "His Majesty's Government wish to make it clear that it is their definite intention to take necessary steps to effect the transference of power to responsible Indian hands not later than June 1948." Attlee urged Indians to sink their differences, for "administration had broken down to the point where Britain was no longer effective." Another item of considerable importance was contained in the dramatic announcement that Lord Wavell was recalled as viceroy and Lord Louis Mountbatten was to take his place.

Lord Mountbatten was sworn in as the new viceroy on March 24 and immediately plunged into the task of arriving at some agreed plan that would push aside the mounting danger of civil war. Conferences were held with the various leaders, and at the end of May the viceroy was back in London explaining why the Cabinet Mission plan would not meet the emergency and what an alternative might be. On June 2, back in India, Mountbatten met with various leaders and outlined Britain's final plan for the liquidation of her rule. The following day he made a broadcast to the country in which he expressed his great regret that no plan for preserving the political unity of India was acceptable and said there would be no coercion. The solution to the dilemma was the transfer of British power to two governments, each having dominion status, the changeover to be made "within the next few months."

In the plan as outlined by Mountbatten the Muslim majority provinces not represented in the constituent assembly should have their legislative assemblies vote to determine whether their constitution would be framed by the constituent assembly already in session or by another body. Jinnah, it will be recalled, had demanded all of the Punjab, Bengal, and Assam as part of Pakistan. This claim would mean that a huge non-Muslim minority would have been created in Pakistan. In the case of Bengal and the Punjab, therefore, the legislative assemblies met in two sections—one Muslim and the other non-Muslim—to give the latter an opportunity, if they wished, to join the constituent assembly that had been in session since December 1946. As for Assam, provision was made in this Hindu-majority province for one district, predominantly Mohammedan, to join the Muslim area of eastern Bengal.

By this time the Congress leaders had come to realize that partition was inevitable, and they accepted the plan. The Muslim League got much less by the proposals than it had demanded. India was to be divided, but self-determination was also to be invoked in Bengal and the Punjab, which would now have to be dissected. There was, however, no choice, and reluctantly the League also tendered its acceptance.

It was no easy matter to unscramble the old governmental system that had presided over a united India and to set up two distinct and independent governmental structures in its place. A boundary commission under Sir Cyril John Radcliffe was created to define the frontiers of the provinces that were to be divided. There was also the matter of the division of the Indian army and the small navy. There had to be a division of the old regime's assets and liabilities, agreement on the public debt, and arrangements made in the realm of currency, exchange, and coinage. International agreements had to be duplicated, office equipment and records divided, and arrangements made for the division of office and administrative personnel. All of these details were turned over to ten expert committees made up of senior Indian officials, plus some British in the case of the army, and these bodies in turn presented their recommendations to a supreme partition council that was responsible for fundamental policy and decisions.

In all the matters pertaining to the complex arrangements necessary for partition, Lord Mountbatten took the lead as a disinterested and friendly third party. During July 1947 the viceroy announced that his interim government would divide into two groups. These would meet separately, to work on their own particular problems, and from time to time jointly under the chairmanship of Mountbatten as they were forced to consider matters of joint concern. The process of partition had now begun.

The Mountbatten plan reiterated the policy on the princely states expressed in the proposals of the Cabinet Mission of May 1946. The British government took the view at that time that the former overlordship, or paramountcy as it was called, exercised by the British crown over the princely states would lapse once Britain ceded her authority and would not be transferred to any new government. In theory, at least, each princely state had three choices: it could join with Pakistan, enter the Indian Union, or remain unattached to either and endeavor to go it alone. Once British power had been removed from India, however, it was inevitable that the states would have to join one or the other government, Pakistan or the Indian Union. Practically, there was no other choice. They were not strong enough to stand on their own. The only question to be solved was on what conditions they would be united and how much autonomy they would be permitted to enjoy. The final outcome of this matter of the states will be discussed in the next chapter.

On July 4, 1947, the Indian Independence Bill was introduced into Parliament and quickly passed. Speakers all deplored the sundering of Indian unity but agreed that this was a matter for the people themselves to decide. Final discussion on the bill took place in the Commons on July 15, at which time a number of eloquent valedictory speeches were made as members bade farewell to India and the responsibility Great Britain had exercised since Lord North's Regulating Act of 1773. On July 18 the bill for the transfer of power to two dominions on August 15 became law.

Independence became a reality at midnight, August 14, for both Pakistan and the Union of India. In New Delhi the constituent assembly, meeting in an exultant yet solemn mood, paid tribute to Gandhi, sent friendly greetings to the new sister state of Pakistan, and observed two minutes of silence for patriots who had died for freedom in India. Equally impressive ceremonies were being carried out in Karachi, capital of Pakistan. The following day, the fifteenth, Lord Mountbatten became governor-general of the new dominion of the Union of India and swore in his cabinet with Pandit Nehru as prime minister. In Karachi, Mr. Jinnah assumed office as governor-general and Liaquat Ali Khan then took the oath as prime minister. Independence for the two new dominions was celebrated in many parts of the world. Impressive ceremonies were observed at the headquarters of the United Nations at Lake Success, New York, as the flag of the Indian Union was raised to join those of fifty-four other member nations. In the West Indies and in South Africa Independence Day was celebrated by Indian communities with parades and displays of the flags of the two new dominions. In Great Britain, the London *Daily Mail* signalized the new dispensation by changing its traditional masthead from "For King and Empire" to "For King and Commonwealth." And at the ceremony held in London for the hoisting of the flag of the new Dominion of India, A. V. Alexander, who had been a member of the Cabinet Mission, declared: "The Indian Empire dissolves— the British Commonwealth of free nations welcomes two free peoples into their association."

8. Establishing the New Nations

THROUGHOUT INDIA AND PAKISTAN patriots rejoiced in their new-found independence, which had seemingly been achieved so peacefully. A feeling of spiritual exaltation suffused the people as they listened to the hopes and programs for national greatness propounded by their leaders. Unfortunately, this mood of nationalistic exuberance was soon shattered by the impact of violence and wholesale slaughter in the Punjab and the dark prospect of war between Pakistan and India. Never in modern times have two nations in the first hours of freedom been confronted by such serious problems. As we will see, this initial emergency was surmounted, and India and Pakistan happily were able, toward the end of 1947, to turn to the tasks of constitution making, social reform, and economic advancement. By 1950, both Pakistan and India were sobered and chastened by the responsibilities of statehood. The world was not quite so simple, kindly, or secure as it had appeared in August 1947, and there was the realization that Gandhian Soul Force of itself would not bring national security, nor the mere exit of alien rule guarantee the solution of fundamental domestic problems.

English newspapers in the summer and fall of 1947 were filled with reports describing the end of British rule in India and the details of "packing up." The world in general and India in particular had been amazed at the rapidity with which Britain had pushed the arrangements for complete independence. Lord Mountbatten was largely responsible for insisting that the British departure be carried out as soon as possible. Mountbatten, the last of the British viceroys, has described how the law officers of the crown in London, together with the Lord Chancellor, worked all night on the draft

228

of the Indian Independence Bill to insure its passage in Parliament during the summer of 1947.[1]

This rapidity of abdication of British power may be criticized by later historians. It should be kept in mind that Attlee's original plan called for a transfer of power to Indian hands by June 1948. This date had been moved up to August 15, 1947, and, as the decision was announced on June 3, only seventy-two days were available for the division of the country. While intransigent and frustrated Indian nationalism may have been responsible to a large extent for the speed with which the independence plan was carried out, there are observers who believe Britain could have slowed down the process and thus have helped to avoid the confusion and later the bloodshed that was visited upon India in the fall of 1947. One Indian judge is said to have declared, "The British are a just people. They have left India in exactly the same state of chaos as they found it." [2]

Whether or not the British withdrawal was at the end too precipitous, all observers agreed that no imperial rule had ever before ended like this. Jinnah declared, "Such voluntary and absolute transfer of power and rule by one nation over others is unknown in the history of the world." [3] British officials stayed on to assist the new dominions either as administrators or as officers in the armed forces. The first British troops to leave India after the transfer of power were sent a message by Prime Minister Nehru in which he said:

> I know the good qualities of the British soldier and I should like our own army to develop those qualities. . . . It is rare in history that such a parting takes place not only peacefully but also with goodwill. We are fortunate that this should have happened in India. That is a good augury for the future.[4]

The British left behind them the two nascent states of Pakistan and India. During the previous decade numerous warnings and arguments had been advanced to prove that the former would be an economic impossibility and a political anachronism, with its two main areas separated from each other by a thousand miles. In spite of all these arguments, however, Pakistan had become a reality because in essence "the Indian Muslims felt themselves to be Muslims before they were Indians." [5] The new state had a population of 70

[1] Earl Louis Mountbatten of Burma, *Time Only to Look Forward* (London: Nicholas Kaye, 1949), p. 266.

[2] Richard Symonds, *The Making of Pakistan* (London: Faber and Faber, 1950), p. 74.

[3] *Ibid.*, p. 169.

[4] Mountbatten, *op. cit.*, p. 74.

[5] Symonds, *op. cit.*, p. 191.

million, it was estimated by the census taken in 1941, but this figure had probably reached 80 million in 1948, thus making Pakistan the fifth nation in the world on the basis of population. Official Pakistan statistics give 360,000 square miles as the area, a figure apparently including the western part of Kashmir, then under Pakistan control. As will be seen shortly, the status of Kashmir became a bitter issue between Pakistan and India.

The New Pakistan

A political map of the Indian subcontinent after 1947 shows the Union of India occupying its great central bulk with Pakistan separated into two peripheral areas, one in the northwest and the other in the east. The larger, West Pakistan, had an area of over 300,000 square miles with 34,000,000 inhabitants. It embraced the valley of the Indus River and its tributaries, stretching from the coastal plain fronting on the Indian Ocean and running back to the slopes of the great mountain wall of north India. This area is mainly dry country; in the Sind province, for example, the rainfall averages only 8 inches a year. West Pakistan, however, has extensive irrigation systems which have turned arid and desert land into some of the most productive agricultural areas in the world.

East Pakistan, created mainly from the eastern areas of Bengal, is completely different in topography and climate. A flat alluvial plain of 53,000 square miles traversed by many streams and rivers, notably the Ganges and the Brahmaputra, it is a wet country with dense tropical jungles. The rainfall averages from 75 to as much as 160 inches a year. East Pakistan is a fertile area producing great quantities of rice and the world's largest supply of jute. It is heavily populated, having 46 million inhabitants and a population density which in some areas equals 1200 people to the square mile.

In August 1947 the Pakistanis secured an extensive land area for their new nation, but they did not obtain the necessary governmental structure for their state. This had to be built up almost overnight. The old capital of British India at New Delhi, with its great public buildings and many offices, as well as the bulk of its staff, went to the Union of India. Karachi, the main city and seaport of the province of Sind, was chosen as the capital of Pakistan. Here offices and bureaus were improvised in tents and barracks. Meanwhile, an exodus was taking place from New Delhi, from which 25,000 government employees with their families and more than 50,000 tons of personal belongings had to be moved to Karachi. This was just at the time when massacres and train derailments had broken out in northwest India. With great difficulty the Pakistan government succeeded, partly with the help of forty English airplanes, in transporting the bulk of its civil servants to their new capital. Arriving in Karachi, these transplanted officials established themselves in either tents or temporary buildings. Crude tables purchased in the bazaars were their desks, boxes their chairs, and packing cases their files. Somehow the necessary files of records were set up, government departments established, and administrative machinery set in motion.

As hundreds of Pakistani civil servants streamed into Karachi, they brought with them a share of the assets and liabilities of the old undivided India. Pakistan was to receive stipulated amounts of war materials, and 150,000 troops out of a total of 420,000 were transferred to her command. Final arrangements for the division of Indian assets were not reached until December, when Pakistan secured 17.5 per cent of the sterling balances owed India by the United Kingdom, a like percentage of the cash balances of undivided India, and the same ratio of its uncovered debt.

Independence Day for Pakistan found this new state with a serious shortage of trained administrators and army specialists. British experts, therefore, were urged to remain. In three out of four provinces British officials were retained as governors, and in Karachi British civil servants were placed at the head of four of the governmental departments as permanent secretaries. Many British officers remained in the Pakistan army, and as late as the spring of 1949 the commanders of the army, navy, and air force were from the British Isles. In addition, there were about 750 British officers and technical specialists in the Pakistan armed forces.

By provision of the Indian Independence Act, passed by the British Parliament in July 1947, Pakistan was to be governed by the provisions of the Government of India Act of 1935 until such time as a new constitution could be prepared and without, of course, any authority being possessed by the British government. The legislature at Karachi was a constituent assembly of seventy members chosen by the provincial assemblies, and a cabinet following the traditions of ministerial responsibility was subject to the will of the federal legislature. Since Pakistan was a dominion in the British Commonwealth of Nations, the Pakistan governor-general represented the crown; he was nominated by the Pakistan cabinet and formally appointed by the king. Pakistan as a federal state consisted of four governor's provinces (West Punjab, Sind, North-West Frontier Province, and East Bengal).

The following princely states elected to join the new government: Bahawalpur and Khairpur, the four states later to form the Baluchistan States Union, plus the tribal states of the Northwest frontier. Altogether these territories have an area of 118,000 square miles. The state of Junagadh, together with several minor adjoining states such as Manavadar, initially joined Pakistan but later were taken over by India.

As it began its independent existence, Pakistan was confronted with serious handicaps and problems, the most important being the division of its territory into two disconnected parts. The people in East and West Pakistan were followers of Mohammed, but they spoke different languages and belonged to entirely different culture patterns. In West Pakistan there were three main types: the Sindhis, the Punjabis, and the Pathans, with little love lost between the last two. The Pushtu-speaking Pathans, comprising a group of a little more than 3 million, posed a serious problem in the tribal districts of the northwest frontier. These restless, belligerent, and fiercely individualistic tribes had never been pacified by the British; in 1947 their status became uncertain, for across the Pakistan border were another 5 million Pushtoons in Afghanistan, and there were Afghan patriots who envisaged the opportunity of creating a greater Afghanistan by the union of all the Pushtu people under its rule. This irredentist movement was checked, however, when a plebiscite among the tribes of the frontier district registered the overwhelming desire of the people to remain with Pakistan. When Jinnah, the first governor-general of Pakistan, visited the area in the spring of 1948, the various tribes—the Wazirs, Afridis, and Mahsuts—greeted him with friendship. The Pushtu issue, however, was to emerge later on and was to cause deep antagonism between Kabul and Karachi.

The northwest frontier, apparently, was safely under the administration of Pakistan, but other problems remained, of which the status of the minorities and the necessity of rapid industrialization were most important. Muslim self-determination had been achieved, but it had not been a clean break. In West Pakistan 76 per cent of the inhabitants were Muslim and in East Pakistan the figure was 71 per cent. Translating these percentages into figures, there were 20 million non-Muslims in Pakistan, mainly Hindus; at the same time in the Indian Union there existed a huge minority of 40 million Muslims. These large minority groups in 1947 were like hostages challenging each nation to protect minority rights, thus insuring like treatment for all. In the event, however, that fanaticism were to override reason and communal rioting should break out, the minority groups would be completely helpless, an easy prey to violence.

In the realm of economics, in good harvest years Pakistan fortunately enjoyed a food surplus, together with large yields of jute, cotton, hides, and wool. But it had practically no industries, no factories to process its jute, no mills for its cotton, and no tanneries for its hides. If Pakistan was to become a modern nation, industrialization would have to be one of the first aims.

The Muslim League controlled the new state, and its leaders were not as numerous or as well known as those of its counterpart, the Congress, in India. During the first year of independence the main burden was carried by Mohammed Ali Jinnah, who had assumed the post of governor-general. A weary old man of seventy-one, Jinnah yet proved to be a tower of strength for the new nation; but his heavy responsibilities became too great a burden, and he succumbed to a heart attack in September 1948. He was buried with impressive ceremonies and honored as the Quaid-i-Azam (The Great Leader) because the Pakistanis realized that their new state stood as his monument. Yet he was only the skillful leader rather than the creator of the forces that ultimately brought about Pakistan, and it has been said, "If there had been no Jinnah, it still seems probable that there would have been a Pakistan." [6]

Associated with Jinnah and well prepared to carry on his work was a group of capable administrators. Liaquat Ali Khan, the prime minister, had been Jinnah's chief associate. Born in the Punjab in 1895, he had been educated at Aligarh and Oxford and had a long record of political experience in India, both in the legislature and as secretary of the Muslim League from 1936 to 1947. Pakistan's foreign minister was Sir Mohammad Zafrullah Khan, who had received a legal education in Britain, had been a judge in the Indian Federal Court, had held various posts in the Viceroy's executive council, and had represented India at several international conferences. He was to uphold Pakistani national interests with eloquence and skill before the United Nations.

Following Jinnah's death, the post of governor-general went to Khwaja Nazimuddin, formerly the prime minister of East Bengal. A statesman whose long experience went back to the post of provincial minister under the Government of India Act of 1919, the governor-general performed his official tasks with dignity and high-minded patriotism.

[6] *Ibid.,* p. 193.

The Union of India

Beginning the new state of the Indian Union did not pose as many difficulties as did the establishment of Pakistan. There was no need to search for a new capital, and the bulk of the civil servants, the army, and the navy remained. India also possessed the largest cities, government buildings, most of the museums, colleges, laboratories, banks, and practically all the industries of the subcontinent. With an area of 1,246,000 square miles and a population estimated at 337 million, the Indian Union was one of the greatest states in the world. The main territories comprising India when Britain transferred power were nine governor's provinces, including Bombay, Madras, Central Provinces, the United Provinces, Orissa, Assam, Bihar, East Punjab, and West Bengal. In addition there were some relatively small areas known as chief commissioner's provinces.

The princely states posed a serious problem to India. The great majority of them were mixed up in and around Indian provincial territory. What was to be their status? Unless they could be in some manner effectively assimilated, India would be Balkanized and fragmented. Some of the princely states desired complete independence, a course which, the government of the Indian Union declared, "threatened to bespatter the country with a vast number of independent enclaves, large and small, an eventuality which if not prevented . . . could have wrecked the economy of the country, broken its unity as a nation, menaced its security every moment of its existence, vitiated its resurgent democratic spirit and brought about Balkanisation whose effects would be irreparable." [7]

The British Labour government had consistently refused to encourage any idea of complete independence on the part of the princely states. The governor-general, Lord Mountbatten, took a leading role in convincing the states that their proper destiny lay in joining one of the two dominions. In an important meeting of the Chamber of Princes, held in July 1947, Mountbatten explained that two states departments had been set up, one for each dominion, to conduct negotiations with the states, and that a draft instrument of accession had been prepared, under which only three basic powers would be surrendered by the princely states when they merged with a dominion, these powers being defense, foreign affairs, and communications. Mountbatten explained to the princes that the power of paramountcy had lapsed, that it could not be

[7] *Indian Information, Independence Number* (New Delhi: Government of India, 1948), p. 5.

retained or transferred, and thus technically the princely states had now become independent political units. The governor-general pointed out, however, "You cannot run away from the Dominion which is your neighbor." [8] He added that "there are certain geographical compulsions that cannot be evaded." [9] Under the capable direction of Sardar Vallabhbhai Patel, who made a conciliatory appeal to the states, all of the states within what might be regarded as the geographical confines of the Indian Union had signified their intention of coming into the Union. There were three states, Junagadh, Kashmir, and Hyderabad, whose status was uncertain, and serious difficulties were to arise in each of them. At the outset of independence, the problem of the majority of the states had been settled in principle, with only the details left to be cleaned up, and, while India had lost the territory of Pakistan, she had effectively consolidated the great heartland of the subcontinent.

India faced many internal problems. Politically this new nation would have to consolidate its peoples into one nation and its provinces and princely states into a unified governmental structure. India's inhabitants were extremely diverse: Sikhs, Jats, Tamils, Bengalis, Mahrattas, and Punjabis, all with different languages and cultural traditions. In the past, before the advent of the European invader, we have seen that no princely ruler had ever succeeded in uniting all of the country; and that when it had been politically unified in part, the forces of disintegration were not long held in check. Would the new militant Indian nationalism, born in the late nineteenth century, prove an effective deterrent to the age-old political defect of India—political fragmentation?

Economically also the new India had difficulties. It had lost its richest granary to Pakistan, and disturbed conditions in independent Burma cut down the bountiful amounts of rice which Burma had exported to India in the past. India had important industries to be developed, while it had at the same time a huge population, the second largest in the world, which had already in 1947 outstripped its food supply. The nationalization of agriculture and the modernization and expansion of industry were the two prime economic goals in the minds of India's new statesmen.

These leaders were better known throughout the world than their counterparts in Pakistan. It was logical that Jawaharlal Nehru should be prime minister, but close at his side, as Deputy prime minister, was Sardar Vallabhbhai

[8] Mountbatten, *op. cit.*, p. 56.
[9] *Ibid.*, p. 53.

Patel. If Gandhi was the mystic and Nehru the socialist reformer and national idealist, Patel was the new India's man of action. Born in 1875, he had grown up to become a successful lawyer and then, like Motilal Nehru, gave up a lucrative practice to follow Gandhi. Becoming active in the nationalist crusade in the 1920's, he was imprisoned several times for his part in civil disobedience movements, and during the Second World War he spent most of the period from 1940 to 1945 in prison.

While Patel was perhaps not as influential as his two distinguished colleagues, Gandhi and Nehru, he nevertheless deserves to be included with them in the outstanding triumvirate in contemporary Indian leadership. A man of the political right, deeply conservative, realistic and practical, Patel was what John Gunther called the "party-boss" of the Indian National Congress. In the tumultuous days just before independence it was Patel who dominated the arrangements for the transfer of power from Britain. Like Gandhi, Patel did not live to see the Indian state reach an even keel (he died late in 1950), but in the early years of independence this strong and sometimes ruthless man rendered great service to his country. Even the liberal *Manchester Guardian*, which might be expected to shy clear of Patel's authoritarian tactics, remarked on his death, "It can be said that the only disservice which he did his country since it gained its independence was to die at a very critical moment." [10]

Another leader high in the ranks of Indian statesmen was Chakravarti Rajagopalacharia, whom we have already discussed in connection with Gandhi's Quit India campaign of 1942. With Patel and Nehru he was the leader closest to Gandhi, although on occasion he disagreed completely with the Mahatma's tactics. A good administrator with a keen mind, "C.R." was deeply religious but in no way mystical. During the Second World War he had realistically called for an all-out effort against Japan. He was the foremost political leader in the province of Madras, and was to be India's last governor-general.

A few other leaders deserve mention. Dr. John Mathai, India's finance minister, was an economist and author of note who had been educated at Madras, the London School of Economics, and Oxford University. He was a Christian and had been a professor of economics and a member of the Indian tariff board. Maulana (Very Reverend) Abul Kalam Azad was a Muslim theologian and philosopher, the author of one of the most famous commentaries on the Koran.

---

[10] *Manchester Guardian Weekly*, December 21, 1950, p. 8. For a recent evaluation of Patel see K. Shridharani, "India's Uncertain Future," *New Republic*, CXXIV (February 26, 1951), pp. 10-12.

Born in Mecca in 1888, Azad had been educated at the Al Azhar University in Cairo and had founded an Urdu newspaper in India in 1912. Azad sought to bring Indian Muslims into the Congress movement, which he regarded as a non-religious, nationalistic organization. Azad became minister of education in the new Union government.

Another scholar high in the circles of Indian leadership was Dr. Rajendra Prasad, who early in his career had made a name for himself at Calcutta University and then proceeded to gain fame as a lawyer. In 1920 he became a disciple of Gandhi and was imprisoned several times. Prasad was named president of the Congress on four occasions and in 1947 became president of the Indian constituent assembly. In 1946 his book *India Divided* was published; it contained a strong indictment of Britain for helping to create what was charged to be artificial Muslim nationalism and of Muslim leaders, including Jinnah, for their Pakistan program.

The only important Indian leader educated in the United States was Jayaprakash Narayan, the founder of the Indian Socialist party. Early in the 1920's Narayan came to America, where he earned his living at a variety of jobs, being in turn a waiter, a farm laborer, and a salesman. He attended five universities in the United States and became an ardent Marxist. In 1929 he returned to India, and with the help of Jawaharlal Nehru he organized the labor research department for the Indian Congress. Gradually the young Socialist became the leader of the left wing in Congress, and in 1934 he helped to found the Congress Socialist party. For a few years the small Socialist group continued to work within the framework of the more conservative Congress. The rift between the right and left wings widened, however, and in 1947 the Socialists led by Narayan cut all ties with the larger organization and set about trying to bring "democratic socialism" to India.

Leadership in both India and Pakistan in 1947 seemed quite adequate, in some cases brilliantly so, for the tasks at hand. In both states, however, there was too much reliance upon three or four leaders and, further, the leaders in the main were old men. Young men were not being encouraged and trained to take over from the aging team of patriots who had fought the long campaign against British imperialism.

The Shadow of Conflict

During the latter part of the war, as India paid off its debts to Britain and even ran up a huge credit account of blocked sterling in London, and as Great Britain began to evince

unmistakable signs of her impending departure, Indian nationalists viewed the future with expectancy and complete confidence.
And even after independence with partition, leaders of the two
new nations still envisaged rapid progress in raising the standards of living of the masses and reducing the triple blight of
poverty, disease, and illiteracy among the masses.

Unfortunately, in the first few months of their national
existence both Pakistan and India were confronted by a
state of crisis that left little opportunity for study and work
on social reform and economic development. In the fall
of 1947 there was real danger that the entire subcontinent
would be convulsed by massacres and suffer the collapse of
law and order.

Sporadic communal rioting had been going on ever since
the major outbreak in Calcutta in August 1946. Just before
the partition, August 15, 1947, numerous reports of riots
and killings were received from Delhi and Calcutta, and
from Amritsar and Lahore in the Punjab. This last-named
province was a tinderbox of suspicion and even hatred, with
the Muslims pitted against the Sikh and Hindu communities.
In western Punjab the Muslim majority could vent their
antagonism against the Sikh and Hindu minority, but the
reverse was true in eastern Punjab, where the Muslims were
outnumbered. No clear picture can as yet be drawn of
how the rioting began, and each side accuses the other of
premeditated massacre.

Religious fanaticism and mob violence were unchecked
in the last two weeks of August and throughout September.
On both sides of the Pakistan-Indian border in the Punjab,
village after village went up in flames, their inhabitants,
regardless of sex and age, butchered without mercy or compunction. A gigantic movement of people now began as
hundreds of thousands of terrified villagers and townspeo-
ple tried to flee to safety—Muslims rushing out of eastern
Punjab and Hindus and Sikhs fleeing to the sanctuary of
Indian territory. As this migration got under way, trains
were derailed, their passengers were dragged off and killed,
and refugee columns were ambushed along the road. The
Punjab Boundary Force had to be disbanded as its soldiers
took sides and refused to fire on rioters of their own communal group.

Faced by one of the most terrible disasters in modern
times, India and Pakistan momentarily forgot their differences and pooled their resources to set in motion a joint
military evacuation organization. Relief camps were established, refugees were evacuated by an air shuttle service,
and in little more than two months special trains carried

nearly 2½ million refugees. Huge foot convoys were organized, some numbering as many as 60,000. Moving slowly across the countryside, these convoys were guarded front and rear by men on horseback armed with spears and swords, with regular troops not far away, and with a system of bugle calls that warned of attack. There was much marauding, however, and many stragglers were picked off. Food had to be dropped from planes from time to time when a column was beleaguered. The outbreaks subsided in October, and by November 21 more than 8 million refugees had crossed the India-Pakistan borders. All in all it has been estimated that by the end of the year 6½ million refugees crossed into Pakistan territory and that 500,000 Muslims were killed or, in the case of many women, abducted. More than 5 million Hindus and Sikhs fled from the Punjab, and large numbers of them were massacred en route.

Outside the Punjab there was a serious outbreak in Delhi, and for a brief period it seemed that partitioned Bengal would follow the terrible example of northwest India. It was Gandhi who almost singlehanded prevented this disaster by an appeal and fast; never had non-violence won a more important victory. Nehru also displayed personal courage and magnificent leadership in appealing to the people of India to control their communal antipathies.

These massacres aroused resentment and anger in both dominions, but the very enormity of the tragedy forced both governments to cooperate in the saving of thousands of lives. But other events were taking place which brought Pakistan and India to the verge of conflict by the end of the year and in the spring of 1948 into a state of limited but undeclared war. This added acrimony sprang from rivalry and disagreement over the status of certain princely states, namely Junagadh, Kashmir, and Hyderabad. The first of these was a small state on the Kathiawar coast where 800,000 inhabitants were ruled by a Muslim Nawab although they were more than 80 per cent Hindu. Although Junagadh was entirely surrounded by the territory of the Indian Union, the ruler acceded to Pakistan in September 1947. This action brought a strongly worded protest from the government of India, which declared that it violated the facts of geography stressed by Lord Mountbatten in his speech to the Chamber of Princes on the eve of partition and, furthermore, that Junagadh's ruler was bound to follow the wishes of his subjects, 82 per cent of whom were non-Muslim. Dismissing the argument of sheer legality, the Indian government stated: "Every Ruler claiming sovereignty over his people can have the sanction of law even now for oppressing his people as much as he pleases. Legal sanction is not everything." [11]

Following the Nawab's accession to Pakistan, disturbances broke out in Junagadh, and the ruler fled to Karachi. On November 11, 1947, Indian troops entered the state and took over the administration, promising an early plebiscite to determine the real wishes of the people. Pakistan immediately protested, declaring the ruler's action legal and stating that Junagadh had acceded to Pakistan voluntarily and freely. The plebiscite was duly held, however, and the great majority of Junagadh's people voted for union with India. This incident aroused widespread feeling in Pakistan against India, but its real importance, as will be seen shortly, is its connection with the Kashmir controversy.

Located well within the center of the territory of the Indian Union was the important princely state of Hyderabad, the largest area in the subcontinent where medieval Muslim rule and government institutions had been perpetuated with little change down to modern times. Most of the people were Hindu peasants, and over them was a small Muslim elite of landowners and civil servants. As the date of the British exodus drew near, the Congress party in Hyderabad was determined that this state should accede to the Union of India. On the other hand, the Nizam and the Muslim aristocracy were equally resolved that Hyderabad would not come under the control of India. Most determined to block this eventuality was an organization called Ittehad-ul-Muselmin, which sought to protect Islamic culture in the Deccan. This group had come under the leadership of a militant Muslim, Qasim Razavi, who created a private army called the Razakar Volunteers. In the spring of 1947 the Nizam toyed with the idea of Hyderabad securing recognition from Great Britain as an independent dominion in the British Commonwealth of Nations. This possibility was firmly ruled out by the Labour government. At any rate, in June 1947 the Nizam stated that for the time being his government would not accede either to Pakistan or to India. He added:

> When the British go I shall become an independent sovereign. But this does not mean that I wish Hyderabad to stand aloof either from old allies or old neighbors. . . . I greatly hope that some kind of Standing Conference may soon be established, with regular meetings which may assist the new Dominions and such States as may decide to remain autonomous to co-operate actively in all matters concerning their common welfare.[12]

[11] Press Release, New Delhi, October 10, 1947 (Washington, D.C.: Government of India Information Services).

[12] Quoted in *Chronology of International Events and Documents*, Vol. III, No. 16, August 4 to August 24, 1947 (London: Royal Institute of International Affairs, 1947), pp. 466-467.

This announcement touched off a civil resistance campaign on the part of the Congress party in Hyderabad and led to the arrest and imprisonment of several thousand of its members.

Negotiations between the Nizam's government and that of India were carried on just prior to the resignation of British authority and continued on into the fall of 1947. New Delhi demanded nothing short of accession. It was argued that the facts of geography demanded Hyderabad's incorporation into the Indian Union. India could not countenance an independent state located as Hyderabad was in the very center of its territory. As the London *Times* put it, "Hyderabad is regarded as a possible ally of Pakistan deep in the heart of India." [13] Indians also argued that the will of the people had expressed itself in favor of accession. In reply, the Nizam's negotiating committee stood mainly upon the legalistic aspects of the matter, stressing that, once British paramountcy had been withdrawn, Hyderabad was automatically a sovereign state. As in the Junagadh imbroglio, the Indian government discountenanced the strictly legalistic arguments put up by Hyderabad, and maintained: "The future of political communities and States is not governed by such declarations. An issue like this involving the defence of India, the integrity of her territory, the peace and security of the country . . . could not be allowed to be solved by mere legalistic claims of doubtful validity." [14]

The Nizam's position in the fall of 1947 seemed to be a strong one. India was beset with crises and there was the possibility of its soon being at war with Pakistan. There was the prospect that the subcontinent might break up into a number of political units, and that Hyderabad might eventually emerge as one of the strongest powers. While agreeing, therefore, to a treaty with India which would give this state adequate control of foreign relations, communications, and defense, the Nizam absolutely refused to accept accession. Finally, in November 1947, a standstill agreement was signed for one year, whereby India was given the same rights over foreign affairs and defense as had formerly been exercised by Great Britain, but India was not given the right to send her own troops into Hyderabad. The agreement also provided that any dispute that might arise between the two signatories was to be settled by arbitration.

In this dispute the Pakistanis naturally were sympathetic with their coreligionists and with the Nizam, for his state was the most important center of Islamic traditions and cul-

[13] *The Times* (London), September 27, 1947.
[14] *White Paper on Hyderabad* (Government of India, 1948), p. 6.

ture in the Indian subcontinent. What particularly aroused the Pakistani statesmen at Karachi, however, was what seemed to them the open hypocrisy of the Indian government at New Delhi. To Pakistanis all the arguments based upon the facts of economics and geography and the will of the people seemed to be completely repudiated by the Indian government in the case of Kashmir. According to Pakistan, legalism was being made the foundation for India's claim to Kashmir, while the will of the people and the compulsions of geography were being completely ignored. It seemed to Karachi that India was resolved to have her Junagadh and get Hyderabad and Kashmir too.

Just as India naturally looked forward to the accession of Hyderabad, so Pakistan believed that Kashmir logically belonged to her. All the rivers and the roads that are open the year round go into western Punjab from Kashmir. The main import and export trade of this state is also with Pakistan, and the most important commodity produced for export by Kashmir, timber, was marketed by floating it down the streams into Pakistan. Referring again to the logic of geography, the Pakistanis pointed out that their huge irrigation works, servicing 19 million acres of land, depended upon rivers rising in or flowing through Kashmir—i.e., the Indus and its tributaries, the Jhellum, the Chenab, and the Ravi. The economic life of Pakistan depended upon the control of these rivers.

It was also argued that 80 per cent of the inhabitants of Kashmir were Muslims who had long been oppressed by their Sikh maharajas, who had obtained the throne only by an accident of history, when the British in the 1840's turned over the country to a Sikh nobleman. The ruling clique in Kashmir was Hindu. Laws discriminated against the Muslims, and there was continual popular unrest punctuated by sporadic revolts. Early in the 1930's politically minded Muslims in Kashmir organized their Muslim Conference to undermine the absolute power of the ruler, Sir Hari Singh. A few years later the Muslim leader Sheikh Abdullah seceded from this organization and founded the Kashmir National Conference. This body accepted the aims of the Indian National Congress and was in close touch with such leaders as Nehru, Gandhi, and Azad. In 1946 Sheikh Abdullah launched a Quit Kashmir movement against the Kashmir ruler and was imprisoned as a result. On the eve of partition and the departure of the British there were, therefore, two popular and anti-maharaja movements, the Muslim Conference, tied to the Muslim League, and the Kashmir National Conference, oriented to the Indian Congress.

After Independence Day on August 15, 1947, the Kashmir ruler gave no indication of what his choice would be—accession to Pakistan or union with India. As an interim measure, however, he did sign with the former a standstill agreement providing for the management of the railway line, the postal services, and the customs by the government of Pakistan. During the third week of October reports were received of revolts and severe fighting in Kashmir, and on October 27 an official statement that Kashmir had acceded to India was issued by New Delhi. This action, it was explained, had been taken in order to secure the assistance of India in re-establishing law and order, and it was planned that just as soon as normal conditions were restored the will of the Kashmiris would be ascertained by plebiscite.

There has been much conflicting testimony as to what actually happened during the latter part of October in Kashmir. Pakistan claims that it was apparent to the Muslim tribesmen in Jammu and Poonch that their unpopular ruler was setting the stage for union with India in order to save his position. A spontaneous revolt thereupon broke out, which was put down with extreme severity by the soldiers of the maharaja. There was pillaging and terrorism, and large numbers of Muslim Kashmiris, fearing for their lives, fled to Pakistan. The news of this terror reached the fanatical Muslim tribesmen of the northwest frontier, and they immediately rushed to the aid of their coreligionists in Kashmir. Most of these tribesmen had to cross Pakistan territory, and there is little doubt that their movement was expedited by the Pakistan authorities. Pushing into the Vale of Kashmir, they defeated bodies of the Maharaja's army, rescued columns of Muslim refugees, and regrettably were unable to resist the temptation of looting any property that came their way. These Muslim tribesmen got within eighteen miles of Srinigar, the state capital; in the meantime, in order to give his government the semblance of popular support, the maharaja had released Sheikh Abdullah from prison and made him the head of a new provisional government. The pro-Pakistan Kashmiris proceeded to establish their own regime, known as the Azad Government.

In reply to the maharaja's plea for assistance, the Indian government immediately dispatched armed forces by air to Kashmir. These troops managed to hold back the tribesmen and save Srinigar. The news of the accession stunned Pakistan leaders, and Jinnah for a time considered moving his regular troops into Kashmir. But such an action would have meant war with India, and fortunately his British military advisers dissuaded the governor-general from taking this course.

During November and December heavy fighting took place between the tribal invaders and Indian battalions. At this time Sheikh Abdullah declared, "If present conditions continue, conflict between India and Pakistan is inevitable." [15] Relations between the two nations rapidly deteriorated as heated recriminations were exchanged. Liaquat Ali Khan declared that India wanted to outflank Pakistan so that she could be in a position to throttle its very existence, and, further, that India had welshed on its partition arrangements in not turning over the cash balances and military stores due Pakistan. Nehru, on the other hand, accused Pakistan of assisting the tribesmen to invade Kashmir and of using force to gain their objectives.

Feeling that it had the better case, the Indian government appealed the issue to the United Nations, invoking Article 35 of the charter and charging Pakistan with aggression. On January 15 Pakistan filed countercharges, and two days later the Security Council asked both parties to refrain from any action that might worsen the situation. India had expected the United Nations to support its action in Kashmir and, consequently, to condemn the action of Pakistan. Instead the Security Council was concerned more with investigating the basic elements in the problem than with trying to assign blame for the civil war. Nehru, deeply disappointed, complained in the Indian Parliament of the "strangely narrow view that people in the Security Council have taken in this matter." [16] Finally, in April 1948, the Council established a commission to study conditions on the spot in Kashmir with the purpose of bringing about a free and impartial plebiscite to determine the wishes of the inhabitants. This commission succeeded in obtaining a cease fire line in January 1949.

It is interesting to compare the arguments used by both sides in the Kashmir controversy. Indian leaders took the view that the Kashmiris were not justified in revolting against the constituted authority of their maharaja and that the tribesmen had no right to come to their assistance. Nehru in supporting this view stated: "The issue in Kashmir is whether violence and naked force should decide the future or the will of the people." [17] Again he observed, ". . . there has been aggression, aggression of a shameless kind and this has to be resisted. There should be no surrender to aggression." [18]

Above all, the legal aspects of the case have been used

[15] *Chronology of International Events and Documents*, Vol. IV, No. 1, December 22, 1947, to January 9, 1948, p. 13.
[16] Lawrence K. Rosinger, *India and the United States* (New York: The Macmillan Company, 1950), p. 107.
[17] Jawaharlal Nehru, *Independence and After, A Collection of Speeches, 1946-1949* (New York: John Day Co., 1950), p. 65.
[18] *India Record* (October 11, 1950), II, p. 7.

to buttress the Indian position. Speaking before the Security Council the Indian representative, Sir Benegal Rau, declared:

> The Maharajah of Kashmir executed an instrument of accession in favor of India on October 26, 1947, and Lord Mountbatten accepted it the next day. This completed all legal and constitutional requirements for accession to the Indian Dominion. Nothing more was required. . . . Therefore, it is elementary that Kashmir now is legally a part of India; that Indian troops are legally in Kashmir, going there to restore law and order.[19]

Pakistani spokesmen stressed the economic, geographical, religious, and cultural ties of Kashmir and Pakistan and argued that India played the game with two different sets of rules, one for Junagadh and Hyderabad, the other for Kashmir. Sir Mohammed Zafrullah Khan pointed out that while India dismissed all arguments based on legality in the first two states mentioned and took her stand on the wishes of the people and the facts of geography, she made legalism sacrosanct in the case of Kashmir, ignored the traditions and wishes of the people, and denied the plain implications of geography.[20]

The intervention of the United Nations in the Kashmir dispute early in the spring of 1948 may be thought of as marking the conclusion of this period of great tension and danger of war. Tempers cooled somewhat, and both Pakistan and India, reprieved from the possibility of destructive conflict, now began to inaugurate another phase in their recent history which might be called the period of recovery and promise.

In January 1948, the very same month in which the U.N. became concerned with Kashmir, a tragic event took place which in a sense also served to mark an end to an unhappy period of confusion and strife and the beginning of a new era of confidence and progress. During the holocaust of blood in the Punjab, similar outbreaks in Calcutta and elsewhere in Bengal had been averted primarily by the exercise of Gandhi's unique leadership. The Mahatma's appeal for forbearance, for mutual respect and tolerance between the Muslim and Hindu communities, enraged extremists in the latter group.

Amid the passions of the massacres in the Punjab and the acrimony of the Kashmir dispute the Hindu Mahasabha was violently anti-Muslim, espousing a Hindu empire covering the entire Indian subcontinent and passionately defending

---

[19] Quoted in *Pakistan Affairs* (Washington, D.C.), March 3, 1950.
[20] *Kashmir Question*, pamphlet of the Pakistan Government, published in New York, 1950.

caste and cow protection. Closely associated with the Mahasabha was the R.S.S.S. (the Rashtriya Swayam Sewak Sangh),
a highly disciplined group whose members wore uniforms
and drilled in military formation. Both these organizations
were regarded with deep suspicion by Indian liberals, who
regarded them as Fascists willing, if the opportunity arose,
to use force for the establishment of a Hindu theocracy.
Some of these ultra-Hindu nationalists made the following
demands:

> Remove the present government, which is composed of men
> of straw, and replace it by men who would be strong Hindus
> ... declare the Indian Union a Hindu State; prepare the country
> on a basis of war with Pakistan; impose conscription on all
> Hindus; treat all Muslims as fifth columnists; and declare the
> professing of Islam as unlawful.[21]

On January 13, 1948, Gandhi started his last fast to induce
Indian leaders to pledge their opposition to any anti-Muslim
program. Five days later a solemn promise was made by outstanding leaders, including Nehru and Azad, that the life
and property of Muslims in India were not to be molested.
Meanwhile, a plot had been hatched, and a Brahman editor
of a Mahasabha weekly was picked to assassinate Gandhi.
The deed was done on January 30, when the Mahatma was
shot to death by four pistol bullets fired at close range as he
walked to a prayer meeting in the grounds of Birla House
in New Delhi. The assassination was linked to extremist elements in both the Mahasabha and the R.S.S.S. For the time
being the former suspended its political activities, while the
latter was outlawed by the government.

All the world paid tribute to the frail, diminutive man
whose biography had been so much the history of India during the preceding thirty years. In death he made one of his
great contributions, for the murder brought many people in
both Pakistan and India to their senses and made them realize that this evil act was the symptom of chaos waiting to be
unleashed upon the subcontinent of India. Gandhi occupied
an important place in Indian and world history, and many
books and hundreds of articles have attempted to evaluate
his contributions and appraise his worth. It may be said that
in too many of them Gandhi ceases to be a man and becomes
a myth. He was too great a leader and patriot not to have
all the truth told about him.

The Great Awakener of Indian nationalism, Gandhi transformed the Congress movement from a limited crusade of
intellectuals and bourgeois professional and business classes

[21] *The Times* (London), September 19, 1950.

to a great mass movement in which the common man played an important part. His championship of *Ahimsa*, or non-violence, while at times utterly devoid of solid reason and practicality, was at least a salutary corrective in a world increasingly convinced of the rightness of sheer force. Gandhi correctly saw the snares and evils inherent in the gadget civilization and materialism of the West. He called upon his people to be aware of the Western Mammon. Finally, Gandhi always stood by the side of mercy and love. Compassionate above all, he was the spokesman of the lowly and downtrodden all over the world, and more particularly of the Untouchables in his own land.

But Gandhi suffered from the defects of all these virtues. Only a holy man, a mystic, could so strongly influence the Indian people. It would be a mistake, however, to identify this situation as part of a democratic process. An American historian sagely observes: "Hindus looked upon Gandhi as the mouthpiece of their gods. When your gods told you to vote the Congress ticket, you did not disobey. It was an effective argument, but it cannot be called democratic." [22] The trouble with a mystic and saint as a leader is that his followers must accept with his religiosity a confused ideology made up of worship of the past, medieval economics, attacks on modern science and medicine, and hazy goals. As Nehru has sadly commented, "What, after all, was he aiming at? In spite of the closest association with him for many years, I am not clear in my own mind about his objective. I doubt if he is clear himself." [23]

Gandhi's civil disobedience campaigns and his attacks on constituted authority tended to bring all government into contempt, not only the British but later that of an independent India. And after 1947 on several occasions fanatics seriously embarrassed the government by resorting to civil disobedience and other extrademocratic techniques to force the authorities to their will. For example, a new political party was formed in West Bengal in the fall of 1950, dedicated to the attainment of a "democratic classless society." Its spokesmen declared that this goal would be sought by constitutional means, but if these failed "mass satyagraha might be necessary." [24]

The charge of inconsistency may also be leveled against Gandhi. The Mahatma asked Britain to surrender to Hitler in 1940, thus scoring a victory for non-violence, but in 1947

[22] Lennox A. Mills, "Problems of Self-Government," *The New World of Southeast Asia*, ed. Lennox A. Mills (Minneapolis: University of Minnesota Press, 1949), p. 304.
[23] Jawaharlal Nehru, *Toward Freedom* (New York: John Day Co., 1942), p. 313.
[24] *The Statesman* (Calcutta), November 25, 1950, p. 5.

he found it possible to support the dispatch of Indian soldiers to fight against the Muslim tribesmen in Kashmir. Furthermore, he always sought to assuage communal differences, yet it was his authoritarian attitude at the second round-table conference, his insistence that he alone could speak for the Indian people, that violently aroused the Muslim community and did much to make Pakistan possible. Gandhi fulminated against Western materialism and its factories, but had no compunction about making a strong alliance with industrialists in his own country. He violently attacked Western medicine, but permitted an English doctor to save his life by surgery early in the 1920's.

Gandhi at his best was the Holy Man subtly combining the wisdom of the ancient Vedas with the doctrines of John Locke and Thomas Jefferson. He awakened his people and set them in motion toward a noble yet distant objective, the real nature of which was never clarified in Gandhi's own mind. In truth, as India neared the day of independence, the country no longer needed a seer or mystic as a leader but rather a statesman who could think clearly and precisely. During the negotiations between the Muslim League, the Congress, and Britain in the fateful spring months of 1947, Gandhi seemed ineffectual. As he himself ruminated in September of that year, "There was a time when India listened to me. Today I am a back number. I have no place in the new order where they want an army, a navy, and an air force and what not." [25]

Yet Gandhi, with all these inconsistencies and what to the Western mind seem to be serious defects, was a noble and heroic character great enough to be revered as the Father of the New India. And even Englishmen, who might be expected to dismiss the Mahatma with a jeer or a growl, on the whole treat his memory with sincere respect. One of them has written:

> And time will enable us to see the triumphs and blunders of Gandhi in a gentler light. He has harboured no enmity against us. Posterity will certainly number him among the friends of England. One day we shall raise a statue to his memory, as we have raised statues to Washington and Lincoln, and to the memory of others whose universal spirit transcended the conditions of their time. Perhaps that statue will be placed within one of our great cathedrals. . . . It would not be more incongruous than the statue raised in Winchester Cathedral to the memory of St. Joan. [26]

[25] *Chronology of International Events and Documents,* Vol. III, No. 19, September 22 to October 5, 1947, p. 568.
[26] Glorney Bolton, *The Tragedy of Gandhi* (London: George Allen and Unwin, 1934), p. 322.

Recovery and the Return of Confidence

In the spring of 1948 the stream of refugees had practically ended, all-out war between Pakistan and India had been averted, and both nations could now turn their attention more to the urgent problems of economic development and social reform. On the whole, the refugee problem was handled remarkably well. At one time the Indian Union was running 160 camps accommodating as many as 1,250,000 homeless refugees. A tremendous amount of food, tents, clothing, medicine, and other supplies had to be furnished by both nations to their homeless migrants. Housing schemes and programs of vocational and technical training were worked out, and hundreds of thousands were settled on the land. While this refugee problem was handled better than one might expect, considering its dimensions, hundreds of thousands of displaced persons remained stranded and homeless in the cities. It was natural that they should become restless and disgruntled with the government. Furthermore, tension at times mounted between the newcomers bent on obtaining jobs and the old residents who saw their employment jeopardized.

The United Nations Commission on Kashmir arrived in India in July 1948 and immediately set about its task of bringing an end to hostilities and setting up plebiscite machinery to determine the wishes of the inhabitants. This commission ran into an intransigent attitude on the part of both disputants and had to report its failure to the Security Council. Negotiations continued, however, and in January 1949 a cease-fire agreement was achieved. On January 15 the commanders of both armies met and agreed to exchange prisoners, and in March Admiral Chester W. Nimitz was named as plebiscite administrator by the secretary-general of the U.N. The outlook for a peaceful settlement of the Kashmir issue seemed promising.

India in 1948 registered considerable achievement in the drafting of a new constitution, the integration of the princely states, the study and formulation of numerous plans for economic development, and the introduction of social reform. In Pakistan, the less than a dozen princely states harbor only 4 per cent of the total population, but in India there were about six hundred states containing 25 per cent of the population. Under the vigorous leadership of Sardar Patel the Indian government laid down three fundamental principles to guide policy on the status of the princely states: (1) Despotism, however benevolent, must be displaced by democratic government. (2) The states must be effectively subordinated to the central government. (3) The absurd multiplicity of states, large, small, and minuscule, must give way to an integration into larger and more economically viable units.

By the spring of 1950, 216 states had been merged with the former British provinces; 61 states had been taken over by New Delhi to be centrally administered; and 275 states had been joined to make new political units called unions of states. While the original word of the Indian government in 1947 had been that the states would yield only the powers of defense, foreign affairs, and communications to the central government, by 1950 the old states had been completely subordinated to a position no different from that of the old provinces of British India. In this process the princes naturally have lost their earlier powers and privileges. A few have remained as the constitutional heads of states, but the great majority have been "pensioned off" and bereft of any influence.

In this process of state integration, Hyderabad posed a serious problem to Indian statesmen. The Nizam was determined to maintain his state's independence. However, as India became stronger in the spring of 1948, its government began to apply pressure upon Hyderabad, demanding its accession. Tension mounted, border raids took place along the Nizam's frontiers, and Communists took advantage of the uncertainty to harry and raid villages in Hyderabad. As the crisis developed, fanatical Razakars terrorized Hindu villages, looted shops, and took the law into their own hands. Negotiations between the Nizam and Nehru's government broke down in June 1948, and India thereupon initiated a complete economic blockade of the state. The Nizam appealed to the Security Council for its good offices in settling the dispute, but India immediately insisted that Hyderabad was not competent as a sovereign state to bring the matter before the U. N. Finally, on September 13 the Indian army invaded Hyderabad and after five days of fighting took over the Nizam's government. It has been claimed that many Muslim civilians were killed, one authority putting the number as high as fifty thousand.[27]

In the Hyderabad quarrel, legality was undoubtedly on the side of the Nizam, but facts of geopolitics—defense, economics, communications—were on the side of India. The use of force, albeit in the name of restoring law and order, weakened the case of India in Kashmir, especially in the minds of Pakistanis. It must also be said that the press in Europe and America was critical of India's action. Said the

[27] William Cantrel Smith, "Hyderabad: Muslim Tragedy," *Middle East Journal,* IV (January 1950), p. 47.

London *Times,* "Its present use of force against a weaker neighbour which resists its claims comes badly from a government that owes its existence to the principles embodied in the Charter of the United Nations." [28]

The draft constitution for India was published in the spring of 1948. It was presented to the constituent assembly early in November, was approved late in the same month, and became the law of the land on January 16, 1950. India, or Bharat as it is called, became a sovereign, democratic republic. The new constitution owes much to the political liberalism of Europe and the United States, and Nehru acknowledged this fact when he spoke before the American Congress on October 13, 1949. It is also apparent that the lessons of federalism in Canada, Australia, Switzerland, and the United States have been studied. The Supreme Court, for example, is borrowed from American experience.

In form a federation with powers divided between a central government and state governments, the Indian Union is almost unitary in function, with emphasis placed upon the authority of the central government. From the nine former British provinces, or parts thereof, and from the welter of princely states, large and Lilliputian, only twenty-eight states now constituted the Indian Union (excluding Jammu-Kashmir, whose status continued in doubt). And among these only two princely states survived intact—Hyderabad and Mysore. Although there is a list of state subjects, the central government can legislate upon any subject it may consider to be in the national interest. Furthermore, the president in Delhi can promulgate ordinances and suspend any state constitution. The central parliament is bicameral, consisting of the House of the People and the Council of States. Heading the Union's executive is a president who is the constitutional head, together with a prime minister and cabinet responsible to the House of the People. The vice-president, while chairman of the council of the States, is in reality a non-political figure and in the person of Dr. Radhakrishnan, the world-famous philosopher and student of religion, acts mainly as the focus for important cultural and ceremonial activities.

The constitution contains an imposing statement of fundamental rights, which abolishes Untouchability and guarantees such rights as free speech, free assembly, religion, and due process of law. An interesting feature is the section on directive principles of state policy, which asserts that the government should be guided by certain principles in making its laws. Among them might be mentioned equal pay for the

[28] *The Times* (London), September 14, 1948.

sexes, humane conditions of work, free education, adequate nutrition, and a living wage. It is also stated that the economic system must not result in the concentration of wealth and "that the health and strength of workers, men and women, and the tender age of children are not abused and that citizens are not forced by economic necessity to enter vocations unsuited to their age or strength." [29]

The constitution makes Hindi the official language of the Union, and the government has zealously propagated it as the national language. There has been strong opposition to this policy, especially in south India, where Hindi is regarded as a foreign tongue.

Constitution making has proceeded slowly in Pakistan, the only important achievement being the publication in the spring of 1949 of "Fundamentals of Freedom," containing the basic aims and objectives guiding the constituent assembly. While this statement endorses such principles as representative government, social justice, equality, and the protection of the rights of minorities, the implication is that Pakistan is to be a Muslim state. Some fundamentalist circles assert that non-Muslims cannot expect to hold positions of great trust under the new constitution, but on the other hand, the prime minister, Liaquat Ali Khan, stated that a non-Muslim could be the head of the government. While, in theory at least, the Indian Union is based on the principle of a secular state, it remained to be seen whether Pakistan would tend to be theocratic.

In addition to creating a democratic federal government in India and the first steps toward a Muslim state in Pakistan, both nations between 1947 and 1950 had astonished the world by their stability and by their determination to tackle basic problems. Herculean efforts had been made to resettle hundreds of thousands of refugees, and the frightening specter of full-scale war over Kashmir had been averted. In addition, India and Pakistan feverishly pushed forward plans to modernize industry and agriculture, as well as initiate reforms in education and health. These socio-economic developments will form an important part of our story in the next two chapters.

[29] *The Constitution of India* (New Delhi: Government of India, 1949), pp. 19-20.

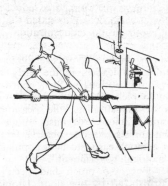

9. India: The Quest for Social Justice and Livelihood

Working with Democracy in India

WITH INDEPENDENCE AND PARTITION SAFELY ACHIEVED and with the machinery of a democratic government ready to be utilized, India's statesmen began to realize the magnitude of the ta s ahead. While under British rule, all patriots, no matter what their personal views, were united solidly in the ranks of the Congress party. There was only one goal— freedom. But independence brought with it a choice of objectives and a confusing array of social and economic alternatives. In the economic realm, should the nation follow the strict path of laissez faire, with no interference in business, or should it pursue the destination of the welfare state? Should there be social and religious reform, based on concepts borrowed from the Western world, or should the status of women, the traditional bonds of the family, and the structure of the caste system adhere to the strictest orthodoxy of Hinduism? In the effort to achieve better standards of living, should the answer be all-out industrialism or the Gandhian return to the rustic simplicity of self-sufficient villages? And in this economic field there were those, the Communists, who believed that the goal of livelihood for the masses could only be achieved by force and revolution; there were others, adherents of the democratic way, who championed gradualism and peaceful means of social and economic change. In other fields there was the issue of whether foreign capital should be invited and on what terms; the choice to be made of staying in or out of the Commonwealth of Nations; and the all-important decision whether, in world affairs, India should align herself solidly with the West or with the Soviet bloc, or endeavor to be on good terms with both sides.

Congress found it difficult to secure agreement on these and other questions. Its leaders in the early 1950's became more conservative and cautious in their approach to reform, because they had to pick their way carefully amid the conflicting interests of industrialists, the peasant agrarian reformers, the Hindu religious extremists, moderate Socialists, and militant Communists. As one observer put it, Congress "is discovering it is much easier to be a popular revolutionary than a popular national government." [1]

Before independence, so much had been promised the masses. As the British left by one door, Utopia would enter by another. But instead, food prices soared, educational reforms lagged, and land reforms scarcely got beyond the blueprint stage. At the same time, job hunters and fortune seekers flocked to get on the Congress band wagon. No wonder there was considerable complaint against corruption in government, and Dr. Rajendra Prasad, President of the Republic, called attention to the bribery, corruption, and black-marketing that were sullying the nation's moral life. Serious dissensions broke out in Congress ranks. Dr. Ambedkhar, brilliant leader of the Untouchables and one of the main architects of the new constitution, became disgusted at the government's failure to pass protective legislation for the Untouchables, or the Scheduled Castes, as they are officially designated. He resigned from the Congress cabinet as law minister in October 1951. Earlier, the Socialist wing in Congress had set up political shop on its own. Its popular leader, Jaiprakash Narain, long-time friend and colleague of Nehru, had been dissatisfied with the conservative trend of Congress. In 1948, therefore, Narain founded the Socialist party of India. Another schism further weakened Congress strength in 1951. Acharya Kripalani, an old Congress stalwart and devoted disciple of Gandhi, became genuinely convinced that Congress was not fit to run the country because of inefficiency and corruption. He did not disagree so much with Congress principles as with its execution and application of them. Having lost out in a struggle for power in the party, Kripalani founded his own political organization in 1951, the Peasants, Workers, and People's party, or the Kisan Mazdoor Praja.

Within Congress, Prime Minister Nehru was also having his troubles. A feud had developed between what one might

[1] *Christian Science Monitor* (Boston), September 8, 1948, p. 2.

term the orthodox and the Western wing. The former, led by P. Tandon, opposed vaccination and all other forms of modern science and medicine; he sought to block the reform of any Hindu customs or institutions, such as cow protection. Tandon, over Nehru's opposition, became president of Congress in September 1951. Finding his reform and developmental program blocked by the conservative wing, Nehru, by bold tactics, forced the resignation of Tandon, and assumed the presidency himself. By reasserting his leadership, Nehru could now dominate Congress, ensure its unity, and dictate its program. In the party proclamation aimed at the approaching general election, the new president stressed the need for high moral standards and a rededication to the ideals of Gandhi.

India's first national election, held in the winter of 1951-1952, took four months. It was the largest ever held in history, there being an electorate of 176 million, of whom 107 million men and women voted. The voting lists had to be compiled in more than a dozen languages and would have made a book twelve feet thick. As 83 per cent of the voters could not read, each party and independent candidate was given a box with a symbol on it. Altogether, 224,000 polling booths had to be set up at 90,000 stations, and the number of ballots provided ran more than 600 million. In spite of the vastness of the operation, the election was conducted in an orderly fashion under the supervision of a nonpartisan body—the election commission. And as an English observer commented: "The entire tone of the Elections was reminiscent of Hyde Park on a rainy day." [2]

There was a multiplicity of parties, but only half a dozen are worth mentioning. There was Congress, of course, with its leader Nehru stressing the new five-year plan for economic development, the Hindu Code Bill sponsored by his party for giving women equality with men under Hindu law, and the secular state with its equal opportunities for all. Nehru was the dominant figure in the election. In nine weeks he traveled 26,000 miles by air, making on an average five public speeches daily. Apart from Congress the most optimistic party was the Socialist. It hoped to get a substantial number of votes and become the main opposition party in parliament to Nehru's followers. The Socialists stood for the abolition of the landlord class without compensation, for nationalization of foreign capital, neutrality in the cold war, and creation of a third Asian bloc in world affairs. In the main Narain's program was Utopian and academic.

A number of parties can be grouped together, the most

important being the Mahasabha, the Jan Sangh, and the Ram Rajya Parishad. These can be classed as Hindu communal parties standing for a Hindu theocratic state which would be violently anti-Pakistan, in which only Hindus would be citizens, and in which the traditional customs of Hinduism would be perpetuated without change. Another group, the K.M.P. or Praja party under Kripalani, stood alone as the champion of Gandhism with its belief in non-violence, redistribution of the land, and rehabilitation of the villages.

On the extreme left, the Communist party of India electioneered for a working-class government, for withdrawal from British ties in the Commonwealth, and adherence to the "peace" camp led by the Soviet Union. Considering the widespread poverty of the masses and the frustrations of the educated unemployed, it would seem likely that communism would have grown rapidly in India after its genesis in the early 1920's. But the Communists have been their worst enemies. The history of their tactics and policies has been one of frequent change and inconsistency. One American correspondent rightly referred to them as those "crazy, mixed-up Communists." In the late thirties the Indian Communists were following an anti-British, pro-Congress line. When war came in 1939 it was dubbed by them "an imperialistic adventure." In 1942, however, after the Nazi invasion of Russia, the Indian Communists switched their tactics to all-out support of the war effort and cooperation with the British government.

This sudden shift had a disastrous effect upon the party's popularity. Frustrated by their inability to gain strength by persuasion, the Indian Communists in 1948 decided to resort to force and armed revolution. A district in the state of Hyderabad was seized and made into a miniature Soviet. This insurrectionist policy was patterned after the tactics of the Chinese leader, Mao Tse-tung. For many months the Indian Reds carried on a reign of terror, but in 1948 the central government used military force to end their threat.

Insurrectionary methods having failed, the Indian Communists performed another ideological somersault. In 1951 the party reverted to political gradualism and prepared to enter the first national election.

These, then, were the most important parties in the Indian political scene, and after the counting of the ballots in the 1951-1952 national election it was obvious that the Congress had won a decisive victory. It had won 362 out of the 500 seats in the *Lok Sabha,* the lower chamber in Parliament. In the state legislatures it had achieved a dominating position, securing over 65 per cent of the seats. Perhaps the major surprise of the election was the poor showing of the Socialists. Their party polled 10.5 per cent of the votes, but in the all-important lower house of Parliament secured only 12 seats. On the other hand the Communists, with little more than 5 per cent of the ballots behind them, gained 27 seats. The Communists emerged as the second largest party. And while their strength was insignificant from an over-all view, it was solidly intrenched in certain regions of south India. Another feature of the election was the eclipse of the Hindu communal parties. All together they polled less than 5 per cent of the votes cast. Hindu orthodoxy and religious issues seemed to be definitely on the wane.

Analyzing the election, the Congress party victory stemmed in large part from the fact that it had been the party that had achieved independence. There was considerable residual loyalty among the masses because they associated freedom with Congress. The personal leadership of Nehru was undoubtedly a major factor. Universally loved and respected, this statesman conducted a campaign of dynamic electioneering that was a pillar of strength to his party. And most important, opposition to Congress was splintered. If there had been only two parties, Nehru's followers would not have been victorious, for they polled only 44 per cent of the votes cast for the national lower house, and in most of the state assemblies they secured only a minority of the votes.

Despite these misgivings, Congress in the mid-1950's was the dominating political force in India, and it seemed to gather strength from year to year. By-elections indicated that it was not only holding its own but gaining somewhat. In the spring of 1955 it won a smashing victory against the Communists in the state of Andhra. This was considered the most significant electoral event since the general election. In this critical contest the Communist party had its greatest local strength. Congress waged its campaign on a straight plank of democracy versus Communism. And despite Nehru's reluctance to assail Communism in the international field, he and his Congress lieutenants felt quite free to lambaste it in this domestic arena. One speaker declared that the real motive of the Communists was "to establish Russian sovereignty in this country." Other Congress orators denounced the Communist system for its lack of freedom and for its despotism. The outcome was a clear-cut victory for Nehru's party.

Within Congress, Nehru in the dual role of party president and prime minister in the national government did much to rejuvenate Congress and adapt it to the basic movements of the times. After his visit to Communist China, and seeing the herculean if ruthless program of industrialization, Nehru made it plain that India must keep abreast of China. Feeling a sense of urgency, he was fearful that economic improvement was not moving fast enough to satisfy the Indian masses. With some like-minded colleagues he convinced Congress that it should adopt socialism as its aim. In January 1955, at its annual meeting Congress adopted its famous Avadi Resolution laying down the goal of achieving a "socialistic pattern of society." This meant an outright welfare state, the expansion of state economic enterprise, the limitation of private business, and a concerted movement in the direction of economic equality.

This move to the left strongly buttressed Congress power. In 1956 India had all the appearances of being a one-party state. In explanation we have the clever political tactics of Nehru as well as the inept moves of his opponents. After 1952 the communal parties, such as the Mahasabha, became quite ineffectual. As to the Socialists, they joined ranks in 1952 with Kripalani's K.M.P. group to form the Praja Socialist party. Notwithstanding this success, to the disappointment of many who considered the Socialist party the only constitutional alternative to Congress, the followers of Narain proceeded to weaken and disorganize their own ranks. First the Praja Socialists lost a large segment that splintered off, taking the name of the Socialist party of India. Another blow was the withdrawal of Narain from politics. This leader, next in national esteem to Nehru, joined the land-gift movement initiated by the ascetic Gandhian Vinoba Bhave. And while the Socialists were weakened by defection and confused by academic and doctrinaire debates over Socialist goals, Nehru—as we have seen—had stolen their thunder by calmly adopting for Congress the aim of a "socialistic pattern of society."

While there was strong criticism in the United States of the visit of the Soviet leaders, Bulganin and Khrushchev, to India in 1955, because apparently diplomatic ties were being strengthened between New Delhi and Moscow, there was another side mostly neglected by Americans. In a subtle way the interests of the Indian Communist party were sacrificed for the inscrutable interests of Russia. Bulganin and Khrushchev spoke glowingly of India's progress. In Calcutta, Bombay, and New Delhi they saluted the efforts of Nehru to ensure world peace. Congress had become respectable in the eyes of Communists—at least of those who lived in Moscow. How could Indian Communists attack the Congress party as reactionary and the tool of the West?

Four years after the first general election in India, Nehru's party appeared stronger than at any time since independence. The most important reason was Nehru. Without him Congress might soon break apart; with him no two-party system seemed likely to materialize. Nehru commanded in the mid-1950's the largest personal following in the world. He was the country's greatest single asset. His activity in the life of the country was amazing. He traveled constantly and spoke perpetually. Everything in India was his business: education, art, the writing of history, the value of sport, the responsibilities of the scientist, the evils of caste, and the horrors of war. From many platforms he spoke to vast audiences, instilling into them the idea that Asia has at last come into its own, that India has gained independence but the greater struggle is to achieve the welfare state, that all in all India is embarking on a challenging and exciting adventure.

The towering stature of Nehru, of course, was not an unmixed blessing. Occasionally in the Indian press one could find evidence of this fact. Writers spoke of his indispensability, of his being the "fountain-head of all activity, relevant and irrelevant. There is not a subject in contemporary life which daunts his remarkable mind or his eloquent tongue. And we encourage him. We want him to inaugurate conferences, lay foundation stones, cut ribbons, open institutions, preside over benefit performances, distribute prizes." [3] But there are warnings about this over-reliance on a single leader, however gifted:

> The consequences of such over-abundance of the Nehru personality in our lives is that the Nehru magic is getting stale. . . . He talks too much. He talks beautifully, but still he talks too much. . . . We are prodigally overspending our Mr. Nehru. We are doing him and ourselves an ill turn by making of a great leader a mere god.[4]

We will return to the political prospects in India in the concluding pages of this study.

Toward Freedom from Want

For some time, even before World War II, the Congress party, while concentrating on the first target—independence —had realized that its greatest task in the long run must be

[3] Santha Rungachary, "The Expendability of Mr. Nehru," *Swantantra* (Madras), Vol. X, No. 50, January 14, 1956, p. 42.
[4] *Ibid.*

the bringing of the better economic life to India's teeming millions. In November 1947 the All-India Congress Committee had declared:

> Political independence having been achieved, the Congress must address itself to the next great major task, viz., the establishment of real democracy in the country and a society based on social justice and equality. Such a society must provide every man and woman with equality of opportunity. This can only be realized when democracy extends from the political to the social and economic sphere.[5]

As early as 1931 Congress had been seriously advocating comprehensive schemes of socio-economic reform.

Up to 1939 the government of India had little interest in planning. The orthodox view was held that the function of government was to enforce law, protect property, collect taxes, and defend the country, and that all other functions of society were better left in private hands. In June 1941, however, the government of India created a postwar reconstruction committee, which was enlarged in 1943; and when Lord Wavell became governor-general in 1944 he proceeded to establish a new department responsible for planning and development.

This step was taken in May 1944. Only a few months before—in January—the Indian people had been startled by the publication of the so-called Bombay Plan ("A Plan of Economic Development for India"). The work of eight of India's most prominent industrialists, the scheme provided for three successive five-year plans involving the expenditure of 30 billion dollars, the doubling of agricultural production, and the quintupling of industrial output in fifteen years. The plan aroused widespread interest, and one Indian economist rightly observed, "It has made the entire nation planning-conscious." [6] So enthusiastic was Indian public opinion over the Bombay Plan and national programs for reform that another economist wrote, "The whole world including ourselves is today mad about planning." [7]

The authors of the Bombay proposals laid down minimum standards to be secured in food, clothing, housing space, education, and health. Every village was to have its school, dispensary, and doctor. It is important to keep in mind that

[5] Shankarrao Deo, "The New Congress," pamphlet (New Delhi, 1949).

[6] P. S. Lokanathan, *India's Post-War Reconstruction and Its International Aspects,* published for the Indian Council of World Affairs (Bombay: Oxford University Press, 1946), p. 57.

[7] Bimal C. Ghose, *Planning for India* (Calcutta: Oxford University Press, 1945), p. 11.

the plan assumed the economic unity of India, as its makers expected that the partition proposals of the Muslim League would not be successful. Priority was given to the expansion of basic industries, such as electrical power, mining, chemicals, and transport. While agriculture was to be improved, the main emphasis was upon industry, nearly half of the entire 30 billion dollars being earmarked for this purpose. The Bombay Plan necessitated the expenditure of huge sums of money, and it was this aspect of it that many economists criticized as unrealistic. In short, the money was to be obtained by tapping the huge supply of hoarded wealth in the country, from sterling securities, foreign loans, the savings of the people, and a favorable balance of trade, and by the creation of new money. The last source, in particular, was strongly rejected by many leading Indian economists.

Another ambitious postwar reform project was the People's Plan, issued in April 1944 by the Indian Federation of Labour. In this document there was much greater emphasis upon the intervention of the state, for the government was to control industrialization and nationalize all the farm lands. The Bombay Plan, while accepting the principle of a planned economy, would maintain a large measure of private enterprise. The People's Plan would have instituted a socialist state.

Meanwhile, the Department of Planning and Development of the Indian government under Sir Ardeshir Dalal, who had been one of the authors of the Bombay Plan, encouraged government officials to scan the possibilities of postwar planning in each of their respective fields. As a result numerous schemes were devised, one of the most discussed being the Sargent Plan for a system of universal and compulsory education for boys and girls between six and fourteen. This was to cost 30 million dollars in the first five years, and by the fortieth year the cost was to rise to the huge sum of 832 million dollars. In the field of public health, the Bhore Committee in its report laid down a blueprint for a healthier India, rightly concentrating upon the village. The plan was commendably ambitious, calling for a great increase in the number of doctors, the expansion of hospitals, and the building up of a network of public health agencies all over the country.

In April 1945 the Department of Planning and Development issued a statement that left no doubt that after the war independent India would follow the policy of a planned economy in which the government would direct and control industry; it might nationalize basic industries, while all others "will be left to private enterprise under varying degrees of control." [8]

As Indian leaders feverishly set about initiating the measures that would bring about a planned, and at least a semi-socialist, economy, it became quite apparent that there was little use, with independence just around the corner, in continuing to harp on the evil economic consequences of British imperial rule. Realistic thinkers, especially economists and sociologists, now began to warn that while a political revolution would soon be achieved, and with it national freedom, there was a comparably important revolution that would have to take place in the social and religious customs and habits of the Indian people. One of these economists wrote: "Rural poverty is not a social disease which large-scale public expenditure can cure nor . . . is it a problem which can be met through the indirect influence of industrial expansion. It is rooted deeply in the present structure and economic basis of our rural society." [9]

Obstacles to Reform in India

The general framework of caste, outworn custom, and traditionalism in India has already been discussed. At this point in our narrative, where we find India eager to initiate economic reforms and to raise the standard of living of its people, it is important to understand just what were some of the specific evils and uneconomic customs that required abolition.

One of the most serious obstacles to raising living standards in India has been the sanctity enjoyed by practically all animals, especially the cow. Cow protection is one of the main tenets of Hinduism, and Gandhi has said, "Man through the cow is enjoined to realize his identity with all that lives. She is the mother to millions of Indian mankind. The cow is a poem of pity." [10] This belief in the sanctity of all life springs from the belief in reincarnation and means that the animal world rather than man rules India. Monkeys, rats, crows, peacocks, pigeons, and all kinds of rodents multiply unchecked, consuming tremendous quantities of food. The depredations of rats alone have been calculated at 200 million dollars a year.

India supports 215 million out of the world's total of 690 million cattle. This means 60 cows for nearly every 100 people.

8 Press Release, Government of India Information Services, Washington, D. C., April 30, 1945, p. 8.

9 Tarlok Singh, *Poverty and Social Change* (Calcutta: Longmans, Green and Co., 1945), p. 16.

10 John Gunther, *Inside Asia* (New York: Harper and Brothers, 1939), p. 393.

Yet these cattle have little economic value. Hindus will not consent to the control of their cow population or to the practice of selective breeding. Millions of aged and maimed cows continue to exist miserably, and in general all the cattle are small and underweight by Western standards. In Bengal, for example, the live weight runs from 425 to 750 pounds, while in the United States a herd often has an average weight of 1400 pounds. Most Hindus will not eat beef, and, because of the poor quality of the cattle, milk production is limited. An American missionary who attracted much attention by his attempts to teach efficient stock management in India has declared, "Over 90 per cent of the cows of India do not pay for their keep. They are an economic drain on the country." [11] This statement is borne out by the testimony of the Indian Board of Agriculture, which has put the annual loss incurred by the maintenance of useless cattle at 585 million dollars.

Closely related to this cow problem and the sanctity-of-life complex is the difficulty of providing the average peasant with secondary occupations. In many areas it has been estimated that the work done by the farmers consumes only 150 days a year. The small farmer in Europe, on the other hand, can always be busy. He has his dairying, poultry, calf raising, and his pig pen. In Japan there has also been the cultivation of silkworms. All of these rural projects, however, are ruled out for the great majority of farmers in India, in part because of their poverty, but mainly because of the religious sanction against animal killing.

One of the most serious evils in the structure of Indian life is the expenditure of relatively large sums of money by the Hindu peasants for uneconomic festivals and ceremonies, such as weddings and funerals. A man will spend the equivalent of twenty years of his land rent for a marriage feast for his daughter. On occasion the peasant must feast his caste-fellows, pay the priest for some service, or spend a large sum on a pilgrimage. So strong is the tyrannical force of custom that no one dares to reduce the customary expenditures. This unproductive spending gives the moneylender, the bania, his opportunity; and it has been estimated that the total rural debt runs to the incredible figure of 4 billion dollars. Excessive rates of interest are charged, and once in debt, the ryot usually stays there the rest of his life. No wonder the peasants have a saying, "The bania goes in like a needle and comes out like a sword." [12]

[11] Sam Higginbottom, "The Cattle Drain in India," *Asia*, XXXVIII (1938), pp. 473-482.
[12] Sir Edward Blunt, ed., *Social Service in India* (London: His Majesty's Stationery Office, 1939), p. 109.

Two other conditions which spring from belief and custom are the maintenance of a large number of unproductive mendicants and beggars and the practice of hoarding wealth. One Indian writer estimates that in undivided India the Muslim and Hindu communities supported about 3 million holy men and beggars, a heavy burden for a poor country. This writer states that these people must be turned to useful vocations, observing that "when young men are able to earn a living the elders are ashamed to beg." [13] From time immemorial large amounts of gold and silver have been placed in temples, or buried, or fashioned into women's jewelry. The value of this immobilized wealth is tremendous, and it could be used to finance extensive schemes of economic development.

The great central problem of the Indian subcontinent is the pressure of its people upon the land. As modern sanitation began to make some impression in India, the mortality rate fell while the birth rate remained the same. Thus it was that between 1931 and 1941 the population increase was nearly 51 million. The Indian subcontinent now supports 20 per cent of the world's people and has a population one and one-half that of all North and South America. This population increase in India has not been something unique in comparison with other countries. In India between 1872 and 1941 the rate of increase was 54 per cent, but in the United Kingdom it was 56 per cent and in Japan during the same period it was more than 130 per cent. The distinctive element in the Indian situation has been that this country experienced a large population increase without at the same time developing its economic productivity to keep pace with the people's needs. It is not too much to say that independent India's most fundamental problem is one of population. A well-known English authority on Indian economic history has observed:

> It is difficult to avoid the conclusion that no matter how productivity is increased, economic organization is improved, public health is promoted, or industrialization progresses, the standard of the masses will not and cannot be raised to a satisfactory level until changes have been introduced which will enable the size of the population to be better adjusted to economic resources.[14]

In India, however, the marriage customs and associated religious beliefs make it almost impossible to exert control over population. Marriage is a social and religious necessity. Hindu belief has it that girls should be married before puberty, and the necessity of having a son to perform the

13 Singh, *op. cit.,* p. 35.
14 Vera Anstey, *The Economic Development of India* (London: Longmans, Green and Co., 1936), pp. 474-475.

sraddha ceremony at the funeral of the father, thereby ensuring his salvation, helps explain the universality of parenthood among Hindus. The unmarried state is practically unknown, divorce is rare, and there is the lowest proportion of unmarried women in the world. Too many girls are married at an early age; in the 1920's it was estimated that 40 per cent were married before the age of fifteen, that 2 million were married before the age of ten, and that 100,000 were already widowed at this age. Of course, child couples do not live together immediately after marriage, the usual age being fourteen or fifteen. This means the first child is born when the mother is sixteen or seventeen, and thousands are mothers of six children before the age of thirty. Early marriage and the burden of too many children explain the high maternal mortality in India and, contrary to the situation in Western countries, the lower life expectancy of women than of men. "It is clear," writes one Indian student of this problem, "that such a universality of marriage, especially early marriage, must tend to shorten the Indian woman's period of education, affect her health and restrict both her professional and public activities." [15]

Actually there is in India a serious disparity in the ratio between the sexes, for there are about 930 women to every 1000 men. This problem is made worse by Hindu law, which prohibits the remarriage of widows. It is this shortage of marriageable women that further encourages child marriage.

Springing from this population problem in India is the pressure of the people upon the land and its subdivision into uneconomic holdings. Roughly throughout the country one-half of the holdings are less than five acres and three-fourths of them are less than fifteen. Many surveys have been made, and all tell the same story of farmers making a bare subsistence on three or four acres, indifferently tilled, and usually not fertilized. Among Hindus land is generally equally divided among the heirs, and the laws of inheritance among the Muslims lead to the same result. A greater evil than land subdivision is that of fragmentation. The fields are broken up so that various heirs may secure a small portion of the several types of crop or wood land. In the Punjab there are fields only a few yards wide but over a mile long. The prevalence of small farm holdings in India makes it almost impossible to carry on modern, mechanized farming without the equivalent of an agrarian revolution. It is not surprising that there is a great gap between agricultural productiveness in India and in the United States.

[15] L. N. Menon, "The Position of Women," *Oxford Pamphlets on Indian Affairs*, No. 2 (Bombay: Oxford University Press, 1944), p. 18.

Two final factors influencing the Indian economic picture demand comment. The Indian peasant has insufficient land to support him in a reasonably comfortable living, while out of the pitiably small yield that is his, he must often hand over a large sum to the landlord, the zamindar. In Bengal, for example, landlords take £3,750,000 annually from the tillers of the soil. This zamindar class has been described as "an incubus on the working agricultural population, which finds no justification in the performance of material services, so far as agricultural improvements are concerned and fails to provide any effective means for the development of the resources of the land which is the greatest asset of the province." [16]

As already indicated, the lot of the urban worker is no better than that of the rural villager. The second serious economic problem is the over-all maldistribution of wealth in India, the tragic gulf which exists between opulence and dire want. In the entire country it has been calculated that 33 per cent of the wealth is owned by 5 per cent of the people, another like amount by 30 per cent, and the last third by more than 60 per cent. Or the picture can be described another way, by stating that in India 20 million people are very wealthy or enjoy substantial middle-class status, some 130 million live in respectable poverty, and 240 million endure a bare subsistence.

It was these economic problems of Indian life that demanded study and rectification if the governments of both India and Pakistan were to secure for their people the better life that had been an essential objective of the nationalist movement before independence.

Immediately after independence, in the realm of industry, agriculture, transportation, and medical and educational facilities, India seemed about to become a planner's paradise, as economists, reformers, and statesmen enthusiastically set to work to achieve a richer livelihood for their people. The financial position seemed sound, with a public debt less than half the national income and with a huge credit account amounting to several billion dollars held in blocked sterling in London. The great need of the country was to increase its food output. In industry, after partition, India retained most of the great factories, together with huge deposits of coal and iron potentially greater than those of any other country except the United States and the Soviet Union.

Numerous industrial projects were either planned or ac-

[16] Quoted in Gyan Chand, "The Problem of Population," *Oxford Pamphlets on Indian Affairs*, No. 19 (Bombay: Oxford University Press, 1944), p. 16.

tually initiated in the Indian Union in 1948. These included two large steel mills, a newsprint factory, fertilizer and gasoline plants, and three automobile assembly factories. In textiles, the largest industry, the plan was to import thousands of spindles and looms from Japan. A seven-year plan for modernizing the railroads at a cost of a billion dollars was blueprinted. The rapid expansion of air services was planned, together with a five-year scheme for highways, and another for creating 2 million tons of shipping. Most spectacular were the multi-purpose power schemes based on the American Tennessee Valley Authority model. These projects aimed at flood control, irrigation, better navigation on the rivers, and the generation of electric power. In India at present only 6 per cent of the water resources are being used, and it is estimated that ultimately more than 30 million kilowatts yearly can be produced. In 1950 the annual production of electric power was equal to only one week's output in the United States. And as for food production, energetic measures were undertaken to increase the supply. Irrigation by means of hundreds of tube wells was planned, better seeds were procured, and various schemes were initiated to reclaim waste land. Public sanitation, education, and labor also received the attention of the planners. There was talk of eradicating illiteracy in five years, and training 2 million new teachers. As for public health, the recommendations of the Bhore Committee were accepted and a target was envisaged of 300,000 doctors and more than 750,000 nurses. There was also a program for labor calling for better working conditions, more housing, social security, and other benefits.

It soon became apparent to the Indian government that it was one thing to plan oneself into prosperity but quite a different matter to bring the plans to fruition. There was a decided decline in confidence as plans failed to reach their goals and capital was not forthcoming to finance the new schemes. On November 14, 1950, in a broadcast to the nation, the late Sardar Patel, then deputy prime minister, declared: "I can tell you quite frankly that the time for preparing paper schemes has gone; we cannot indulge any longer in the pastime of conjuring before our vision idealistic utopias." [17]

In addition to the heavy burden of military expenditure occasioned by the tragic quarrel over Kashmir, there was evidence that industrial development in India was being throttled by the government's policy of nationalization of industry and deep suspicion of foreign capital. In the spring of 1948 the Indian government made the following statement on in-

[17] *The Statesman* (Calcutta), November 14, 1950, p. 6.

dustrial policy: (1) The generation and distribution of electric power will be regulated, and in some instances will be the function of the government. (2) The state will have an exclusive monopoly in the case of munitions, atomic energy, and the railways. (3) All new projects in certain key industries will be the responsibility of the government, and after ten years private enterprise in this area will be reviewed by the state. (4) In addition the government must have power to plan and regulate basic industries even if run by private enterprise. (5) Foreign capital is welcome, but the major interest and effective control of all projects financed from abroad must be in Indian hands.

The amount of capital, both foreign and domestic, forthcoming for economic development in the two or three years after independence was not adequate for India's needs. Furthermore, both industrial and agricultural production showed alarming declines. Most serious was the problem of inflation and the growing deficit in food supplies. Each year witnessed larger and larger imports of foreign food grains, the figure in 1949 being close to 4 million tons. Largely because of this need to import such huge food stocks, India had an unfavorable balance of trade, which in 1949 was close to 600 million dollars. In 1950 the country reeled from a series of calamities—droughts, floods, earthquakes—and by the end of the year was facing famine conditions. Supplies were obtained on a cash or barter basis from the United States, Canada, Australia, Russia, and China. And in the spring of 1951 the United States made a loan of 190 million dollars at 3 per cent with which to buy surplus American grain. With this transaction the crisis disappeared.

The First Five-Year Plan

With all this disturbing economic background, there came to India's leaders the realization that provision must be made for a bold and comprehensive program of economic development. Speaking in July 1951, Nehru referred to the lack of success in basic economic matters and defended the creation of a planning commission a year before. This body was to "make an assessment of the material, capital, and human resources of the country" and to "formulate a plan for the most effective and balanced utilization of the country's resources."

Following these instructions the commission issued its draft outline for a first five-year plan in July 1951. The program called for expenditures by the central and state governments of more than 4 billion dollars with new expansion in the field of private enterprise of around 250 million dollars. Eyes were set on the target of raising national income by 11 per cent, which, by allowing for population increase, would mean a real per capita increase of 7.5 per cent. The government's main effort in the plan was to increase the supply of food, hence the allocation of 45 per cent of its plan capital into agriculture and irrigation projects. Twenty per cent was set aside for social services, health, education, etc., and 8 per cent on industry. Industry was not to be neglected, however, for 200 million dollars were to be spent in the fields of ship-building, iron and steel, machine tools, and fertilizers. Private industry, both domestic and foreign, was likewise expected to expand, with particular attention to oil refineries, steel, textiles, chemicals, and cement.

The most spectacular feature of the first five-year plan was its huge multi-purpose power projects. These dams were among the greatest engineering achievements in the world, and their design and construction owed much to American technicians. Bhakra-Nangal, for example, when finished would be the second highest dam in the world, making a lake 56 miles long and 550 feet deep. This project will eventually produce almost as much electricity as all India had in 1950, and its first target for irrigation was set at 1⅓ million acres. Power, flood control, water for irrigation—these, the fruits of the multi-purpose projects, would go far in revolutionizing the lives of millions of peasants.

Side by side with the major effort on food production came a substantial advance in industry. Among state projects one of the most important was the huge fertilizer plant at Sindri with a capacity of 1000 tons daily. In addition factories for turning out penicillin and DDT were established, together with others for the manufacture of machine tools, newsprint, and railway coaches. Private industry has developed new lines of industry in the manufacture of dyes, chemicals, pharmaceuticals, and industrial explosives. Two huge oil refineries were also put in operation with the aid of foreign investment. The index of industrial production was 105 in 1950 (base year 1946), and in the first quarter of 1955 it had reached 152. A year later it had climbed to 170.

Indian leaders understood that somehow the masses must have a part in the economic reconstruction of their country. New industries and multiple-power projects would mean little if the people living in more than 500,000 villages did not take a hand in the five-year plan. In these rural communities lived 300 million people. The problem of disease, under-nourishment, poverty, and illiteracy largely had to do with these peasants. Most of the 500,000 villages were a dreary collection of mud-walled huts, roads that were dusty or muddy depending on the weather, dirty unhygienic wells, and spindly

children with running noses and festered eyes. The symbol of
the primitivism of the villages was the dung cakes plastered
on every wall. This humus, which should go back into the
soil, was used for cooking and for warmth in the cold season.

Gandhi had always taught that there could be no basic
improvement in India without the reconstruction of its villages. This view was also held by a number of British officers,
such as F. L. Brayne, who, before the war, had had remarkable success in village improvement. The pilot project for
village improvement was started at Etawah in the state of
Uttar Pradesh in 1948. The scheme was suggested by a New
York architect—Albert Meyer—who had been in India during the war. He believed that India had to have a mass effort
involving all aspects of life in her villages. The pilot project
came under the direction of Horace G. Holmes, an American agriculturist from Tennessee, who increased the project's
yield of crops 50 per cent in three years.

On Gandhi's birthday anniversary, October 2, 1952, a
nation-wide campaign of village community development was
initiated in 28 Indian states. In the formulation of the program Chester Bowles, then the American Ambassador, had
a prominent role. He offered substantial help from the United
States, and the Ford Foundation assumed important responsibilities in the training of the necessary personnel. The initial
phase launched 55 development projects covering 16,000 villages and 11 million people. A community project was usually
made up of three blocks, each with 100 villages and a population of 66,000 scattered over 150 square miles or more. In
two years the program had reached out to cover 23,450 villages, and at the same time a less concentrated national extension in agriculture was started to reach villages not yet covered
by community development. A veritable army had to be
trained for service in the villages. At the head of each unit
was the project officer, and in each of his three blocks would
be an engineer and three agricultural officers. And for every
5 to 8 villages there was a village-level worker who has been
called a "rural first-aid man." It is the job of these officers
to train villagers in the essentials of modern agriculture, public health, village industries, sanitation and animal husbandry.
At the same time, in cooperation with the educational staff,
programs in social education for the abolition of illiteracy
are carried out. No wonder that a U.N. mission reported that
the community projects are "the most significant experiment
in economic development and social improvement in Asia
at the present time." [18]

[18] Quoted in *India in 1954: Annual Review* (London: India House),
p. 57.

During the course of the first five-year plan rural development saw exciting progress. More than 400,000 acres of formerly useless land have been reclaimed, 1 million acres have been put under irrigation, 8,000 new schools built, and 68 million peasants reached. As one visited various villages undergoing this rehabilitation, the visitor was amazed by the many signs of progress: compost piles, clean wells, access roads ending a village's isolation, community halls, and improved latrines. While the central government contributed large sums to the scheme—about 65 million dollars—one of the basic objectives was to get the people of the villages identified with the work of improvement. "Self-help" under government direction was an essential part of community development. Thus the villagers were urged to make contributions in cash, materials, or labor, and their participation between 1942 and 1955 was estimated to come to a value of 40 million dollars. In evaluating what has been called India's quiet revolution, it has been said that her foreign policy in the 1950's may be given a few pages in histories a century from now, but that the community-development program will be given a substantial chapter.

Toward Social Justice and Welfare

Before independence one of the shrillest denunciations made against British rule was its neglect and mismanagement of education. Only 18 per cent of the people were literate in 1947, and the educational system was not fitted to the real-life needs of most Indians. It was bookish, literary, and dominated by an examination system that emphasized memory rather than thought. After independence, educational reformers put ten years as a target date by which time illiteracy would be completely removed. But it was soon found in independent India that mass education—together with provision for improved facilities at the university level—for more than 300 million people is a herculean task.

Notwithstanding serious problems in the way of inadequate finance and a shortage of teachers, encouraging progress has been made in the schools. An important commission studied the system of secondary education, which has been one of the weakest links in Indian education, and made its report in 1953. It was emphasized that secondary schools should stress a diversity of studies and cease to be mere feeders of the colleges. Multi-purpose schools should be opened to encourage technical education at an early age. Most important, the report urged that secondary education ending at about 17 should be a terminal stage preparing for life. In the primary—our elementary—stage the central ministry of education is trying to get all schools oriented to a pattern advocated by Gandhi. This system is known as basic education. It shuns the idea of "reading and writing" learning, believing that elementary schooling should be related to the environment and life situation of the child. Arts, crafts, gardening, and citizenship are important elements in the program. In the villages, also, social education, as we have seen, forms part of the community-development program. Radio, posters, and films are used to reach the illiterate adults. Over the period 1950-1955, some 5 million people have achieved the rudiments of reading and writing.

There is a tremendous demand for college education, and since 1947 universities have increased from 19 to 30, with tremendous increases in enrollments. In fact, it can be said that the number of students in the colleges has outstripped facilities and also the capacity of the country to absorb the tens of thousands of graduates, all too many of whom are still just educated clerks with no special training. Another disturbing problem is the low status of the teaching profession. At all levels teachers are overworked and underpaid, and the average teacher can barely survive unless he gives "tuitions." Overcrowding of schools, underpaid teachers, and a curriculum too often ill-suited for the requirements of commerce and industry has not only brought about a deterioration of standards but also the serious problem of what is known in India as "student indiscipline." There have been demonstrations and boycotts by high school and college students. At Calcutta University authorities were held prisoner because they refused to postpone the date of the final medical examinations. In 1953 strikes began at Lucknow University and spread to other colleges in the state. This ended with attacks on public property, such as post offices, and resulting loss of life. Students have taken over their fathers' example of defying authority when schools were an important battleground for civil disobedience against British rule. This indiscipline in the schools and colleges of independent India remains a constant source of anxiety to officials.

While problems on the educational front are many and substantial, there are grounds for optimism. Officials in the ministry of education at New Delhi, often American-trained, are professionally competent and dedicated civil servants. A scholar and educator like Humayun Kabir, secretary and educational adviser to the government of India, could not be frequently duplicated in educational circles in the most advanced Western nations. Quantitatively at least, there have been encouraging signs of educational progress. In nearly every branch facilities have been doubled, and the literate population has been enlarged to 22 per cent.

Vital statistics have always been a sad chapter in the Indian story. Just before independence it was estimated that the average annual death rate was 21.8 per 1000 of population, whereas it was only 9.6 in the United States. The infant mortality rate was 158 for India and 29 for the United States. Nearly 40 per cent of all deaths in India took place within the first year of life; and the life expectancy of an Indian was no more than 26, as compared with 65 in a number of Western countries. Back of the lamentable health situation in India was the lack of hospitals and health centers, the high prevalence of communicable diseases, absence of good water supply, poor sanitation, and insufficient doctors and nurses.

Under the first five-year plan nearly 300 million dollars was earmarked for health, and definite progress can be observed. At the start of the plan there was one doctor to 6,100 of the population. At the end there was one to every 5,100. The number of nurses rose from one per 21,000 to one per 16,000 of the population. Hospitals and health centers were substantially expanded. The net result of this work was the rise of life expectancy to 32.

One of the most dramatic programs aiming at securing equality and better welfare for the Indian rural masses has been in land-tenure reform. Land inequalities and exploitive forms of tenure have long been one of the heaviest burdens of the people in the countryside. Perhaps as many as 40 per cent of the workers in agriculture are landless, and as the population of India has mounted upward in the past quarter-century, farmlands have been forced to support more and more people. In addition to the landless laborers there is a vast army of tenants who have rented from landlords, often rightly termed parasitic.

The Congress party, even before independence, had pointed to this land inequality as one of the greatest economic problems. After 1947 the various states in India began to enact land-reform legislation. The main object was to eliminate the so-called "intermediaries," the landlord zamindars. Other features of agrarian laws were the limitation of rents, the protection of tenants from landlord abuse, and careful supervision of moneylenders' activities in rural areas. Ceilings were also placed on individual landholdings, the general plan being to have a ceiling of 30 acres and a floor of 5 acres to a family.

Apart from this governmental approach to the land problem, one of the most colorful and dramatic features of agrarian reform has been the crusade of a dedicated holy man and disciple of Gandhi, Vinoba Bhave. This saintly reformer is the most revered religious leader in India today. His message of peace, service, and humility has made him in the eyes of the people the true successor of Gandhi. In 1951 in the state of Hyderabad, he began his now famous Bhoodan, or land-gift movement. Traveling on foot from village to village, he asked those who had land to give it to those who had none. He asked his audiences: "If you have four sons and another is born, you give the last his share. Make me your fifth son, and give me my share." By June of 1955 the contributions made reached the figure of nearly 4 million acres; and by 1957 the figure may have been as much as 50 million acres. Vinoba Bhave is not only a land reformer but the would-be builder of a new society. He seeks the moral improvement of the Indian people. His program is an interesting fusion of the old and new. While he advocates the equality of women, decrease in the worship of old gods, and the end of Untouchability, he sees India's golden age based on a return to village industry.

How well are the state governments and the mission of Vinoba Bhave solving the land problem? The answer is a mixed one. There is no doubt that the situation is improving. Where still a tenant, the peasant has been given security of tenure and fairer terms of rent. In a few years from one-third to one-half of the peasants in India may have adequate land holdings. The state governments compensate the landlords for their estates. In turn the peasants, in a series of payments, reimburse the state. Thus the peasant—at least for this generation—has to bear the same economic burden. The least aided will be the landless workers. As to the Bhoodan movement, the good that has been done should not be minimized. Some landless workers now have small parcels of land, and the people of the countryside have been touched and uplifted by a message of "help thy neighbor." But the land problem in India is not just one of maldistribution. It is a case where there is just not enough land available to be divided to provide the average rural family with a farm holding large enough to provide a good standard of living. Cultivated land per capita is now less than 1 acre. It follows that the future of industry is also the future of the land in India. Urban employment must be expanded to draw off the uneconomic surplus now living in the rural areas. Only thus can the excessive fragmentation of land be halted and bad production give way to efficient methods of farming.

A new India is taking shape not only in industry, education, life in the villages, and better health facilities but—

largely because of the impact of Western influences—much of the social structure and habits of the Hindu people are being modified: the status of the traditional joint family, the legal position of women in relation to property and divorce, the participation of women in public life, and the force exerted by the age-old caste system. All these facets of Hinduism are rapidly changing.

Throughout the entire structure of Hindu social and religious life new forces, some obvious and strong, others subtle and weak, are transforming the ways of life of the people. Despite the prohibitions of caste there is increasing intermarriage between Hindus and Europeans, between the former and Muslims, and between Hindus of different caste groupings. The old joint family is breaking down. Young men now set up their own homes, not taking their brides to live with their parents and other relatives. Wives of middle-class families are going out to work because of economic pressures. It is in this field that there has been the most revolutionary change. In the Indian constitution women are given complete legal equality. Since long before independence, educated women in various organizations have been working for and demanding that the ancient principles in Hindu law be amended in the fields of marriage, divorce, and inheritance. Leaders in the women's movement in India have also campaigned against child marriage and the seclusion of women, and for maternity welfare and adult education. In 1952 women organized the first international conference in India—and the third in the world—on planned parenthood. The very active birth-control movement in India has behind it the full force of women's groups.

A committee as far back as 1941 had drafted legislation for the general revision and codification of Hindu law. Because of the bitter opposition of orthodox groups, Nehru and his government decided to proceed with the program on a piecemeal basis, item by item. In 1955 the Hindu Marriage Act outlawed polygamy and made divorce possible for the first time. Other installments gave women the right to be guardians of their children's property, to have an equal share in their father's inheritance, to have a place in the paternal home if widowed or if a spinster, and to inherit a husband's property on his death. Child marriage has been outlawed for nearly fifty years, but recent revelations indicate that there is much to be done before this custom is abolished. In 1951 the census report estimated that more then 9 million couples had been married between the ages of 5 and 14. While it still exists, there is also evidence to show it is definitely on the wane. The terrible lot of womanhood depicted, and exaggerated somewhat, by Katherine Mayo in her *Mother India* in the 1920's, no longer has relevance to India in the closing 1950's.

On every hand there is abundant evidence that India as a "man's world" is radically changing as women become doctors, lawyers, air hostesses, actresses in films, and social workers. In public life a number of women have risen to high prominence. Mrs. Pandit, sister of Nehru, has served her country abroad in various high diplomatic posts, notably as president of the General Assembly of the U.N. Rajkumari Amrit Kaur has been minister of health in the central government, and in 1950 became president of the World Health Organization. And in the 1952 election a number of women were elected to the central and state legislatures.

Occasionally one hears the assertion that "caste has been abolished in India." This is, of course, quite untrue. The whole traditional structure of caste still remains intact. What has happened is that the constitution has declared that there shall be no "discrimination" against any citizen on the grounds of caste and the practice of Untouchability is abolished. No matter, therefore, to what caste a man may belong—or in the case of an Untouchable, who in a sense is outside and below the caste hierarchy—he cannot be denied access to hotels, restaurants, and places of entertainment, or the use of wells, roads, and "places of public resort" maintained by the state.

Generally speaking, the whole system of caste is on the defensive. In the cities, caste has little meaning in government offices, factories, and stores. The old taboos against intercaste marriages are weakening, and young people increasingly disregard them. Prohibitions against eating with members of another caste are often ignored as interdining, as it is termed, becomes more common. Enlightened opinion in India has been most concerned about the degraded and miserable Untouchables. Numbering more than 55 million, their lot has been described thus: "It is as if a pale had been built round the British Isles, and every man, women, and child condemned to intolerable indignity and extreme poverty."[19] Despite the constitution and special protective and developmental programs of the government, the condition of the Untouchable community has not improved materially. The report of the commissioner for the Scheduled Castes reported in 1953 that "there has been no appreciable improvement with regard to the practice of untouchability."[20] In the villages, still the citadel of orthodox Hinduism, discriminations against Un-

[19] *The Times* (London), May 2, 1955, p. 13.
[20] *Report of the Commissioner for the Scheduled Castes and Tribes* (New Delhi, 1953), p. 77.

touchables have not materially lessened. Laws on the statute
books can do little without the support of public opinion. While
Hindus often severely castigate other peoples for their practice of racial or religious discrimination, as in the case of
the Negro in the United States, it may be kept in mind that
India has a like problem.

From the First to the Second Five-Year Plan

In the spring of 1956, India looked back over nine years
of independence and more specifically the fruits of the first
five-year plan. Its leaders were gratified to know that most of
its targets had been achieved and in important fields over-
fulfilled. Most important, the plan target for food production
had been exceeded by some 4 million tons, and food imports
had virtually ceased. The output of cotton had increased by
45 per cent. It was mainly the reduction of food and cotton
imports that explained, after 1951, India's favorable balance
of trade. Industrially, production in five years registered a 50
per cent advance. The target of an 11 per cent increase in
national income had been exceeded by some 7 per cent, which
could be regarded as a new per capita income gain of about
8 per cent. As a symbol of this economic achievement the
Indian Industries Fair had been held at the end of 1955. It
was the largest ever held in Asia, covering an area of 73
acres and with some 20 nations being represented. It gave
hundreds of thousands of Indians at the fair grounds in New
Delhi an opportunity not only to see the latest marvels of
science and industry from countries such as the United States,
Great Britain, and Russia, but to witness with pride the
achievements of their own land.

In May 1956, another momentous step in the struggle for
welfare and livelihood was taken in India when the final
draft of the second five-year plan was presented to Parliament. A year before a tentative draft had been drawn up for
public study and analysis. The second plan called for the expenditure of about twice that spent on the first—some 48 billion rupees (16.25 billion dollars). Of this huge sum one-third
would be spent by private enterprise in the so-called private
sector and the remainder by the state in the public sector. The
plan aims are: to increase national income a little over 25
per cent, to expand steel production 250 per cent, to increase
coal output 60 per cent, food grains 15, and electric power 100
per cent. Power, industry, minerals, and transport are to receive the most attention, some 57 per cent of the expenditures
in the public sector. By the end of the plan the national extension and community-development programs will cover a

population of more than 300 million. Substantial attention is also given to reforms in the areas of education, health, and land problems.

With this second plan the area of the public sector is materially widened. In 1948 the government's policy resolution set aside the state's exclusive responsibility for six industries. But in 1956 the state widened the public sector to include seventeen key industries under its management, with twelve more to be progressively state-owned. The main goal will be advance toward a socialistic pattern of society. This means the steady reduction of disparities in wealth and income; Congress has gone far into the realm of the welfare state in contrast to its conservative tone in matters economic when India gained its freedom. Some Indian economists, however, point out that even at the end of the second plan the private sector will still produce 80 per cent of the national income.

This second plan brings India several difficult, almost unsolvable, problems. One of these is how to secure the necessary and competent administrative staff to run the various state enterprises. Poor management will mean failure to reach the targets set in the plan. The most serious problem is where to obtain the necessary finances to carry through the program. Estimates vary, but the gap between the amount needed and expected revenues in loans and taxes is over 800 million dollars. Since much of its equipment for new industries, such as steel plants, will have to be imported, the bill will have to be paid in "hard currencies." This foreign exchange problem means finding the equivalent of more than a billion dollars in the next five years. Indian economists hope that adequate funds will be secured by external assistance. During the first five-year plan the total finances made available from abroad ran to 630 million dollars. This did not include the United States wheat loan or private American philanthropic aid. If these two avenues are counted, the total American aid would run in the neighborhood of 500 million dollars. Under the Colombo Plan, Australia, New Zealand, Canada, and Britain have made substantial contributions in money and technical aid. The World Bank has also made available, up to 1956, some 125 million dollars. It will be noted that all this aid has emanated from Western countries.

A visitor to India, say at the end of the first five-year plan, might after a superficial tour have believed that the country was changing very little. There were the vast, sprawling slums of the great cities, the hordes of beggars that congregate around the historic spots visited by foreign tourists, and unchanged villages bowed down by poverty and disease. But a keen observer would have noted the modern new factories, not many of them, but a symbol of India's industrial revolution. He would have visited the great multi-purpose projects such as Damodar Valley and made a tour of the villages that had been touched by the work of the community-development projects. These signs of a new India emerging were accompanied by a dynamic spirit of confidence and enthusiasm. As a U.N. mission reported, "There is a sense of urgency and responsibility among the Indian leaders with which they are endeavoring to enthuse the people and capitalize upon it to provide the motive power for economic development and social progress."[21]

[21] *India in 1954: Annual Review*, p. 57.

Liaquat Ali Khan

10. Pakistan: The Struggle for Democracy and Unity

Divided: Can We Stand?

DIRECTLY AFTER INDEPENDENCE AND PARTITION, enthusiasm for the future was prevalent in Pakistan. Most of its people expected quick realization of their hopes for a good life in proportion to the sacrifices that had been made to create their new nation. Alas, these hopes did not materialize. There were too many burdens to carry, too many problems to solve. There has been the tremendous task of building almost from scratch a viable national economy. The staggering burden of military expenditures occasioned by the cold war with India —which became hot for a brief period in Kashmir—has diverted funds from such nation-building services as health, education, and irrigation. There has been the threat of a secessionist movement in the North-West Frontier Province supported by Afghanistan, as well as the potential blow of losing the waters essential for irrigation in West Pakistan because of India's control of their source.

Pakistan lost the main cities of India and the great centers of government. With much of her banking and commercial activity in the hands of a Hindu middle class, she lost these services when Sikhs and Hindus fled to India. On the whole, her people were less well educated and less politically mature than those in India. These facts were abundantly clear when an observer, visiting the subcontinent in the 1950's, compared Karachi with New Delhi or Lahore with Bombay.

In the decade after partition and independence, Pakistan was harassed by endemic unrest, the fall of governments,

280

riots, and serious emergencies. The greatest threat came to be recognized as internal, not external. While Muslims in Bengal and their coreligionists in the Punjab united to defend their religion and culture, as they believed, in 1947, after freedom East and West Pakistanis, divided by some thousand miles, found increasingly that they were different people. After ten years of independence, the great question was, Can Pakistan maintain her unity?

It was ironic that, after sacrificing so much to be able to leave predominantly Hindu India, the people of Pakistan soon gave evidence after 1947 of not being able to stick together. The reason lay primarily in the thousand miles separating East and West Pakistan and in the different people and their contrasting environments in the two wings. In the west lived descendants of the white-skinned Aryan invaders or the later Muslim invaders. They were a martial, energetic, and proud people who had been the backbone of the old British Indian Army. Their small clique of educated leaders were good administrators, accustomed to giving orders and having them obeyed. Their homeland of West Pakistan, some 300,000 square miles, was dry and sparsely populated and really was a projection of the vast desert expanses lying to the west. East Pakistan, on the other hand, was a riverine area, lush with jungle vegetation, drenched with heavy rainfall, and densely settled. Its people were dark descendants of pre-Aryan stock converted by their Muslim conquerors and racially quite dissimilar to the Punjabis or Sindhis in West Pakistan. The latter "is a land of donkeys, camels, purdah, mullahs, and Arabic scholars: it is a hodge-podge of the Middle East. East Pakistan is a land of timid men, of green jute and paddy fields, of lazy rivers and heavy rains: it is in Monsoon Asia." [1] Before partition the Muslim population in East Bengal had been exploited and used by the commercial and banking Hindu communities centered in Calcutta. Independence to the Bengali Muslim meant freedom from the foreigner and the chance to develop his neglected homeland. This ambition had been recognized in the famous Lahore Resolution of 1940 stating that Pakistan was to be a state "in which the constituent units shall be autonomous and sovereign."

In the crisis months first following independence the need for strong unity and the lack of experienced administrators in East Pakistan led to strong centralization in the hands of the central government in Karachi. From West Pakistan, especially the Punjab, came numerous officials to fill posts in the East Wing. While mainly honest, a goodly number of these imported officials had little sympathy with the Muslim Bengalis,

[1] *Manchester Guardian*, January 13, 1955.

whom they regarded as backward and crude. Soon the governed began to complain that they were being neglected in the way of developmental schemes and the allocation of revenues. It was even claimed that, after several years of independence, there had in fact been a decrease in schools so urgently needed. The university at Dacca actually was badly neglected, and a visiting American Fulbright Professor referred to the institution as a "pedagogic shambles."

Another irritant was the apparent determination of the central government to adopt Urdu as the official language—this despite the fact that perhaps only half of the people in West Pakistan speak Urdu and among the Bengali-speaking people of the other wing not more than 10 per cent. Another cause for grievance among the Bengalis lay in the proposed constitution. To the Muslims in the West Wing, made up of the old provinces of the Sind, North-West Frontier, the western part of the Punjab, and several princely states, Pakistan comprised a number of political units, among which was East Bengal. The Muslim Bengalis, however, challenged the justice of this point of view. They demanded political, linguistic and cultural, and financial parity with West Pakistan. In support of this claim they pointed out that East Bengal was not a mere province, to be set alongside Punjab or Sind, but a veritable country worthy of being equated with all the units in West Pakistan. Their most important ammunition was the fact that they had a majority of the population of all Pakistan—some 56 per cent—and, furthermore, that the export of their jute crop brought the nation the bulk of its foreign exchange.

After 1951 discontent and a sense of grievance mounted steadily in East Pakistan. There was serious rioting in the provincial capital, Dacca, and elsewhere in 1952. The trouble arose over the apparent determination of the central government to make Urdu the official language, ignoring the claims of Bengali. Since independence, the Muslim League party had run political affairs in both East and West Pakistan. It had been the party of Jinnah, the party that had fought for and won partition. In East Pakistan, however, it had lost contact with the people. It had failed to alleviate economic difficulties and had been more responsive to the views of politicians in West Pakistan than sensitive to the needs and desires of the Muslim Bengalis. The popularity of the League plummeted to zero. When elections were scheduled for the spring of 1954, Fazlul Huq, a venerable Bengali political figure, became the leader of a coalition—the United Front. This opposition was a diverse and unstable group containing all elements of politics, from the most conservative to Communist.

The United Front issued a 21-point program reflecting the frustrations of Bengali nationalism. It made such demands as: (1) Bengali to be a state language, (2) steps to be taken for the rapid industrialization of East Bengal, (3) radical changes to be made in the education system, with the mother tongue as the medium of instruction, (4) political prisoners to be set free, (5) East Bengal to get complete autonomy—defense, currency, and foreign policy to be joint subjects with the central government. The election, held in March 1945 was a complete rout for the Muslim League, this party getting only 10 seats out of 309 in the legislature.

Victory for the United Front was a heady concoction, and both its leaders and their followers seemed to lose all restraint. Fazlul Huq was reported as saying he "did not believe in partition." On another occasion he said, "I do not believe in political division of a country. I am in fact not familiar with two words—Pakistan and Hindustan. When I speak of India, I mean both countries. India exists as a whole." [2] While Pakistanis, especially in the West, regarded these statements as treason, Indian public opinion was naturally gratified.

Meanwhile, early in May, serious trouble had broken out between Bengali workers and those from other parts of Pakistan. The government was unable, and not very eager, to restore order. In the riots more than a thousand lives were lost. The central government at Karachi moved quickly. Ten thousand troops were sent to the troubled area; Fazlul Huq, the new head of the Bengali government, was dismissed; and Major General Iskander Mirza, one of the top civil servants from the central government, took control. Under martial law order was restored and many grievances were rectified. In the spring of 1955 parliamentary government was restored, and in a more chastened mood both wings of the nation set about building a better-united Pakistan.

Ups and Downs in Politics

While what became almost a Bengali separatist movement was the most serious problem in the political life of Pakistan after 1947, the whole trend of politics was a checkered one as Pakistani leaders sought to develop a democratic and stable form of government as expressed in a constitution supported by the majority of citizens, whether in the West or the East Wing. The rather turbulent chronicle of Pakistan politics following independence began in 1951, when a serious plot to overthrow the government was disclosed. This Rawalpindi conspiracy case involved the chief of staff of the army and other officers. It was believed that the conspirators had secured Communist support. The government of Liaquat Ali Khan had little trouble arresting the ringleaders and removing the foci of treason, but later in the year constitutional progress received a heavy blow when Liaquat, the prime minister, was murdered by a Pathan fanatic. The mystery of this evil deed has never been cleared up. Some thought the assassin was acting on Afghan orders; other observers held that the murderer was merely a disgruntled rebel.

In this crisis, Governor-General Khwaja Nazimuddin resigned to become prime minister, his post being taken by Ghulam Mohammed. Following this abrupt change in leadership the initial drive of dedication and enthusiasm that had been so evident shortly after partition lost its momentum. As we will note later in our discussion of Pakistan economics, the country was faced by grave problems of famine and budgetary difficulties. Another weakness was the slow progress being made in constitution making. Shortly after independence, as we have seen, India rapidly made strides in this field. Pakistan scarcely moved at all. This was a mistake, as it permitted the initial drive of enthusiasm to be lost amid growing local prejudices and loyalties. Realizing this fact, Liaquat Ali Khan began the work of constitution making in the spring of 1949 when an *Objectives Resolution* was passed by the legislature. Laying down the general principles of the constitution, this document made it quite clear that Pakistan was to be an Islamic state.

A *Basic Principles Interim Report* was also drafted, but unlike its companion document it aroused much opposition. East Bengal was not happy over its balance of political representation of the two wings in the central government. Bengalis were also aroused at Urdu being chosen as the official language. The report also offended the orthodox Muslims, who championed a completely theocratic state. Their leaders, the Mullahs, demanded that Pakistan be ruled by the letter of Islamic law. The civil servants and intellectuals strongly opposed this claim. In their belief, while Pakistan should be regarded as a state deriving its cultural and spiritual legacy mainly from Islam, religion and politics should operate in separate spheres. An amended version of the report presented in December 1952 leaned toward the orthodox Muslim position. It provided that all laws should be consistent with the Koran and Islamic law and that a board of Muslim experts should be set up to review all bills.

Throughout the summer of 1952 there was bitter acrimony

over the constitutional proposals and increasing bitterness between the orthodox and modernist schools of Islamic thought. The Mullahs began an agitation against an offshoot of Islam, the Ahmadiya Community. Mobilizing the forces of bigotry, they demanded that it be expelled from Islam. In January 1953 rioting began in Karachi over student grievances. Then the Mullahs began to direct demonstrations, and disturbances broke out in various parts of the nation. The riots in Lahore were especially menacing. Martial law was proclaimed, and the central government took stern measures.

In April the governor-general dismissed Nazimuddin's government. His cabinet had allowed the country to drift, there was political discord among the provincial politicians, and law and order were deteriorating. The new prime minister, Mohammed Ali, a modernist and friend of the West, was recalled from his post as Pakistan ambassador to the United States. We have already noted that 1954 was not a tranquil year, witnessing as it did serious riots in East Pakistan and the imposition of martial law in Dacca. The general tone of politics deteriorated rather than improved. The prime minister in one of his speeches referred to "bribery and corruption," saying that these "were another poison corroding our body politic" and "permeating all levels of government and business." [3] Politics was also too dominated by personal rivalries and party patronage. Between 1949 and 1954 a number of the provinces had witnessed the suspension of parliamentary government, and between 1947 and 1954 some nine provincial ministries had been dismissed by the central government on various charges of misconduct.

In October 1954, the governor-general decided that resolute action was essential to save the country from chaos. A state of emergency was declared, the constituent assembly dissolved, and Mohammed Ali was asked to head a new government. It was a ministry of strong men who had no backing from the politicians. Its main support came from the civil servants, many of whom had received their training and principles from the old British Indian civil service, and the army fortunately gave the new regime its loyalty. By this time there were influential circles in Pakistan who had given up hope that democracy could be made to work. There was wide belief that politicians and legislatures would be put indefinitely into cold storage.

This, however, was not to be. While political and economic measures were taken to restore national stability, the government decided to call for national elections in the spring of 1955 and to restore parliamentary institutions. During the

[3] New York *Times*, September 12, 1954.

summer a new prime minister was selected to head Pakistan's first coalition government. This was the former finance minister, Chaudri Mohammed Ali, who had been a distinguished civil servant. From the fall of 1955 to the following spring the new government pressed forward in the task of reform and building political stability. In East Bengal good work was done to rectify the old "poor cousin" treatment of the past. Above all, the process of constitution making was speeded up. A prerequisite was the passing of the One-Unit Bill integrating the three provinces and six states of West Pakistan into one unit. This was the most important legislation passed since 1947. It was, by this time, obvious that East Pakistan would not be satisfied with anything short of parity with the West Wing. But a like parity could not be given to West Pakistan unless its various administrative divisions were welded into one. This unity was achieved by the passage of the One-Unit Bill in October 1955.

The Constitution

Work now proceeded on the drafting of the constitution, which was introduced as a bill into the constituent assembly in January. After spirited and sometimes stormy discussion the bill was passed in the latter part of February 1956. The new constitution became operative on March 23, when an Islamic republic was proclaimed, amid parades and celebration, throughout Pakistan. The new government, federal in structure, is an interesting amalgam of the American presidential and the British parliamentary system. Maximum autonomy is given to the two provinces of West and East Pakistan. Powers of the federal government at Karachi are carefully listed; then those that are provincial, and those that are concurrent. Unlike the parliamentary system in Britain, the independence of the judiciary is provided for, with competence to pass upon the constitutionality of all legislation. Because of the political inexperience of Pakistan in constitutional matters, the argument had been made that she would do better with a strong executive similar to the President of the United States. This need is met, in part at least, by the President of the Republic, who is given certain powers, such as the passing of ordinances, the veto of bills, and supreme command of the armed forces. Nominally, however, the president must accept the advice of the cabinet headed by the prime minister. The legislature is unicameral, consisting of a national assembly of 300 members—half from West and half from East Pakistan.

The preamble states that "Muslims of Pakistan should be

enabled . . . to order their lives in accordance with the teachings and requirements of Islam, as set out in the *Holy Quaran* and *Sunnah.*" But at the same time the preamble lays down that "adequate provision should be made for the minorities freely to profess and practice their religion and develop their culture." The Islamic features of the constitution are not as prominent as the orthodox Muslims initially demanded. The only official who must be a Muslim is the president; all other offices are open to any citizen regardless of faith. It is also enjoined that "no law shall be enacted which is repugnant to the Injunctions of Islam." Instead of giving a board of orthodox Muslim experts the power to review all bills, as was provided in earlier drafts of the constitution, the president is given power to appoint a commission which will make recommendations on how existing law can best be brought into conformity with the injunctions of Islam and to advise the national and provincial assemblies on how the law and custom of Islam might best be given legislative effect. While the new republic is termed an Islamic state, Pakistani spokesmen deny that it is theocratic. They assert that constitutional recognition is given to the fact that Moslems had to fight "in order to preserve their culture and tradition and their entity as Moslems." The debarring of non-Moslems from the presidency is justified on the grounds that this is a natural reflection of the fact that the great majority of citizens are Moslems. This principle, it is pointed out, applies in most Western democracies either explicitly by law or by custom.

The constitution lays down a long list of fundamental rights of the citizen. These include freedom of speech, association, and religion, equality before the law, and the abolition of Untouchability. The directive principles of state policy define the general philosophy and aims of government. It is recognized that it must be the purpose of the state to promote the social and economic well-being of all its citizens. An interesting feature of the constitution is the provision for an economic council. This body will plan the entire economy, have a membership taken equally from the East and the West Wing, and distribute all the available national assets between the two parts of the country.

Political trends since the adoption of the constitution have not been reassuring. The new pattern of government set up in 1956 has been strongly attacked in both wings. In East Pakistan the United Front, so victorious in 1954, has been falling apart. Hindu parties in the province attack it for supporting a constitution that discriminates against non-Muslims. The Awami party, the main opposition, is against the constitution

—not because this document is opposed to the interests of the nation, but because such opposition suits the tactics of personally ambitious politicians. In too many political circles in Pakistan it is not "My country right or wrong," or even "My party right or wrong," but rather "Myself right or wrong." To make matters worse, in the East Wing floods in the spring of 1956 brought about serious food shortages. Amid these difficulties the legislature met late in May, the first time since the spring of 1954, and amid bitter debate the speaker adjourned the assembly indefinitely. A few days later the president, Major General Mirza, suspended the constitution and invoked emergency regulations. After only a week parliamentary government was restored, but the prospects for stability looked dim.

Politics have had no steadier a course in the West Wing. Here the rule of the once dominant, but now aging and deteriorating, Muslim League, has been challenged by a new party known as the Republican. This party was formed after its leader became head of the West Pakistan provincial government. This official, Dr. Khan Sahib, declared, "Free and fair elections held at the earliest possible opportunity followed by the introduction of land reform by a popular government is the only panacea for the evils that exist in Pakistan to-day." [4]

After a decade of independence Pakistan's political future remained uncertain. Too many splinter parties, not enough party responsibility, and too much personal enmity and ambition—these features and more would have to be expunged from the body politic before it could hope to approximate a healthy democratic organism.

But while sincere friends of Pakistan regretted these conditions, at the same time they believed that there was no need to lose hope for the future. In spite of initial disadvantages of the worst kind, in spite of bad luck such as the loss of outstanding leaders like Liaquat Ali Khan, Pakistan has survived all these strains. A balanced evaluation of its past achievements and future possibilities has been made difficult because of its proximity to India. This country had an adequate supply of outstanding leadership, more political experience, and a good start toward industrialization well before independence. As a correspondent of the London *Times* has observed, "If its people lived anywhere else between Lebanon and Japan they would be regarded as a nation temporarily bedeviled by internal problems, but with its heart in the right place. Compared with efforts of other Asian countries its development program is sensible and successful. . . . It is necessary for foreign observers from India to remember this and to remember the conditions prevailing in neighboring Middle East countries

4 *Hindu Weekly Review*, June 11, 1956.

and south-east Asia. Against this broadened horizon Pakistan becomes a country where law and order is [*sic*] still firmly imposed, where the majority of literates still firmly believe in the processes of parliamentary democracy, and where a small but determined leadership [mainly career administrators] knows where it is going." [5]

The Long Road to Plenty

When Pakistan secured independence in 1947, it appeared that her economic problems would be the most serious and difficult to solve. It has been surprising that her most notable achievements have been in this field rather than in the area of politics. Despite the most discouraging conditions—no industry to start with, inadequate personnel, no power resources, and few natural resources outside of agriculture—Pakistan has made astonishing strides in building an economically viable state.

As Pakistani leaders surveyed the economic possibilities of their country, they saw a land of 100,000 villages, some dozen large towns and cities, inhabited by 76 million people (census of 1951; the figure for 1956 is 82 million). This means that a rapidly growing population, nearly half the size of that of the United States, is living in an area only one-tenth the area of the forty-eight states. In East Pakistan the density is one of the highest in the world; more than 43 million people live in an area of only 55,000 square miles. This would be similar to about one-quarter of the population of the United States crowded into an area little more than one-half the state of Oregon. Pakistani leaders, planning their economic program, understood that poverty and underdevelopment pervaded every aspect of their country's life. In the first years of independence the Pakistan federal budget ran to little more than 300 million dollars, as compared to one of more than 60 billion in the United States. The life expectancy of the people was 31 years, the percentage of literacy less than 19, and the national income per capita was about $60.

Pakistani statesmen had to secure capital, especially foreign exchange, in order to build new industries, power projects, and adequate irrigation schemes. To do so they had at their disposal a surplus of some half-dozen agricultural products, mainly cotton and jute, to sell in the world's markets. The story of Pakistan's economic struggle since 1947 is one of advances, setbacks, natural catastrophes, invaluable "Good Samaritan" aid from friendly nations, and finally—by the late 1950's—the prospect of substantial improvement in the living standards of the people and the productivity of their country.

[5] *The Times* (London), September 12, 1955.

In the early years, through 1950, the main emphasis was upon consolidation, planning essential new industries, organizing channels of trade and banking, and enunciating the government's policy toward industry. In the spring of 1948 the government issued a statement of industrial policy. This defined the aim of the state thus: to provide gainful employment to all its citizens, to assure them freedom from want, and to realize the more equitable distribution of wealth. The policy of semi-socialization, economic planning, together with a fear of foreign economic imperialism was also reflected in this official statement. In addition to posts, telegraphs, and railways already state-owned, the statement announced that the following industries must be government-owned and -operated: arms, hydroelectric power, railway cars, telephones, telegraph and wireless apparatus. In addition, twenty-seven other industries would be subject to central planning by the state. It was also stated that "the government of Pakistan must, however, reserve their right to take over or participate in any other industry vital to the security or economic well-being of the state." [6] Foreign capital was also welcomed so long as monopolistic practices were avoided. In a selected list of industries, Pakistani capital should be allowed to subscribe up to 51 per cent of the investment, in other categories at least 30 per cent.

As what can be termed the period of consolidation came to a close at the end of 1950, an ambitious six-year development plan was drawn up. This formed part of the larger Colombo Commonwealth Plan for South Asia. There now ensued what might be referred to as a boom-and-bust period. In 1951 the Korean War resulted in a hectic demand for Pakistan exports. Remarkable prosperity followed, with mounting surpluses in foreign exchange and a flood of imports. This boom was followed, with the tapering off of hostilities in Korea, by serious depression and a world recession in the prices of primary products. In late 1952 prices of Pakistan main exports dropped to 50 per cent of the levels of the previous year. Imports were still allowed to flow in, resulting in a serious deficit in the balance of payments. To add to the mounting economic crisis, between 1951 and 1953 there were serious crop failures and the country faced famine conditions. Tragic consequences were averted by wheat loans from Canada and Australia and, above all, by a gift from the United States of a million tons of wheat in the summer of 1953.

The subsequent economic history of Pakistan may be described as the period of initial austerity and growing development. In 1953 the government in its budget took drastic steps to curtail nonessential imports. At the same time every effort was made to increase production and the shift from an agri-

6 "Industrial Policy" release of Pakistan government (April 1, 1948).

cultural to a semi-industrialized economy was well started. Generous gifts from abroad helped, a succession of favorable harvests brought about a measure of self-sufficiency in food production, and in industry the long-range planning began to show encouraging results.

Up to the spring of 1955, the three Commonwealth countries of Australia, Canada, and New Zealand had given substantial assistance amounting to more than 90 million dollars. The United States had been the greatest benefactor, having made grants, loans, and commodity credits amounting to 360 million dollars.

The combined results of austerity, planning, and foreign aid add up to an encouraging achievement. Between 1950 and 1955 production of seventeen major industries increased by 280 per cent. Between 1950 and 1956 some of the specific advances registered were: cloth and yarn 347 per cent, sugar 130, crude oil 52, coal 27, and electric energy 173 per cent. By 1954 Pakistan stood first in the world in jute, sixth in cotton, and third and fourth in rice and tea respectively. In tobacco and wool it took third place among Asian nations.

Unlike India, which has moved steadily toward a socialistic pattern of socialized industry, Pakistan has modified her original 1948 policy in favor of private enterprise and encouragement of foreign investment. For the latter full repatriation at any time of profits and principal is now guaranteed, plus the condition that foreign capital can hold absolute control of its investment up to 60 per cent. The best example of the economic philosophy followed by Pakistan and its achievements can be seen in the operations of the Pakistan Industrial Development Corporation. This agency was organized in 1952 with a capital investment of 170 million dollars obtained jointly from the government and private capital, from foreign aid, and a loan from the World Bank. Between 1952 and early 1955 this P.I.D.C. built the following: three paper mills, one cotton mill, ten jute mills (one of them the largest in the world), a DDT plant, two cement factories, several woolen mills, a sugar plant, and two dockyards. In 1955 twelve large industrial projects were completed, and in the following year a huge fertilizer plant and a steel plant were built. The interesting feature of the P.I.D.C. is that it is not interested in nationalization. It is the partner of private investment, and as soon as possible it aims to hand each of its projects to private enterprise. In both West and East Pakistan, in the field of government-owned and -controlled projects, a number of huge multi-purpose projects are in process with the aim of turning out hydroelectric power, controlling floods, and increasing water available for irrigation. There are also numerous irrigation projects, either in process or already completed. Intensive surveys have been carried out to search for natural gas, oil, and iron. Encouraging results have been obtained. In 1952 the Sui gas field was discovered, and in its first year of operation the equivalent of 500,000 tons of coal was produced as fuel by the gas. Another significant discovery was the unearthing of rich iron deposits which will make possible the development of iron and steel industries supplied by domestic ores.

In the area of social welfare Pakistan's need is, if anything, greater than that of her neighbor, India. Educational facilities are pitiably inadequate, with 80 per cent of the population illiterate; housing in the towns and cities is quite frequently substandard, and tens of thousands of refugees still live in unspeakable hovels; public health is in a distressing state, with too few doctors, health centers, and hospitals. Correspondents report that in most areas compulsory elementary education is "seldom more than a politician's campaign talk." This somber picture is not what the Pakistani leaders wish to see. There are simply not enough funds available to develop industry, advance social welfare, and provide for the military budget. From 1947 to 1955 the sum of 2 billion dollars was spent on defense, primarily because of the Kashmir quarrel with India. This amounted to 61 per cent of all central revenue. In 1954, as we will see in the following chapter, Pakistan and the United States signed a defense-assistance treaty by which the United States made available substantial amounts of military equipment. This military aid, plus the increase of American economic assistance for village aid, education, health, and water projects, was doing much to help Pakistan become an economically healthy state.

The Pakistan budget for 1955-1956 showed that its domestic accounts had been balanced, that national income continued to rise, and that the balance of payments in foreign trade showed an improvement over the previous year. The year 1955 ended with a comfortable balance of foreign exchange. Progress, however, was not to be uninterrupted. During 1955-1956 Pakistan suffered heavily from floods. In the spring of the latter year, East Bengal was plagued by torrential rains and the overflowing of rivers. A serious shortage of food developed. Rationing was introduced, and relief shipments of food were imported. The United States provided a free gift of rice.

These floods were a grim reminder of the delicate balance on which Pakistan teetered, between famine on the one hand and bare subsistence for the masses on the other. Many years would intervene before the country would have an adequate reservoir of industrial and agricultural productivity ready to serve her in the face of natural calamities.

Nehru   *Jinnah*

II. Pakistan and India in the World

INDEPENDENCE FOR PAKISTAN AND INDIA coincided with one of the most troubled and menacing periods in world history. Unlike the United States, Canada, and Australia, nations whose infancy was more or less insulated from the interplay of power politics, these new Asian powers were plummeted at birth in 1947 into the very center of gigantic revolutionary forces and power rivalries. During the first decade of their new nationhood, India and Pakistan were confronted with the menacing repercussions of the cold war, the uncertain designs of the rising might of Communist China, and war in Korea, together with unrest and instability throughout much of southern Asia. Absorbed in domestic problems and consolidation of their national unity, India and Pakistan strongly desired peace and the general stabilization of Asia. As we will see, in the pursuit of this common aim each nation utilized different means.

The defense of India and Southeast Asia had been the responsibility of Great Britain for the 150 years preceding independence. The whole area of the Middle East, Southeast Asia, and the great Indian Ocean basin was guarded by British sea power. Following the liquidation of British rule, a new defense arrangement became essential for what an Indian publicist has defined as "the Indian Ocean area with Afghanistan, Sinkiang and Tibet as the outer northern ring constituting the real security region of India." [1] This same

[1] K. M. Panikkar, "The Basis of an Indo-British Treaty," pamphlet of Indian Council of World Affairs (Bombay: Oxford University Press, 1946), p. 44.

scholar, just before the grant of independence, pointed to Soviet power controlling all of the Eurasian heartland and insisted that only by the organization of the maritime rim of Asia in an alliance with Great Britain could Russian power in Southeast Asia be contained.

While India and Pakistan have not made specific bilateral alliances with Britain, they have continued to be members of the unique association of nations now termed the Commonwealth. In addition Pakistan joined two regional security alliances: the Baghdad Pact for the defense of the Middle East and SEATO for the protection of Southeast Asia from aggression.

The question of membership in the Commonwealth was much discussed in India after the adoption of a constitution that would make her a sovereign republic. The problem arose how this republican status could be squared with allegiance to the crown, the one common feature that had, heretofore, united the dominions in the Commonwealth. In April 1949 the prime ministers of the various dominions met in London to see if some formula could be devised that would keep the republic of India within the Commonwealth. Agreement was quickly reached whereby India could remain a full member, giving up her former allegiance to the crown but now acknowledging the king "as a symbol of the free association of its independent member nations and, as such, the Head of the Commonwealth." When Pakistan became a republic in 1956, she too continued as a part of the Commonwealth. From time to time, the statesmen of both countries—especially Nehru—have publicly acknowledged the value and importance of membership in the Commonwealth. Adherence to this informal association of sovereign nations now means nothing more or less than the opportunity for intermittent, friendly consultation on world problems affecting the interests of all members of the Commonwealth.

Since 1947 India and Pakistan have played important roles in world affairs. The former, particularly, has been astonishingly active in exercising a decisive influence in international relations. India wielded important weight in the affairs of the United Nations; she had an important part in the Korean truce; assisted materially in securing the end of hostilities in Indochina; acted as a mediator in Chinese–United States relations; and in general worked with considerable success for the preservation of world peace.

What have been the obectives of Indian foreign policy? In 1948 the Congress party defined them as follows:

"These principles are the promotion of world peace, the freedom of all nations, racial equality and the ending of imperialism and colonialism ... It should be the constant aim of the foreign policy of India to maintain friendly and cooperative relations with all nations and to avoid entanglements in military or similar alliances which tend to divide up the world in rival groups and thus endanger world peace." [2]

The basic tenets of this policy have been simply defined by an American scholar as "friendship with every nation, attachment to no bloc, sympathy with struggles for freedom and opposition to racial discrimination everywhere." [3] Nehru in his many utterances on foreign policy has usually stressed that peace can only be achieved by peaceful means and that military alliances and armaments only intensify rivalries and bring closer the prospect of world war. Nehru has attempted to obtain acceptance for his Five Principles of coexistence, the so-called *Pancha Shila*. These consist of respect for the territorial integrity of other nations, nonaggression, noninterference in internal affairs, equality, and peaceful coexistence.

The amazing prominence of India in world affairs can be explained, in part, by the stature of its leader Nehru as a statesman, orator, writer, and dynamic personality in the cause of peace. As the largest "uncommitted nation" India naturally is more important as an independent, disinterested party than if she aligned herself with any bloc. Like an attractive woman, she is constantly wooed by a number of suitors. Elizabethan England used much the same kind of policy against her European rivals. By reason of India's pioneer effort against colonial rule and the world prominence achieved first by Gandhi and later by his follower Nehru, she has enjoyed a position of leadership conferred upon her by the nations recently emancipated from Western imperialism and by those people, as in western and northern Africa, who are endeavoring to throw off colonial rule. India has also gained a strong following in the world for her championing of moral principles in the conduct of foreign affairs. Idealists, pacifists, and seekers of peace everywhere have been moved by India's advocacy of non-violence, disarmament, and peaceful coexistence—in short, adherence without equivocation to the teachings of Christ and Buddha.

Pakistan, in contrast with her neighbor India, has had to be content with a less important role in world affairs. She has not had behind her the same resources in industrial potential, population, and extent of territory as her neighbor. Unlike India, she has not been able to carry on an independent policy in world diplomacy, the friend of all and the recipient of all. Pakistan has felt too insecure. She has inherited the main burden of defense in the north against a potential foe, Russia. Under British control the burden on the northwest frontier was an all-India responsibility. Furthermore, Pakistan has not had friendly relations with India since 1947. On several occasions the two countries were on the brink of war; and in Kashmir actual undeclared hostilities were carried on between the regular armies of both sides for about a year. Pakistan's foreign policy has had three main objectives: (1) security from any attack that might materialize in the north, (2) adequate defense from her more powerful neighbor in the event of war, and (3) undoubtedly, a position of comparative bargaining strength vis-à-vis India in the long-drawn-out dispute over Kashmir.

Immediately after independence it seemed likely that Pakistan would follow the same non-alignment policy carried out by India. In 1950 Liaquat Ali Khan accepted an invitation to visit Russia. Instead he went to the United States and Canada. Apparently it was the prime minister's tactic to use the possibility of Russian ties as a means of exerting pressure on Western nations, especially in obtaining support in Kashmir. But by 1952 it was apparent that Russia had definitely taken the side of India in the Kashmir imbroglio. From this time, Pakistan definitely moved away from a position of non-alignment in the direction of closer relations with the West, especially the United States.

The first step in this direction was a mutual defense treaty with Turkey, signed in the spring of 1954. In May of that year, Pakistan signed a defense assistance agreement with the United States under which substantial amounts of military equipment were available to the former. Some estimates of United States help ran as high as 50 per cent of the total amount budgeted by Pakistan on defense. The next move was a Turkish-Iraqi defense treaty signed in Baghdad, to which Britain, Iran, and Pakistan later adhered. Thus was created by the end of 1955, largely by American inspiration, the "northern tier" of allies pledged to withstand aggression from the north. In yet another area Pakistan had accepted the principle of collective security. In September 1954 she had signed, along with seven other allies, the South East Asia Collective Defense Treaty designed to block Communist aggression in this area. While Pakistan cannot throw the same amount of weight in diplomacy as her larger neighbor India, her geographical position does endow her with unique strategic value. Through Turkey, Pakistan's western territory joins up with NATO in Europe, and its eastern wing in southern Asia forms the link with SEATO. It is these facts of geopolitics that make Pakistan such an important ally of the United States.

So much for the general orientation of India and Pakistan in world affairs; now to an examination of the relations be-

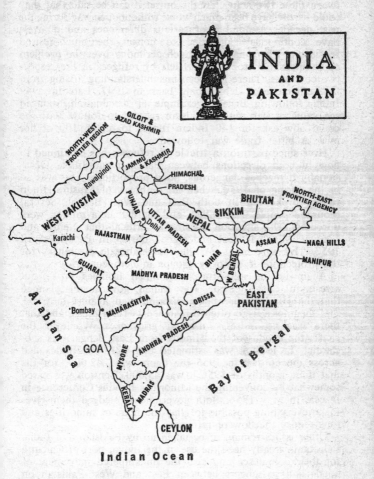

INDIA
AND
PAKISTAN

GILGIT &
AZAD KASHMIR

NORTH-WEST
FRONTIER REGION

Rawalpindi

JAMMU
& KASHMIR

HIMACHAL
PRADESH

WEST PAKISTAN

PUNJAB

UTTAR PRADESH
Delhi

NEPAL

BHUTAN

SIKKIM

NORTH-EAST
FRONTIER AGENCY

Karachi

RAJASTHAN

ASSAM

NAGA HILLS

GUJARAT

MADHYA PRADESH

BIHAR

W BENGAL

MANIPUR

Arabian Sea

Bombay

MAHARASHTRA

ORISSA

EAST
PAKISTAN

GOA

MYSORE

ANDHRA PRADESH

Bay of Bengal

KERALA

MADRAS

CEYLON

Indian Ocean

tween these two states. At the outset it can be said that they could hardly have been much worse without open war during the past decade. A number of serious differences and quarrels have continuously operated to poison the much-desired friendship. There has been much acrimony over the problem of compensation for property left by refugees in the respective countries. There has been misunderstanding arising from the settlement of debts going back to 1947. Late in 1949 India, following Britain's example of devaluation, reduced the value of her rupee. Pakistan refused to follow suit; she could now ask for 140 Indian rupees to match 100 of her own. A bitter trade war followed.

Ever since partition a trickle of refugees has continued to flow in both directions between Pakistan and India. Occasionally it reaches dangerous, flood proportions. This was so in the spring of 1950, when an outbreak of Muslim-Hindu rioting broke out in both East and West Bengal. Several thousand people were killed, and more than a million were uprooted. The situation became so critical that Nehru and Liaquat Ali Khan met and signed the Delhi Pact in April 1950. This agreement provided for elaborate machinery for the protection of minority groups in both countries.

Again in the mid-fifties, communal troubles broke out afresh in East Bengal. The Indian government claimed that the Hindus were being discriminated against in trade, that their lives were often threatened in rural areas, and that there was no redress for their grievances. Whatever the cause, the exodus of the Hindus from East Bengal was substantial. In 1954 it was estimated that 121,000 Hindus fled across the border; in 1955 the figure was 242,000; for the first three months of 1956 it was 43,000. Tension was eased somewhat by convening the Minorities Exodus Conference in Dacca, in May 1956. Both governments pledged themselves to do everything possible to allay the fears of minorities and thus reduce the flow of refugees.

Other issues remain to be taken up by Pakistan and India. Pakistanis greatly need the use of the Indian port of Calcutta for their commerce and also the unhampered movement of goods and passengers between East and West Pakistan on the Indian railway system at normal fare rates. Aside from the Kashmir problem, to be discussed below, the most potentially explosive issue between the two nations has been that of the use of the Indus waters for canal irrigation purposes. Before partition a single irrigation system watered 20 million acres in the Punjab and Sind provinces. Partition left most of the canals in Pakistan but their water supply in India and Kashmir. There has been abundant fear that India might withhold or divert these vital water supplies. Furthermore, the intent of India to build great irrigation projects based on this water will—so the Pakistanis argue—inevitably seriously reduce the amounts available to Pakistan. David Lilienthal, formerly head of the famous T.V.A., in the United States, advocated joint international control for the entire Indus basin. After agreement on this basis had failed, the World Bank offered its good offices in helping the disputants come to an agreement. It was proposed that of the six rivers involved, three would go to Pakistan and the full use of the remainder to India. As late as the spring of 1957 negotiations were being carried on in Washington with the hope of arriving at an agreeable plan for the utilization of the waters.

The genesis of the Kashmir controversy has already been discussed (in Chapter 8). This quarrel, the most serious between Pakistan and India, defied all attempts at solution in the 1950's. We recall that a cease-fire agreement had been secured in January 1949. By this cease fire and division of territory, Pakistan controlled the area of Kashmir west and north of the demarcation line and India the remainder of Kashmir. The area protected by Pakistan organized its own government, taking the name of Azad (Free) Kashmir. This had been obtained through the happy auspices of the U.N. Commission. Admiral Chester W. Nimitz failed to make any progress as plebiscite administrator, and in the spring of 1950 an eminent Australian jurist, Sir Owen Dixon, was named by the Security Council as mediator to supervise the demilitarization program. In his report he did agree (in order to placate India) that Pakistan had committed *de facto* aggression. Reporting the failure of his mission, Dixon declared that India's agreement would never be obtained for an arrangement which would ensure a fair and unintimidated expression of opinion in Kashmir.

In January 1951 the Commonwealth prime ministers convened in London. Mr. Liaquat Ali Khan insisted on the Kashmir question being placed on the agenda. During the deliberations, Mr. Attlee and his colleagues strove mightily to help the disputants arrive at agreement. Various suggestions were made, the most promising being that Commonwealth troops from outside the Indian subcontinent should take over the policing of Kashmir while the plebiscite was undertaken. While the Pakistan prime minister accepted this and two other basic alternatives, Nehru refused in each case. This Indian intransigence did much to win world opinion over to the side of Pakistan. During the course of the next two years an American, Dr. Frank P. Graham, was given the task by the U.N. of arranging demilitarization and a plan of plebiscite. On a number of occasions success seemed just around the corner for Dr. Graham, but in the last analysis all efforts failed because of Nehru's intransigence on one basic point. India must retain an overwhelming ratio of her troops, viv-à-vis Pakistan's, in order to "maintain order." Recalling Dixon's comments about a fair plebiscite, Pakistan refused to accept India's terms.

By the mid-1950's the Kashmir situation had changed radically from within. The development had been in India's favor. A constituent assembly had been elected which had ensured Sheikh Abdullah's pro-Indian party, the National Conference, of overwhelming control of the country. To all intents and purposes only one party had been allowed to participate in this selection. In the summer of 1952 agreement was reached in New Delhi by Nehru and Sheikh Abdullah on the terms by which Kashmir would become part of India.

One of the architects of this agreement was not to remain in political office very long. Following the agreement, Abdullah became increasingly suspicious of some of the Hindu fanatical organizations in India. Furthermore, influential Hindus in Kashmir began to attack his program of land reform. Aroused by what seemed to be largely an anti-Muslim movement, Abdullah came to have serious doubts about placing the rights of dominantly Muslim Kashmir under the control of dominantly Hindu India. In a number of speeches he aired his doubts. The result, in August 1953, was his dismissal from office and imprisonment of him and some colleagues. A pro-India prime minister took his place—Bakshi Ghulam Mohammed—and in the spring of 1954 the Kashmir constituent assembly ratified the accession of their state to India. These events touched off widespread demonstrations in Kashmir supporting Abdullah. Thousands were imprisoned and many killed. In Pakistan there was a prevailing mood of indignation.

While these dramatic events took place in Kashmir, the Indian and Pakistani prime ministers were conferring in New Delhi. An accord was reached stipulating the appointment of a plebiscite administrator by the end of April 1954. But before this official could be appointed a new complication—according to the Indian view—had cropped up. Rumors of a Pakistani–United States military assistance pact began to arouse Indian opinion, and suspicions were confirmed by the signing of the pact in May 1954. As we have already seen, in little more than a year Pakistan became a member of the Baghdad group.

These diplomatic moves were strongly condemned by the Indian government. Nehru characterized the Pakistan-American pact as a "step towards war." He accused the signatories of bringing the cold war to the Indian subcontinent. At the same time, there was much talk in India about American "plans" to secure military bases in Pakistan and in Azad Kashmir. A prominent Kashmiri politician declared that America wished to use Kashmir as a war base in its global strategy. This controversy became more heated during the visit of the Russian leaders Khrushchev and Bulganin to India during December 1955. The Russians took an "unambiguous stand" in favor of India in the Kashmir question, declared that Kashmir was now one of the states in the Indian Union, and castigated Pakistan for her alliance with the United States.

Pakistan immediately sought support from her friends and allies. Horace A. Hildreth, the U.S. Ambassador in Karachi, reaffirmed the support of the United States for a free and impartial plebiscite under U.N. auspices. A few months later, when the SEATO Council met in Karachi, it went on record as supporting a settlement "through the U.N. or by direct negotiations." Nehru strongly attacked the SEATO resolution, declaring it was a military alliance's support of Pakistan in its dispute with India. Previously he had also charged that American aid to Pakistan was not to strengthen the latter in the event of any attack from the north—such as the Soviet Union—but primarily to increase Pakistani military power as a counter in its rivalry with India.

As the 1950's neared an end, it seemed that the Kashmir question had reached an impasse. There was no longer any talk in India of a plebiscite such as had been promised by Nehru late in 1947. Nehru now stated that the whole context of the dispute had changed since American aid to Pakistan and the Baghdad Pact. He added that the old arguments used by Pakistan were now quite out of date. High-ranking Indian officials argued that no decisions could now be made that would not be acceptable to the Kashmir assembly. In retort the Pakistanis charged that this body was a hand-picked group of Indian stooges. Speaking in Srinagar, Kashmir's capital, Krishna Menon—a member of the Indian cabinet—declared that Kashmir was a part of India and would remain so, for all time to come.[4] Nehru also let it be known that the only practical settlement now was a recognition of the present *de facto* cease-fire line as the Pakistan-Indian border.

[4] Krishna Menon, *Hindu* (Madras), May 21, 1956.

What do outsiders to this dispute have to say about the merits of the disputants' cases? The great majority of observers in the Western nations have gone on record as saying that Pakistan has much the better of the argument but admit that possession is nine-tenths of the law. The usually carefully objective Robert Trumbull, formerly New York *Times* correspondent in New Delhi, went on record in his book *As I See India* thus: "I would estimate that 99 per cent of the foreign observers . . . who visited Kashmir . . . were convinced that in a fair plebiscite an overwhelming majority of Kashmiris would vote for Pakistan. The same opinion was also held by many Indians." [5] The *Manchester Guardian*, usually completely tolerant and often effusive in its praise of Nehru as a statesman, lashed out at his arguments on Kashmir, "which look like chicanery." The London *Times* referred to Kashmir as an "Indian colony or protectorate," but said it was a pampered one. Considerable economic aid is being spent in Kashmir with the view that a rising standard of living will ultimately woo the Kashmiris to the Indian connection. Meanwhile the Azad Kashmiris, tied to Pakistan, are frustrated and discontented. They have no wish to be separated from their brothers. Among the Kashmiris who do not support Bakshi, the prime minister, there is a substantial number who are not so much pro-Pakistan as pro-Kashmir. They would prefer to have Kashmir go it alone but realize that this probably would be a dangerous alternative. With suitable terms to protect their interests, they realize that the Pakistan tie would be the best solution. While there are arguments about these alternatives, there is no argument over the fact that the majority of Kashmiris have no use for Indian occupation and want an opportunity to express their desires in a free plebiscite. It is extremely probable that the Kashmir question will continue to simmer. It is a powder keg of Islamic irredentism that might explode at any time.

As far as Pakistan's differences with her neighbors are concerned, her cup of foreign affairs has certainly flowed over. In addition to disputes with India there has been a stormy controversy with Afghanistan. Under British rule, where the plains of north India touched the first ranges of mountains that lead to "the roof of the world," there was constant serious trouble with the fierce mountain folk—the Pathans. In 1893 a British administrator, Durand, negotiated with Afghanistan in fixing India's boundary well into the tribal, mountainous country. The purpose was to create a buffer zone between this Durand line and the settled, ad-

[5] Robert Trumbull, *As I See India* (New York: William Sloane Associates, 1956), p. 99.

ministered area under British rule. The new boundary left a considerable number of Pathans on each side of the line—some in Afghanistan and some in British India.

When Pakistan became a nation in 1947 she claimed that the old Durand Line was the rightful frontier between her and Afghanistan. This claim was hotly disputed by the government in Kabul, which asserted that all the Pathan people living in the so-called Tribal Territory and the North-West Frontier Province should have the right of self-determination. A number of dissident tribal leaders in the latter area thereupon proclaimed the independence of what they called Pakhtunistan.

Since 1947 Afghanistan has carried on a shrill propaganda campaign for Pakhtunistan. Several armed clashes took place on the Afghan-Pakistani border, and in March 1955 a mob attacked the Pakistan Embassy in the Afghan capital. Protest demonstrations followed throughout Pakistan. It is interesting to note that Afghanistan insists upon the freedom of some 7 million Pathans living in Pakistan but has nothing to say about the same right of self-determination for the slightly less numerous Pathans living in Afghanistan. It is extremely unlikely that the Pakhtunistan movement will gather much strength. Since 1947 the mountain tribal areas have been tranquil under Pakistani sovereignty. These fierce and martial mountaineers are permitted to rule themselves by their traditional assemblies or *jirgahs*. Considerable economic development is being carried on by Pakistan to raise standards of living in the tribal areas. It has been said that in this territory alone, Pakistan is spending probably double the entire Afghan revenue. There is deep suspicion in Pakistan that India has been covertly encouraging the Pakhtunistan cause. Spokesmen for the movement openly publish periodicals in Bombay and Delhi and organize Pakhtunistan meetings. Thus yet another fagot is added to the fire of suspicion between India and Pakistan.

India in the World

Outside the subcontinent India has played a prominent part in world affairs, partly for the promotion of amity and peace in the world in general, and partly to safeguard her vital national interests. The first of these is her security. Because of bad relations with Pakistan, India has been interested in keeping her military preponderance over her neighbor. New Delhi also frowns upon Pakistan's membership in any military alliance that might enhance her prestige and strengthen her bargaining power in disputes like that over Kashmir. It has been said that the number one fact of international life in the late 1950's to the Indian Ministry of Foreign Affairs was American aid to Pakistan.

The enmity of Pakistan may be India's immediate worry, but the most serious concern to her security is the future policy of China. This huge and resurgent state has an imperial tradition of expansion; at one time her armies and power controlled much of central, southern, and southeastern Asia. Maps have actually been printed in Communist China showing parts of Burma, Assam, Kashmir and Nepal under the rule of Peking. Another disturbing feature is the existence of substantial immigrant Chinese communities in Southeast Asia. Some publicists believe that a clash is inevitable between the two giants of Asia—China and India. Even before the former had come under Communist domination, Arnold Toynbee had written: "In the end the current of Chinese expansion in the tropics will meet the current of Hindu expansion over the submerged heads of the smaller and weaker and less efficient peoples in between, who are already fast going under." [6]

No matter how true or untrue Nehru may believe this eventuality to be, he has taken no chances. His government has been especially interested in the northern mountain area, where, under British rule, such states as Tibet, Bhutan, Sikkim, and Nepal were maintained as buffers protecting northern India from invasion. Tibet, which had come to acknowledge the suzerainty of China in early modern times, had been forced by Britain in 1904 to agree not to lease any of its territory to a foreign power. This move was directed against Russian expansion. In 1911, after the fall of the Manchu dynasty in China, the Tibetan government at Lhasa proclaimed its independence. The Nationalist government of China under Chiang Kai-shek, however, continued to assert sovereignty over Tibet.

In the fall of 1950, Communist Chinese premier Chou En-lai declared that Tibet "must be liberated." In October an army easily invaded and subdued the country. This attack aroused consternation in India. Two notes of protest were sent to Peking, whereupon New Delhi was told in effect that Tibet was none of its business. The sequel was the signing of a non-aggression pact between India and Communist China. This document recognized the conquest of Tibet, and both signatories agreed to abide by the Five Principles of *Pancha Shila* in foreign affairs. Undoubtedly, the Chinese invasion of Tibet was a rude shock to Nehru and his colleagues. As nothing short of force could alter the situation, Nehru ob-

[6] Quoted in Eustace Seligman, *What the United States Can Do about India* (New York: New York University Press, 1956), p. 53.

tained China's signature to the Five Principles. This public pledge, he earnestly hoped, might discourage Peking from further expansion in the future. The same motive of containing Chinese military and political power was certainly in Nehru's mind at the 1955 Asian-African Conference held at Bandung. All the Southeast Asian powers were eager to have Communist China again pledge adherence to the principles of peaceful coexistence as contained in the Tibetan pact. Thus it was that they occupied an important place in the final communiqué issued by the conference.

With Peking's conquest of Tibet, the only buffer states standing in the way of a Chinese advance to Indian borders are the tiny protectorates of Sikkim and Bhutan and the Kingdom of Nepal. The last-named, home of Mount Everest and recruiting ground for the famous Gurkha soldiers by the Indian Army, is vital for India's security. Nehru has declared that his nation has a special position in Nepal and that while it will not interfere with its independence, neither will it permit any interference by other powers. In Parliament, the Indian prime minister has stated, "It is not possible for the Indian Government to tolerate an invasion of Nepal from anywhere." [7] The same position holds true in the case of Sikkim and Bhutan. The situation, however, is delicate in Nepal. Under pressure from New Delhi it has been striving to democratize its government. Democracy, however, has made little headway. The ruling monarch is liberal and progressive but is beset with a combination of greedy politicians, ignorance and lack of experience of his people in democratic government, and the serious challenge of Communist groups. In 1953, for example, Indian troops crossed into Nepal to help put down a Communist-inspired peasant uprising. Nehru's government has been trying to strengthen and stabilize the little kingdom by supplying equipment to the Nepalese army, encouraging the reform of the civil service and the tax system, and expanding the health and educational facilities. New Delhi ruefully understands that Nepal is no longer isolated from the tug of power politics: "Once a hermit, then a buffer, she now has become the meat of the sandwich." [8]

Apart from the immediate responsibility of defending its frontiers and in the broader field of world politics, India has been motivated by a pro-Asian, anti-imperialistic policy. As part of Asia, proud of its newly won freedom, India has insisted upon recognition of the dignity and worth of the

[7] Jawaharlal Nehru, *Speeches: 1949-1953* (New Delhi: Government of India, 1954), p. 149.

[8] A. M. Rosenthal, "Grim Shadows over the Cobra Throne," *New York Times Magazine*, May 27, 1956, p. 47.

Asian people. Nehru and his colleagues have, on every possible occasion, stressed India's and Asia's proud historical legacy, their unique culture, and their promising destiny. Any assumption of superiority by the West over Asia, any slight by the former, is deeply resented by Indian leaders. Racial discrimination by whites over men of color stirs the strongest antipathy in the Indian Union. From the day of independence, Indian leaders have been implacably anti-colonial. As one well-known Indian publicist has observed: "The antipathy to imperialism is deep-rooted in the minds of everyone in India, and that has been acquired not from books, but from national experience." [9]

India's concern for Asian rights was reflected in the convening of the First Asian Relations Conference in New Delhi in March 1947. The various speeches made at this conclave, especially the utterances of Nehru, called attention to the new importance of Asia in world affairs. They insisted that in the present crisis in world affairs Asia must play a vital role. The speakers maintained that the whole spirit and outlook of Asia are peaceful and that its emergence in world affairs would serve the cause of international peace.

The Indian prime minister took a leading part in the famous Asian-African Conference, held in April 1955. This conference, which was declared to be a mark of Asia's coming of age, called for increasing cultural cooperation between the Asian and African peoples, condemned racialism, and lashed out against colonialism. In his closing address Nehru declared: "Asia is no longer passive today; it has been passive enough in the past. It is no more a submissive Asia; it has tolerated submissiveness for so long. Asia of today is dynamic; Asia is full of life. If there is anything that Asia wants to tell . . . it is this. There is going to be no dictation in the future; no 'yes-men' in Asia, I hope, or in Africa." [10]

As an Asian Nehru has deplored the exclusion of Communist China from the United Nations. As an Indian he may, sometimes, have moments of disquietude about the might of the New China, but nevertheless as an Asian he has shared what he has considered a Western slight to a great power. In 1953 he observed: "If China is not there (in the U.N.), then from the point of view of population, from the point of view of world importance, nearly a quarter of the world is not there." [11]

[9] A. Appadorai, "Indian Foreign Policy," *International Affairs* (London), January 1949, p. 38.

[10] Quoted in George McTurnan Kahin, *The Asian-African Conference* (Ithaca: Cornell University Press, 1956), p. 73.

[11] Quoted in Chester Bowles, *Ambassador's Report* (New York: Harper and Brothers, 1954), p. 244.

Ever since its independence, India has uninterruptedly taken up its cudgels against imperialism. In 1949 it convened an Asian conference to consider the problem of Indonesian independence. Again in 1954 the Colombo powers, consisting of India, Ceylon, Pakistan, Burma, and Indonesia, met to discuss problems affecting their interests. Nehru had considerable influence at this conclave, which urged a cease-fire in Indochina, a U.N. seat for Peking, the end of all H-bomb tests, and self-determination for Morocco and Tunisia. In the U.N., Indian representatives have given strong support to Arab nationalism, especially the struggle, eventually won, for Tunisian and Moroccan independence. British, French, and Belgian colonialism has also been frequently criticized by India in this international body; and in 1956 Nehru, deeply concerned by the Algerian problem, advanced five suggestions for its solution. In addition to championing self-determination in areas such as Africa, India has made carefully studied efforts to gain the friendship of peoples in former colonial areas, such as the Gold Coast, or territories on the verge of freedom like Nigeria. In these and other African areas, Indian representatives sedulously cultivate friendship and extend the influence of their country.

India herself has also been involved directly with colonial and racial problems. For more than fifty years discriminatory treatment of Indians in the Union of South Africa has caused deep resentment in the country of their origin. We recall that it was this issue that first brought Gandhi to prominence. After the Second World War this problem became more explosive. The Dutch nationalists first under the prime minister Dr. Malan, and then under J. G. Strijdom, began to carry through their program of *apartheid* (separateness). This policy called for absolutely no mixing between the Europeans, African Bantus, and Indians. Furthermore, they insisted upon the maintenance of European supremacy in politics. The Indian and Pakistan governments, aroused by several laws they considered discriminatory, brought the matter before the United Nations. A commission was appointed to study and report on the problem. This body was boycotted by the South African authorities. While the Pretoria government refused to budge, India instituted a trade boycott and closed its high commissioner's office in South Africa.

When India secured its independence in 1947, a number of small enclaves belonging to France and Portugal survived. They were vestigial remnants of the old days of European expansion. In the case of France, after some bitter and protracted negotiations, Pondicherry and other tiny holdings were ceded to India after 240 years of French rule. A formal treaty to this effect was signed in November 1954. In the case of Portugal there was an uncompromising stand against cession. Involved were Goa and two other possessions, all in Bombay state, amounting to 1500 square miles with a population of 600,000. To most Indians Goa was a symbol of imperialism, an irritating reminder of Western exploitation in an almost completely free motherland. Nehru called the Portuguese possessions "a continuing interference with India's political system." [12] After 1947 India made repeated requests to Lisbon to open negotiations for cession. Portugal maintained that Goa was an integral part of the homeland, that much more was spent in Goa and its two other possessions than was obtained by local revenues, that it was absurd to talk about exploitation. Lisbon also argued that there was no essential connection between Goa's being in the Indian subcontinent and its having to belong to India. The Portuguese asked if this should also be true for Pakistan. From time to time clashes took place on the Goanese border as passive resisters, non-violent agitators, sought to cross the frontier of Goa to further a liberation movement. In August 1955 some fourteen people were killed by Portuguese soldiers and a number wounded. Despite the rousing cry in India for armed intervention, Nehru insisted that the problem could only be solved by peaceful negotiation. Nehru, in this dispute, was in a difficult position. If his soldiers crossed the borders of Goa, what would this action do to his oft-repeated adherence to *Pancha Shila?*

India: Mediator and Emissary for Peace

In addition to her anti-colonialism and her concern for security and for Asian prestige and solidarity, India has been eager to use her influence and leadership in reducing areas of friction in the world. She has been active as a mediator in disputes, encouraging disarmament—especially in nuclear weapons—and has stood before the nations as a disinterested party working for the common good of humanity. While there has not been complete agreement in Western nations about the over-all balance sheet of this role, it is indisputable that India has exerted tremendous weight in the affairs of the world. Her hand was active in the Korean armistice, in the admission of new members, especially in 1955, to the United Nations, in the truce secured in 1954 in Indochina, and in reducing some of the tensions stemming from differences dividing Communist China and the United States. In a general way, Nehru worked assiduously after the death of Stalin and his dethronement from the inner circle of Soviet "Greats," to sell the idea

[12] *Hindu* (Madras), August 1, 1955.

that Russia was changing in the direction of reasonableness. This point of view was presented by the Indian prime minister at various Commonwealth conferences. Nehru argued that this change of heart deserved a gesture of appreciation from the Western powers.

In seeking to give the widest currency to his ideas, Nehru in the mid-1950's became one of the most widely traveled heads of state. He made numerous visits to London and visited the United States in 1949. In 1954 he made a state visit to Communist China, stopping off at most of the capitals of south Asia. In 1955 Nehru paid official visits to Russia and a number of east European countries. He received a tumultuous welcome in Moscow. Everywhere he went he spoke for peaceful coexistence in accordance with the Five Principles. In 1956 he set off on his travels again, attending the Commonwealth conference, visiting West Germany, France, and Yugoslavia. In the latter country he conferred with its leader Tito and with Colonel Nasser of Egypt.

In addition to the peregrinations of its prime minister, India has been the host of a goodly number of distinguished visitors. Among them can be mentioned the United States Secretary of State, John Foster Dulles; the British Foreign Secretary, Selwyn Lloyd; King Saud of Saudi Arabia; the Shah of Iran; and the Canadian Foreign Minister, Lester Pearson. Above all, there was the much-publicized visit of the Soviet Premier Bulganin and the First Secretary of the Communist Party, Khrushchev. These visitors had tremendous success as they acted with gusto, orated without much regard to the truth, and traveled the subcontinent from one end to the other. They delighted their hosts by using the formal salutation, the *namaste;* they ate Indian dishes, and wore on occasion the traditional Gandhi cap.

Spirit and Practice of India's Foreign Policy

So much for the manifold actions of Nehru and his colleagues on the world's diplomatic stage. What has India claimed to be the spirit and philosophy of her foreign policy? There has been constant criticism of other powers, especially those of the West, for their practice of power politics and reliance upon force. On the other hand, India is said to follow the principles of non-violence, of *Ahimsa,* and the dictates of peace and love expounded by Buddha some twenty-five hundred years ago. Speaking on "The Indian Way in International Affairs," Mr. Nehru in December 1956 stressed that "the Indian people seemed to have developed a tradition to do things peacefully. . . . If there was any message which India offered to other countries, it was this message of doing things by peaceful methods to solve any problem." [13] In recent years India has been purposefully resurrecting the teachings of Buddha to publicize and strengthen her foreign policy. In May 1955, extensive celebrations were carried out in India commemorating the twenty-five hundredth anniversary of Buddha's Great Emancipation. President Prasad in a radio broadcast called upon all people to dedicate themselves anew to Buddha's teaching. He said his gospel was the only way to avoid strife and violence; he also added that the *Pancha Shila* was based on the message of Buddha. In a previous chapter the importance of religion in Indian tradition has been stressed. In part this explained Gandhi's tremendous following; and now Indian leaders are endeavoring to give the sanctity and authority of religion to their purposes in world affairs. The spiritual, the non-violent, approach of India in her relation to other nations is a constant theme. Many well-informed observers in the West have been impressed by the spiritual motivation of Indian foreign policy. Professor Norman Brown has commented that "it is in the light of India's moral idealism" that her approach to world affairs must be viewed.[14]

What would appear to be an objective appraisal of the Indian claim to high idealism and principle in foreign affairs? The term "neutralism" is sometimes applied to Indian policy. This is not accurate. India has been neutral only in her refusal to join military pacts; she has certainly aligned herself in many disputes. She has aligned herself with Asian-African nations in the pursuit of certain economic, political, and cultural aims. She has exerted her influence in many troubled areas—Korea, Indochina, Palestine, and North Africa. In the United Nations she has placed herself closely by the side of the Arab bloc.

In truth India has followed a realistic policy in international affairs calculated to protect her national self-interest. That policy has been as benevolent as attainment of this objective has allowed, and it has been very shrewd. This basic motivation of national interest has often been obscured by a camouflage of philosophical and moral platitudes.

That India's foreign policy has elements of opportunism, inconsistency, and expediency—as does that of any great world power—is seen in the fact that she has not hesitated to use force when her unity or security has been threatened, as in the

---

[13] *Indiagram,* (Washington, D.C.: Indian Embassy), No. 851, December 29, 1955.

[14] W. Norman Brown, "Indian National Ideals Today," Mary Keatings Das Memorial Lecture, Columbia University.

case of Hyderabad and Nepal. While continually advocating disarmament in the United Nations, India has turned down a number of reasonable proposals for demilitarization in Kashmir. And on this issue of Kashmir, the general principle of self-determination for all peoples hardly squares with the obstacles Nehru has placed in its path in Kashmir. Indian spokesmen make much of adhering to basic principles of right in guiding one's role in world affairs. Thus India castigated Dutch rule in Indonesia, French rule in North Africa, and military operations by the British against a small minority of Communist terrorists in Malaya. Yet Indian leaders have never criticized Communist totalitarian rule in eastern Europe, never interested themselves in the rights of the people of the Baltic republics overrun by Russia during World War II. Little has also been said about the question of German reunification and the rights of the East Germans to self-determination. These blind spots, so conveniently ignored by India in her conduct of foreign affairs, were well exposed by Krishna Menon's much-publicized masterful and equivocal performances before a TV forum—*Meet the Press*—in 1955 and 1956. Another ideological inconsistency to many observers in the West is how Nehru and fellow members of his Congress party can accuse the Communist party in India with about every crime in the book and yet cultivate the friendship of the inspiration and fountainhead of this evil in India—Soviet Russia.

It would clear the air and improve understanding between India and the West if the former would not take such a holier-than-thou attitude in world affairs. Basically her policy is a very natural and logical one. She is in a sense only following the American example of isolation as practiced from 1783 to the First World War. India will not take sides in any gigantic international tug-of-war, such as that between Russia and the West. But India has acted as mediator and honest broker in peripheral disputes and has in a general way tried to infuse the international scene with reasonableness and conciliation. This has been a positive and a valuable contribution and India could not have made it if she had aligned herself, militarily, with any bloc.

Stripped of distracting claims, India's real aims in international affairs have been:

1. to prevent Pakistan becoming militarily a threat and to retain her present hold on Kashmir;
2. to spread Indian prestige throughout Africa, the Middle East, and Southeast Asia—fertile areas because of India's role as the great colonial emancipator;

3. to do nothing to antagonize China and Russia, for residing in these powers are latent threats much more serious than any now obtaining in the West;
4. to do all possible, without becoming involved in the cold war, to help maintain world peace;
5. to spread India's prestige and mission throughout the world.

In the United States there has been much criticism of Indian foreign policy. India has been dubbed a "stooge of Moscow," and an "international fellow-traveler." Americans, however, should understand the extreme urgency for India of concentrating on her internal problems just as their forefathers did up to less than a century ago. Westerners might also realize that, putting themselves in Indian shoes, it is easier to point out the defects of one's friends than those of one's potential enemies. During and after the visit of the Russian leaders in late 1955, Nehru made it abundantly clear that India had not joined the Russian camp, that friendship with one nation is not aimed against another. Americans should understand better than they apparently do that a critical contest for leadership is now being carried on in Asia. It is between two ways, two ideals, two approaches to life. On the one hand there is India believing in the parliamentary way, the Bill of Rights, and the importance of the individual. On the other, there is Communist China dedicated to force, disdain of the individual, and the collective way. Both are striving to solve their economic difficulties, and their degree of success or failure will be watched closely by other Asian peoples. If India falters it will result in the dominance of China throughout Asia, with dire consequences to the rest of the world.

Even if the message of non-violence, Gandhian ethics, and spirituality in foreign affairs have been unduly stressed in supporting Indian actions on the world stage, her best minds should continue humbly to publicize these precepts, while admitting that India, like her fellows in the family of nations, has not been able fully to realize them in practice.

Prospects

In the late 1950's the pattern of politics in the Middle East and southern Asia moved with inexorable speed toward some, as yet, unperceived destination. Only one thing was certain—these areas were in a state of flux. Western influence was rapidly declining. Nationalism was at white heat, and dreams of greatness beckoned to rising leaders such as

Colonel Nasser of Egypt. And in southern Asia hovered the expansive might of Soviet Russia and China.

The course of history in the Middle East and southern Asia would depend in large measure upon events in Pakistan and India. Would these states be able to bury the hatchet? Only thus could they inherit imperial Britain's old role of protecting and stabilizing the Indian Ocean area. If this function is tried out, its success will depend upon the inner strength of the two nations. There must be rapid economic development and with it rising standards of living. In the case of Pakistan, an ambitious five-year plan was set in motion in 1956. As we have seen, India about the same time started her second plan to develop her latent resources and improve the miserable living conditions of her masses.

The inner strength of India and Pakistan in the future will depend not only upon economic development but on national unity. Before independence both peoples took unity under British rule for granted. We have seen that there has been serious sectionalism in Pakistan and in India in 1955-1956 there was disturbing evidence that national unity versus group and linguistic nationalism loomed as the foremost problem. Because there had been dissatisfaction with the administrative divisions of various states as laid out by the British, a commission had been appointed to study and recommend a new and more acceptable system of state frontiers. The commission's report, when published in 1955, set off a violent wave of excitement and agitation from various linguistic regions in India which were not satisfied with the recommendations. Disturbances and even bloody riots, as in Bombay, broke out in numerous parts of the country. Each language group, some running to many millions, is proud of its language and past culture. In southern India, especially, there is strong resistance to the language of the north, Hindi, becoming the official language in place of English. Will loyalty to the central government, in New Delhi, prove strong enough to prevent regionalism from seriously weakening Indian national unity? This will be one of the crucial questions to be answered in the next decade or so of Indian history.

In both India and Pakistan there were disturbing signs in 1957 of the magnitude of the task to be surmounted. In Pakistan political instability seemed to get worse instead of better. Three different prime ministers held office in 1957. In India there were growing symptoms of old age and hardening of the political arteries of the Congress Party. In national elections held in 1957 the Congress still held a comfortable lead. The Communists, however, doubled their vote and gained control of the government of one state. The most dangerous development was India's economic deterioration. The Second Five-Year Plan faltered as it became evident that one billion dollars would be needed in foreign aid to carry it through. The United States, however, indicated its willingness to advance a loan of more than $200 million.

And so we leave two new nations—India and Pakistan—part of a troubled area in transition. The dynamics of south Asian history depend primarily upon increasing cooperation between India and Pakistan, strengthening their economic potential, and consolidating their newly won national unity. No one can hazard how successfully these three basic challenges will be met—even in the near future. But upon the nature of the response made by India and Pakistan rests, one can be sure, the future course of history in southern and southeastern Asia.

12. The Passing of the Nehru Era

India and Pakistan in the 1960's

JAWAHARLAL NEHRU DIED ON MAY 27, 1964, following several months of ill health. Indian prime minister since 1947, he had been the revered leader of more people than any public figure in the modern world. Since the end of British imperial rule he had been the outstanding personality in the Indian sub-continent and also one of the most important figures in world politics. His passing definitely marked the end of an era in Indian history. The Indian scene will never be quite the same, its problems never the almost exclusive responsibility of a single hand.

Although the passage of time must give better perspective, Nehru's place in Indian history is secure. He stands along-side such great figures as Asoka, Chandragupta II, Ram Mohan Roy, and Gandhi—and Akbar, Sir Syed Ahmad Khan, and Mohammed Ali Jinnah—if Muslim Indian greats are in-cluded. Nehru's contributions to the new India were im-measurably great: leading to independence and consolidating the new nation, and guiding it past many dangers and pitfalls. Nehru deserves most of the credit for establishing a stable parliamentary system based upon the twin concepts of sec-ularism and progressive social-economic democracy.

Nehru's grasp of domestic and international realities was both firm and positive during his first decade of leadership. In world affairs his policy of non-alignment kept India clear of Cold War involvements and yet friendly with both the Free and the Communist worlds. In the domestic arena Nehru's genius held together various oddly contrasting political groups within the dominant Congress party. And in the economic field, he vigorously pushed forward his Socialistic pattern of better livelihood for all.

After 1957 some of Nehru's basic premises of statesmanship proved to be false or at least highly suspect. His belief in the good faith of Communist China proved to be tragically misplaced and non-alignment to be somewhat out of date. His adamancy on the Kashmir dispute came to haunt him during the dark aftermath of the Chinese invasion, when it became apparent that India could ill afford the enmity of both Communist China and Pakistan. It was also clear that the Prime Minister's control over the Congress party was increasingly ineffective. He was not able to put in order the party house, which was showing the twin evils of too little dynamism and too much corruption. Nehru was out of touch with what has been called the new and third generation of leaders within Congress; and notwithstanding his long championship of the secular state, where people of all creeds could live together amicably, there were alarming evidences of anti-Muslim feeling and a burgeoning Hindu nationalism. Nevertheless, Nehru was a heroic and truly great figure. An unkindness of fate presented him with titanic, mounting problems in the last few years of his life, when his mental and physical powers were in decline.

The Rise of Regional Nationalism in India

In the long history of India the subcontinent was seldom united before the British conquest. Western imperialism gave India this unity and also a lingua franca, English. During the British period the Indian people developed a common nationalism in their struggle for independence. But subsequently, ancient cultural and regional loyalties emerged to challenge national unity. Nehru was increasingly confronted by this tendency after 1957. Shortly after independence and the integration of the Princely States, the Indian Union consisted of twenty-seven states. There were growing demands for state boundaries to conform to language, especially in South India. In various areas "linguistic nationalism" led to agitation and, on occasion, riots. In 1952, in South India, a Telegu-speaking advocate of a separate state fasted to death.

Nehru fully realized the danger implicit in this regional nationalism but reluctantly gave way, and the new state of Andhra was created. A States Reorganization Commission was then appointed and its *Report* issued in 1955. The next year, following its recommendations, state boundaries were redrawn largely on a linguistic basis. India now had fourteen states, each with a dominant language. Bombay was an exception with its Marathi- and Gujarati-speaking areas, and, following much agitation and violence, was divided into two states in 1960. Discord also continued in the Punjab, where a Sikh minority asked for a separate state, and in some quarters, even an independent Sikhistan. Assam, where a Bengali minority has been at odds over language with the Assamese, remains another regional area of unrest. And on the Indo-Burmese border a continuous struggle against central control from Delhi has been waged. The warlike Naga tribesmen demanded independence for an area of some 6,000 square miles of jungle and rugged hill country. In 1963, Nehru's government recognized the area, Nagaland, as a distinct state (the sixteenth) within the Indian Union, but some opposition continues.

Regional nationalisms have been further exacerbated by the "official language" controversy. The constitution prescribes Hindi as the official language but also provides for the continued use of English until 1965, and even after this date for special purposes, especially in the law courts. The non-Hindi areas, especially the Dravidian South and Bengal, strongly oppose the elimination of English and the adoption of Hindi. They claim that their regional languages are more developed and also that there can be no satisfactory substitute for English in science and as a world language. Whereas in the northern Hindi areas, Hindi and a second language could be easily mastered, in other parts of India three languages would have to be learned: Hindi, the mother tongue, and English. The better educated would thus be at a disadvantage in competing for government service and other lines of endeavor. South India has been vehemently opposed to what is termed "Hindi imperialism"; and in 1958 demonstrations were held in Madras against the planned change from English to Hindi in 1965. Southern nationalism went so far as to demand the creation of a separate Dravidian state with a population of one hundred million.

Endeavoring to soften this linguistic rivalry, Nehru supported the extension of the 1965 deadline. In 1963 legislation was passed extending indefinitely the use of English as an associate official language. National Integration Council was also created to study how India's many groups could be better integrated into a homogeneous community.

India's Struggle for Social and Economic Advancement

Only extreme poverty—on occasion famine—widespread human suffering, and blighted lives lie ahead for India's masses unless industrialization continues to be rapidly advanced, agricultural production substantially expanded, and the great majority of the population located in the villages stirred out of their age-old inertia. In the early 1960's India was in the midst of her third five-year plan (1961-1966). The three plans represented a total investment of nearly fifty billion dollars.

The first two plans showed some striking advances: steady increases in the production of steel, aluminum, cement, chemicals, textiles, and many consumer goods, and a bicycle boom, which meant "that Indian villages are at last getting on wheels." By 1960-1961, using 1949-1950 as a base year, industrial production had risen from 100 to 194 and the national income had risen 42 per cent. The third plan's goals were the creation of fourteen million new jobs, a 32 per cent increase in farm production, and a 47 per cent increase in school enrollment. Visible and encouraging signs of economic progress could be seen in many parts of the country: new factories, steel mills, dams, irrigation projects, oil refineries, and pipelines.

Despite these changes, the true magnitude of India's economic task became more apparent after 1961. Estimates of population growth had been too low, and the incredible increase threatened to nullify the gains of the five-year plans. The 1961 census gave a population figure of 438 million, an increase of 79 million over the past decade. The estimated unemployed were seven and one-half million, indicating that between 1962 and 1976 some forty million jobs would have to be created; and the population estimate for 1976 was 625 million.

These figures became alarming when food production failed to reach the designated goals. In fact, in some cases crop yields per acre actually declined. An important factor in this disappointing situation was and still is the listlessness and conservatism of the Indian villager. There are constant examples of the lack of rural initiative and the unwillingness of the farmers to adopt modern methods. The much touted Community Development Program, which had meant to remove the incubus of outworn custom and superstition from the villages, failed. New methods had been introduced in 1959 to stir the countryside, and more responsibility delegated to such local bodies as the village council, the cooperative society, and the school. But these measures did not solve the problem.

The graveness of the economic situation was highlighted in 1964 by a serious food shortage. The hope of bumper crops had not been realized, and food shortages became evident. Food prices rose 16 per cent in the year ending March 1964, and many areas saw rioting and looting of grain stores. Grain supplies could still be drawn from the United States, but inadequate facilities for unloading at the docks further complicated the crisis.

Assessing the overall accomplishments of the five-year plans, there are some critics who believe they have been too timorous of vested interests, in short too painless. These critics point to the inadequacy of landholding reform, to the government's failure to tax rich farm income, and to the growing gulf between the very rich and the miserably poor. They add that there has been too little regard for a leveling down process and that there is more concentration of wealth in India than in any country in Western Europe. Perhaps a germane statistic is the per capita income for 1961, which, in spite of many economic achievements stemming from the plans, was estimated to be a miserable $69.30.

Tribulations of Democracy in Pakistan

The domestic problems of India are paralleled—with some important variants—in its neighbor, Pakistan. A serious regional dichotomy exists between the Eastern and Western parts, which are so different in culture and economic geography. Only Islam and some fear of India act as a bond. Pakistan has the same economic backwardness as India: low income, shortage of foreign exchange, widespread low living standards, and inadequate industrialization. Unlike India, however, she suffers from a chronic political instability that became critical in 1958, when General Ayub seized power. At that time the country seemed to be falling apart. Politicians schemed at the expense of the state, economic development was static, and corruption rampant. As one Pakistani put it: "the leaders were conspiring, the common man perspiring, the nation was expiring, and alas, not a soul was inspiring."

With Parliament dissolved and the constitution abrogated, the General cracked down on the black market, order was restored, and corrupt politicians put out of circulation. The new regime's notable achievement was land reform, directed against the parasitic landlords. A limit was placed on holdings and some two and one-half million acres distributed to landless peasants.

By 1958 economic conditions had deteriorated. Food production was short, requiring the importation of large quantities of grain. Foreign exchange reserves had fallen dangerously low and the first five-year plan was not achieving its goals. In 1959, General Ayub's government gained control of the economic situation and a second five-year plan (1960-1965) was formulated—one more realistic and modest than the first. The first had not paid enough attention to improvement of the agricultural output. As a consequence, economic advances had barely kept up with the increase in population. The second plan gave priority to agriculture, with substantial sums allotted to industry, public utilities, education, and general welfare. As in the case of India, Pakistan has been dependent on large amounts of foreign aid. Up to the spring of 1962 about two and one-half billion dollars had been secured from this source, together with over one billion in arms aid from the United States. The second plan called for an estimated expenditure of the equivalent of four billion dollars, of which one billion seven hundred million dollars would be needed in external assistance, not including United States food grain loans. A World Bank *Report* spoke optimistically of the plan's prospects of success, and it would seem that the evaluation was realistic. In the spring of 1964 the index of farm production was put at 139 in comparison with a figure of 107 in 1958. The rate of growth of the economy was estimated to be 4.2 per cent annually; thus the second plan objective of a 24 per cent increase in the gross national product (GNP) will be fulfilled. The economic auguries for Pakistan appear more favorable than for India.

General Ayub had nothing but contempt for the politicians who had brought their country to the edge of disaster in 1958. He was convinced that the Western type of parliamentary government could not work in Pakistan, where the masses were illiterate and politically inexperienced. In 1962 martial law was ended and a new constitution announced. It established a new scheme of government based on the "Basic Democracies" program. This interesting scheme insures mass participation at the grass roots level of local government. By manhood suffrage, 80,000 electors, so-called, are selected. They have the responsibility of electing the president, and the national and provincial assemblies. In local government, a five-tiered system of councils gives the peoples' representatives, elected indirectly, an opportunity to work with nominated official members.

In what is, in effect, a system of enlightened despotism, the President, Ayub, has sweeping powers. Neither the judiciary nor the legislature can effectively block his will. President Ayub has declared: "Our ultimate aim is to restore democracy." His hope, however, is that the transition will not take place before the common people have gained sufficient political know-how to protect the state and themselves from the discredited politicians. Meanwhile, the Western-educated classes are restive and will remain so until full democratic practices are restored. Supported in his role as president by a national plebiscite, when the Basic Democracies system was first introduced, General Ayub has signified his intention to contest for the presidency in the next national election, in the spring of 1965. The election was held early in January. After a very spirited and tumultuous campaign in which Miss Fatima Jinnah, sister of the late Mohammed Ali Jinnah was leader of the opposition, President Ayub won a decisive victory. The result was a clear mandate for his government to continue with its ambitious program of social and economic reform.

India and Pakistan at the Crossroads

The situation in the subcontinent was completely transformed by Communist China's invasion of India's northern frontier in 1962. Under British rule defense policy had been based on the outer buffer states of Afghanistan and Tibet—both within the British orbit. Then there was an inner ring of some tribal areas, such as the North-East Frontier Agency, plus small states in close relation with India, such as Nepal, Sikkim, and Bhutan. The exit of British power from the scene left a vacuum that was not fully understood by either Pakistan or India. Afghanistan soon began to make claims on the northern border of Pakistan and Communist China followed suit along India's north frontier. For nearly a decade following independence, however, there seemed to be little real danger from the north. Pakistan and India were absorbed in their own quarrel over Kashmir; and India kept her army relatively small—some 600,000 men, most of whom were kept on the Pakistan border. At the same time Nehru did everything possible to gain the friendship of Communist China, whose membership in the U.N. he continually and stoutly championed.

Indian leaders had been somewhat disturbed when it was revealed that Peking maps portrayed as Chinese large areas that India considered her own territory. But no moves were made by China to extend its influence until 1950, when it exercised its claimed sovereignty over Tibet by sending in an occupation force. There was some anxiety over this move in Delhi, but Nehru's only response was to sign a treaty with China in 1954, whereby India gained certain trading privileges in Tibet and obtained Peking's assent to the Five Principles of Peaceful Coexistence, or *Pancha Shila*. In 1956, however, encroachment of Indian territory along the northern border began. By 1957 the Chinese had surreptitiously penetrated into Ladakh, part of Indian Kashmir, and built a strategic road connecting the Chinese province of Sinkiang and Tibet. While checking on this intrusion, an Indian patrol was captured by Chinese forces in the spring of 1958.

The controversy became acute when the Tibetans rebelled against Chinese control in 1959. The Dalai Lama, together with thousands of Buddhists, made their way over the towering mountain passes and were given sanctuary in India. Peking thereupon accused Nehru's government of supporting the revolt and called for the "liberation" of Ladakh, Sikkim, and Bhutan. Prime Minister Nehru had tried to play down the Chinese incursions and, while denying the worst, continued to hope for the best, but now Indian public opinion became sharply anti-Chinese and pro-Tibetan. The Indian people were further aroused when, in August 1959, the Chinese captured an Indian patrol along the border of the North-East Frontier Agency.

Early the next year, Chou En-lai—the Chinese Premier—visited New Delhi, but there was no agreement, and tension continued. The Indian government admitted that China now claimed 52,000 square miles of Indian territory and had occupied over 14,000 square miles, mostly in Ladakh. During 1961 notes and diplomatic sparring continued between Peking and New Delhi. The only important development was the integration of Portuguese Goa into the Indian Union by force. Contrary to all Nehru's previous statements, army units took over the territory in December. Britain and the United States expressed strong regret over the resort of force, and the tables were to be quickly turned and India to find herself the victim of aggression.

In the summer of 1962 several armed clashes occurred in Ladakh and the North-East Frontier Agency (NEFA). Late in October, Chinese Communist forces launched a major offensive at points all along the border, and on the twenty-second Nehru broadcast sadly to the nation, asking for unity in India's hour of peril. A wave of patriotic enthusiasm welled up; political parties forgot their rivalries; and recruiting stations were swamped. Anti-Chinese demonstrations were held in the large cities, and, as news of Indian defeats came from the fighting front, a search began for culprits responsible for the disaster. Undoubtedly, Indian troops were ill prepared and ill trained. Their equipment was obsolete and could not match Chinese weapons. Amid mounting public criticism, Krishna Menon, the Defense Minister, was forced to resign.

Toward the end of November the military situation had become critical. A national emergency had been declared, and Nehru had dispatched an urgent request for military aid to Britain and the United States; badly needed equipment was quickly flown in to the war zone. Here fighting was carried on under the most difficult conditions. Soldiers suffered from frostbite, from lung sickness induced by the high altitudes

—in some cases over 14,000 feet—and light artillery in many cases had to be pulled up mountain trails by hand and by mule power. The Chinese forces seemed ready to debouch upon the plains of Assam and to threaten the entire Brahmaputra valley, when they announced a cease fire and a withdrawal of some twelve miles back to the lines of control held on November 7. India was to do the same. New Delhi would not agree to these terms, but the fighting halted. Indian casualties were placed at one thousand killed and five thousand missing. Communist China continued to hold a large part of Ladakh and some areas in the NEFA. As the year ended, representatives of six Afro-Asian nations met in Colombo and drew up proposals seeking peaceful agreement of the points at issue. As 1963 closed, however, no progress had been made. The nations of the Free World and the Afro-Asian states tried to determine the motives for the Chinese invasion. One commonly advanced explanation was that China wished to discredit India's prestige in Asia, and another, to cripple her economy by forcing her to spend huge amounts on arms rather than on economic development; finally, some observers believed China had a more limited objective: the control of the strategic road across Ladakh, connecting the Chinese province of Sinkiang with Tibet. The Malayan Prime Minister's harsh appraisal was "that China can no longer tolerate the existence of a great rival such as India, a successful democracy which is giving leadership to Asia."

Pakistan was a concerned observer of China's confrontation with India and the ensuing turmoil. India's embarrassment was seen as Pakistan's opportunity. For some fifteen years the dispute over Kashmir had simmered, occasionally bursting into flame. India's unwillingness to negotiate had created continued resentment and frustration. In January 1962, Pakistan made a formal request to have the issue reopened in the U.N. Security Council. In the ensuing debate the Indian representative described Pakistan as an aggressor, since Kashmir was an integral part of India. Nehru also made it clear there could be no talks as long as Pakistan persisted in bringing the matter before the U.N. Following the Chinese attack, British and American officials, visiting India in connection with military aid, persuaded Ayub Khan and Nehru to initiate talks on Kashmir with the purpose of achieving an "honorable and equitable settlement." Discussions were carried on early in 1963 but proved fruitless. In Pakistan, frustration mounted at Nehru's longtime pledge to honor a free plebiscite and anger at being labeled an aggressor by a government that had not hesitated to use force in Junagadh, Hyderabad, and lately in Goa.

Meanwhile Kashmir's opposition to the tie with India had been growing. In December the mysterious theft of a sacred relic from a Muslim shrine in Kashmir appeared to have political overtones. A grave crisis followed, accompanied by anti-Hindu riots. In March 1964 a group of Kashmiris demanded that their country's status be "settled by free plebiscite." Since 1953 Sheikh Abdullah, Kashmir's first prime minister since 1947, had been imprisoned by the Indian authorities, who feared his lukewarm support of his country's integration into India. Abdullah was released in April 1964, in order to allay Kashmiri feeling. In his first public appearance, he was welcomed by thousands of cheering Kashmiris, who were told of their country's right to self-determination. Arriving in New Delhi for talks with Nehru, Abdullah let it be known that his object was to bring friendship between Pakistan and India. Although it was plain that the Kashmir leader wanted a free choice for his country, it was not clear whether this choice involved a completely independent Kashmir or one tied with Pakistan. India's choice in 1964 was either to grant self-determination or to employ repressive measures.

During and immediately following the Chinese attacks, Pakistan's foreign policy underwent substantial shifts. In the words of her foreign minister, Z. A. Bhutto, she went through a "period of great cataclysm and painful reappraisal"; she was profoundly disturbed by the failure of her allies, Britain and the United States, to pressure India into settling the Kashmir dispute when Nehru requested military aid. A Pakistani correspondent wrote of "The West's failure to respond to Pakistan's steadfast loyalty." Resentment mounted when massive military supplies were pledged to India by Washington. Speakers in the Pakistan National Assembly called for closer ties with China and withdrawal from the United States sponsored military alliances of SEATO and CENTO. President Ayub Khan insisted that the Chinese military menace was over-exaggerated, that Peking's aims were limited to border rectification and did not involve all-out war. Military aid, therefore, was unjustified for it upset the military balance in the Indian subcontinent, thus endangering the security of a loyal ally of the United States. Other Pakistan sources asserted that with United States aid India would shortly have an army ten times the strength of her neighbor.

Adjusting to what she considered an untenable position, Pakistan moved toward Communist China. China's prime minister visited Ayub Khan in the spring of 1964, and important commercial and air agreements were signed by Peking and Rawalpindi. Most important, against Indian protests, Pakistan made concessions of territory along the Sinkiang-Kashmir border. Trade pacts were also made with various members of the Soviet Bloc. While the United States was somewhat perturbed by this new orientation in Pakistan foreign policy, the Pakistan government let it be known that there would be no basic change as far as its ties with the West were concerned. The most ominous development, however, was the increasing involvement of Communist China in the affairs of the Indian subcontinent. Peking announced support of Pakistan in the Kashmir imbroglio, and its foreign minister declared that if India attacked Pakistan, China would assist the latter.

The Prospect

The next few years may be critical for both India and Pakistan. The most urgent need is a détente between New Delhi and Karachi (the Pakistan capital is to be moved to the new site of Islamabad). Continued obduracy over Kashmir paves the way for possible Chinese intervention in the affairs of the subcontinent and can only result in mutual tragedy. Not only external security but internal tranquillity is at stake. The Kashmir quarrel and Pakistan's rapprochement with China has kindled communal antagonism, i.e., Hindu-Muslim antipathy. In 1964 there was bloody rioting in both nations. Thousands of destitute, bewildered refugees had to flee their homes, crossing into either Pakistan or India. Religious fanaticism is increasingly evident. In the summer of 1964, for example, a conference of Indian Muslims met in Lucknow to express their "confusion, helplessness, and despair."

Only with the two countries' reconciliation is there reasonable hope that they can surmount their internal problems. Pakistan's economic prospects appear assuring. She must try to achieve political stability, accompanied by an orderly transition to sound parliamentary government. India celebrated her seventeenth anniversary of independence in August 1964, in a humble and chastened mood. Political stability was not the immediate concern. Nehru's heirs had formed a new government under Lal Bahadur Shastri, and the transition, early in June 1964, was achieved quietly and smoothly. But the challenges are still of herculean dimensions. The country's serious food shortage has to be remedied, if disaster in the near future is to be averted. The dread uncertainty regarding Communist China remains, and "the agonizing question" is whether an adequate program of economic development can be carried forward in addition to greatly increased military expenditures. The amount provided for defense spending in the 1963-1964 budget doubled that of the previous year.

India passes into her post-Nehru era guided by Prime Minister Shastri. Unlike the heroic and colorful figure of his predecessor, he is quiet—even meek—and somewhat colorless. His health has also given some cause for alarm. But he is a competent administrator, a dedicated patriot, and, above all, one gifted in the art of conciliation. These are qualities that India now urgently needs.

Index

327

MENTOR Books of Related Interest

ASIA IN THE MODERN WORLD, *Helen G. Matthew, ed.*

Prominent authorities study the people, culture, and political history of Asia and provide the background for understanding its current role in world events. Illustrated with maps. (#MT542—75¢)

EAST AND WEST *by C. Northcote Parkinson*

A stimulating, sometimes irreverent look at the traditional alternations of power between East and West. By the author of the satirical classic, *Parkinson's Law*. (#MT612—75¢)

PEKING AND MOSCOW *by Klaus Mehnert*

A truly inside view of the past, present, and future of the Sino-Soviet alliance by a foremost expert on Russia and China. (#MQ598—95¢)

THE CHANGING SOCIETY OF CHINA *by Ch'u and Winburg Chai*

The nature of Chinese civilization as revealed in its social institutions, philosophy and religion, art and literature, and the impending threat of Communist totalitarianism.
(#MT365—75¢)

THE NATURE OF THE NON-WESTERN WORLD *by Vera Micheles Dean*

A noted expert on foreign affairs throws new light on the conflict between East and West as she probes the beliefs, traditions and emotions that motivate the people of the non-Western nations. (#MT580—75¢)

THE ORIGINS OF ORIENTAL CIVILIZATION *by Walter A. Fairservis, Jr.*

An archaeological and anthropological study of the beginnings of culture in China, Korea, Japan, Mongolia and Manchuria. Illustrated with drawings and photographs.
(#MP445—60¢)

A SHORT HISTORY OF JAPAN *by Malcolm D. Kennedy*

The cultural and political development of Japan from the time of its first emperor through the Second World War—to its present position as a member of the Western alliance.
(#MT559—75¢)

THE SONG [...] *lated by Swami Prabha[...] od*

The time [...] roduction by Aldous Hu[...]   (#MP466—60¢)

THE UPANISHADS: BREATH OF THE ETERNAL *Translated by Swami Prabhavananda and Frederick Manchester*

The ancient Hindu scriptures that focus upon the knowledge of God and the highest aspects of religious truth.

(#MP386—60¢)

GANDHI: HIS LIFE AND MESSAGE FOR THE WORLD *by Louis Fischer*

The life story of one of the greatest inspirational and political leaders of our time gives insight into India's pivotal place in world affairs.   (#MP390—60¢)

ISLAM IN MODERN HISTORY *by Wilfred Cantwell Smith*

A noted scholar discusses the impact of Mohammedanism on Middle Eastern political life today.   (#MP537—60¢)

THE TEACHINGS OF THE COMPASSIONATE BUDDHA *edited with commentary by E. A. Burtt.*

The best translations of the basic texts and scriptures, early discourses, the Dhammapada, and later writings.

(#MP380—60¢)

THE WAY OF ZEN *by Alan W. Watts.*

A modern American's interpretation of Zen Buddhism as a means of living serenely and fully in a confused and frustrating world.   (#MP476—60¢)

A TREASURY OF ASIAN LITERATURE *edited by John D. Yohannan.*

The literary classics of the Orient: a collection of poetry, stories, and scriptures from Arabia and the Far East.

(#MT340—75¢)